In loving memory of Myra
and
for Daniel, Marion and Laura, Caroline and David
and for all my grandchildren
who bring so much joy into my life.

Contents

Foreword

It is a great pleasure to join in celebrating Greville Janner's tremendous lifetime of service and dedication to our country. He had a distinguished career in the Commons, not least as Chair of the Select Committee on Employment, and now in the Lords, and he has been and remains tremendously influential and important, both in the parliamentary world and because of the work he does on behalf of the Jewish community and for charities up and down Britain.

His greatest parliamentary achievement was probably his part in the passage of the War Crimes Bill. I remember at the time that there was a very strong campaign against it and opinion could have gone either way. It was very much due to the enormous strength of the campaign that Greville mounted and the sincerity with which he put across the case – the fortitude and the courage but also the sincerity that persuaded many people to back the Bill.

I know how much Greville owes to the redoubtable Janner family, and to Myra in particular. There can never have been a better partner, a more solid helper or someone who backed up his every achievement and achieved so much in her own right. We all miss her.

We are very proud of the Janner family and in particular, of Greville's lifetime of service. It is great that he is now telling both the story and the stories of his remarkable life. I am sure that you will enjoy reading it, as I have done.

The Rt Hon. Tony Blair MP
2006

Prologue

The 15 April 1947 was the second anniversary of the Liberation of the Belsen concentration camp. I stood by the mass graves, surrounded by survivors, most of them weeping. Wooden signposts: 'Here lie 1,000 dead' . . . 'Here lie 500 dead' . . . Long mounds of murder.

All my family in Lithuania and Latvia had been slaughtered by Nazi locals, who had burned or buried their bodies and stolen their possessions. I shivered. Almost certainly, none of my family had died here in Belsen. But tens of thousands of others did.

One single gravestone for one small child. Awful. But then it is easier to picture one Anne Frank than a thousand skeletons. I looked around at my hosts from the Jewish Relief Unit, but none were looking at me. So I broke down and sobbed.

Then anger – sheer blinding fury. Anger, as I had never known it. Hatred of the killers. Compassion for the survivors, standing around me as the rabbi led the chanting of the Jewish memorial prayer, '*Yiskadel ve'yiskedash shamei raba . . .*' By a miracle, my parents and sister were alive, so I had never recited this prayer. But now, I did – in memory of fathers and mothers and children who had been slaughtered. I cried and prayed with the rest.

That moment was the start of my new life. This book is the story of that life – of its origins and its pathways, its realities and its dreams, its joys and its failures. Before Belsen – childhood. After Belsen – from War Crimes Investigator to student, from lawyer to politician, from son and brother to husband and father and grandfather. But since 1947, always with the shadow of that day in Belsen, hovering over my world.

Belsen was death. 'To life!' became the focus of my days – and the central theme of my memoirs.

PART ONE

Youth

ONE

In the Beginning

In the early hours of the morning of 11 July 1928, I arrived – three weeks late. I have spent the rest of my life trying to catch up. I was born in Cardiff to Elsie and Barnett Janner. Their families had emerged in the 1880s from Latvia and Lithuania, escaping from persecution, or from conscription into the Tsar's army, or both.

By age-old Jewish custom, we name our children after relatives, loved and departed. My father's adored mother, Gittel (or Gertrude), died in childbirth when he was ten years old. Since I could scarcely be called either Gittel or Gertrude, they followed Jewish tradition and looked for a similar name. Hence, in Hebrew, Gavriel. My English equivalent name came from some obscure cricketer whom my mother admired. As a child, I disliked it, but I learned later that an unusual name is useful in public life and at least I do not have to add my surname when I sign personal letters.

My father's parents came from a tiny Lithuanian village called Vitumjan (Chapter 21). When my grandfather left home, he took the surname of Vitumjaner – the man from Vitumjan. On arriving in England, he dropped the Vitum and we acquired our surname. Father's mother came from the nearby and much larger town of Tels. She was tall, beautiful and cultured; she spoke several languages; and she was Father's idol. Her death tore him apart.

Eventually, the family settled in Barry, South Wales. Towards the end of the First World War, Father served in France and he was gassed in the trenches and returned to Cardiff, where he set about earning a living as a local, one-man solicitor.

My mother's father, Joseph Cohen, had emerged from Lithuania, when he was seventeen. He escaped over the border in a haycart and ended up as a door-to-door salesman in Dublin. A few years later, he fell in love with a photograph of the beautiful Yetta Natanson and travelled back to

Lithuania. After ten days, they were married – and soon moved to Newcastle, where my mother, Elsie, was born. Barney (as Father was known) and Elsie met at a friend's wedding, fell in love and were married on 12 July 1927. A year later, I was born in our Cardiff home.

We did not stay long in Cardiff. While Father loved the place and the people, Mother hated both and was delighted to get away. She found it provincial and parochial and when some lunatic accused Father of making off with the synagogue silver, she determined to get back to the glories of Hampstead – and of Whitechapel, where as a youngster she had joined in founding and running the Brady Girls' Club in what was at that time a thriving and largely immigrant Jewish community, physically deprived but culturally and educationally throbbing.

My father, Barney, continued to earn his living as a solicitor and to work on his political career. After he stood unsuccessfully as Liberal Candidate for Cardiff Central, Lloyd George invited him to London to contest the 1930 by-election in Whitechapel – a Labour seat, but winnable and in a Jewish area, which Mother knew well. So Father's political ambitions overcame his attachment to Wales. To Mother's delight, they pulled up their roots and replaced them in the decent soil of Hendon, then a semi-rural area, with a field grazed by horses at the end of our garden.

Father fought a vigorous by-election campaign, but lost by 1,099 votes. His best-known poster portrayed a scrubbing brush and a lump of coal as 'arguments used against Janner'. Happily for him – and Father was never happier than in political life – he won the seat in the 1931 General Election. Barnett Janner, proud of his immigrant Jewish roots, became Liberal Member of Parliament for Whitechapel and St George's, a job that he hugely enjoyed.

He was then and remained a devoted servant of his constituents, whatever their background or however they had voted. And as a proud Jew and Zionist, he campaigned for the creation of a Jewish state. His political problem was that he found himself voting steadily in the Labour lobbies. He believed profoundly in Liberal philosophies but found the Party impractical, disorganised and unlikely to achieve the results it sought.

In the 1935 Election, young Janner was once again beaten. Many Jewish constituents who had praised and loved him as a man did not vote for him as their MP. They deserted to Labour. And largely under the influence of

Morgan Phillips, agent for Jimmy Hall who had beaten him, Father followed the voters and joined the Labour Party. Morgan Phillips became his lifelong friend, together with his wife Nora, later Baroness Phillips. And their daughter, Gwyneth – now Gwyneth Dunwoody, MP for Crewe and Nantwich – became my valued inheritance from Father's political past.

Father was thoroughly miserable as an ex-MP. Too often, I heard him at Jewish meetings, making speeches that began: 'When I was in the House . . .' He poured his energies into battles against Fascism and Nazism and for the creation of a Jewish state in Palestine. Fourteen years his junior, Mother was his assistant, his confidante, his chauffeur, his adviser. They worked as a brilliant and quarrelsome team.

We were comfortably off. When Father came to London from Cardiff, he was employed at first by Woodhouse & Co., my grandfather Joseph's high street furniture-retailing company. Mother had always resented the fact that her brothers were in the business but she was not. They had been sent to university and she had not. It was as much independence as she could wrest from them to be allowed to go down to the East End of London to work in the Brady Clubs – which in itself was at that time a most unusual freedom for a young woman from a nice Jewish family. Mother's sister, Edith, was allowed to study and became a barrister. But like Elsie, she had to make do with some modest money in a trust. And to compound the indignity, its trustees were their brothers.

Father soon found that he was intensely unhappy, working for his in-laws. So he left and started his own solicitors' firm. It was never mighty, but when combined with Mother's modest income, it provided us with all that we needed.

My childhood was typically middle-class and largely uneventful. A comfortable home, with a cook and maid and education at a local preparatory school. I always told my mother that I wanted a brother, a sister, a cat and a dog. A quarter of my wish was granted in 1932, with the arrival of my sister, Ruth. When I discovered that I had a rival for the attention of Mother, and occasionally of Father, I was irritated. I decided that I would have preferred a brother, a cat or a dog. So as we grew up, I teased and tormented that good-natured, happy little girl. I was eventually sentenced by my parents to a week as a boarder at my school in

Hampstead. I hated being a boarder and since then, I have always regarded boarding school as only one up from an open prison. I hope that my behaviour towards my sister improved. Happily, from the time that Ruth and I went to Canada, some seven years later, she became and remains my most beloved friend.

My other and most respected pal was my cousin, Edmund Cohen, eighteen months older than myself. We were both at The Hall School, a Hampstead institution renowned for its pink caps and blazers and a redoubtable headmaster called G.A. Wathen. Cohen E.G. (Egg for short) was my hero. A good footballer, an excellent cricketer, popular with all and especially loved by me.

My time at The Hall was reasonably happy and unmemorable. Someone told my mother that everything about my appearance was one stage lower than it should be – hair in eyes . . . glasses at end of nose . . . tie around chest . . . shirt out around trousers . . . trousers down by knees . . . socks around ankles and shoelaces on the ground. I did not do very well either at my work or at any sport other than running. So much so that my favourite teacher, a bustling young woman called Beryl Grant, once said to me: 'Now come on, Janner. Perk up, you'll be famous one day.' When Miss Grant was in her middle nineties, living in Taunton, I was appointed to the House of Lords. She wrote to me: 'There, young Janner – I told you, didn't I?'

In 1935 we joined the rapturous, cheering, waving crowds, watching the coronation procession passing through Whitechapel, with King George V and Queen Mary gracefully saluting us from their open, horse-drawn state coach. By contrast, in November 1936, from the top floor of The Hall, I watched the blazing fire of Crystal Palace. We were silent with excitement and awe.

In the summer of 1938, my grandparents Joseph and Henrietta Cohen took their family on a Mediterranean cruise on the *Empress of Australia*. There were thirteen of us and I was the youngest. My eyes and mind were set alight by the glories of diversity, a vision which has focused my world ever since. Gibraltar, with its caves and tunnels and monkeys . . . Algiers, with its market and Edmund's mother, Eva, covering her fine nose to block out the combined smells of sewage and strange spices. Then, the glorious island of Corfu . . . the temples of Athens . . . the mosques and markets of Istanbul. . . . What a parade of joy, shared with our laughing tribe, including my recently acquired aunt from Canada, Sylvia, scooped up by my discerning Uncle Sidney, and with whom I fell in love. The family won most of the prizes in the ship's games. It was a glorious prelude to the darkness of war, about to descend on us all.

In September 1938, Hitler invaded Czechoslovakia. My parents shipped me off with my school, to Northampton, with a tiny rucksack. Its contents included pyjamas and a can of condensed milk. We, the children of The Hall, ended up in a suburb called Moulton. Ruth was by then in the junior section of South Hampstead High School, who were evacuated to Berkhamsted, in Hertfordshire.

I shared a billet with another Hall lad, in the home of the Chambers family. One evening, about a week later, we were eating supper when our host hushed us. Prime Minister Chamberlain was speaking on the wireless. He had returned from a place called Munich and a meeting with German Chancellor Adolf Hitler, clutching and waving an agreement. Yes, the Germans would stay in Czechoslovakia. But he had brought us 'Peace in our time'. We could all return home. Hurrah for Chamberlain! Little did we know.

I treasure an original letter, dated 20 October 1940, and written by Neville Chamberlain from his home at Highfield Park, near Basingstoke. It was addressed to Herbert Samuel, who later became Viscount Samuel and the first and only Jewish Governor General of Palestine. It reads:

My Dear Samuel,
It was very kind of you to write to me and I appreciate very highly the fact that I retain your approval for my efforts to maintain peace. Though that proved to be impossible, it did give us breathing time and that may in the end make all the difference.

An extraordinary comment from an appeaser who was an international disaster to a man who should have known better than to have approved of that appeasement. Had there been no 'breathing time' for Hitler, history would have been very different.

When the crisis was over, we all returned home. By then, my family had moved to 3 Lancaster Gate Terrace. Our home had become a centre for refugees – people with curious foreign accents. The adults were too senior to be called by their first names. There was 'Uncle' Charles – Charles Stockler. And 'Uncle' Hans – Hans Weiss, also from Vienna. Then 'Auntie' Irma Ehrlich, whose husband we were told was a brilliant scientist, in Czechoslovakia. She came to stay with us with her son Paul. Her husband was murdered by the Nazis in Prague.

Dr Desider Friedman came to us from Austria. I remember his name because he gave me a set of festival prayer books, inscribed with his love. He was the head of the Viennese Jewish community and I heard my parents repeatedly but uselessly begging him not to return to his community and to Nazi dangers. He died in Dachau Concentration Camp, before the war began.

Then the Stiassny family moved in. Their daughter, Hannah, was almost my age. One day, Mother told me to take Hannah across to Kensington Gardens. 'Go and play, you two. Mind how you cross the road.' We walked over the Bayswater Road and into the sunshine of that happy park. I commanded Hannah: 'Catch me', and I leapt over the low railing and onto the grass and skipped away. 'Come on, catch me.'

Hannah stayed rooted to the spot. I ran back to her. 'What's the matter?'

'Are we allowed to go on the grass?' she asked.

'Of course,' I replied. 'Why not?'

'In my country,' she said, 'Jewish children are not allowed on the grass.'

I did not understand. We stayed on the paths and when we got home I asked Mother: 'Why can't Jewish children where she comes from run on the grass?' Mother sat me down and told me for the first time why Uncle Hans, Uncle Charles and the Stiassnys and so many others had come to London. I asked her if that could happen in England. 'Of course not. We are very lucky we live here. But in the countries which Grandpa and Grandma Cohen and Grandpa and Grandma Janner came from, it's not like in England. There, the Jews are still persecuted.'

'What does "persecuted" mean?' I asked. As gently as possible, she explained to me. But it was all summed up for a child in those terrible words: 'In my country, Jewish children are not allowed on the grass.' Much of my later life has been spent trying to ensure that Jewish children – and black, Muslim, Indian, South African and Christian children – all children – are free to run on the grass, wherever they may live.

A year later, the war arrived. I was just eleven years old. We listened to Chamberlain declaring war in a grim broadcast. Mother said: 'It's about time we taught those bloody Nazis a lesson.' Father remained silent. He knew the horrors of war. He had survived by a miracle. Gassed in the infamous Battle of Passchendaele, an unknown comrade had pushed a gas mask over his face and he had woken up in hospital, alive but with chest trouble which stayed with him all his life. He had said his prayers to God for his salvation. One morning, he was putting on his phylacteries (*tefilin*), winding them onto his left arm, when he heard the man in the next bed saying to an orderly: 'These Jews are so clever. Look, Janner's taking his own blood pressure!'

My cousin, Edmund, and I joined The Hall School evacuation to the glorious but scarcely heated mansion of the Verney family, in Claydon, Buckinghamshire. The food was poor and inadequate and Edmund and I used to wait outside the staff room, enjoying, when we could get them, the crusts off the teachers' toast. Our greatest disappointment came when a boy from Hungary received a food parcel. It turned out to be a whole chicken – preserved in lard. We were not worried about eating non-kosher food, but lard was beyond our limit and his. We ceremoniously sank it in the Verney lake.

Claydon Manor was too magnificent and too cold for us. The glorious staircase, with its metal sheaves which rustle when you touch the banisters – that was out of bounds. But we found that if we opened the great wooden doors behind our beds, there was a space before the doors to the next room. There we stored our precious food – our 'tuck'. The fireplaces seemed to have been specially built to avoid heating the rooms. Their backs sloped away and the heat fled from the wrought iron grates, straight up the chimneys. We were frozen. It was a chill autumn, a bleak winter – and none of us was sorry when, before Christmas, the school decided, war or no war, to return to its native Hampstead.

Then my parents had a bright idea. The war was returning to London; Blitz or no Blitz, I should go to boarding school, in Pontypool – Jones's West Monmouthshire School – the 'West Mon', in all its Welsh, rugby glory. It was academically a good school and well away from the likely bombing of London. Why Wales? Father loved the land of his youth. Why Pontypool, which was not quite Wales but on its borders? Because that was the constituency of Father's friend, Arthur Jenkins, then Minister of Education, and father of a schoolboy later to become much better known than his father – Roy. I remember him then as a good-natured, slender teenager. Arthur promised that he and his wife, Hattie, would keep an eye on me.

So away I went, armed with my winter clothing, a few books and a packet of yeast – the revolting, pre-antibiotic antidote for the boils on my neck and in my nose, plagues of my youth. Mother used to camouflage my yeast in a spoonful of honey, which is why for many years I could not abide the product of the bee.

At the West Mon, both pupils and masters were kind to me. But I was lonely. I was the youngest boarder. And I was different. We used to swim in the local indoor baths. We wore nothing, not even the slivers of an excuse for swimming trunks, required by The Hall at the Hampstead Baths. The very first day, I found myself surrounded by a crowd of curious class mates. 'Ooh, look at him now,' one of them sang out, pointing at my private parts. 'Look, lads. There's something missing!' He was right. There was. Their curiosity was only matched by my own, because I had never seen anyone in his undisguised, uncircumcised totality. In one naked moment, I had become famous at the West Mon, an object of laughing curiosity.

There was no anti-Semitism at the school. They had simply never met a Jew nor even heard of one, at least not since the days of Jesus Christ. Father always regarded Wales as the least anti-Semitic of places, and he was right. But certainly the lads of the West Mon thought that we Jews were very odd people, to lose part of our necessary apparatus for no apparent reason.

My great hate at that school was the bell which mercilessly tolled at seven each morning. Clang . . . bong . . . clang . . . bong . . . I would push my tired head under the pillow and wish it away. Another day had begun.

Sundays were fun. I would go off to Newport for Hebrew lessons and for lunch with a local Jewish family. Or to Neath, where my cousin Shirley Nathan lived with her scientist husband. I spent my half-term with them, too. They took me to see Judy Garland in *The Wizard of Oz* and Shirley and Judy joined my list of favourite women; Shirley has remained on it ever since.

Then one day, I received a letter from Mother. I still have it, stained with my tears. 'Daddy and I have decided that you and Ruth should go to Canada, where you will be safe and happy. You will travel with Aunt Edith,

Michael and Derek', the Tarshes. 'And you will spend the war in Montreal, with them and with Grandpa and Grandma Cohen. Daddy and I will stay on in London.'

I never thought I would be sorry to leave the West Mon, but I was. Mother and Father took us onto the train from London, to Liverpool. Mother was in her Mechanised Transport Corps uniform. She told us that we would never have to worry. Grandpa had a shop in Montreal. Father gave me his father's gold watch. They told me that if I was in trouble, I should always go to any of my uncles – especially Uncle Isie Graham, husband of Father's sister, Sally.

I asked Mother: 'Why are you sending us away? We will be so lonely.'

'Because Daddy is on Hitler's blacklist. We are sure that the Germans will never come here, but we want to be sure that you will be safe. And you won't be lonely because you and Ruth will be together.' It was a moment too fraught to comprehend – a strange combination of childish fear and sadness, mixed with anticipation and excitement.

So, on 1 July 1940, Ruth and I and Aunt Edith and her two boys sailed from Liverpool to Canada on the *Duchess of Richmond*. Mother stood upright in her khaki uniform, together with Uncle Jack Tarsh, waving from the dockside and smiling bravely. We cried for a moment, then ran off to explore the great ship.

To us, this journey was a huge adventure. We leapt around the decks, waving our arms and shouting to each other. Yes, we felt sad for our parents, but what a treat this was for us in a new world. Our parents were choking with misery, because they knew that they might never see us again. We just believed that we were off on a hugely exciting holiday, sailing indeed into a new world. Wow! How jealous my friends at the West Mon would be, if they knew I was leaping round the deck of a great passenger liner, heading out into the mighty Atlantic.

On 2 July 1940, twelve hours after we sailed, the Germans torpedoed an evacuee ship called the *Arandora Star*. The wireless simply reported this fact without the name of the ship. For twelve hours, our parents were riveted with anxiety. Three months later, another evacuee ship, the *City of Benares*, was torpedoed and sank in mid-Atlantic, en route to Canada. Three hundred and twenty-five passengers were drowned. They were people like us . . . evacuees, as we were called . . . mainly families and children, seeking transatlantic safety. Mother told us later that if either of these ships had been sunk before we were at sea, they would have kept us at home. Still, they expected the Germans to invade Britain and if they had taken over our great land as they had done most of Europe, Mother and Father would have been among the first to be murdered or taken off to a concentration camp.

As it was, all five of us shared a rocking, lurching cabin, full of the reality and stench of seasickness. Yuk! Then and throughout our time in Canada, Aunt Edith was saintly in her patience. Ruth and I obeyed parental strictures and behaved as well as children could, as did Derek – who later used his middle name Nicholas (or Nick, as he is now known). His older brother, Michael, was totally honest and always spoke his mind, good-natured and well-intentioned, but uncontrollable and uncontrolled. Not easy for his Mum, or for us.

Some five days later, we entered the St Lawrence river, passing under the Quebec bridge. By a great optical illusion, you stood on deck and it seemed a certainty that the funnel would strike the arch. It did not and we landed safely in Montreal, to be greeted by Sidney and May Levitt – Uncle Sidney and Auntie May, to us.

Long ago, Joe Levitt had been the capital provider and partner of Grandpa Joseph Cohen. Despite the break-up of the partnership or perhaps because of it, the families remained friends and Joe's nephew Sidney was now in charge of the large Woodhouse furniture store in Montreal. That shop would provide wartime sustenance for us and for our grandparents, who joined us a few weeks later.

On our first night we stayed at the Levitt home in the comfortable, hilly Montreal suburb of Westmount. Before going to sleep and as a good and well-trained little English boy, I put my shoes outside the door for cleaning. The following morning, Auntie May marched into my room holding up the diminutive shoes with a look of disgust. A sprightly lady of gypsy aspect and dress, she was clearly cross. 'What are *these*?' she demanded to know.

'My shoes, Auntie May,' I replied, with downcast eyes. 'And why are they outside your door?' 'To be cleaned, Auntie May.'

'In Canada,' she said, 'if you leave your shoes outside the door, they will be thrown away. If you want them cleaned, you either clean them yourself or you pay for a shoeshine boy to do it for you. This . . .' she paused. 'This country . . . is a democracy!'

I thought of Auntie May when I went to the movies in Los Angeles many, many years later. The fat woman beside me was chomping and rustling a bag of popcorn. After ten minutes of suffering, I turned to her and said, very politely: 'Please, madam, please . . .' 'If you don't like it, you should go out and watch the movie at home,' she shot back at me. So I got up and as I filed past her, the woman alongside said: 'You know, people *here* are free to eat popcorn if they wish. The United States is a democracy.' I muttered something about Americans being very courteous and thoughtful – but with exceptions. Then I thought of Auntie May and decided that it was not worthwhile arguing. It would indeed be better to watch a movie at home.

Both incidents convinced me that while democracy is a gem, to be cherished and polished, it has different meanings for different people. And for Ruth and me, the Allies' fight for its preservation meant four difficult years. The love and friendship between us began when we left for Canada and will last, deeply cherished by us both, for the rest of our joint time on this earth.

A few days after our arrival in Montreal, Aunt Edith took us off to a small hotel on the shores of Lac Ouimet in the Laurentian mountains, where we spent three glorious weeks. We were soon joined by my mother's parents, Joseph and Henrietta Cohen. I roamed through the woods and learned to love their silence and the smell of pine needles. A friendly fellow guest taught me how to strip bark off silver birch trees and use it to make model canoes. And Aunt Edith, who in her day had been a champion diver, gave us all swimming lessons in the cool beauty of the lake.

Then back to Montreal, where Grandpa had rented an apartment in Kensington Avenue, immediately next door to the great Shaar Hashamayim Synagogue. I was sent to Westmount Intermediate High School where I was taught with children of my own age. But as my British standard of school knowledge was way ahead of theirs, I did not have to study too much. Which was just as well, because I was so often absent.

In those days, if any child in the family contracted any infectious disease, not only was that child put into quarantine but so were the rest of the family. With four children and nearly always one of us having measles, mumps, chickenpox or some other childhood illness – which later on, people hoped children would get while they were young – we were incarcerated in the flat. Out of sheer boredom, I went to the local library. There I borrowed a children's book on magic, which started a lifetime's hobby.

When I checked out the book, the man behind the desk said: 'Would you like to be a magician, young man?'

After a moment's thought, I said: 'I certainly would.'

'Well, I do magic for fun,' he said. 'I'll teach you.'

From then on, whenever I was away from school, I went into the library. We talked magic and he taught me. I put on my first magic shows for the other three children, producing a fried egg out of an empty straw hat. Magic had entered my life, where it has remained as the great ice-breaker, ever since.

In the summer of 1941, Grandpa, Grandma and Aunt Edith packed all of us off to Camp Hiawatha, a Jewish children's camp near the resort town of St Agathe, in the Laurentian mountains. In eight joyful weeks, I was happier and developed more than at any other time in Canada. Mother had shown me how to run, very fast, crouching down for a quick getaway. I had won the 100 yards race in the local Wolf Cubs sports. Now I found that I was by far the fastest runner of my age in the camp. Then came the camp election – a lesson in politics and democracy. We were to elect our own Prime Minister. I stood against a bright youngster who whopped me. He offered the campers more control, better food, less discipline – all promises which we all knew he could not fulfil. But he won anyway. And I learned my first lesson in the innate dishonesty of some politicians!

I shared a ten-bedded bunkhouse with people of whom many became lifelong friends. We sang camp songs . . . savoured the wilds on glorious canoe trips – shooting rapids and all. I took part in camp plays and delivered such solo epics as *The 11.69 Express*, and poems by Stanley Holloway, to receptive audiences of counsellors and campers. Forget the war in far-off England and parents and family, it was on with life. I was appreciated, stretched and happy.

On the far side of the lake, Ruth was equally contented. But on the trails that led from the boys' camp to the girls' camp, I savoured my first, joyful trysts. With vivacious Dorothy Solomon, who later married my 'bunk' chum, Cyril Reitman . . . with the wondrously beautiful Sheila Golden, who became a heroine of Montreal through her work for the disadvantaged and the disabled and who herself suffered the amputation of a leg. We had camp dances, filled with laughter and with little finesse, but fun galore.

After two months at camp, I was not ready to return to our Montreal apartment. I was nearly thirteen and approaching my barmitzvah – the great day when a Jewish lad is accepted as an adult into the congregation of Israel. The date had been fixed for November. But then the family came to a fateful decision. My good, honest, outspoken cousin Michael could not be handled at home. They decided that he needed the discipline of a boarding school. They would enrol him at Bishop's College School, the Eton of Canada, in a year or two. But Aunt Edith was not prepared to have her lad go on his own. I, too, would have to be a boarder. So that I would arrive at school at the start of term, they brought my barmitzvah forward. It was a day of honey and of tears, of joy and of very great sadness. On one side of the Atlantic, I read a portion of the Law in the huge synagogue, together with another English evacuee. On the other side, in London, my parents went to an East End synagogue and celebrated their only son's barmitzvah, in his far-off absence. On both sides of the water, we wept. We could not even speak by telephone. Only letters. Inadequate, censored and delayed. For me, that was the true horror of the war. I was an orphan. Yes, blessed with family, but no parents within sight or sound, and heading for a school where I would be deeply unhappy and wretchedly lonely.

TWO

Bishop's College School and St Paul's School – Seeds of Socialism

I became a dissenter, a radical, an anti-racist and a socialist at what was then – but is happily no longer – one of the least radical, most old-fashioned, most conformist, least innovative and most unsocialist places in the Western world. Bishop's College School, Lennoxville – BCS – was the Canadian over-reflection of that academically excellent but physically and emotionally cruel place, the traditionalist, British public school. The atmosphere was riddled with dislike. Sunk in the heart of Francophone Quebec, most of the boys despised French Canadians. I could never understand why. An Anglican stronghold, they also despised Roman Catholics, few of whom were French speakers. And the school allowed only a minute quota of Jews – about ten in the senior school, and a handful among the juniors.

We Jews were forced to attend Christian prayers, not only in hall each morning but also in church each Sunday. Easter was horrendous. '*You* killed Christ,' my mates informed me. I had nothing whatever against Christ, and could not understand how I could have killed him as I was now after all only thirteen years old and he, alas, was crucified in biblical times. I learned slowly that I was their means of seeking revenge.

I was walking to church on my first Sunday when an amiable, rotund and musical Jewish fellow sufferer called George Hurst came up to me. George was popular because he was good-natured and responded to taunts with a genial smile. He took out his misery on a piano, in a corridor outside the top-floor dormitories. He was later to become conductor of the Bourne-mouth Symphony Orchestra.

'Take care, young Janner,' he said. 'You will discover in the middle of the service that everybody gets up and forms a queue. On my first Sunday, I joined it and when I reached the priest, he gave me a mouthful of wine, and a piece of dry bread, which I put in my pocket. When I pulled it out a few weeks later and showed it to a friend, he called it "the host" and said that I had been carrying Christ's body around with me in my pocket!'

'What do I do?'

'When the others get up, you sit still.'

I did – and the others just glared at me.

It was after a church service that I suffered my first migraine, and George emerged from BCS with a mighty, facial twitch. As a Jew, you could get nothing right. 'Lend me a nickel.' 'Sorry, I haven't got a nickel.' The supplicant would rub together the finger and the thumb of his right hand and screw up his nose. 'Jew . . .'

'Lend me a nickel, please.'

'OK. Here's a nickel.'

'Thank you. How much interest will you charge me, Jew?'

We had to study *The Merchant of Venice*. I formed a deep affinity with the awful Shylock. Had I not also got eyes and ears and feelings? If you pricked me or beat me up or caned me, did I not bleed?

A prefect used to distribute the mail. He would stand on the stairs and call out the names of the recipients and flick the letters towards us. Sometimes they would even call out the names of the sender. 'Janner . . . from Rabbi . . . Rabbi . . . Levy . . .' Someone would call out: 'Oy oy . . .'

One day, a classmate asked me with apparent kindness whether I missed my family. I said, 'Yes – I miss my mother very much.' So he started singing, to the tune of a current South American tango hit: 'Ay-ay my Mamma, I vant my Mamma – oy-oy, I vant my Mamma . . .' I suppose I should have hit him, but that was what he wanted. Anyway he was bigger than I was and I have never believed in physical violence as a sensible retort. I learned there a lesson which often proved useful in later political life. If you give other people the fight they seek, the pain will usually last longer.

Not surprisingly, most of my friends were fellow Jewish sufferers. Like poor Adrian Levitt – also sent to Bishop's to cure him of his non-conformist approach to life and son of my 'sponsors'. Or Leo Rothschild, my lifelong friend and a gentle and cultured soul. We sometimes escaped together on Sunday afternoons and cooked on camp fires in the woods. Edward Bronfman was another soft-spoken and kindly young man, sent away to get the best education. He and I shared High Holy Days together, with the Echenberg family in the town of Sherbrooke. Sam Echenberg was a Colonel –

the highest-ranking Jewish officer in the Canadian army. We were very proud
of him. Before the days of Israel, Jews were not regarded as fighters. Then
there was Ralph Paull, a burly friend, whose parents kept him well supplied
with salami sausages. And Don Faerman – it was at his fourteenth birthday
party that I was first introduced to the joys of what was then called 'necking'.

My non-conformist BCS hero was a lad whom nearly everyone else
despised because he admitted to being a Socialist and would when older
vote for the Canadian version of the British Labour Party. But on the
whole, my political reactions were instinctive, rather than intellectual – an
approach which has endured.

From the moment you entered the door of Bishop's, you were part of a
class system. The 'new boys' were the underclass. After a year of
endurance, you became a 'neutral', looking down on the 'new boys' and up
at the third year – the 'seniors' – and with it at their privileges. The prefects
had the power, which included the right to beat.

If you were guilty of any sort of misdemeanour, which I was constantly,
you got 'sent in'. You lined up outside the prefects' room in the evening.
You were then called in to account for being late or untidy or cheeky or
whatever and when found guilty, as I always was, you bent over and a
prefect beat you hard across the buttocks with a cane. I was a scared,
wretched, lonely child. As a somewhat sloppy, unkempt little boy who was
often late, I found myself 'sent in' most nights. I would creep out of the
prefects' room, clutching my backside and determined not to cry. I could
not have been more miserable. At one stage, I was beaten so often and so
hard that my buttocks were a criss-cross of painful red and white weals.
I took myself to the school Matron, who applied some ointment. She said
nothing to me about the cruelty, but I was not beaten again.

I never complained to anyone about my miseries. I never even mentioned
the beatings. My father had only hit me once as a child, and then with total
justification. Mother had told me to go to sleep and stop reading and had
taken away my torch. So I had lit a candle and was reading by its light,
under the covers. Not unreasonably, Father explained to me that I might
easily have burned the house down and cremated myself in the ashes. He
then slapped my face.

I could not understand why the boys at BCS were so vile to each other.
So what did I do? I spent hours in the library, reading voraciously,

everything from Howard Spring's *Fame Is the Spur* to all the novels of Charles Dickens. And something inside me made me want to beat those nasty bastards at everything. I was determined to excel – which I did.

I hated Latin and found it extremely boring and difficult. So I memorised every Latin text and ended up winning the Lieutenant Governor's Prize for Latin. When I was later sent to St Paul's School and received my first Latin report, it read: 'Janner's knowledge of elementary Latin grammar has improved. As well it might. When he arrived here, from Canada, it was virtually nil!' In my matriculation, I even got nearly 100 per cent in maths – a subject which I have always found monstrously difficult. And my French became excellent, especially after a Cours d'Été, French Summer School, at Montreal's McGill University Queen Victoria College. I was the youngest person there. We were not allowed to speak English – a rule which I regarded as sensible and hence to be obeyed. I emerged with a love of French, and anyway, it was a language spoken by French Canadians who in those days were another despised ethnic group.

My main outlet for triumph was on the sports field. I was a superb sprinter, I could outrun the lot of them. I was useless at ice hockey. My ankles hurt too much. And I was terrified of the ski slopes, but I managed to get on the school's junior ski team anyway, through determination, not talent. I even excelled at American football. I ran like a hare, once scoring six touchdowns in a triumphant match against a local school team. But in one tumble, I dislocated my right shoulder, the greatest physical pain that I have ever endured. Hauled off to hospital in an ambulance and anaesthetised by an ether mask, I thought I had been under for at least an hour, while they heaved my arm bone back into its shoulder socket. I remembered a long and vivid dream and was astonished to learn that I had been 'out' for no more than thirty seconds. But I have not forgotten the boom-boom drumming in the head as the ether sent me under.

The finest and most graceful skier in the school was a tall, lithe youngster called Phelps, who was very kind to me. One Christmas, he invited me to join his family at a Laurentian ski resort called Mont Tremblant. A few days later he apologetically withdrew the invitation 'because,' he told me, 'the hotel had restricted clientele'. That was the current, revolting shorthand for: No Jews. I could not understand. Why should they exclude people because they were Jewish?

I was too frightened to ask my grandfather and did not want to upset my Aunt Edith by telling her of my misery and Ruth was too young. I just put up with it. But I made up my mind then that when I grew up, I would somehow stop the nonsense and fight back. Meanwhile, my cousin Michael endured a year in the junior school, before the family brought him back to Montreal, en route (for them all) to home in England.

I soon learned that the persecution was not confined to BCS. Grandpa took me to a meeting in the Montreal Forum, addressed by Mikhoels and Pfeffer – Soviet Jewish activists, later annihilated in a Stalin purge. They told us about the Holocaust. That, I could not absorb into my mind or soul.

My only other approach to physical punishment in my childhood was on the eve of the Passover, in a hotel in Bournemouth. Grandpa Cohen had gathered all the family together as his guests for a huge table at the hotel 'seder' – the occasion when we read the story of the Exodus, the going out from Egypt. My cousin Edmund and I were upstairs, playing blackjack, and we lost track of the time. So we were not present to perform the required rite of Jewish boys – to ask the four questions about why we celebrate the Passover.

When Grandpa stormed upstairs he looked at us and pronounced the memorable words: 'I'll smack your little *tokhus* until it bleeds!' But he never did. My bottom remained unsmacked.

As so often in life, it improved with seniority. The BCS 'new boy' year was hell; the second 'neutral' year, not so bad; and when I became a senior, with power to 'send people in' to be beaten by the prefects, I abused that power for about a month, before I realised what was happening to me . . . that I was becoming part of the system that I so despised. . . . From then on I never 'sent in' anyone, ever again.

During my four years in Canada, I only once heard my parents' voices. Each week, the BBC brought together a group of parents to speak to their evacuee children overseas. One morning I was called into the study of the amiable but insensitive headmaster. Instead of leaving me alone for those precious moments, he sat in his chair, smiling at me as I tried not to cry. The tears poured out of my eyes but I clamped my lips shut. I was immeasurably lonely.

Unwittingly and certainly unwillingly, BCS sowed in me the seeds of socialism. A burning hatred of inequality and of racism and an abiding sympathy for those who were despised because they were different. It provided my first bitter taste of mindless anti-Semitism.

So BCS gave me a first-class education, not only in English, history and French, but also in life as a persecuted member of a harassed minority. In Canada, Camp Hiawatha had fostered my pride, my leadership and my confidence. And my Canadian Cohen relatives – Aunt Sylvia and her sons, Gordon and Lyon – gave me happy refuge in their Montreal home after Ruth, my grandparents, Aunt Edith and her boys returned to England, leaving me to complete my year at BCS. But I took to counting the number of days before I could go home and they stretched out into agonising infinity.

'Enough,' the Janners and the Tarshes and the Cohens all decided. Hitler was not going to invade. It was time for the evacuees to return home. Which was fine for everyone except me. Mother had arranged for me to be accepted at St Paul's School, but only if I took my matriculation and got decent results. I would have to stay behind at Bishop's.

I worked and studied and ground my way through those exams, like never before or since. My results were spectacular. The family arranged for me to be taken from New York to London aboard HMS *Arbiter*, a US 'Woolworth' aircraft carrier, supplied to Britain under the Marshall Plan. En route, I spent a wondrous week in New York, as a guest of family friends, who gave me literally the time of my young life. I marvelled at Paul Robeson, playing the Moor, in *Othello* . . . I was enraptured by the musical glories of *Oklahoma* – and of the New York Philharmonic Orchestra . . . and at the Metropolitan Opera, I was mesmerised by *Carmen* – still the only opera which I truly enjoy.

I was whipped up to the top of the Empire State Building and down the river to the Statue of Liberty. I craned my neck at the skyscrapers and wondered at the traffic, the noise, the sheer exuberance of that great city. And then I took my bag, filled with gifts from my hosts, and marched up the gangplank to HMS *Arbiter*, joining a host of other young men, all hitching a ride at His Majesty's expense, because we would soon be called up for our military service.

The first day was fine. Then the lurching, heaving, rolling began. Whoever invented the flat top did not intend it to be used to carry people. We vomited our way across the Atlantic. The crew tried to teach us boat drill and gun drill, but we were just too sick. One of my mates was a skilled bridge player and between our rushes to the rail or to the 'heads', I learned the elements of that intellectual game. Which is perhaps why I still bid and play like a drunken sailor.

In Liverpool, the family were waiting for me. Mother and Father, Ruth and Edmund, Aunt Edith and the rest of the Tarsh family. After a joyful holiday in Prestatyn, in North Wales, where I won the sprint race in the village sports, it was back to London – to 3 Lancaster Gate Terrace – and to school. St Paul's.

To and for me, St Paul's was everything that Bishop's was not. About one third of the pupils were Jewish. The High Master, Walter Oakeshott – a brilliant, soft-spoken and witty man who later became Master of Lincoln College, Oxford – told Mother: 'I choose our pupils by merit, not by religion. We look for people for whom the school can do most and who can do most for the school.' As with choice, so with education. In my two years at St Paul's, I endured not one incident of anti-Semitism.

The teaching was excellent and in some ways eccentric. As I entered the school two years away from taking a scholarship exam in history and one year from the top history form, I was put into a remarkable form called 'Modern Special'. Our three teachers were all fantastic. History, Paul Longland – a committed left-winger. I could not imagine any teacher at Bishop's who would openly admit to left-wing views. This man told yesterday's story as his story of today. It lived. Then Philip Whitting, another laughing Socialist, and atheist. He told us how when he was called up into the army, they asked him for his religion. 'I haven't got one,' he replied.

'You've got to have one, young man,' his interviewer snapped back.

'Why?'

'Because otherwise, we can't bury you.'

'Very well,' said Mr Whitting. 'I'm Church of England – for burying purposes only!'

Rubbing his fist against his bald head, he demanded our attention. He asked us questions and expected answers, right or wrong. And he challenged us, whatever we replied. So did Mr F.G.S. Parker. Every time I answered a political question with a Labour answer, he would attack me, tearing at the roots of my logic and making me try to justify my view.

I always regarded him as a right-wing Tory. When I visited him at his home a year after I had left the school and told him this, he roared with laughter and produced his Labour Party membership card. Now, that's education. Training the mind. Honing the intelligence. And not just feeding ideas and facts for exam purposes.

When I joined St Paul's, in September 1944, it was still evacuated to East Hampstead Manor, a reasonably stately Berkshire home. The pupils either lived in hostels or, like myself, were billeted with local families. I found myself at a house called 'Le Nid' – pronounced locally, Lee Nidd. My host was Bill Hull, a warder (or male nurse) at Broadmoor psychiatric hospital. His wife, Nan, was a buxom, warm, outspoken lady, to whom I was a puzzle. At election time, Mrs Hull assured me that she was going to listen to speakers from each of the parties and then make up her mind. But we all knew that she would end up, as always, voting Tory. They were proud Scots and in the outside loo they kept a Scottish newspaper with a cartoon character called 'Oor Wullie'.

I was warned when I arrived that you always used the back door of the house. You went out of the front door only in a coffin. I was allowed to do my homework in the front room, which was used for special occasions only. They found it odd that I could not study in the living room, under the light of the gas mantles and with the huge wireless blaring. This was kept alive by accumulators, which we carried up to the grocer on Crowthorne High Street, who put them on charge.

The family moved at a sensible, normal pace. I whooshed in and out; Mrs Hull called me 'the whirlwind'. They were not in the least worried by the fact that I was Jewish. They just could not understand why I did not eat my bacon ration, but as I gave it each week to them, they were totally satisfied with my odd habits. My only misery: when I tried to adjust one of the gas mantles, it poured soot across their kitchen. The cost of redecoration went onto my parents' bill.

I parked my bike in the back yard; cycled to East Hampstead Manor, five miles each way, whatever the weather; and was happy in a school where, unlike Bishop's, they neither sought uniformity nor despised the different. I was sorry when, at the end of the summer term, the school and all its pupils returned to London.

Elections, I enjoyed. Mother had only once stood on her own account, in East London, where she was trounced by the then famous Communists, Phil Piratin and Willy Gallagher. But the 1945 election not only saw the triumphant election of Attlee's Labour Government but, happily, the return of Father to his beloved House of Commons, this time as Labour MP for Leicester North West. He had been hunting for a seat ever since 1935. At the 1935 Labour Party Conference, a friend had introduced him to the man who controlled the Leicester seats, the local power broker, Councillor Fred Jackson. The sitting MP was Harold Nicholson, the distinguished writer and former Labour man, now Independent. His majority was sixteen, the smallest in the country. Father beat him by a spanking margin of 7,593.

As in Crowthorne, the more so in London – my life at St Paul's was as vigorous, energetic and varied as it was not, alas, academic. Everything new that I tried, they encouraged.

I was a good sprinter and beat the school record for the 100 yards. Fine – but there was no school athletic club. 'Then why not form one?' I did. We built up a team and organised matches against other schools. And on one of the great days of my life, at a track called Motspur Park, I won the Southern Counties Junior 100 yards. I was the fastest runner for my age in all of the South of England and I was dead chuffed. My family were thrilled, especially Mother, who had taught me so long ago how to burst off to an explosive start. As a girl at South Hampstead High School, she was on every sports team. Sadly, she still looked back on those days as the happiest in her life. Now she took pride in my moment of glory.

I thought that the school magazine was boring and uninspired. So the teacher who ran it told me to go to the school library and look at *The Debater* – the magazine started by G.K. Chesterton, when he was at the school. Never mind that he would turn in his grave if he learned that a Jew was recreating his journal – just do it. Together with a group of friends, I sold advertising. We produced a reasonable product; and we learned much.

The school had two debating societies, the Union and the Chesterton. To me, the Union was too establishment. I joined the Chesterton and was soon elected chairman.

When High Master Walter Oakeshott had scanned my Bishop's reports and agreed to my Mother's plea to admit me to St Paul's, he told her: 'He'll never be a prefect, I'm afraid. He's coming in too late.' But one great morning, a senior prefect ran up to me, beaming. 'Congratulations!' he shouted, giving me a bear hug. 'You've been made a prefect!' He was right, and I was put in charge of Jewish prayers. At Bishop's, we all had to attend both Christian prayers and Sunday Chapel. At St Paul's, they respected students' right to be different. You could attend Christian prayers or Jewish prayers or neither. Wonderful.

We even had a Jewish Youth Study Group. Its central organisation held winter schools and summer schools, in Birmingham, Leeds and London. Most 'study groupers' were far more traditional Jews than myself. No matter. Provided that you respected the rights of the orthodox to follow their ways, they would leave you alone to follow yours.

My father often told me that we British Jews are very lucky people. We combine two marvellous cultures and we should be proud of both. At Bishop's, Jews were a despised minority. At St Paul's, we were part of society, and treated as individuals with such respect as we earned. At the Jewish Youth Study Groups, I learned to relax totally in young Jewish company.

I had one problem – no time to study. At Bishop's, I had studied like a demon. At St Paul's, I was making up for those lost years. So I scrambled through adequately in my Higher School Certificate and, probably as a result of lively interviews, I won an Exhibition – a minor scholarship – to Trinity Hall, Cambridge. I was hugely lucky. But first, I had to endure my 'National Service'.

THREE

Army Days

I was due to be called up in June 1946. Meanwhile, I was to enjoy a few months' work experience in Father's office. Alas, there was little enjoyment. My Victorian Dad considered that the right way to train me was to require me to take on tasks far beyond my reach and to berate me when I failed; to issue orders and to require immediate obedience; and with the best intentions, to achieve the worst results from his son. My sanity was saved by his secretary, Miss Mabel Vickers: hair cropped short; horn-rimmed spectacles; and full of laughter. When Father told her off, she laughed. When he required me to do the filing which I found impossible and excruciatingly boring, she laughed and stuffed the files under the massive armchair. She knew exactly how to handle Father. I did not.

Father was Victorian in his approach to his children. I respected him deeply, both for having lifted himself out of his humble origins into political and communal leadership and for his total integrity. But, sadly, we were never close. He considered that it was a son's duty not only to obey instructions from his father, but not to disagree with his views, nor still less to argue with him. That put our relationship at a respectful distance. We were emotionally and intellectually so far apart that when he died and I came to the hospital to say prayers at his side, I wept. We could have given each other so much comradeship and pleasure. Now it was too late. He was wrapped in white sheets and life had gone from his face. Now there was no chance of having a real relationship with my father.

How odd that was, I thought. I had followed his trail into the law – although I could not stand being in his solicitor's office, and so had become a barrister. I had followed him into politics and, indeed, become the first Labour son ever to succeed his father in the same parliamentary seat. We had so much in common but he had kept us apart. I choked with emotion, in memory of what this body beside me had been and in misery at the chance, now gone for ever, of our enjoying that special friendship which would have had added so much to both our lives.

Then I stood up and said our Jewish memorial prayer – and I determined that I would learn from our non-relationship and that I would listen to my children and to my grandchildren and that we would discuss and debate, with mutual respect . . . and that we would have the deep friendship which I had missed so bitterly. And I thanked God for the understanding and friendship of my mother and sister. Without them, my youth would have been off balance.

So I decided that I had learned much from my father, but not what he had intended to teach me. Victorian youngsters must have had tough lives.

After a few weeks in Father's office, I decided that the Army could not be worse. I marched off to the nearest recruiting office; told them that I was due to start my two years' National Service in June; and pleaded with them to call me up right away. They agreed.

It was a freezing cold March winter's day when I climbed onto the train, heading for Reservoir Camp, Gloucester. At the camp entrance, I joined a laughing group of fellow recruits, all with broad Gloucestershire accents. We collected our uniforms and moved at the double across a snowy field towards our hut. Seasoned soldiers, eighteen-year-olds who had been called up a few days earlier, shouted at us: 'You'll be sorry . . . You'll be sorry . . .'

I found the training immeasurably mindless and boring. Marching up and down and saluting to the front by numbers . . . dismantling, cleaning and assembling my rifle . . . polishing the floor and folding and squaring off my blankets. I soon found that of our platoon of twenty-four, I was the only one who was fully literate. So, I read my mates' girlfriends' letters to them and helped them to write back. In return, they made my bed and cleaned my rifle. In our hut, we huddled around the inadequate oil heater. There was no heating in the ablutions block. The water for shaving was ice cold and I learned the true meaning of that army expression about what freezing cold does to the private parts of brass monkeys.

Still, the lads were good-natured and fun. To them, I was a curiosity, whom they appreciated and thought funny. To me, they were a hilarious, good-natured and delightful novelty. And I was enchanted to learn from them how you could use one word in the English language as a verb or adverb, noun or adjective. 'Well, fuck me!' as our Sergeant used to say. 'Never in my fucking life have I seen such a fucking lot of useless fuckers as you lot!' I was not just learning how the other half live, but especially how they talk.

Off duty, we headed for town. The lads preferred the pubs and I wandered through the glorious Gloucester cathedral, with its unique gargoyles, some of them with the faces of the medieval stonemasons who created them. To my surprise, I was sorry when the four weeks' initial training froze to their end.

We had all been invited to choose our regiments. I selected the Royal Artillery, naively believing that I would ride in vehicles pulling the guns. On arrival at the training centre in Larkhill, in the centre of Salisbury Plain, I soon learned that we marched in front, pulling the guns behind us. My unit had been selected as potential officer material. I did not tell them that I knew that if you went on to officer training – at OCTU, as it was called – you might well have to spend an extra year in the army, which was definitely not for me.

My platoon were an amiable lot, including a man called Mike, who rode a huge motorbike. When we had weekend leave, I would sit on the pillion, holding on to him like grim death, as he charged down the roads to Salisbury station. No helmets in those days. Terrifying.

Our Sergeant was a wizened, battle-hardened veteran called Holloway, small in stature but loud in voice. 'Come on lads, Bags Of Guts . . . Bags Of Guts . . .' he would yell. He was known as 'BOG Holloway'. But 'Sarge' to his face, of course. He regarded me as an amiable sort of idiot. I just about managed to conquer the technicalities of handling the gun – roughly for line, roughly for elevation, cross level, accurately for elevation, accurately for line. We covered our ears when we fired the guns and hoped for the best.

The big question: What to do next? I decided that I wanted to see at least a little of the world . . . to get out of England . . . which probably meant, Germany. Father decided that I should use my army time to learn some law and prepare for my future. Combining the two ambitions meant getting me into the Directorate of Army Legal Services (DALS), in Germany.

Father had two Labour MP neighbours in Leicester seats. One was Bert Bowden, who later headed the BBC; the other, Terence Donovan, who became a distinguished High Court Judge. Terence's brother was a General whose territory included DALS. In September 1947, he put in a good word for me and I was posted to its Legal Aid Section at HQ BAOR – the headquarters of the British Army of the Rhine in the spa town of Bad Oenhausen, affectionately known as BO.

I travelled by train to Harwich and then embarked on a troopship to the Hook of Holland. Standing by the railings, an old soldier asked me: 'Do you speak German?' I shook my head, regretfully. 'You need to learn,' he said, 'otherwise you can't have fun with the bints. Anyway, the best place to learn the fucking language is in bed!' I got his point.

Off the ship and onto a Dutch train. Scrawny children lining the embankments, their hands held out for food. We threw our rations to them, out of the windows. This was my first glimpse of Hitler's hungry legacy.

Life at DALS was relaxed. We lived upstairs and worked downstairs and our sergeant treated us with courtesy. I soon discovered that our main job was to help the squaddies who wanted to divorce their English wives to marry German girls. 'Ah well, it's a job,' we used to say.

Each Friday night, there was a BO service and dinner for the Jewish soldiers, most of whom were serving in the War Crimes Group, North-West Europe. Knowing them changed my Army service and my life. Eighteen years old, I was about to become the youngest War Crimes Investigator in the British Army of the Rhine.

The Chaplain to the Jewish forces in Germany, Rabbi Brown from Leeds, conducted the service for us. Then the Jewish Hospitality Unit provided us with a homely and traditional Sabbath repast. Chicken soup and chopped liver and roast chicken and apple strudel. There, I made many friends, including a swashbuckling young captain called Saul Rosenberg of the Gordon Highlanders. To us, he was known as 'MacMoishe'. After demob, he emigrated to Israel, acquired the name of Shaul Ramati and became an eminent member of the mixed Armistice Commission and then an ambassador. It was also at those gastronomic evenings that I made friends with the War Crimes mob. These included a joyful, capricious, wilful young character called Freddie Granville (né Gottlieb), who tucked me under his vivacious wing. He was in Search Section. Job: 'To track down Nazi bastards who murdered Jews and prisoners of war'.

Freddie told me that the head of the Search Section was one Peter Priestley, whose surname used to be Cohen. The first Cohen was the Temple High Priest, Aaron. A brilliant name change. Captain Priestley had been interned in the Dachau concentration camp, before the war, when they still removed the dead in coffins. Peter decided that he needed a coffin more than the deceased and changed places with one of them. Fellow prisoners carried him out and he escaped from Germany and volunteered for the Special Air Service where all the paratroopers with Jewish names changed them. If they were captured by the enemy and known to be Jewish they would be murdered and not treated as prisoners of war.

One Friday night, Freddie challenged me: 'Don't you want to do something useful with your army life? Why don't you join us in War Crimes?'

'How could I do that?' I asked. 'For a start, I don't speak German.'

'Then learn it,' said Freddie.

'How do I get into your work?'

'You just learn German and leave the rest to me,' he said.

So I did. Four times a week, I took evening classes, with a statuesque blonde at the Army Education Corps Centre. Within weeks, I told Freddie: 'Right. I can now get around in German. But that wouldn't get me very far in the Nuremberg trials, would it?'

'You're not going to be an interpreter,' said Freddie. 'It's Search Section for you. We've a list of thousands of these filthy murderers. Concentration camp guards. Some killed Jews and others shot our British escapees from Stalag Luft III.'

A week later, I received instructions to report for interview to Captain Peter Priestley. I asked Freddie how to handle the interview. 'Don't worry,' he said. 'You'll get in. I've told the Captain about you. He loves the idea of having Barnett Janner's son in his unit!' So there was some advantage to my ancestry after all.

Priestley approved and passed me on to the head of the unit, Colonel Nightingale. To my joy, on 30 December 1946, Lance Bombardier Janner, all of eighteen years old, became a War Crimes Investigator. I found myself surrounded by my smiling Friday-night friends. Freddie was charged with my training. I sat with him in his standard Army-issue green Volkswagen Beetle and we careered around the British Zone, on the trail of culprits.

Freddie was a heavy smoker. One sunny day, he was driving his Volkswagen at great speed, puffing at his cigarette and swerving every now and again to avoid a pedestrian and then only at the very last second, laughing joyfully as the civilian leapt out of his way. 'You ought to try a cigarette,' he said. 'It's very pleasant. Have one.' Keeping two fingers of one hand on the wheel, he pulled a packet of Players out of his pocket and held it out to me. I thought: Why not? He lit a match. I sucked in the smoke. Acrid. Unpleasant. 'Persevere a little,' said Freddie. 'You'll love it.' So I did. After two cigarettes, I was hooked. Within weeks, I was smoking two packets a day and that went on for twenty years, wherever I was and however unpleasant for others and every day of the week. I was a chain smoker. To hell with my running, I gave that up. Politics was more enjoyable, anyway.

Soon, I was assigned my own targets, plus my own Volkswagen. My nearest brushes with death did not come from the Nazis. The first was when my Volkswagen's brakes gave out, at the top of a hill. I raced down, swerving to avoid parked cars and mercifully missing both humans and lampposts and steering the vehicle until it ran halfway up the hill on the other side. Another time, I was in a truck, driven by a colleague. He swung to the right. I was flung against the door to the left and fell out, the wheels missing me by a hair's breadth. Happily, I was then assigned my own driver.

My first job: escorting a captured woman guard from Auschwitz-Birkenau. She was an ugly, loathsome person whom my driver and I and a military policeman were glad to leave at our military prison, known by the code name of 'Tomato', in Minden. I hated her and found her the ultimate argument in favour of the death penalty.

My first capture was another prison guard. In my hand, I held my instructions. A photo, in SS uniform, at the top right-hand corner. Details of background and infamy filling the sheet. This man was a farmer. He was sitting in his massive kitchen, surrounded by children, dogs and cats. Yes, he resembled the photograph, but he was such an ordinary man. Such an undistinguished, undistinguishable ordinary human being. How could he have been the monster described in the document? It was then I learned that most of the Nazi murderers were just ordinary people. That was the horror of it. Ordinary people who took pleasure in killing ordinary Jews and gypsies, ordinary socialists and gays, and ordinary civilians in Nazi occupied lands. I felt sick.

I thought of that farmer many years later, in 1999, when I watched a vicious killer called Sawoniuk, standing trial at the Old Bailey. The main accusation – that he had lined up a group of fifteen Jewish women, stripped them of their clothing, and machine-gunned them down so that they fell into the grave behind them. Sawoniuk looked like an elderly, very ordinary clerk person. The jury decided that he was a mass murderer.

Our War Crimes Group instructions: when you catch someone, do not say to him: 'You are a vile killer. Your time has come. Say goodbye to your family because you will never see them again.' No. Resist the temptation. Instead, smile and say: 'So sorry to trouble you, but we've been asked to take you to somewhere nearby, for a few questions. You'll probably be home tonight, but perhaps you'd like to pack a few clothes, just in case you're away for a night or two.' Then get the person into the car and, with renewed apologies, put on the handcuffs. 'So sorry, it's just a matter of routine. They'll be off in a few minutes when we reach our destination. We'll be there in time for lunch . . .' Arrest in daytime if you must, but the middle of the night is better. People are a lot less likely to cause trouble when they are dozy. Ordinary people are like that . . .

I arrested a man called Hans Diessner, wanted for the murders of British airmen who had escaped from the prisoner-of-war camp known as Stalag Luft III. I knew he lived in Hamburg and on the off-chance that he might have been careless enough to allow his name to be on the list, I did a search at the Meldamt – the local registry. Behold, under a slightly different name, my man. I immediately called HQ, who sent over a Dutch investigator. We knocked at the door of Diessner's suburban apartment at about 3 a.m. An ordinary looking hausfrau opened the door. What did we want? 'So sorry, madam. We'd be grateful for a quick word with Herr Diessner.' The man emerged in his pyjamas, rubbing his eyes. Yes, he was Hans Diessner. 'Please would you be kind enough to get dressed and come with us?' said my Dutch mate. 'You should be back this evening.' I noticed an Iron Cross and some other medals and arm bands which I duly 'liberated'. Diessner kissed his wife goodbye. Into the car and on with the handcuffs and off we drove to Tomato Prison, where we handed him over to the guards in apparently good condition.

The following day, Captain Priestley called me into his office. 'Well done with Diessner. But you're going to have to go over to Tomato at once to identify his body. Last night, he committed suicide in his cell.' At Tomato, I recognized the body of Diessner. It was the first corpse I had ever seen. There were red cord marks around his neck. He had hanged himself. I was surprised that I felt no emotion. Was that because I knew he was a cold-blooded murderer and that I was pleased that he had done justice to his unworthy life? Or because I reckoned that if he had been tried and convicted, he would one day again be a free man? I wondered at the time, but I lost no sleep over his demise.

When I had arrived at the Directorate of Army Legal Services, I had been promoted to Lance Bombardier – the artillery equivalent of a Lance Corporal. Later, I was made up to full Bombardier. In January 1948, after I captured Diessner, I was promoted to the mighty rank of Sergeant, Local Acting Unpaid. With it went welcome access to the Sergeants' Mess, decent food and accommodation, and a touch of comfort.

Our work was painstaking. Our failures were many and our successes few. Our best allies were the KRIPO – the German criminal police – most of whom at that time were anti-Nazis who had previously either been ineligible for the German police or turfed out of it.

In August 1948, we were shocked to learn that War Crimes Group was to be disbanded. Priorities had changed, we understood. What mattered now was the Cold War against the Russians and for that we needed German help. One of my mates said bitterly: '*They* don't care about those criminal bastards, even the ones who murdered Brits.' *They* were, of course, the same people who were preventing Jewish survivors from settling in Israel. The British Government of the day, Ernest Bevin's Government. I was ashamed of them.

So War Crimes Group was wound up and I was transferred to the Judge Advocate General's Branch (JAG), dealing with alleged offences committed by our British troops. Meanwhile, much of my life centred on my weekend work in the Bergen-Belsen Jewish Displaced Persons' (DP) Camp.

FOUR

Bergen-Belsen and its Shadow

Bad Oenhausen boasted a military cinema. It was there I first saw Belsen. With my friend Edward (Ted) Greenfield, I watched the film of the liberation of Belsen concentration camp by our British troops. With cold horror, I endured the bleak, savage, unspeakable misery of that foul place. As Ted and I stood up to leave, at the end of the newsreel, I heard two women talking in the row behind us. One said to the other: 'I don't like Jews. But they shouldn't have done that to them.' Yuk!

I knew that the former SS Barracks in what was known as Bergen-Belsen now housed the only Jewish Displaced Persons' (DP) Camp in the British Zone of Germany. It was north of Hannover, near a town called Celle. I determined to get there, as fast as possible. That Friday night, I talked to my Jewish friends. They introduced me to members of the Jewish Relief Unit (the JRU), stationed not far away in a town called Eilshausen, who invited me to come over for dinner. So two days later, I met that devoted, staunch and admirable group of British volunteers, whose job was to bring relief to the Jewish survivors. They told me that the following Sunday was the second anniversary of the liberation of Belsen. They were going to the ceremony and to the DP Camp. Would I like to go with them? Yes, please.

That Sunday, I joined a JRU leader called Pearl Ketcher. It took us about two-and-a-half hours' driving before we entered the village of Bergen. 'The people here say they never knew there was a concentration camp up the road,' said Pearl, contemptuously. 'Bloody liars. Truckloads and trainloads of people going by in one direction and none ever coming back. Where did they think they were going – to some permanent holiday camp? Couldn't the villagers smell the stench of death? Didn't the guards from the camp come here to swill their beer and tell their tales of bravery?'

We drove past the lines of German barracks and onto the site of the death camp. It was a desert. Buildings burned down, to destroy the seeds of typhus and typhoid. Among the rubble, I found a child's shoe . . . a rusted, tin mug . . . rags. . . . The whole area was covered with blood-red moss. No birds flew. You walked on the moss and it crackled, as if you were treading on bones. We passed mass graves. 'Hier ruhen 1,000 Tote' – 'Hier ruhen 500 Tote' – here lie 1,000, there 500 dead people. Murdered human beings, most but not all of them Jews. Incomprehensible to a lad of eighteen. I was numbed. We walked across to the simple Jewish memorial – a granite and marble obelisk, topped with a round ball. Grouped around it were survivors, now displaced persons (DPs) and representatives of the Control Commission for Germany (the CCG) and of the JRU. The Chairman of the Camp Committee, Yossel Rosensaft, addressed the gathering in flowing Yiddish. I recognised the words for blood, tears and death – and Jews and Nazis and the hope for a future in Palestine.

Then Rabbi Zvi Helfgott, the Chief Rabbi of Belsen, sang the memorial prayer: El Molei Rahamim. A wail rose up. Together, we chanted the Hebrew prayer for the dead. Together, we wept. After more prayers, the crowd drifted away, in solemn, respectful silence. 'Enough of death,' said Pearl. 'Now we're going to take you to the Kinderheim – the children's home – for tea.'

The Kinderheim was in a long, low, single-storey building, with the Fachschule – the trade training centre – alongside. Opposite stood the great Roundhouse, once the headquarters of the German army. It held a cinema, meeting halls, dining rooms and the British Officers' Mess. It was now our military HQ, but the cinema was sometimes used for major Camp events.

The Kinderheim housed over fifty children. Some were orphans, others were separated from their parents. Many did not know whether their fathers or mothers, their brothers or sisters, were alive or dead. All were dressed in khaki uniforms, cut out of American army blankets. Many of the boys wore wedge caps, from the same material.

I was ushered into the dining hall and sat between a solemn little girl called Ella Blum, and a bright and laughing youngster called Yosef Elster. Ella, aged eight, had survived in a monastery. Her parents had disappeared, presumably murdered. After the war, a Jewish organisation found her and brought her back into the fold, removing the cross from her breast. She was shy, affectionate and wistful. Yosef was a natural leader, and he was very curious. 'Bist ein Englisher Zelner?' – are you an English soldier? Indeed. I was wearing my uniform.

'Ich bin Yosef,' he said, pointing at his chest. 'Ess' – eat – he pretended to shovel food into his mouth. 'Ess . . .'

That was my first word of Yiddish. My first sentence came after I had done my best to eat the pickled herring with dry, brown bread, washed down with sweetened tea. 'Shpielst di ping-pong?' asked Yosef, hitting a pretend ball with an imaginary bat. I nodded. Yes, I did.

So we played ping-pong and I then tried to make conversation and I was adopted by Bronya Stunzeiger, the 'madricha' (or leader) of the group – bright eyes, black-haired and thoughtful, with a hunched back; a survivor in her early twenties. 'Please return,' said Bronya. 'Come for Shabbas. Come Friday night.' Pearl said: 'Do. We'll get you here somehow. Or you can hitch-hike. You can stay at our JRU mess.'

That Friday evening I returned. I was made fairly welcome by the JRU – or at least by some of them. Others resented 'Barney Janner's son' on the 'who-does-he-think-he-is-because-his-father-is-an-MP?' principle. An Australian woman called Ray Rubenstein, a scion of the Helena Rubenstein cosmetics family, was prepared to take me for what I was – a young man who had been knocked emotionally askew by Belsen, by the Camp and especially by the children.

Friday night dinner at the Kinderheim was unforgettable. I sat with Bronya's group. A girl of about ten whose mother was dead turned her face sideways to the wall and sang the Yiddish version of 'My Yiddisher Momma' and we all cried. Then they sang Israel's pioneer songs and we all laughed and I joined in because they were songs I had learned at the Jewish Youth Study Groups at weekends and at conferences that I had attended while I was at St Paul's School. '*Anu alim artza* . . .' they sang. 'We are going up to the Land . . .' 'God will build Galilee . . .' 'We are the Palmach . . . We are the pioneers . . .' The past was disaster, the present was tough, but Palestine was their home and their hope. They sang and dreamed and prepared for their Homeland. I emotionally understood what had until then been an intellectual acceptance of Zionism. How obscene that there was no land where these youngsters could go, as of right . . . nowhere where Jewish children and their families could walk on the grass, as of right. How disgraceful that my own government would not let these children into Palestine.

It was then that I first really hated Ernest Bevin. I had met him once with my father, sitting at the next table in the Members' dining room in the Commons. He speared a potato with his knife and stuck it into his mouth. It was he and his policy that were keeping *my* children – because this is how I now regarded them – in Belsen, forcing *my* children to stay in the Kinderheim, in the building known as RB7, instead of following the beacon of hope to the Promised Land. I determined to do whatever I could to help these youngsters and, when my Army service was over, to fight to destroy the policies of Bevin and his ilk. But what could I do now?

One of the JRU team suggested that if I would like to be in Belsen on Sundays, when the school was open, I should teach a class in English. I agreed. The experience was dire. There were about thirty children in my class, ages ranging from about eight to fourteen, depending on how much schooling they had lost during the war years. They spoke half a dozen languages, none of them English. Most spoke Yiddish but the Hungarians did not. I had to teach by what we laughingly called 'the direct method' – I spoke to them in English because I knew no better or no different. They responded in Hungarian, Romanian, German, Yiddish, Hebrew . . . Chaos!

My solution was – songs. I taught them the 'Hokey Cokey' and made them dance it with me. Then 'One Finger, One Thumb, Keep Moving' and 'Underneath the Spreading Chestnut Tree'. It worked, but not very well. Most of the fault was, of course, mine, but the children were not known for being ruly. One of the JRU women was a teacher in the school. I met her over Sunday lunch. She was looking distraught. 'What's the matter?' I asked. 'I couldn't keep them quiet,' she said. 'So I decided to teach them a lesson – and I left the school!' Some lesson . . . some school . . .

I became friendly with two teachers at the school. One was a Russian called Munie, who taught me how to drink down vodka in a gulp. The other, Shlomo. We two did a deal. Shlomo taught me Hebrew and I taught him English.

In Belsen, Passover was special. The JRU asked me to conduct the Seder service in the Kinderheim – the annual recitation of the story of the Exodus from Egypt. The 'seder' was fun, especially the songs. As for the story of the Going Out from Egypt, that was a tale of hope. Our ancestors, too, had escaped from Nazi bondage and were on their way to freedom in their Promised Land.

Bronya's group had adopted me and accepted me as part of their extended family. Shoshana Ilush and her little brother Yosef spoke six languages, which they had learned while they shifted from country to country; they could read and write in none of them. Bruno Krawzik and Benjamin Stein were waifs from Poland.

The JRU people were extraordinary. In charge were the determined Sarah and the tiny Evelyn; David, boss of Camp Security; Issy, who commanded the German workmen who dealt with the plumbing and the sewers as well as maintenance of the buildings and roads. I was proud of them all.

Quietly, many of them helped with so-called 'illegal immigration' – spiriting Jews into Palestine, under the noses of the British troops and contrary to the rules laid down by Bevin. We all approved, except for Rose Henriques, wife of the redoubtable Sir Basil Henriques, 'the Gaffer', the renowned magistrate and youth leader. Rose considered that what mattered was to comply with British law. Most of her colleagues believed that bad laws were there to be broken when necessary to save lives and what laws could be worse than those which blocked the Jews of Belsen from entering their own Homeland and which kept them in hated Germany, the land of Jewish death and bondage?

Being Jewish has its hazards, the ultimate of which these people had looked straight in the face. Death. But there is also a warm camaraderie, forged in the flames of shared persecution. If you are '*amho*', then you are one of us. I have found this family warmth in Jewish communities throughout the world – in the Yemen . . . on the Island of Djerba, in Tunisia . . . everywhere, from Australia to Alaska, from Johannesburg to Jerusalem. We Jews are a quarrelsome lot, like most families, but we do also enjoy a family warmth, created by our religious and cultural heritage, but heated in centuries of anti-Semitic racism.

The Jews of Belsen had very mixed feelings towards Britain, its troops and its authorities. On the one hand, we had stood alone against the Nazis; without us, there would have been no victory. But with us, there was no way out of the hated land of Germany. Nearly all legal paths to the Promised Land were closed. They spat out the word 'Bevin' like some foul poison.

I was soon known in the camp as the 'Englisher Zelner' – the English soldier, or, to be more precise, 'the Yiddisher Englisher Zelner'. Belsen had more influence on me than any other experience in my young life.

Yom Kippur – the Day of Atonement – was a real horror. On Kol Nidre night, the most solemn occasion in the Jewish year, I joined Bronya and her colleagues in taking the children to the service. It was held in the Roundhouse, which had been the Germans' camp theatre and meeting place. A huge cry of pain echoed through the place. We all wept. Aye, what a catastrophic world. And still no one wanted our children. And still Bevin would not allow even the children to find new lives in their ancient homeland.

In July 1947, the ship named *President Warfield* sailed from France with over 4,500 survivors of the Holocaust crammed between and on its decks. It was headed for Palestine. During the voyage, the passengers renamed it, the *Exodus*. All on board knew that unless they were lucky enough to run the British blockade off the Palestine coast, they would probably be taken off and shipped to Cyprus or to Mauritius. What they had never considered was the possibility that even Bevin's Government would send them back to Germany, to the land of Nazi persecution and death. Sadly, Bevin and his team decided that the time had come to teach these unruly Jews a lesson. The *Exodus* landed at Haifa. Its passengers were not even allowed to greet their families but were mauled, manhandled and pushed onto two smaller vessels. Then back to Germany and to the humiliation of British-run internment camps at Wilhelmshaven and Amstau.

When they landed, some of the children were ill and were sent to the hospital at Belsen. Three of the lads were transferred to the Kinderheim, where I first met them. One was Aharon Taler, a pleasant, charming, good-looking lad of about fourteen, who had quietly accepted the pain of life, since he was wrenched away from his mother in Lodz, Poland. The second was his brother, Yehoshua, universally known as Shiele – bright, bespectacled and full of questions. Their main question, of course: when do we leave for Eretz Israel? To answer that question, the Jewish Agency – then, as now, the Jewish organisation in charge of immigration (*aliya*) into the Land of Israel – needed permission from their mother. I wrote the appropriate letter to their mother, who had remained in Poland, in what was by then a reasonably fluent but grammatically appalling Yiddish hand. The third youngster was Yosef Dauerman, who travelled with his father, who was in the new camp. 'Gavriel, please help us,' he pleaded. 'We don't want to stay in Germany.' He was sent to join his father in Amstau.

The following weekend, I again scrounged a lift from my JRU friend, Pearl, to Wilhelmshaven and to the *Exodus* camps. We travelled in an ambulance. When we arrived at the gates of the camp, I climbed out. I was in civilian clothes. The camp was guarded by its inmates, one of whom came up to me and asked me in Yiddish: 'Who are you?' I told him. He shook his head. 'We can't have English soldiers in here,' he said. At that moment, Yosef Dauerman appeared and launched himself at me like a rocket, with a mighty bear hug. 'Gavriel, Gavriel, you found us!' he proclaimed. The guard and everyone around laughed. 'OK, Gavriel, you are *amho* – one of us – *baruch haba*'. Welcome.

I was deeply shocked by the primitive hutted camps. I was humiliated that my own government and especially a Labour one could return these sufferers to Germany, of all places. It was cruelty. I was blazing with anger.

A man called Bollek took me round the camps. He spoke good English and his shipmates had appointed him their interpreter and negotiator. He was famous and appreciated for giving the appropriate instructions in a way that the Jews would understand and their captors would not. Much depended on a pun. The word 'lo' in Hebrew means: to him. When the same word is spelled not with the Hebrew letter 'alef', but with the letter 'vav', it means: no. In other words: don't do it. So Bollek would be driven round the camp in a truck. He would cry out, in Yiddish, through a loudspeaker: 'Today, all children over the age of twelve will register. *Lo mit ein alef.*' Don't do it. They didn't.

To my surprise, I came across a group of young Brits. Zionist by action as well as by word, they had joined the *Exodus* in Marseilles and shared the journey, the agony and now the incarceration with the survivors. What could I do for them? They asked for toothpaste. Whether from the British Naafi or the American PX, our troops in Germany had access not only to toothpaste but to almost anything else they might require, at very reasonable prices.

I was proud of the people in Wilhelmshaven and Amstau. Their spirit I later recognised in the South African fighters against apartheid, so movingly chronicled by Nelson Mandela in his epic memoirs: *The Long*

Walk to Freedom. My father's Parliamentary Zionist friend and head of the chinaware family, Josiah Wedgwood, used to refer to Jewish people who would not campaign for a Jewish State as 'cringeing Jews'. The people of Wilhelmshaven and Amstau never cringed. Instead, no sooner had they arrived than they started slipping away again, onto trucks and then to boats; leaky, inadequate, crowded, dangerous boats, like the *Exodus* – back on their path to freedom.

One great day, the British authorities allowed a trainload of Jewish children from Germany to emigrate to Palestine. It was called the 'kinder aliya' – the children's 'going up' to the Promised Land. They included Bronya and my children from the Kinderheim. I drove over to the Dutch border town of Bocholt to bid them farewell. As I stood in my uniform, revolver on hip, looking for the youngsters I knew, I noticed a group of young men behind me. I heard one say to the other: 'Vos iz dos epis, a English khaya?' What's that – an English beast? Not a compliment. A 'khaya' does not have human attributes. 'Zoll er zein mein kapora' – may he be my scapegoat!

'Gib a kik oyfn nooez,' said one of his colleagues. Look at his nose. 'Efsher er iz amho'. Perhaps he is 'amho' – one of us Jews.

The first man came over to me and asked me in broad Polish Yiddish: 'Ferzeiung khaver' – excuse me, friend. 'Amho?'

'Avada' – I replied. 'I certainly am.'

The young men all beamed. '*Oh, Shalom aleichem,*' they chorused. Shalom and hello and what are you doing here and of course we'll help you find your children. They did.

As the train pulled out of Bocholt station and the youngsters waved farewell on their road to freedom, all of us left standing on the platform – including the young men who had challenged me – stood and silently and unashamedly wept. It was a day of hope.

All my life, I had taken for granted that there had to be somewhere in the world where Jewish people had the right to live. Not just to be tolerated. Chaim Weizman, Zionist leader and later Israel's first President, had said: 'We should not endure intolerance, but we must not endure tolerance.'

In Belsen, it was Zionism for some and religious Judaism for others which kept the flame of hope burning. Some of my friends went on 'aliya alef' – authorised emigration to Palestine, with certificates. Others took their chance with 'aliya bet' – so-called illegal emigration, without certificates. Most just waited and hoped. Some got visas to the USA or Canada or Australia and even a few to Britain. Most were lost in a morass of depression.

Each family lived in a room in the white stone barrack blocks. Some survived on their 'Joint zuteilungen' – their rations from the American Joint Distribution Committee ('the Joint'). If anyone left, no one informed the authorities. The vanished were referred to as 'Toyten' – dead people – and their rations were shared among the remaining survivors.

Some opened tiny businesses. With a scrubbing brush, a bar of soap and a tub for heating water on the stove, plus a flat iron and a board, you were in business with your laundry. Or you could start a stall, selling what little property you might have at a profit and buy more. Nothing new in that. My Grandpa Joseph Cohen began his eventually huge furniture business as a peddler, in Dublin. But the Belsen circumstances were grim. The black market flourished, especially in cigarettes and in currency. For concentration camp survivors, the laws deserved no respect. The Germans were their former persecutors and we British, preventing them from reaching their Promised Land in Israel, were now the perpetrators of their present plight.

People tended to clump together in barrack blocks with others with a similar approach to life. There were the Socialist Zionists . . . the religious Zionists . . . the ultra-orthodox. 'How could anyone believe in the existence of God, when He had allowed His people to be persecuted, tortured, annihilated?' I asked Chief Rabbi Helfgott. That intelligent and cultivated man came from Yugoslavia, where he had fought with the Resistance. 'Gavriel,' he replied, 'I too have asked that question. But only He has the answer. And He has preserved us – you and me and all the rest of the people here – for His purpose.'

I was glad that the Rabbi and the rest had found solace in religious practices. Faith had kept many of them alive through their hideous trials and would preserve them on their way to what the great Arthur Balfour described in his Declaration as the 'National Home for the Jews'. He had not used the word 'State' but that was his diplomatic language. A State there had to be.

I discussed these problems with my Jewish army mates who used to come up to Belsen with me. We knew that the Jewish people were commanded to devote their lives to 'Torah' – Jewish law – and 'Avoda' – work, meaning striving to put His law into effect. Torah was primarily for others. Avoda was ours. And it meant – getting the people out and into Palestine as their homeland. So my weekends were full of life and learning. I was maturing fast. And each time my Belsen friends told me their story, I became even more determined to be useful.

From Israel, my Belsen children wrote to me. Bruno Krawzik had changed his name to Boaz Karvy. 'I am sorry, Gavriel. I have forgotten my Yiddish. Please learn Hebrew so that I can understand your letters.' He was in Meshek Afek, a kibbutz north of Haifa, together with Bronya and her new husband. Shy little Ella Blum was in Beersheba and Tsipora and Yosef Ilush in kibbutz Ein Harod. Yosef and Bella Elster were with their parents in Tsfat; Benjamin Stein and his father in Haifa. All of them were writing, saying: 'When are you coming?' Their places in the Kinderheim had been taken by new children, decanted from the immigrant ship *Exodus*. The treatment of the ship and its passengers had swung international opinion into recognising that a Jewish State was a moral imperative and a political certainty. About time, too.

When your time in the Forces was drawing to an end, you were offered the chance of a two-week 'demob course' – an educational course to prepare you for your demobilisation – and your return to civilian life. Mischievously and with little hope, I applied for a course in Hebrew. To my amazement, they found one for me, at the University of Göttingen, in South Germany. My teacher was a venerable academic, whose Hebrew language had not advanced since biblical days. I was his first pupil since 1937 and he most courteously made me welcome. I asked him if any Jewish people lived in Göttingen. 'Yes,' he replied. 'There's just one family. A woman and her son, both of whom have survived concentration camps. Their name is Buergenthal.'

I found them. Tom, aged fourteen, had been in Sachsenhausen concentration camp. He had been forced to carry bodies into the crematoria. He was befriended by a fellow inmate, the Norwegian explorer,

Odd Nansen, and survived with his help and that of a friendly camp guard who brought him food. His father was murdered but, by another miracle, his mother survived. They made me welcome. We kept in touch and the Buergenthals emigrated to the United States, where Tom became a distinguished professor, and in 2001 I was hugely proud to learn that he had been appointed a judge at the International Court of Justice in The Hague. What a marvellous survivor he is.

We were also allowed a period of local demob leave. I took mine in Denmark, with my relations, the Rudaizky family. The Nazis and their allies murdered my entire family in continental Europe, with only one exception – the Danes. Not a Jewish soul was left alive in Riga or in Ritover, in Luknik or in Tels, in Latvia or in Lithuania. We had learned that it was not Germans but locals who had murdered most of them. In Ritover, the villagers had rounded up Jews, including my family, and herded them into a synagogue, locked them in and set light to the place. Not one survived.

Mercifully, the people of Denmark were different. Whether or not their Royal Family sewed yellow stars onto their own clothing is not certain. What we do know is that the Danes smuggled out most of their Jews, in small boats at night, across the water to Sweden and to life and safety. These included my cousins, Meyer and Anna Rudaizky, and their three small children, Liba, Finn and Lilian. After the war, they returned to Copenhagen and I decided to spend my demob leave with them.

In England, food was carefully rationed. Thanks to Mother's doctors' certificates – the one happy side-effect of her gall bladder and other internal problems – we had a little more milk and other essentials than some families. Here in Denmark, dairy produce was plentiful and wonderful. The family feasted me on eggs and butter and cheese.

When I returned home at the end of my Army service, I was proud both of my work at Belsen and of my knowledge of the Yiddish language. My family soon brought me down to earth. Mother told me that my concern over the DPs had become 'an obsession' and Father that the time had now come for me to 'get stuck into your studies and get ready to earn a living'. When I tried out my Yiddish on my grandmother, she shuddered, visibly. 'You talk Yiddish like a Polak,' she said. 'You are a Litvak' – a Lithuanian.

'You should not be speaking the language like a Pole!' Ah well . . . most of my Belsen chums were escapees from Poland.

All that said, my experiences at Belsen and with the War Crimes Group were then and have remained massive influences on my life and work. I have never since lost my focus on the battles against racism and anti-Semitism nor on the fight for human justice, individual and communal.

It was the visions of modern terrorism that fuelled my blazing determination to concentrate on these issues. Its need grows, day by dangerous day. Suicide bombing . . . in Palestine, Iraq, Turkey . . . from New York to London: the vile and senseless murders of the innocent. Whether on the London tube or in an Israel café . . . in an Egyptian market or on an Iraqi crossroads – turn on your TV and the odds are that you will see some mass murder, somewhere in our crazy world.

In 2004, I was the guest of Crown Prince Alexander and Princess Katherine, who had returned to their Serbian capital, Belgrade. The first morning, they took me, together with my parliamentary aide, Terry Newman, to the mosque near the Palace. Right-wing extremists had set light to the building. No one had taken action against them. We talked to the Imam and to his sons. No, there was no government intervention, no compensation, no help to rebuild. That was evil Islamophobia.

A few weeks later, we visited Amman, the capital of Jordan. We met with Prince Hassan bin Talal, whom I had known for years and who had been Crown Prince until shortly before the death of his brother, King Hussein. He agreed that we should set up a new organisation, at political level, to deal with both Islamophobia and anti-Semitism. I asked him to be our President and he said: 'Only if you will be joint president with me'. So we put our heads and our good names together and our Council has grown hugely. Among our members are world-renowned politicians and statesmen, from some forty countries. At least there is now a weapon which we can use, against these two growing and almost twin forms of dangerous racism. Prince Hassan agreed that we should run this new organisation out of London. We have set up a powerful Executive of leading British Muslims and Jews, mainly parliamentarians.

So the seeds planted in me, in the postwar misery of Bergen-Belsen, have remained a pivot of my existence. My mission: to do everything in my power to battle against racism, whether against my Jewish people or our Muslim brothers and wherever we find it in this world.

How, then, have these past horrors merged into the present world of British Jewry? How do they affect our community of some quarter of a million souls, who identify as its members? How can we cope, when our community has normal age spread, while there are well over 1.6 million Muslims in Britain, predominantly with young families?

The British Jewish community is as mixed in its membership as it is in its politics. Of course, it is united against Nazism and racism. But its young people continue to marry out of the faith – certainly over 30 per cent of them. This is a far lower percentage than in the United States, but it is the main source of our communal shrinkage.

Those who remain are deeply divided, politically and religiously. Many leaders of the Conservative Party are Jewish, as are many members of the Parliamentary Labour Party, in both Houses of Parliament. Our religious communities vary from the extreme orthodox to the ultra-Liberal. Between come those who are known as 'Reform' – who include my daughter, Laura, whom I am proud to salute as a practising rabbi, ordained in 2004.

At the other end of our religious scale come those who are Jewish by birth but not by belief, most of whom do not identify as Jews. That is totally their right in our free world, but I sometimes look back on the Nazis, who slaughtered their Jews in concentration camps, like Belsen and Auschwitz, or threw them into pits in Lithuania and Latvia, Poland and Estonia. They did not care whether or not these Jews identified with their community in life. In death, they shared the same mass graves.

In jocular mood, the French proclaim: '*Vive la différence*'. I believe that we must indeed recognise and respect our world of difference. But we must battle to ensure that others who are different do the same. Belsen built a fire of anger into my soul, which has emerged into my life and work ever since.

How, then, have postwar Jewish communities, in Britain and in Europe, reacted to the horrors of the Holocaust? In Britain and in many European communities, we took a deep and grateful breath. To whatever extent we and our families had survived the war and the Holocaust, we now had to rebuild our lives. To our children and grandchildren, the Holocaust histories are just that – history. His story, not theirs.

I believe that it is only by remembering the past that we can hope to prevent the same miseries spreading into the future. So colleagues and I created the Holocaust Educational Trust. Each year, we take planeloads of students and teachers, and even some politicians, to see the ruins and mass graves, the remains of the hell of Auschwitz. We have had a part in bringing Holocaust education into our British schools syllabus. And we send survivors and lecturers into schools and colleges to talk about the Holocaust.

Of course, this has not prevented human hatred. We are ashamed of the disgrace of Darfour, mirrored in too many other lands. But we try. In Britain, we battle against anti-Semitism, together with other revolting forms of racism. And colleagues and I liaise with political and communal leaders of like mind, in Europe and beyond. We ask: how can we help, in their battles against racism, whether against Jews or Muslims or anyone else?

For Jews, the situation in France is grievous and growing in its danger, and especially sadly, relations with the French Muslim communities are deteriorating. Similar racist miseries are growing in Belgium and the Netherlands and in other European lands, especially sadly and surprisingly, in Denmark. There is no visible end to our task.

FIVE

Demob Happy

OK, so I was demob happy, as we used to call it. I was as free as a travelling bird. I was young, ready to absorb new places, new friends, new sensations. Yes, it was a break from the realities of communal stress, racist violence and military discipline. For once, just glimpses of the overflow of war and politics. For once, only one joyful, useful breath of wisdom – that there must be a time in every young life when the world is yours.

My granddaughter, Isabel, recently spent five months of adventure, from India to Singapore, from Thailand to Australia, from New Zealand to Fiji and beyond – now, that's youth and life and freedom. Today, youngsters usually enjoy that in their gap year between school and university, at the age of eighteen. When I was that age, I was a soldier in Germany. How lucky they are today – but in its own way, how much I learned in the army, and how much I enjoyed the contrast with the freedom of demob.

In March 1948, I was out of the army, demobbed, free. The time had come to travel, first stop: Spain. I asked the Spanish Embassy to recommend a village where they speak 'Castellano' – classical Spanish and not a dialect. They suggested Laredo, on the north coast between Bilbao and Santander, and recommended the local inn. So, armed with the sediment of my schoolboy Spanish and a pocket dictionary, off I went.

Laredo is now a thriving tourist town, with a massive ocean strip of tourist hotels. Then it was a fishing village, mainly built around a church on a hill. My inn – the Hostal de Laredo – was the only tourist accommodation. I was the only tourist in the Hostal and, it soon turned out, the only Jew that the Laredo people had ever met. How did they know I was Jewish? Because nearly every day was a fiesta, in honour of a saint. The priests processed out of the church, carrying images ahead of them. The population fell to its knees – all except their new friend, Gabriel, who remained standing. When they asked me why, I told them I was Jewish. They could not believe it. No horns, no spiked tail. Just an ordinary person.

I soon made friends with the younger set. I learned the art known as '*pelar la pava*' – literally, plucking the turkey – chatting up the birds; and some of the turkeys were youthful Spanish beauties of high order. I also learned the '*piropo*' – the untranslatable, cheeky approach. Example: along came a lady with a good-looking girl who was obviously her daughter. One of my new mates went up to her and bowed. '*Señora*,' he said. '*Vaya usted con Dios y su hija conmigo.*' Roughly: Madam, may God go with you and your daughter with me!

So up and down we paraded in the cool of the evening, eating delicious *churros* and with my mates laughing at my pathetic Spanish. But they liked my guitar and we sang songs and if sufficiently provoked I could sing: '*La Vaca Lechera*' – the milk-giving cow. They taught me other ballads, including two love songs with which I later serenaded my girlfriend, fiancée, wife and love of my life, Myra.

I learned to play pelota – banging a hard type of squash ball against a wall, with your bare palms, which soon swelled up. I enjoyed fresh sardines from the sea, cooked on open grills on the hill by the church. And I became friendly with the two monks who ran the local school – La Escuela de los dos Frailes – the School of the Two Friars. They were white-clad Franciscans and while leading a celibate life, enjoyed it to the full, with excellent wine and conversation. In return for their hospitality, I was required to teach the schoolchildren some English songs. Once again, and with memories of the Belsen school, the 'Hokey Cokey', 'Underneath the Spreading Chestnut Tree' and 'One Finger, One Thumb, Keep Moving'.

Then I made friends with the fishermen. They were curious to know about England and the new Labour Government and whether we cared about them. At first, they said little. Then they took me out on their fishing boats and when we were well offshore, they talked and listened. They told me how they despised Franco and his regime and how they prayed for his downfall, but could do little to speed it. Could my Labour Party and I be of help? My Spanish was stretched, along with my understanding of the complications of life, in that most hospitable of villages.

My friends took me to a bullfight in a nearby village. Cruel, indeed, but the local *torreros* were not only brave but, I thought, amazingly reckless.

Somehow, the battle between bull and man seems just a little fairer in a village than it does in a mighty bullring, like the one in Pamplona where Myra and I would start our honeymoon, before moving on to Laredo. I was very sorry to go. I promised to return. But the time had come to travel to Italy.

I had learned French in school in England and in Canada; Spanish, in Canada; German and Yiddish, during my national service in Germany; Hebrew, from childhood, and then more in Belsen and in Israel. Now I had decided that I wanted to learn Italian, so I had taken some lessons from an Italian student in London. From Laredo I wended my way to Barcelona, then to Madrid, and by a series of trains to Milan, Rome and Venice, making friends and conversation all the way.

I took with me as my guide, Nikolaus Pevsner's marvellous book, *European Architecture*. I gloried in Milan cathedral with its Coca-Cola stand on the roof and with marvellous choral singing echoing through the great building. Then to Rome. The train was packed and I was standing in the corridor with a bunch of young trainee priests. We made conversation in French. They decided that I should not stay in a youth hostel but should come with them to their priestly dormitory. So I saw Rome through their eyes, from the vast glory of St Peter's to the papal, pastoral majesty of Castel Gandolfo.

In Laredo, my friends had tried hard to convert me to Catholicism. They believed that this was the only way that my soul would be saved and that I would achieve what they believed was the greatest of the glories – life after death, through recognition of Jesus Christ as the son of God and through the acceptance of His ultimate sacrifice. For my sake, they never wholly gave up. Happily, my more realistic Roman friends did not bother to try. Instead, they showed profound interest in my Jewish religion. Their Saviour, after all, was Jewish, and they had never met a live member of my faith.

Then to Venice. On the island of Guidecca stood a youth hostel where, for the equivalent of a shilling a night – nearly a pound, today – you shared a room with fifty-nine other sweaty young voyagers from all over the world. In another room were an equivalent collection of assorted maidens. While holiday mates are usually for those holidays only and you never have contact with them afterwards, however good your intentions, on Guidecca I made two lasting friends, Freddie Kerpner and Gordon Message.

Freddie was on his way back from Vienna, where he had seen his mother for the first time since the war. He was half Jewish and in 1940 his family had shipped him off to Sweden, for safety. By a miracle, he and his mother not only survived but found each other. He came back to London and stayed with my family. But the trauma never left him and in spite of a happy marriage, he later committed suicide. His son, Joachim, is a Stockholm journalist, married, with bright children, and we are often in touch.

Gordon was a tall, broad man with a massive laugh. He taught children with learning difficulties. He was a Morris dancer, a repairer of antique watches and a splendid individualist. A few years after our first meeting, Gordon came to see me. 'Am I right that you're not too fond of Germans?' he asked.

I nodded. 'I have had my problems with them,' I said.

'That's a pity,' Gordon laughed at me. 'I'm about to marry one and we wanted you to be best man!'

He calmed my embarrassment with his assurances that his wife had come to England because she also did not like the atmosphere in Germany and hated the Nazis. So best man at their wedding I was, and their son, Andre Greville Message, is my godson. He is a highly talented designer, in the world of advertising.

So the three of us – Freddie, Gordon and I – found three handsome females from the next-door dorm and off we went to enjoy Venice. Accompanied by my guitar, we serenaded the locals, who plied us with wine. Or we sat at a table in the Piazza San Marco, almost totally broke, buying a bottle of Coca-Cola between us and decanting it into six glasses already filled with water, which we kept in front of us during a joyful evening.

No cares, provided that we did not lose our passports and our tickets home. No worries, until we returned to reality. Just youth, at its joyful, decent, laughing best. Demob was great, but the time had come to return to the real life of study and of work.

SIX

Cambridge and Harvard

There could be no greater contrast. On the one hand, the armed forces, with their discipline and class system, their uniform dress and required behaviour. On the other, the glorious undergraduate freedom of Cambridge.

True, as a War Crimes Investigator, I had been entrusted with freedom and responsibility scarcely rivalled for a man still in his teens. But unlike some of my Cambridge mates, I had no urge to run drunk and wild. During my three years at Cambridge I only overdrank once, as an experiment. I was disgustingly sick and never indulged again.

You arrive in the army and are issued with your uniform – a word not chosen by chance. You receive your instructions and your orders and you do what you are told, uniformly. At Cambridge, freshmen were flooded with invitations to join societies – political and religious, sporting and academic. You could spend your entire undergraduate life at social, political and sporting gatherings and events, which some of us did.

I at once joined the Cambridge Union, the Labour Club, the Trinity Hall Athletic Club and the Jewish Society. The best club, though, was the college. All our freshers lived in the handsome medieval buildings – and medieval they still were. I was at the top of G staircase, sharing a room with my old army friend, Ted Greenfield. It worked fine, because by the time I came to bed, he was asleep and by the time I got up, he was gone – like the famous Box and Cox. I talked and argued and debated late into the night, over endless glasses of sherry and cups of coffee. For me, that was post-demob bliss. Ted was an early sleeper and riser.

The nearest loo was at the end of the garden, by the river – down the stairs, into the cold night and across the garden. So we were provided with chamber pots. I was not surprised one morning to find our ancient servant – known as a 'gyp' – disposing of the watery contents down the sink.

Although I was destined for law and my 'exhibition' (or minor scholarship) was in 'history for law', I decided to read first-year economics. The law I would miss was mainly academic and although my father thought that I had wasted enough of my life and should be settling into something useful which would enable me to earn a living, I decided to learn something about the economy. On this issue as on so many others during my childhood and youth, Mother backed me. She was my rock.

Both Oxford and Cambridge universities are blessed with the tutorial system. Each week, in each subject, between two and four of you gather in your supervisor's room, to discuss your work. They set you your essays and criticise and correct them. Above all, they sharpen your mind, through information and challenge.

I soon found that the content of most of the lectures was available in books written by the lecturers. You could buy the books and read and absorb them in your own time, instead of sitting through lectures, which I customarily skipped. Instead and voluntarily, I enjoyed each week Nikolaus Pevsner's illustrated lectures on European architecture and Hersch Lauterpacht's on international law. I was no great scholar but I did concentrate on my studies for the last three weeks before exams and I ended up with a very creditable and probably undeserved 2(1); which was one up on what I managed in my Finals.

My running had not improved since the days when I won the 100 yards at HQ BAOR. But I did make the Freshers' team against Oxford. I came in last. But college athletics I enjoyed and in my third year, I was elected President of the Trinity Hall Athletic Club.

It was politics, though, that gripped my life and filled it with interest plus a touch of fear. I took an active part in the Labour Club, and was soon elected Secretary. When the annual elections came up at the start of my first year, I decided to have a go at the Chair. One evening, a much respected and delightful man, Brian Abel-Smith, came to see me. 'You are a friend and I like you,' he said. 'Which is why I have come to tell you that I shall not be voting for you.'

'Why not?' I enquired.

'Because you don't know how to deal with people. You don't listen enough. You tell them what needs to be done and you are usually right, but you've neither patience nor tact.'

Happily, I had the good sense and maturity to accept the advice in the spirit in which Brian intended it. I thanked him. But I stood as Chairman and lost to my room-mate Ted Greenfield. I then started on the hard path of learning to temper enthusiasm and the urge to get things done, with patience and tact – a battle that continues to this day.

I prepared my Union speeches carefully, but they did not go down well. It took a Labour Club friend to tell me why. 'You are a fountain of words,' he said. 'Your brain and your tongue work so fast that no one can keep up with you.' I had to slow down. But how? I tracked down the Donald Evans School of Languages in Notting Hill. Mr Evans coached me himself. Recording my voice and playing it back on a gramophone, he tightened the tap of the fountain. He taught me how to pause. He played me recordings of Churchill. Harold Macmillan once said: 'The greatest trick of all, if you can do it . . . is the pause . . . just that wait . . . and you've got an audience . . .' From Donald Evans, I learned to use that magical pause and to vary my pace – and much more that I later taught others. Thanks to him, my speeches at the Union greatly improved. I stood successfully for the Committee, and much later his guidance formed the basis of my presentational skills training courses.

Canvassing for Union elections was not permitted but nothing could prevent me from dropping in to see my friends. 'How are you?' they would ask. 'Worried,' I would reply.

'Why?'

'Well, it's Union elections today.'

'Oh, I'd better get along to vote, hadn't I?'

'That would be very kind of you – but I haven't asked you to do it!'

From the Committee, there was a progression – Senior Committee Member, then Secretary, Vice President and President. Once you were on the ladder, no one pushed you off. But a young man called John Silberrad opposed me for President. I handsomely beat him, which made my election even sweeter.

University politics were in their own way as tough, ruthless and nasty as anything you would meet later. I also acquired cultivated cunning. I was blessed with brilliant mentors, including Percy Craddock – later, Sir Percy,

UK Ambassador to China and then head of MI5. A master speaker, he drew his black gown up above his shoulders, like a hawk about to swoop. A warm and humorous friend but a skilful, artful and dangerous opponent. When my presidency was threatened by John Silberrad, my political wizards gathered in a room in Trinity College. I attended upon them, to cull their wisdom. We plotted and we planned, not least how to counter the Silberrad ploy, which was: to hell with tradition . . . let's elect someone who is different and who will bring a bit of fun into the place and who is not just a card-carrying Labour clone.

One friend and admired mentor, who became a lifelong political colleague, was Jack Ashley. He had been the youngest Councillor in the northern town of Widnes. He fought his way to a scholarship at Ruskin College, Oxford, then on to Gonville and Caius, Cambridge.

Jack never forgot his roots. He refused to wear evening dress at Union debates, even when he became President. 'I'm not going to get dressed up like a millionaire,' he said, 'while my mother is still in need.' One day, Randolph Churchill – Winston's unworthy and drunken son – debated against Jack. He was rude, boorish and personal. In the Committee Room, after the main (or 'paper') speeches were over, I heard him say loudly: 'I'm not used to debating with people from the slums.' Jack also heard but maintained his dignified silence.

Jack and his wife Pauline were married in 1951 and left for the ceremony from our home at Lancaster Gate. A marvellously well-matched couple, they retained my fondest regard.

Jack was elected MP for Stoke-on-Trent South in 1966. He took an active part in the House, especially in matters dealing with the disabled and in conjunction with his Labour ally, Alf (now Lord) Morris. I am proud to work at the side of Lord Ashley of Stoke. How sad that his Pauline, like my Myra, has passed on.

In the 1945 General Election, a coachload of my Labour Club mates joined me in canvassing for Father's re-election to Leicester North West. With them, I spread my political wings in NALSO – the National Association of Labour Student Organisations. At NALSO, I first met a number of personalities who became outstanding in varied ways. One was John Stonehouse. He rose up swiftly to become an MP and then Postmaster General, before he plummeted to earth, convicted of fraud.

It was through NALSO that I first knew Gordon Borrie, later Director General of Fair Trading and now a distinguished colleague in the House of Lords, and colleagues and comrades from student socialist movements, in many parts of the world, which all helped my education and preparation for my political future and for my battles for fairness and against racism.

Most Friday evenings, I enjoyed dinner at the Jewish Society. My other social base was the Majlis, the Indian organisation, which proved to be the start of a political, cultural and emotional relationship that became permanent. To my surprise and pleasure, I found that my Hindu and Sikh colleagues and friends had a largely similar approach to life to my own. I became especially attached to three of their undergraduates, who remain my friends to this day and each became a distinguished luminary. There was Jai Mukhi, now a leading lawyer; Milon Banerji, who became India's Solicitor General and is now its Attorney General; and Natwar Singh, who returned to the UK as Deputy High Commissioner, then became Sonia Gandhi's political adviser and then Minister for External Affairs. It was with them that I met some extraordinary Indian leaders, including the brilliant and controversial Krishna Menon (Chapter 26).

At Cambridge, I had friends in all political parties. I learned the truth of the famous saying of Lord Acton: 'It is an evil doctrine that makes a difference of political opinion a matter for personal hatred.'

Sadly but not surprisingly, my support of some human rights causes has meant creating enemies. These were especially vicious in the days of the Soviet extremists and their allies, and they still include Nazis and fascists and their brood. So enough already, without antagonising the Irish, and I have never taken any side in the battles between Unionists and Republicans, Protestants and Catholics. Many years ago, I was driving from Northern Ireland to Eire, when I was stopped at the border. One of the guards smiled at me and said: 'Sir, are you a Catholic or a Protestant?' I replied: 'I am Jewish.' 'That may be,' the guard smiled back. 'But are you a Protestant Jew or a Catholic Jew?' Happily, when I replied that I was 'just a Jewish Jew', he let me proceed.

My first and unforgettable visit to Dublin was in 1950. I was invited to take part in a debate in Trinity College, together with Douglas Hurd, our

Cambridge Union Vice President. The event was well controlled by Moss Abrahamson, the Society's President, and was followed by a remarkable drinking session, in the basement below. We raised our beer mugs and were required to sing a tribute to the governors of the College: 'Hey ho, bugger the Board!'

One day at the end of 1997, shortly after my elevation to the House of Lords, I visited Washington's Capitol Hill. My old pal, Congressman Gary Ackerman, took me out onto their favourite photocall spot, with the background of the great Congress dome. Suddenly, he said to me: 'There's a couple of gentlemen just passing by who I know will want to say hello to you.' I turned round. It was the Sinn Fein leaders, Gerry Adams and Martin McGuinness.

'Good afternoon,' said Mr Adams. 'And who may you be?'

'I'm Lord Janner,' I replied. And I shook his outstretched hand.

'Oh, I'd like to be a Lord,' said Mr Adams.

'I'm afraid you've got a couple of problems,' I said.

'What are they?'

'Well, first you would have to become very respectable,' I smiled at him.

'I think I might just about manage that,' said Mr Adams, happily. 'So what's the second problem?'

'You would have to be a citizen of the United Kingdom.'

'Now, that's a pity,' said Mr Adams, shaking his head. 'I'm afraid that that will not be possible.'

Then he and Mr McGuinness strolled on, and I knew that my chances of welcoming either of them to the House of Peers – at least as members – were not great.

In 2005, I was invited to join the President of Ireland, Mary McAleese, a tall and charming lady. This time, there were no beer mugs, no songs, no debate – instead, a deeply dignified, moving and proud event – at the launch of the Eire Holocaust Educational Trust.

One of my Trinity Hall law tutors was a lovable Welshman, who had lost two fingers in a mining accident, Dr T. Ellis-Lewis, universally known as TEL. When my final exams approached, I panicked. I knew that I had not done nearly enough work to get through. 'Well, boy,' said TEL, 'we can't have you fail, can we? You've done too much for the College for that. Now, I set the tort exam, so I can't help you with that one, but let's go through the rest and do some question spotting. What we have to do is look and see what's new in the law and what questions are topical and likely to be asked.' Question spot we did and with his mighty help I achieved a lower-second-class degree – a 2(2). Not good, but at least not a Third and, because of my political achievements, it was enough to win me a year as a post-graduate student at Harvard Law School.

After two years' National Service, people like myself reached university with a different and more mature approach than those who emerged straight from school or even after a gap year. Certainly, for me those were three fantastic Cambridge years, stretching the mind and the talents. Academically, my time was unremarkable. As the good TEL once told me: 'What's the point of coming to Cambridge, boy, if you're only going to study?' As with Cambridge, so it was with Harvard.

From 1952 to 1953, Harvard and its Law School were my base . . . the lodging house of Mrs Coyle my home . . . but the whole of the United States my oyster. During the Presidential election campaign, I attended Boston meetings of both mighty candidates, Adlai Stevenson and Dwight Eisenhower. Stevenson was incisive, witty and a master of language – an intellectual giant, rare in the world of politics. Sadly, people like to vote for those with whom they can identify . . . with whom they feel at home and who they would like to have in theirs. Stevenson was a star too bright for the political firmament of this drab world. Stevenson's son, Adlai Junior, was at Harvard College, and I silently sympathised with him. I sensed that his Dad would lose.

Dwight Eisenhower was everyone's Dad. A military hero, he came across to his audience as a man who would understand their problems and their anxieties, their hopes and their aspirations. What you want in the White House is someone who represents *you*. Eisenhower was not only the epitome of the average American but also one who showed that if you are both average and honest, decent and brave, you can be a leader of your nation. Eisenhower personified the American dream and was duly elected, and I had learned some major political lessons.

As a Labour Party supporter, I was far to the left of most of my American friends, even the college students. I visited Washington DC and sat in on the grim cruelties of the Joseph McCarthy hearings. I stared at the Senator and hated him. Stevenson and Eisenhower, each in his own way, represented that which was decent and honourable in political life. McCarthy was political dirt.

Harvard Law School was a graduate centre. American students must complete their undergraduate course before they launch into law. They then must excel in three years of legal studies, before they can earn a law degree. Foreign students who had had three years of legal study could get their Master's degree in a year. I had done only two years of law. However hard I studied, I could get nothing better than certificates in individual subjects. So I chose subjects which not only interested me but which would have relevance for my European future: criminology and international law.

The Criminology Department was headed by an extraordinary husband-and-wife team, Sheldon and Eleanor Gluck. They had carried out an intensive study into a hundred juvenile delinquents. They matched boys and girls with others who shared the same ten characteristics, such as age, IQ, financial level of parents, and number and sex of siblings. One of each pair had been in trouble with the law; the other had not. Why? With shattering brevity and after the publication of a fine volume called *Unravelling Juvenile Delinquency*, they came up with a conclusion, simply stated. Most non-delinquents *believed*, rightly or wrongly, that at least one of their parents loved them. Most delinquents did not.

I decided to visit and examine the running of American penal institutions, starting with those for delinquents in our home state of Massachusetts. To my surprise and pleasure, I found that the administrators of those institutions were almost invariably pleased to explain their work.

Until now, my on-the-spot knowledge of criminology came mainly from my undergraduate visits to Kneesworth Hall, a remarkable 'approved school', near to Cambridge. It catered only for brilliant delinquent boys, with IQs of 120 or more. From Harvard, I visited a range of institutions for young offenders, mainly in and around Boston. The oddest man I met was the head of one place who firmly believed that youngsters tended to run off the rails at full moon. 'The word lunatic means one who has been driven crazy by the moon, doesn't it?' he said.

I had taken my first driving test in the Army. It was not too testing. My US test was more difficult but finally the examiner said: 'OK, Limey. I suppose you won't be too much of a menace on our roads.' I bought a car from the editor of the Harvard newspaper, John Sacks. He called it the 'Sackmobile' and let it go for 100 dollars. When I got behind the wheel, it took a look at the first hill, heaved a sigh and coughed and then expired. I got my money back and then bought another more serviceable vehicle. In my new car, I went prison visiting. At Sing Sing, I saw my first electric chair. The sign outside the prison: DEAD END. Later in the year, I drove through Alabama and saw the chain gangs on the road, and when visiting San Francisco, my friends and I and my car were ferried across San Francisco Bay to the Island of Alcatraz.

Until we learned of the iniquities of South Africa's Robben Island and the trials of Nelson Mandela and its other political prisoners, I regarded Alcatraz as the ultimate 'lock-'em-up and forget them' school of criminology. We were at all times accompanied by four warders, so that we would not be kidnapped. None of them carried guns, which could be snatched from them. Instead, armed guards stalked the catwalks above the mess hall and other open spaces. And in the centre of the ceiling of the hall hung tear gas bombs. It was visiting these establishments and recognising their incredible variety that impressed on my youthful mind the vastness of the United States and the variety of its peoples and practices. Often, the way that the individual state treated its deviants reflected the primitive and bleak level – or the depth of sophistication – of its civilisation.

I was blessed with two scholarships for Harvard. One paid my fares and the other my fees and my keep, but there was little left over. I needed to earn so I got a job teaching Hebrew School, two afternoons a week, at the Temple Reyim synagogue in the Boston suburb of Newton. Its Rabbi was named Cassel who, for fun, I called by the English pronunciation of Castle. I taught a mixed class of ten- to twelve-year-olds and they and I enjoyed ourselves hugely. At the end of the year, I asked the Rabbi whether if I had stayed he would employ me again. He replied: 'I'm sorry, but no. Never has a teacher given so much pleasure to his class but never has a class learned so little from its teacher!' Not an ideal reference for any professional educator.

I met Supreme Court Judge, Justice Felix Frankfurter, at a party. Another guest told me that Frankfurter was coming to dinner with him one evening and he found the judge sitting in his car, outside the door of the house. 'What are you doing in your car?' he asked his famous guest. 'Oh, just preparing my conversation,' the judge replied.

By happy chance, another Cambridge Union debater, Anthony Lloyd, was at Harvard at the same time. A wise, thoughtful and delightful young man, who later became a distinguished Law Lord, he willingly joined me in constituting an ad hoc Cambridge debating team. In the US and in Canada, debating was an art and a science, for which teams were awarded points. With what they regarded as unconventional and relaxed style, we did fine on presentation but not too well on content. We debated at Montreal's McGill University and, by contrast, at the Norfolk Penal Colony, a prison near to Boston. Our two Norfolk opponents were Bill Flynn and Buzzie Mulligan. Bill was inside for a series of highly successful confidence tricks. He specialised in passing counterfeit cheques. Buzzie had killed a gay man in a Boston park. Subject of the debate: This House Believes in the Welfare State.

Bill began: 'We live here in a welfare state, don't we?' Cries of 'yeah, yeah . . .'

'Does anyone here wish to stay?' Cries of 'no . . . no . . .'

I spoke next, explaining and praising Britain's efforts to provide fair and decent, equal and honourable opportunities for all. Buzzie retorted: 'The arguments of the gentleman from England are as valid as my partner's cheques!' Roars of laughter – and the death of our case. At the end of the day, they presented Tony and myself with Certificates of Release from the prison, and showed us round some of the cells. In one of them, a man was sitting playing a classical guitar with the skill and feeling of a maestro.

'Would you like to buy this guitar?' he asked me. 'I'm due for release in a fortnight and I am going to need money to live. You can have it for a hundred bucks.'

Bill Flynn was with me. 'What do you think?' I asked him quietly.

'He needs the money and you want the guitar, so why not?' said Bill.

Two weeks later, the guitarist turned up at my Sumner Road digs. I gave him the 100 dollars and he handed over the guitar. Then he said to me:

'I have a special favour to ask. I have a concert tomorrow, which is very important to me. I've been promised I can borrow a guitar, but I have not got one. Please would you let me keep this instrument for just another two days and I'll bring it back to you?' Naively but kindly, I agreed. Two days later, he did not reappear. I contacted Bill at Norfolk, and he gave me the address of a bar in a notorious part of Boston called Sculley Square, plus the name of the man who was the guitarist's boss.

The next day, accompanied by a loyal Harvard friend of mine who also lived in Mrs Coyle's house, I went to the address in Sculley Square, which I later learned was the centre of the local Irish Mafia. I walked boldly inside and asked for the boss. 'Sit down, Limey,' one of his henchmen commanded, pointing to a seat by the bar. 'Give them drinks,' he instructed the barman. My pal and I sat with our glasses of beer in our shaking hands. When the boss arrived, I told him my story. He said nothing, turned his back on us and strode into the next room.

About ten minutes later, the mobster was back, with 100 dollars in his hand. 'Take it, Limey,' he said. 'You are a very lucky man. I'm only doing this because you're English and I don't want you to think that we Yanks are a bunch of crooks.' He smiled at me, kindly; he handed over the 100 bucks; he shook my hand and he pointed to the door. We got out of it just as quickly as dignity allowed.

I needed more money, so I got myself onto a lecture panel, offering themes such as 'Socialism in Post War Britain'. Early in 1953, I travelled by train to Florida, to deliver a series of lectures. At the start of the journey, I chatted with an engaging mixture of blacks and whites. Then I went to sleep. When I woke up, there were only whites in my compartment. 'What's happened to all the black people?' I asked a passenger. 'We're in the South,' the man replied. 'We've crossed the Mason–Dixon Line. We're segregated now.' I was shocked.

My first engagement was at the all-black Bethune Cookman College. One of the two founders, Mary McLeod Bethune, was in her eighties and was waiting in her home to see me. She was white-haired, bright-eyed and powerful of tongue. 'The walls are crumbling,' she said. 'The walls were high, but they're coming down.'

I addressed students from a platform in a large hall. I was the only white person in the room. I felt strange. But the Dean of the College gave me a warm welcome; my lecture went down a treat; and I left for lunch with the Dean and his family, well satisfied. The lunch was excellent and happy and I got on especially well with the Dean's son, who was not much younger than myself. After lunch, I said to him: 'Let's go down to the beach for a walk and a swim.' 'Sorry,' he said, shaking his head. 'We're not allowed on the beach with white people.' I went cold. I felt sick, ashamed. 'It's not your fault,' said my new friend. 'We don't blame *that* on the British!' Well, for that at least, the Lord be thanked.

I did not go to the beach. We talked. They lived in their black bubble while waiting for the day when it would burst. As a Jew – especially as a Jew – I would do all I could to blow it apart. Black, white – Jew, Muslim – colour, race – we share our limited time in this world. The Holocaust was a Jewish tragedy. Segregation, apartheid, discrimination against blacks – that was a tragedy that I intellectually understood before but first felt and endured at Bethune Cookman College. Those walls must come down.

From Bethune Cookman College, it was an intellectually short distance to the creation of the Maimonides Foundation and Coexistence Trust. To share a bright future, moderate Muslims and Jews must work together against the extremists that afflict them both.

At the end of my Harvard year, my close friend and future best man, Tony Cohen, flew over from London to join me on a great trip. We were friends at Cambridge. We had once driven around Italy together, in his open and slightly decrepit MG. Partners in friendship as in marriage tend to be one of two kinds: either they are similar in approach, spirit and temperament, or they are opposites, complementing each other. That was Tony and me. He was soft-spoken and patient, punctilious and careful, gentle and good-natured. Trained in the law, he would become a trusted solicitor; just the friend that I needed, to keep me in line. We never argued or quarrelled. We each enjoyed the assets of the other.

We were joined by three of my Harvard American friends: Michael (Mike) Halberstam; Newell Mack; and Philip (Phil) McCurdy, all of whom had studied at Harvard College and become my friends. Mike was tall, witty and gentle. His brother became famous as a Pulitzer Prize winner. Michael became a doctor and one of his patients, whom I met with him, was the wife of Martin Luther King. When Myra and I were in Pamplona on our honeymoon, we watched the running of the bulls through its streets.

We were astonished to see Mike, out in front, arms flailing, with the bulls' horns perilously close to his rear. Some years later, he was murdered. He had disturbed a burglar inside his house and he challenged the thief, who rammed a knife into his chest and fled. Mike staggered to his car and drove after the villain, ramming him against a post. Then my friend died at the wheel.

Newell Mack was the son of a professor of spectroscopy at Madison University, whimsical and wise. He and his wife both died of cancer. By a marvellous coincidence, I stumbled across the path of his son, Nathaniel, who in 1996 spent three months working for me as a researcher in the House of Commons. Phil McCurdy was as intense as Mike and Newell and Tony were relaxed. A talented artist, he was a lively non-conformist and I much envied his prowess with the ladies.

The five of us packed into the car, with our minimal luggage on a roof rack and in the boot. Our money was equally minimal, so we camped out where it was safe; scrounged accommodation from friends or family, wherever any of us were blessed with either; and sometimes we arrived at a penal institution in the late afternoon and, on the flimsy basis of my interest in criminology, we were shown around and then dined in the evening; slept overnight in the gym hall or wherever there was space, ate a substantial breakfast in the morning and then drove on.

We swept across that huge country, saluting our ancient Chevrolet after it had survived each hundred miles, with a chorus of 'Happy Birthday to You'. Niagara . . . Chicago . . . and across the desert of Nevada, where we stopped at a petrol station to fill the car and to empty ourselves. In my best American, I asked the proprietor: 'Where's the rest room, please?' He spread out his arm and swept it across the horizon in all directions. 'Rest room?' he proclaimed. 'Rest room? Look – fifty thousand square miles of rest room! Do help yourself . . .'

Las Vegas was then only one strip. We allocated ten dollars to each of us from our limited pool, spreading it across the blackjack and roulette tables and the one-armed bandits. Characteristically, Phil disposed of his ten bucks within minutes and the rest of us dragged it out for a couple of hours. We watched shows, enjoyed the brash vulgarity of the flashing lights and the hotel décor and then we drove on through the night, taking turns at the wheel.

The National Parks were joyful. We walked to the bottom of the Grand Canyon and wearily climbed our way back to the top. We gawped at the geysers in Yellowstone Park. We parked our sleeping bags in the open. San Francisco and Alcatraz . . . Los Angeles and Hollywood . . . then back by another route and further south, reaching New Orleans in time for my twenty-fifth birthday.

Phil spent the day earning some money, drawing portraits of visitors, in front of the cathedral. Then my three mates conspired with four girl schoolteachers from Oklahoma to take me for a special birthday fun evening – to the 'My Oh My Club'. We dressed as well as we could and were seated at a table near the stage. Then along came a beautiful brunette called Micki. 'Who's the birthday boy?' she asked. They pointed at me. Micki came over, sat on my lap and cuddled and gently chewed my ear. My seven friends were doubled up with laughter.

'What's so funny?' I asked. 'I always was the most attractive of all of you, to discerning young women.' Which only made them laugh more. Then one of the Oklahomans could keep the secret no longer. 'Micki,' she said, 'is a boy!' They had brought me to a gay club, from which I fled without ceremony, leaving them to pay the bill.

We ended up in New York. The car had now reached its ultimate; it was unsaleable. Our friends took Tony and myself to the boat. Newell bought me, as a farewell gift, my favourite, chocolate milkshake. They emptied the Chevy, pointed it at the river and then jumped out of the way. It had been a great hundred bucks' worth but had reached the end of the road. That also marked the end of my carefree youth.

PART TWO

The Law and Family

SEVEN

The Bar

To qualify as a barrister, you had to attend a bar school. Mine was run by a firm called Gibson and Weldon, in central London. My favourite teacher was an eccentric character named Padley. The tutors would read out notes, which we wrote down, word for word, and then explain them if necessary. We were expected to memorise the notes and to be prepared to spew out appropriate and relevant paragraphs in weekly tests and all of it for our Bar exams. As a result, most of the lectures were the ultimate in dreary boredom. Only Mr Padley's were full of humour. The moment he saw someone's attention wandering, he would pounce and ask a question. He teased, he provoked, he taught. He asked questions and expected you to do the same. There were, of course, sensitive souls who preferred to learn and let learn in peace, but most of us enjoyed Mr Padley. When my turn came to teach, many years later, I shamelessly adapted and copied his style.

As I had a law degree, I was freed from all the Part I Bar examinations, which gave me time for a lively social life and, I hoped, for an entry into politics. I put my name down on the candidates' list at Transport House, the Labour Party HQ. I travelled and read and learned.

Any legal subject with a practical aspect I found interesting. The making and breaking of contracts . . . torts – civil wrongs, like negligence or nuisance . . . even real property, the study of land ownership. All had relevance to human life. But equity, the law administered by the Chancery Courts, was dry, irrelevant and boring. When it came to the Bar Finals, I coped well enough with all the papers except Equity, which I was sure I had failed. I hoped for a provisional pass – that is, a pass provisional on my retaking Equity and scraping through it next time. When the grim day arrived and the results were published, I joined my friends at the Middle Temple notice board. I looked down the list of provisional passes. No Janner. Then the long list of Third Class passes. No Janner. I turned away, feeling sick.

Then someone called out: 'Hey Greville, You've got a Second.' I couldn't believe it. My heart sang. I had passed my last required examination. Little did I realise that most of my life from then on would be examinations. Except that they were called cases and court appearances, selections and elections.

In 1954, I was called to the Bar. I was now a fully fledged barrister. As a champion junior athlete, one of my heroes was a former Olympic champion called D.G.A. (Douglas) Lowe. I applied to him for a pupillage and was promptly accepted. He was in the chambers of a tall, reserved and brilliant Labour lawyer, Gerald Gardiner. The pupillage was a disaster. I shared it with Julian Priest, a good-natured young man who warned me that Douglas Lowe was uncommunicative. Indeed.

Lowe used to sit at one side of a large, highly polished antique table, with the two of us working opposite. If I wished to ask a question, I would wait for a pause in his concentration. 'Could you be kind enough . . .' He would look at me. 'Could you be kind enough to let me ask a question?' Silence. Then: 'Just a moment, Janner.' About five minutes later, he would look up and say: 'Yes?' By that time, I had either forgotten the question or decided not to ask it anyway. 'Most kind of you,' I would say, 'but I have found the answer.' He nodded.

Father fed me work which was well beyond my capabilities. I soon found that very little that I had learned at university or at Bar School was of the least use in dealing with the day-to-day problems of my clients, civil or criminal. Either I was sunk into the mysteries of tenant protection under the Rent Acts, or much more often, dealing with problems of which witnesses' evidence should or should not be believed. Or sometimes, the legal issues were so rare and recondite that no Bar students had ever approached them. Such was the archaic law on mortmain, which surfaced in a remarkable case involving a notorious landlord called Arthur Bertram Walters.

At the Lambeth County Court, the Crown was represented as '*amicus curiae*' – a friend of the Court. As the case had apparent and serious legal ramifications, this was a formidable and experienced man. He treated me with a mixture of courtesy and lofty contempt. For him to be faced by a pupil was clearly inappropriate and demeaning. I thought he was quite right.

When presiding Judge Clothier called out the words: 'Yes, Mr Janner,' I was frozen. I rose to my feet, knees shaking. Voice behind me: 'Come on, son. Get on with it.' I did. A few moments later, I felt Father tugging on my gown: 'Tell him . . .' he said, with his booming Welsh resonance. 'Tell him that . . .' The judge nodded, sagely. I told him as best I could. Clearly, Father was deeply frustrated that he could not do the job himself. In those days, solicitors could only appear in minor cases. Somehow, I reached the end of my submission and answered the court's questions, often thanks to the judge himself coming to my rescue. Thus: 'I expect what you mean, Mr Janner is . . .' 'Thank you, your honour,' I would respond, with profound appreciation. 'I am most obliged . . .'

Then Father pulled at my gown. 'Tell him that . . .' he announced in a resonant stage whisper. 'May I only add, Your Honour,' I said, 'that . . .' Judge Clothier nodded, most kindly. And I then promised myself that if ever I was in a position of authority, whether in the law or anywhere else, I would do my best to help raw youngsters to cope, with the same quiet dignity that the judge had accorded to me.

Soon afterwards, I appeared again before Judge Clothier. I appealed to His Honour to give more time before evicting my client, a woman in her late fifties. 'Your Honour,' I begged, 'please do not put this aged lady out of her home, in the evening of her life – at least without giving her two months to find somewhere else to live.' Judge Clothier snorted. 'Aged lady?' he grunted. 'Aged? Your client is at least ten years younger than I am, and I'm not aged!' I learned my lesson. Today, when addressing anyone over the age of sixty, especially if I cannot remember his or her name, I simply say: 'Good morning, young man,' or 'Good to see you, young lady.' Almost invariably, the person smiles and says: 'Oh, thank you for the compliment . . .'

In June 1955, I was instructed by my friend, David Young, to represent a client of his on 6 July. David – now the very distinguished Lord Young of Graffham – agreed that I should apply for an adjournment. I did. 'What is your reason for seeking an adjournment?' the judge demanded. 'Because, Your Honour, the case is fixed for the 6 July. And that is my wedding day.' 'I have never heard a better reason for asking for an adjournment,' said the judge, smiling. 'Granted – and good luck!'

To earn a living as a barrister meant getting accepted by and admitted to good chambers. All members of chambers, however mighty, or however minuscule, are independent. They share the same rooms (French – *chambres* – chambers) and the same clerks, and much of their success depends on the good name of the chambers and the goodwill of the clerks.

In those days getting a pupillage was no problem, but getting accepted into the right chambers was a totally different and much tougher proposition. I was lucky. I applied at 1 Garden Court. Nominally, the head of chambers was an ancient gentleman called Astell Burt. In reality, there were joint heads: Lewis Hawser and Charles Lawson.

Lewis Hawser was a tall, gaunt and imposing presence and a man of brilliant intellect. But his father was the very man in the Cardiff synagogue who had wrongly accused my father of disgraceful behaviour. Our fathers had become lifelong enemies.

Lewis interviewed me, asking me a series of brisk and probing questions. Then he sat back in his chair and said: 'Is the fact that our fathers are enemies any reason why we should not be friends?' 'Certainly not,' I replied. 'In that case,' he smiled at me, 'you will be very welcome in these Chambers.'

Next, Charles Lawson, tall, burly, genial and with a rich voice, who happily agreed with Lewis. In chambers, Astell Burt was known as 'Uncle'. But Charles took pity on me and became like an uncle to me. There were two clerks. Arthur was shrewd, manipulative, funny and very tough. His junior, William, was young, handsome, and in his relationship with Arthur, the sorcerer's apprentice. They lived off commission. They serviced the mighty and fed crumbs to the youngsters.

The Bar is a curious, unsettled and uncertain profession. You are instructed – 'sent a brief' – for a big case tomorrow? It will last a month, so you clear your diary? Then odds on it will settle. Or the case holds firm and another monster drops into the list for the following week, but you're stuck on the first one, so the clerk tries very hard to have it transferred to someone else in Chambers. If Mr Lawson was unexpectedly busy, then Arthur was pleased to tell the solicitor that Mr Hawser was free. If the solicitor did not want that alternative, for whatever reason, then Arthur would try other members of Chambers. He had plenty of choice – they were a talented lot. Each layer of crumbs fell off the table to one level lower. By the time they reached the new recruits, these crumbs were small, but we fed off them.

I was lucky because I had my father's firm behind me, including his partner and my cousin, Gerald Davis, and later my sister, Ruth. Eric Davis, Gerald's brother, also briefed me when I was raw. They risked their own good practices in the process.

At 1 Garden Court, the atmosphere was totally different from that in the chambers of Gerald Gardiner and Douglas Lowe, where I had spent my pupillage. People here helped each other, readily and without reserve. Above all, Charles Lawson checked my draft documents – especially those for cases, referred to as 'pleadings'. More often than not, he rewrote them for me. Later, his daughter Jennifer married another barrister friend, Eldred Tabachnik, who, like myself, became President of the Board of Deputies of British Jews. I had what we called a knock-about, common law practice. Very little in the Chancery Division, but whatever else came my way I would accept. I especially enjoyed criminal cases.

I learned my first lesson from a well-known QC (or 'silk'), Bernard Gillis. He led me in my first major fraud case. I liked our client and made the mistake of believing him. Gillis fought the case with skill, but we lost. Unanimously and speedily, the jury declared our client to be a wily confidence trickster. I told Bernard that I was convinced of the man's innocence. 'Oh, come on, don't be so naive,' said Bernard. 'Of course he was guilty.'

'But he looked so honest. He appears so honest.' 'Of course,' my leader snorted. 'All con men who are any good appear to be honest or they'd never make a dishonest living!'

I represented another con man, who was involved in an ingenious swindle. For a modest sum, you could buy a share in non-existent pigs and sows and the more they bred, the more money you would get. In due course my client and his fellow conspirators were charged with fraud. I knew that my client would plead not guilty to the charges, but I could see no answer to them. So I visited him in his cell at the Old Bailey. He had no apparent means and I was representing him on Legal Aid, at no cost to himself. 'Tell me, please,' I asked him. 'What is your defence?'

'You tell me,' he replied.

'My job,' I said, 'is to put your case before the jury and the judge in the best possible way. But I cannot tell you what your answer is on the facts.'

'You can't?' responded my client, incredulously.

'You can't?' he repeated.

'No, I can't,' I replied, firmly.

'In that case,' he said, 'in that case, what am I not paying you for?'

In March 1973, I was briefed for a client in a major Old Bailey trial that had a number of other defendants. One of them was represented by a chambers colleague and friend, Ivor Richard, who later became an MP, a European commissioner, UK ambassador to the United States and a peer, and later the leader of the Labour peers. Another defendant was represented by my wise ally and friend, Brian Clapham.

Suddenly an usher approached the judge and whispered something into his ear. The judge stopped the trial. 'There has been a bomb scare,' he announced. 'Members of the jury, will you please retire to the jury room. The accused will be taken to the cells.' The judge then stood up, bowed to the court and retired. Together with Ivor and Brian, I moved sedately into the hall outside the court. Brian pointed through one of the great glass windows. 'Look,' he said. 'Look down there. There are soldiers with guns crouching in the doorways.'

Suddenly, there was a mighty thump. A huge bang. The windows shattered inwards. Like an old soldier, I fell to the ground. My wig flew off my head but my gown flew over it. I was covered in glass. Silence. Then cries and shouts. Someone's leg had been cut by flying glass. Others were injured. One man died and my solicitor's clerk suffered a cut on his leg but otherwise, my colleagues and I escaped unhurt. We were very lucky.

I was involved in several murder trials, sitting behind Queen's Counsel, but only one where I held the responsibility on my own. It finally convinced me that capital punishment is no deterrent. My eighteen-year-old client had been high on purple hearts, a then popular drug, and was busy burgling a house in south London when the owner arrived home. He attacked the householder with a knife and killed him.

Not surprisingly, my client was a man of limited intelligence. He seemed bewildered and not at all penitent. It was clear on the evidence that he had no defence to a murder charge and his best hope of avoiding the gallows was to plead 'diminished responsibility'. I explained to him that if he was convicted of murder, he would be hanged. A verdict of 'diminished responsibility' would probably lead to his imprisonment in a criminal psychiatric institution. I suggested to him that he should be represented by Queen's Counsel, but he said no. He insisted that I do the job for him.

All went well at the trial. It was clear that my client was demented. The plea of diminished responsibility succeeded and he was duly committed to imprisonment at Rampton psychiatric prison, 'at Her Majesty's pleasure'. Immediately after the verdict, I visited him in his cell. He asked me to explain to him what had happened. I told him that I was glad to say that we had succeeded in our plea and that he had avoided the death penalty and would be sent to a full security psychiatric institution. 'For how long?' he asked.

'Until they are quite sure that if you are released you won't kill anyone else,' I answered.

'You mean that I could be in this asylum for life?'

'It's possible.'

He blazed up in fury. 'That's appalling,' he said. 'I don't want to be locked up in that place forever.' I tried to explain to him that the alternative would almost certainly have been hanging. 'I don't believe you,' he said. 'It's your fault that I'll be in that place forever.' So much for the deterrent value of capital punishment. Potential murderers either do not believe that they will be caught, or in the old days, that they would be liable to the death penalty. Or they are not of sound mind. From then on, I campaigned for its abolition, which finally got through Parliament in 1965.

On 28 December 1958, I represented thirty-seven, non-violent, protesters at the North Pickenham rocket site, near Swaffham, Norfolk. My job was to get them out of court, and home as swiftly as possible. My clients were all active supporters of the Direct Action Committee Against Nuclear War. They had all pleaded guilty to obstructing the police at the rocket site. They had been warned not to trespass on the base but they had marched on. The police removed them, but they came back. Then they were arrested. Their motive? To abolish nuclear war. Said the Prosecution: 'That is a cause which must recommend itself to any right-minded person, but this is not the way to go about it.'

Before the case, I had consulted the guru of the anti-nuclear movement, that great philosopher, Bertrand (Lord) Russell. He invited me to visit him at his book-lined home, which I did with alacrity. I found him gaunt, with a pile of grey hair – brilliant in his analysis; deeply focused on his issues; and obviously pleased that I had sought his support. We talked in his library and he promised to send me an appropriate letter to read out to the court. A telegram arrived: 'Hope defendants in trial of Direct Action Committee will be leniently dealt with since they are actuated by conscientious motives in attempting to prevent wanton destruction of many millions of human lives. I think their action deserves general support.' It was signed: Earl Russell.

My clients had made it plain that they would not buy their freedom by undertaking not to behave in the same way in the future. My solution: to ask the court to bind them over to keep the peace, which did not require the defendants' consent. True, they could refuse to be bound over, but that would take a positive act of repudiation, rather than that silence which characterised their approach to demonstrations.

How, then, could I induce the court to take this action? I told the magistrates that my clients were not the ordinary sort of men and women who came before a court. 'They are decent and honest, law-abiding citizens who have never been in any sort of trouble or difficulty before, other than through their beliefs.' My clients believed most strongly that it would be wrong for them to give any promise which they could not be certain they would be able to keep. Only one of them would be prepared to enter into a recognisance and she was a woman with family responsibilities. It would be repugnant for her to sign but she would do so.

I then invited the court to bind over my clients to keep the peace. If that was their intention, then I would rest my case. If, on the other hand, they were proposing to take some other course, then it would be my duty to put forward the circumstances of each of my clients in turn, all thirty-seven of them. Chairman: 'The court will adjourn.' After only fifteen minutes, they returned. My ruse had worked. My clients rejoiced and, however temporarily, I was a hero of the anti-nuclear movement.

Then there was the 1965 inquest on the famous, former light heavyweight world champion boxer, Freddie Mills. He had been found dead in his car. At that time, my father's firm acted for the British Boxing

Board of Control and they instructed me to appear for his family at the Coroner's Court.

So how did he die? Who owned the rifle which Mills used to kill himself? A friend had lent it to him because Mills said that he was dressing up as a cowboy at a fancy dress party and needed it for his costume. Yes, he had financial problems with the club that he owned but he had access to money and had powerful friends; verdict: suicide; speculation: gangland murder; we shall never know.

On 11 November 1963, a man was killed before my eyes. As a result, I gave evidence in court, for the first and only time. I was driving slowly along the north London Finchley Road when an old man, wearing a khaki raincoat, stepped out from between two cars some twenty yards ahead of me. His head was lowered and he looked neither to right nor to left. I stopped, expecting him to wait in the centre of the road for a break in the traffic coming in the opposite direction. He did not. Instead, he walked smack into the front, offside mudguard of a small, black, Ford Anglia, one of a line of traffic going at 15–20mph in the opposite direction. There was a horrible, sickening thud. The man was thrown to the ground, hitting his head on the road; he lay there, blood seeping out of his mouth. The car which had hit him stopped quickly. A woman emerged, young, blonde and screaming; 'I didn't have a chance,' she said. She was right; she could not have avoided the tragedy.

By this time, several people had lifted the old man onto the pavement. I drove round the corner, stopped and got out of my car. First, I wanted to satisfy my own conscience as to whether or not I should go back and make a statement. Long acquaintance with the courts had taught me that giving evidence, even at an inquest, was a time-consuming process. If it came to civil or criminal proceedings involving the driver, I might have to give up days of work. Then I realised that if the man had stepped out even a few seconds later, I would have run him down, and if the woman in the other car had been my wife, I would have prayed that someone would have come forward to testify that it was not her fault.

Whose fault was it? Clearly, the man had walked right into her car. But could she not have seen him? Should she not have swerved out of his way, or hooted so as to break into his reverie? No. I walked back to the scene.

The old man was lying unconscious on the pavement. I walked into the police station to give a statement.

After I had finished carefully writing down what I had seen, an old acquaintance called Harold Godfrey arrived in the room. He had witnessed the tragedy from the other side of the road. To my relief, he said: 'It wasn't her fault.'

On 18 November, Mr Finlay (for that was his name) died in hospital, never having regained consciousness. On 26 November, the inquest was held at St Pancras Coroner's Court. First to give evidence was the uncle of the deceased, who testified to his previous good health. Then came that most charming and brilliant of pathologists, Dr Francis Camps. He made it clear that the cause of death was a fractured skull, caused through the impact. Next, my turn. I walked to the box, feeling peculiarly ill at ease. 'Mr Janner, do you want to take the oath?' queried the coroner's officer. 'You are not appearing in a professional capacity.' Dr Milne, the coroner, smiled.

'I'm afraid that he must take the oath, the same as everyone else.' I did, repeating it after the coroner's officer. I then told the story. Once I got moving, I felt better. Then I was cross-examined by the solicitor representing the relatives of the deceased. Forgetting the old rule that any question you ask at an inquest is likely to be answered in a way contrary to your client's interests, he dragged out of me that the old man had looked neither to right nor to left, but walked across the road with his head down, as if in a dream.

Then came Harold Godfrey, whose account was very similar to mine, but seen from the opposite side of the road. The two young police officers who had come to the body testified next, and then the woman driver. To my utter amazement, this honest, decent person, genuinely attempting to tell the truth, explained how the deceased had stepped off the pavement on her side of the road and had walked in front of her car, leaving her with no alternative but to try to pass behind him. She was, she said, going at about twenty-seven miles an hour.

As the coroner pointed out in his summing up for the jury, the lady was obviously mistaken. She had not seen Mr Finlay until she had hit him, and in retrospect, she had tried to recreate the scene, and failed. The verdict – accidental death.

Lessons to be learned? First, do not give a statement to the police after an accident, unless your solicitor is present. Speak on the spur of the moment and tell what happened, numbed as you are by shock, and the chances are that you will get it wrong. And if you are as wrong as the lady in Mr Finlay's case, you will be convicted of a serious driving offence out of your own mouth – unless you have the good fortune to have two, independent witnesses to testify that you are both wrong and innocent.

Second, note how justice can go astray, through the efforts of ordinary people to tell the truth, even if that truth is contrary to their own interests. Justice is, at best, an attempt to reconstruct what can never be seen again. This attempt will often fail. Which explains one reason why even the best system of justice is fallible.

Myra's father, Emanuel, came to visit us in England. He wanted to see me at work, so I took him with me to the Old Bailey. We went to see my client in the cells. While we were waiting for him to arrive, I watched Father pacing up and down the cell, in both directions. 'What are you doing?' I enquired. 'Just working out the area and how much I could rent it out for!' he replied. I now knew that Myra had inherited her sense of humour from both her parents. By the time our client arrived, our laughter had subsided.

The cases I liked most were those in which the clients were underprivileged and needed my help. I most disliked appearing on behalf of landlords, seeking to evict the helpless from their homes. Barristers are on the cab rank. Our job is to serve our clients, with care and integrity. It is not for us to decide on who is right or who is wrong, who is innocent and who is guilty. That is a matter for the court, and the longer you practise, the more you learn how often your assessment of your client is wrong. So you are not in general allowed to turn down cases because you dislike or suspect clients or their cases. What you must not do is to deceive the court. Your job is to make the best of your client's case.

The only case I ever turned down because I was not prepared to represent the client was when I was instructed to appear on behalf of a Nazi, who had attacked blacks. I told my solicitor the truth – that Counsel should not be emotionally involved in the case on either side and that I did not believe that I could do justice to his client. The solicitor believed that having a well-known Jewish leader represent his client would give credibility to his client's case, but accepted that he had overstretched the limit of my cab rank potential.

The same did not apply to my landlord-and-tenant cases. I could not say to my solicitor: 'I am only prepared to represent tenants.' But I deeply disliked fighting for the eviction of people who may have been legally and entirely in the wrong but who were in my view morally correct. As Mr Padley had warned us, at Gibson and Weldon's Law School: 'Sadly, the law and justice are not necessarily the same. Your job as a barrister is to assist the court to come to the correct conclusion, on the basis of the law as Parliament in its extraordinary wisdom or otherwise sees fit to create it and the courts in their infinite magnificence have interpreted the same.'

I found undefended divorce cases both lucrative and interesting. You could sometimes handle three or four in a row. My favourite: the cruelty case, in which the husband alleged that his wife would only engage in sex with him if he gave her Green Shield stamps!

At the Bar, I enjoyed most the cut and thrust and the camaraderie of advocacy and least the pile of paperwork that I had to take home with me, at nights and weekends. Myra never minded my work, provided that I was at home with her and the children. Often, when I was hard at it long after midnight, my elder daughter Marion would totter downstairs, rubbing her eyes. She had set her alarm so that she could give me a special midnight hug. My earnings at the Bar were not enough to keep my growing family in the style which we enjoyed. So I looked for additions. But I tried never to do so at the cost of my family security. I also enjoyed having my own pupils. Their pupillage fees were quite useful but what mattered much more was that they were all drivers. They would sit behind the wheel of the car while I prepared my case on the way to court. Sometimes, this was inevitable because it was a 'late return' from someone else or a last-minute brief. Sometimes, I had regrettably not allowed enough time to prepare my brief with the thoroughness it required. Sometimes, it was like last-minute revision before an important exam. Whatever the reason, time was precious. I also enjoyed teaching my pupils. I took them through the cases and the arguments and they would draft paperwork, which I always corrected. Excellence, I praised. Errors, especially the startling ones, I marked with appropriate expletives.

My cousin, Nick Tarsh, spent a brief time with me in Chambers. After a few efforts at complex cases and paperwork, he decided that the Bar was no place for him. Instead, he set off on an extremely successful business career. Most who have finished their pupillage do not end up at the Bar.

At the Bar, I was much more interested in helping individuals to improve their lives or to rescue their fortunes, than I was in arguing and studying law. As with politics, so with my work as a barrister – I admired others for their intellectual capacities and recondite interests. My concern was much more about people. And it has been the chance to give that service that has permeated my professional career, for over half a century.

EIGHT

Myra and Marriage

I first met Myra Sheink, from Melbourne, Australia, at a posh, black-tie party. Ruth had told me that I must meet her. 'You'll love her, brother,' she said. I did. It was a chilly evening and the elegant home was not overheated. 'So, how are you enjoying London?' I asked Myra.

'I'm freezing,' she replied. In a moment of youthful inspiration, I unbuttoned my black jacket and held it open with both hands.

'Come in and get warm, then,' I suggested. She did, and she remained for over forty years.

The chemistry was perfect. We laughed at the same jokes. We liked and disliked the same people. One day when we were dancing our way down Oxford Street and Myra was saying how much she liked a smart dress shop, I popped the first question. 'Are you looking forward to going back to Australia?' 'Certainly not. If I can avoid it, I shall,' she replied, without hesitation. 'Why do you think I left there?' She had endured two unsuccessful engagements, entered into, I suspected, as a result of the pressure of her orthodox Jewish milieu, where a girl in her middle twenties surely should have been married. One fiancé was called Bill and the other Ben and, of course, I referred to them as the Flower Pot Men. Then she added: 'But I may have to go back in July.'

'I hope not,' I replied, quietly determining to do my best to see that she did not.

Myra was staying with her mother's brother, Chief Rabbi Israel Brodie, and his wife, Fanny. Uncle Israel, as I later called him, was good-natured and funny and, like so many people in public life, not at all like his public image. Aunt Fanny was a former schoolteacher, crisp and formal, but always kind to me, and one day, she did me a great favour. She inadvertently told me how Myra felt about me. I phoned and asked for Myra and Aunt Fanny said: 'She's in Newcastle.'

'Would you please ask her to phone me as soon as she can? I need to know whether she'd like to come to the theatre with me on Thursday next week.'

'Oh, I'm sure she'd absolutely love to,' Aunt Fanny replied. 'Don't worry, she'll phone you immediately.' She did – but was furious when she discovered that her loving but naive aunt had given her game away.

Everyone liked Myra. Especially, at that time, my mother. She asked me whether I was considering proposing to Myra and I asked her what she thought. 'She's too good for you, dear,' Mother replied, with her usual subtlety. A few weeks later, Mother invited Myra to join a party of young people at our Broadstairs cottage, called 'Janner's Jungle'. And one evening, I took Myra for a drive and we stopped outside the Captain Digby pub on the cliffs, overlooking the sea. 'How about marrying me? Please . . . I'm afraid that I have only myself to offer – plus a life insurance policy!' She hugged me and said yes and we became engaged. When we returned to the Jungle, the denizens were all delighted. Mum gave Myra a hug and said: 'Now, don't spoil him, dear. Start now as you intend to continue . . .'

We soon learned that if a young couple can survive an engagement and still love each other, the marriage will be great. 'Just let them get on with the wedding arrangements,' Myra said. 'They're nothing to do with us, dear.'

Myra's family were well respected, as I told my father one day. He replied: 'Oh, we know that.' I discovered that my parents had already checked. Jewish people believed that a marriage was more likely to last if both sides were of 'good stock' – settled, strong, healthy families. The family, immediate and extended, was and remained at the centre of our world.

We survived the engagement in good heart, especially thanks to a series of joyful parties arranged by our friends. And I took Myra up to Trinity Hall, Cambridge for its May Ball. There she taught me how to dance. Not leaping around, as I used to do at Camp Hiawatha, but standing together as closely as possible, cheek to cheek, eyes closed and rocking gently in time to the music.

The General Election was in June 1955. Three weeks before Election Day, I received a call from Labour Party HQ. 'How about standing for

Wimbledon?' Perfect. A London seat, so until the last week I could continue with my Bar work. Tory majority of over 15,000, so no hope of winning and no stress. The constituency owned and rented out a hall, so they would cover most of the expenses. Problem: how to win the nomination?

The vacancy had opened up so late because the candidate selected by the local Party was regarded as an eccentric left-winger, whom the Labour Party refused to endorse. After an unmemorable but successful Selection Conference, I found myself on the battlefield with Jack Gibson, a veteran official of the Union of Shop, Distributive & Allied Workers (USDAW), as my doughty agent. My opponent was a thoroughly decent old gentleman called Cyril Black. A charitable and religious soul, he was a teetotaller and campaigned against the evils of drink. My canvassers and I enjoyed passing out pamphlets in local pubs and drinking places, quoting from his denunciations of alcohol.

In those days, people still came to election meetings. We held a series around the constituency. I advertised through a loudspeaker, strapped to the roof of my car. 'Labour Election Rally tonight. This is Janner, your Labour candidate. Come and heckle Janner!' They did, by the hundred. I enjoyed the meetings, the loudspeakering, the pamphleting, and I was joined on the doorstep by good-natured and kindly friends of every political complexion. I have especially happy memories of two Tory articled clerks in my father's office, Malvyn and Irvine Benjamin. With bowler hats and rolled umbrellas, they set a precedent which later many other good friends followed. They asked people to vote for Janner. Any political questions, they wisely referred to the grateful candidate.

We lost, of course, but we reduced the Tory majority, from 30,794 to 10,490. In his courteous victory speech, Cyril Black congratulated me on my campaign, without condescension. I responded by praising him and his fairness as an opponent and wishing him well in his return to the House. I then paid my tribute to my team of workers and proclaimed the glory of our result.

Cheerful and cheering, we left the hall. Our mates sat Myra and me in the back of an open sports car and pushed it down the main street of Wimbledon, loudly singing what was then the Labour Party song: 'The Red Flag'. 'So raise the scarlet standard high,' we chorused, joyfully. 'Beneath its shade, we'll live and die. Though cowards flinch and traitors fear, we'll keep the red flag flying here . . .' Imagine the red flag flying in sedate and middle-class Wimbledon. Little did we imagine that in 1997, Labour would win that seat.

My most notable campaign memory? I was working one day in our HQ when Jack Gibson came striding in, smiling and rubbing his left hand on his right fist. A bald, rotund man in his sixties, he was generally good-natured, but when roused, he was a fierce opponent. 'What are you looking so happy about, Jack?' I asked him.

'I was cycling along on my way here,' said Jack, 'when a man signalled that he wanted to talk to me. I got off my bike and went over to him and he said: "Why are you working for a Jew?" So I hit him on the jaw . . . I did enjoy it. The man stood there bewildered. I don't think he liked my argument but I certainly let him know how I felt about his.' I thought then, how immensely lucky we Jews are to live in such a fair and decent land – together with people like Jack Gibson, who know the powers of argument!

Myra and I were married on Wednesday, 6 July 1955. Tony Cohen was my best man and took charge of the wedding ring. On the morning of the great day, Myra was taken off to the '*mikva*' – the traditional Jewish ritual bathhouse. She had never been there before. She dipped one toe in the water and decided that that was more than enough. She left and never returned.

By upbringing, Myra was completely observant. The first time she ever touched electricity on the Sabbath was when I had 'flu and she was alone with me in my family's flat at Albert Hall Mansions. She made me a hot cup of lemon water. As our lives grew together, Myra adopted without much trauma the more relaxed traditions of my side of the family. We kept a kosher home. We observed Friday nights as a family occasion. When Myra had lit the candles, I made the traditional blessings over the wine and the bread; and we sang the Hebrew grace at the end of the meal. On Sabbath and on festivals, though, Myra cooked and we travelled. When we ate out, we avoided forbidden foods – pig products and shellfish – but ate the rest.

We had so many people to invite to the wedding that Uncle and Auntie Brodie held a pre-wedding party in a marquee in their Hamilton Terrace garden. That was mainly for our young friends, who were invited to the wedding but could not be fitted into the marquee for the dinner and reception afterwards.

Our wedding day was sunny and hot. My best man, ushers and I arrived early at the Hampstead Synagogue in Dennington Park Road, and so did the bridesmaids. My parents and Myra's mother and my old teacher, the Revd I. (Harry) Levy stood together on the Bima – the raised platform below the Ark of the synagogue. Harry raised both eyebrows and whispered: 'She's late!' At that moment, the male-voice choir broke into our favourite melody, 'Hariyu' – which, since Myra died, I cannot hear without choking back my emotion. She walked up beside me, veil over her face, she took my hand gently, then blew into her veil. 'Help,' she said, 'I can't breathe!' Then she smiled and I knew that she was not proposing to faint. Tony produced the ring. I pronounced the ancient formula: 'Behold, with this ring you are holy to me in accordance with the law of Moses and of Israel.' The deed was done.

We spent the night at Claridges and then flew to Spain, to Pamplona, where we watched the running of the bulls through the street. Then to my village of Laredo, where we were greeted and serenaded by friends from my previous visit, and stayed in the first of the new hotels in what has now become a tourist strip in a celebrated resort. It was there that Myra was struck down for the first time by an attack of depressive illness. The local doctor diagnosed clinical depression; he prescribed what he described as a 'brilliant new drug' – thalidomide.

In London, we were blessed with the care of an unusual uncle and nephew partnership, Alfred Rudd and George Morris. Rudd (as he was always called, to distinguish him from my Uncle Alfred) immediately said: 'This drug is too new. We don't know what side-effects it has.' Mercifully and to our eternal relief, there was no more thalidomide for Myra. If she had continued with the treatment, there would have been a grave risk of our children being born with serious deformities.

Nineteen fifty-five was a memorable year. Pupillage . . . engagement . . . Wimbledon election . . . marriage, honeymoon . . . a new world, with a wife to keep and care for. We bought a small, three-bedroom, semi-detached home in Northway, Hampstead Garden Suburb. I converted the garage into a study, with French windows opening onto our tiny garden and the Big Wood. It was at the top of a hill and peaceful and we were very happy. The house cost £3,600. Uncles Israel and Abe Brodie chipped in for the down-payment and the rest we borrowed on a ten-year mortgage, with interest fixed at 3 per cent. Those were the days!

About a year later, we were under canvas in the summer camp of the Victoria Youth Club, together with many of our friends. One of the club leaders remarked to me that Myra wasn't looking too good and I told him she was feeling sick and wretched. 'Really,' he said. 'Have you considered whether the next generation might be on its way?' We had not. It was: Daniel was on his way.

Myra was at her best when pregnant. She lost the urge to smoke, and she felt that these were the only times when my mother approved of her. Their relationship had become sadly uncomfortable and Mother, who in so many other ways was such a remarkable and great lady, totally failed to give any love to a woman who so badly needed it.

Daniel arrived on 27 April 1957 and Marion on 16 August 1959. Gloriously active children, we loved them so much that we could not abide the thought of having no more babies. Hence Laura, born on 1 August 1963. All three children were born in the Royal Free Hospital. When they moved Myra into the labour ward for Daniel's birth, I had to wait in her empty room, until the obstetrician, Mitchell Rees, opened the door with the magic words: 'You have a lovely healthy baby.' When Marion was due, Myra asked whether I could be present at the birth.

'I'm sorry,' said Mitchell Rees, 'we don't have fathers in the room because we need to give all our attention to the mothers.' When Laura was arriving, Mr Rees reluctantly agreed to allow me to be present for the last few minutes. It was then that I watched that ultimate miracle. With a boy and a girl as our first two, we did not care about the sex of the third, but I had expected a boy. Myra was sure that it was a girl because her face hadn't changed during pregnancy – such was the scientific basis of sex prediction in those days! Whatever the reason, and after the most careful post-birth checking of the sex of the new arrival, I came to the conclusion that Myra was right again. We were both hugely happy.

A few doors down from us lived the Manning family. John was an official in the Admiralty. His wife, Elena, was once a well-known tennis player. Their four-year-old daughter, Lynn, was beautiful, lively and loveable. So much so that when our first baby was due, we decided that if it was a girl, we would call her Lynn.

In 1966, Myra phoned me at my chambers. 'Come home, please. Immediately. Lynn has just been round to say that she found her mother dead, with her head in the oven.' I rushed home. By then, the ambulance had arrived. Myra was distraught. John's mother moved in to look after Lynn, but Myra found the memory of that horror so upsetting to live with that we decided to move.

We saw John and Lynn occasionally, and late in 1967, Lynn called round and told me that her father, who was a heavy smoker, was in hospital with lung cancer. I immediately went to see him. He told me that he was getting better. I was glad but asked him whether he had made a will. 'Any of us can go under a bus . . .' He replied: 'Don't worry. Everything has been arranged and is in order.' As I would have expected from a well-disciplined civil servant.

Myra had never liked our first, Northway home, and in 1970 we moved a few streets away, to a large, detached house and garden, on a busy corner. The problem there was the noise of the traffic. So some five years later, we moved again, and this time to an even larger home, on the corner of Linnell Drive. It cost £36,000, over £30,000 on mortgage. I was making a modest income at the Bar, but by then we had three children. I was so scared at our extravagance that I had trouble sleeping at night. Little did I know that by the time we sold the house some twenty-one years later, property would have soared so high that we would be able to pay off all our debts. Myra's determination to live in homes beyond our means was our financial salvation.

On the eve of the Day of Atonement in 1968, I returned home to find Lynn standing at our open front door, with Myra who looked pale and stressed. 'Uncle Greville,' said Lynn. 'You are my guardian.'

'I'm sorry, Lynn dear,' I replied. 'But I don't understand.'

'Daddy has died and made you the executor under his will. Our solicitor says that you have automatically become my guardian.'

I was stunned. But yes, she was right. John had made an informal will, of the standard variety, bought from the local newsagent and completed in his own handwriting. An expert on wills in Barnett Janner and Davis confirmed. I was Lynn's guardian. I could renounce probate. I was entitled to refuse to take on the responsibility. We were horrified. We had acquired a new child, off the peg and without warning and at the age of twelve. A child from a completely different, somewhat eccentric, non-Jewish background. 'Well, that's it,' said Myra. 'She's ours now.' But what about Lynn's animals? I knew that Myra could just about put up with goldfish but disliked anything on four legs. She shrugged. 'OK, so Lynn would be very miserable without the dog, and our children would love it. Trixie comes with. But not the parrot. Or the guinea pigs.' So Lynn joined our family. John had left enough to pay for her schooling as a boarder at St Christopher's School. Our children accepted Lynn as part of the family, and until she herself married and had her own son, Tom, she spent much time with us. We love her very much.

In 1987, Myra and I decided that we should invest in a small home by the sea. Bournemouth was best for me, because of the sand and the sea, and for Myra because of the excellent shopping. We found a building near the top of the East Cliff, with a large lawn and swimming pool, but the building itself was covered in scaffolding. The estate agent strongly advised us not to buy it, because there were cracks in the brickwork and that was why it was going so cheap. 'To hell with the cracks,' said Myra. 'The insurers will fix it and we can afford it so let's go for it.' We did, and it became a haven for us all. For me, it provided a place of peace to write books, like this one, and, for my family, it was a happy and inexpensive seaside escape, only a couple of hours from London. So that was magic.

NINE

Israel Brodie – Religions and Beyond

Chief Rabbi Israel Brodie was known to his family as 'Rollick' – origin: his name was Israel – or, in Yiddish, Yisrooel – or Sroolick – hence: Rollick. Uncle Rollick, to Myra and to me. Or, more likely, just plain Uncle. We loved him for his warmth and humour and, above all, because he loved us.

The idea that politics is reserved for politicians is, of course, ludicrous. In business of every kind . . . with academics in every university . . . everywhere from churches to charities, from Westminster to Winchelsea, life includes a political struggle. And as Uncle once told me, the nearer you get to the top, the lonelier you become. 'It's your family who keep you breathing,' he said.

Uncle was of the old British school. A graduate of Balliol, Oxford, he was proud to blend British and Jewish culture and custom, which he conveyed in his sermons and speeches, in his rich and sonorous voice. Rotund, bearded and genial, he was well loved within the Jewish community, except by those who regarded him as an intolerant and unbending enforcer of ancient and antique rules.

To us, Uncle was saintly. He had married Aunt Fanny when they were both middle-aged. They adored each other – but he loved children, had none of his own and treated Myra as his daughter. As her husband, I enjoyed his affection and immense tolerance. Never once did he criticise me for my way of life, directly or indirectly, publicly or privately, to me or to anyone else, even though I had many failings in his orthodox eyes. We kept the Sabbath on Friday nights at our kosher home. I loved and looked after his precious niece. And I served not only my constituents and the country where he and I were honoured to live, but did so with pride in my Jewish religion and people, which was all that he asked from his nephew. I once told him how sorry I was that I had to travel to Leicester on

Saturdays, for my surgeries. He replied: 'Greville, *derekh eretz kadma le Torah.*' The Talmud tells us that 'respect goes before the law'. Uncle had my total respect and my fondest affection.

We enjoyed many of our happiest evenings with Uncle and his bald and good-humoured doctor brother, Abe, at dinner in our home. They told jokes and family stories and laughed and quaffed wine and whisky and rejoiced in God's gift of life. As Uncle once said to me: 'Grasp life while you've got it, my boy. It's not going to last for ever – for any of us.'

When Uncle refused to accept the learned and gentle Rabbi Louis Jacobs as principal of Jews' College, he sparked off a massive communal explosion, led by William Frankel, editor of the *Jewish Chronicle* and a friend both of Rabbi Jacobs and of the Janners. Rabbi Jacobs's outspoken views on the non-divine origins of the Bible were unacceptable to the religious leadership of the United Synagogue in general and especially to the Dayanim – the senior rabbis who make up the Beth Din court.

Uncle was deeply hurt by the attacks on his decision and on him personally, and the family placed the blame for his subsequent heart-attack on the bitterness of his opponents. It was after that attack and during his later and fatal illness that I really got to know the man.

Like nearly all public miseries, however massive, the Jacobs affair gradually faded from memory. Mother and I decided that the time had come to see whether we could not successfully press for Uncle to receive a knighthood. He deserved it. Not only would it make him happy, but especially Aunt Fanny, who was very much a lady.

Now, Mother knew how to work the system. 'Recommendations come from the top, and the religious top at that,' she said. 'How well do you know the Archbishop of Canterbury?'

'Reasonably well,' I replied. 'I expect he'd see me.'

The Archbishop, Lord Coggan, was a great friend of the Jewish people and a pillar of the Council of Christians and Jews. I spoke to him by phone and told him I needed a word with him, please, on a private and personal matter. He invited me in, the following day. When I told Mother, she said: 'Be careful, dear, how you address him. Start by calling him: "Your Grace", then move to "Archbishop".'

'Isn't that just a trifle formal?' I queried.

'Maybe, dear,' Mother replied. 'But you'll find in life that people enjoy the dignities. If they want you to drop them, they'll tell you.'

I followed Mother's instructions. The Archbishop agreed that the Chief Rabbi deserved a knighthood. And in 1981, Uncle was received by Her Majesty at the Palace, frock coat, top hat and all and accompanied by his beaming Lady. They were deeply happy, and their family, friends and community rejoiced with them.

I only once appeared before the Rabbinical Court – the Beth Din – and Uncle kept well away. It was on behalf of a twelve-year-old called Bobby, who had been at the Norwood Orphanage as it then was – an old-fashioned institution for Jewish children, some of whom were orphans but most of whom had come from broken or non-existent homes. I was on the Committee and I hated the entire concept of this huge boarding establishment for deprived boys and girls.

Bobby's problem was that while his mother said that she was Jewish, she could not prove her origins; his father was unknown. Question: could Bobby be barmitzvah – confirmed as an adult of the Jewish faith at his fast approaching age of thirteen? The Beth Din decided there was not enough evidence of his Jewish birth and he would have to go through all the rituals of conversion, even though he had been at Norwood for some six years. One of the Dayanim, Rabbi Meyer Lew, took me aside afterwards and said to me quietly – and to my seething anger: 'Why don't you just let the boy live happily as a non-Jew?' Bobby was not barmitzvah. He did not convert. At seventeen he joined the Army. And a few years later, he committed suicide.

When Uncle fell terminally ill he was brought to St Thomas's Hospital where he lay unconscious, connected to life by drips and tubes. Eventually, I persuaded Aunt Fanny to get some sleep in the nearby guest room while I dozed through the night in a chair by Uncle's side. In the morning, joined by Myra, we stood by Uncle's bed. Aunt Fanny tapped him gently on the cheek and called him by his customary diminutive. 'Rollick,' she demanded, quietly. 'Rollick, wake up. Come on, wake up.' As if in trained obedience and to our wonder and delight, he opened his eyes. 'Where am I?' he asked.

Later that morning, when the ladies had returned home, I asked Uncle to bless me. He lifted his hands, needle in vein, and placed them softly on my head. Then we both wept. 'Strange, isn't it,' he said, 'that it takes this to bring us together.' In his life of hustle and now especially in mine, we had shared time too little and too rarely. That, I determined, would now cease with him and with others.

During the months that followed, Uncle rarely spoke of death. He only once made Myra cry by telling her: 'Darling, there's a man over there – calling me . . .' He only once mentioned death to me and I asked him why our religion lays so little stress on the after-life. He replied: 'Because we are much more concerned about the essentials and the certainties of life here. *"Torah, avodah and gemilut chasadim"'* – the study of the law, the doing of good works and the requirements of charity. Then he told me the marvellous Talmudic tale of the father who died in the Holy Land, leaving his fields divided equally between his two sons, one of whom was married with many children and the other a bachelor, on his own.

One night after the harvest was in, the married brother went quietly to his land and transferred a pile of his sheaves of corn across the border onto his brother's field. Later that night, the bachelor brother came to look over the harvest and found that extra pile and carried it back onto his brother's land. The following night, the brothers both arrived at the same time and they met at the border, each carrying sheaves intended as gifts for the other.

'What are you doing?' the bachelor brother demanded.

'Making you a present of some of my sheaves,' the married brother replied.

'But I have no children and you have many. Your need is greater than mine,' said the bachelor. 'It is for me to give you my sheaves, not for you to give me yours.'

'Not so, dear brother. I have the blessings of a wife and children. You are on your own. Your need is greater than mine.'

The two brothers looked up to heaven and demanded of the Holy One Blessed Be He: 'Which of us is right?' And a mighty voice came echoing down to them: 'You are both right, and upon this land will I build my Temple.'

Uncle had a private room on a high floor at St Thomas's Hospital, looking out over the Thames and towards the Palace of Westminster. One evening, he said to me: 'You know, Greville, your Parliament building reminds me of the Bible.'

'Why, Uncle?'

'Because when you read the Bible, you always find something new. And every time I look at the Palace of Westminster, it looks different.'

One evening, as Big Ben was striking six thirty, I walked across Westminster Bridge and up to Uncle's room. I found him lying in bed, chuckling. 'What's so funny, Uncle?' I asked him.

'There's a nurse,' he said. 'One of my favourites. She's big, black and kind. All day, she fusses around me, making sure I've got everything I want. Then suddenly, as Big Ben strikes six – poof – she vanishes. She's gone. Not one second after the sound of your clock does that woman remain. She reminds me of Enoch – remember him?'

'You mean Enoch Powell?'

He chuckled. 'No. The man he was named after, Enoch in the Bible. He was the only man who didn't die. Everyone else did – but Enoch simply vanished. *V'aineno* – he wasn't there. Just like my nurse. She vanishes – she's not there – she's gone.'

Later that evening, I queued up at the Members' cafeteria in the Commons. By chance, Enoch Powell was behind me in the queue. I told him this story, which he knew well. He then invited me to sit with him and he regaled me with detailed biblical and talmudical commentaries on his ancient namesake. He was a forbidding man, with piercing eyes and a smile that did not warm but chilled. But his brain and his intellect, his knowledge and his learning were unrivalled in the political world. How sad, I thought, that he lacked just those qualities of humanity and gentle kindness and humour that made Uncle so great in my life, and so missed by Myra and by me when his ended.

The wife of the well-known Jewish publisher, Anthony Blond, once told me that she met Enoch Powell at a party and it turned out that they lived in the same street. He had said to her: 'Ah, you must live next door to the Jew.' 'Oh no,' she replied. 'I live *with* the Jew!'

From time to time, Uncle returned home, apparently recovered. I had no idea of the seriousness of his illness until one day I spoke to his doctor about getting him some sort of medicine.

'You do realise what's wrong with your Uncle Israel, don't you?' the doctor enquired.

'No, I don't. It's something to do with his heart problem, isn't it?'

'Oh, come on,' said the doctor. 'Don't you know he's got leukaemia?'

I put down the phone and wept.

Myra and I were with Uncle when he died in hospital. I wished we had spent more hours together while he was well. They took his body home and I stayed with him that night, only leaving him while his body was washed and prepared for the grave. In the morning, the cortège set off for the Willesden cemetery, but stopped at his own St John's Wood Synagogue on the way. One of the rabbis pronounced his epitaph:

'Rabbi Brodie,' he announced, 'was a good man. *He* was not a politician!'

I was in the front row and all eyes turned to me, mouths twitching with suppressed laughter. The Dayan continued: 'Rabbi Brodie was a generous and a kindly man. *He* was no politician. Rabbi Brodie was a man of religion and of good deeds. *He* was no politician!' And so it went on, casting precisely the sort of unconscious humour on that grim occasion that Uncle himself would have enjoyed.

Uncle's death destroyed Aunt Fanny. She soon ended up in the Westmount Old People's Home. She kept repeating: 'You know what Rollick's last words were? "I love you, Fanny."'

Our Chief Rabbi has an impossible task. He is appointed by the United Synagogue, which is not necessarily as united as its name, and certainly not with other sections of our religious community, including the ultra-orthodox on the right and the Reform and Liberal on the left. So while Uncle did not find his job easy, nor did his successor, the outspoken and distinguished Immanuel Jakobovits. On the Middle East and Israel, he leaned to the left but generally and especially on United Kingdom affairs, to the right – for which, to the delight of our community, Margaret Thatcher rewarded him with a peerage.

In 1991, Immanuel Jakobovits died and was succeeded as Chief Rabbi by Jonathan Sacks. Articulate and witty, learned and outspoken, he remains a powerful advocate for the Jewish people, in Britain and throughout the world. Like both of his predecessors, he has had to withstand criticism and attack, mainly from within his own community. I hope that before long, his resonant and focused tones will, like the fearless voice of Immanuel Jakobovits, be heard in our Parliament. Meanwhile, we rejoiced when he – like Uncle Israel before him – became a knight.

With the Anglican bishops and our Jewish clergy represented in the House of Lords, that left the Roman Catholics as the major gap. I had become very fond of Cardinal Basil Hume, not least because of his efforts to encourage the Vatican to return to the Jewish world the works of art that had been placed by Holocaust victims in monasteries and churches for safekeeping. One day, when I was in his office in the Archbishop's House, I asked him: 'Isn't it about time that Roman Catholics were represented in our Parliament? Surely your voice should be heard, along with those of the Church of England and, now, that of Rabbi Jakobovits?'

After a long silence, the Cardinal said: 'Yes, you are probably right. But my first loyalty is to the Pope, and to accept an appointment in the Upper House of a national parliament would be regarded by some as a breach of that prime duty.'

'Surely not,' I said. 'You would serve in Parliament specifically as a priest of your church, which should then be heard as a respected voice in our Parliament?'

'Maybe, one day,' the Cardinal replied. 'But not yet, alas.'

Alas, indeed, that the day of Roman Catholic representation in our Parliament has not yet arrived – and that the day for Jewish representation had not arrived in time for Israel Brodie to be elevated to the House of Peers.

PART THREE

Politics and Public Service

TEN

Candidate and MP

At about 7.30 one morning, early in June 1970, the telephone rang. It was Mother. 'Dad's not well. He won't be standing for Parliament. Do you want to have a go at getting the nomination for Leicester North West?'

I woke up with a start. 'What's the matter with Dad?'

'His doctor says that his chest is so bad that if he stands, he won't be responsible for his life.'

The old problem. Some years ago now, Father had suffered a flare-up of his First World War chest trouble and they thought it was cancer. I had rushed round to see them and found my parents lying together in the double bed at their home in Lancaster Terrace. 'Your old Dad's on his way out,' he had said to me. Happily, it turned out that he had pneumonia and, with the help of antibiotics, he had recovered quickly. Now, a decade later, the pain had returned.

'Do you want to have a try at fighting the seat?' Mother repeated.

'Never mind that. I'll be round to see Dad right away.' When she rang off, I rubbed my eyes, thoughtfully.

'Get moving,' Myra said. 'You go and see them.'

'What about Leicester North West?'

'We can think about that later. Go.'

I went. My parents were in bed. 'Dad will be better in a few weeks, if he stays indoors,' said Mother. 'But if he goes out canvassing, Rudd says that it could be the end.' Our cousin, Rudd, was one of the few doctors whom Mother trusted.

'You're not going to give up the Commons, are you?' I asked Father.

He smiled. 'Doesn't look as if I've got much alternative, does it?'

'It's not as bad as all that,' said Mother. 'Bob Mellish has been on the phone.' He was the Labour Chief Whip. 'He has told your Dad that he must under no circumstances stand. And as soon as he's better, they'll put him up in the Lords. Now then – what about having a go yourself?'

'Would they have me?'

'We don't know,' said Mother. 'But I've had a chat with Lily Marriott.' She was a very influential Labour Councillor and a good friend. 'She thinks she can pull it off for us.'

'What do you think?' I asked them.

'It's up to you. This could be your big chance.' I said that I would go home and talk to Myra and let them know.

'You'll have to make up your mind quickly,' said Mother. 'If you want to have a crack at it, then you'll have to go up to Leicester tomorrow and see the Party.' Now, I knew the Leicester Party well. I had canvassed for and with Father at every election for twenty-five years, and they knew me. But the Labour Party does not believe in hereditary seats. No son had ever succeeded his father in our Party. I returned home and told Myra the story. She said: 'I'll think about it.'

That evening, we finished our dinner and Myra was doing the washing-up and I was drying the dishes. 'I've decided,' said Myra, with her usual Australian directness. 'Let's do it. But on terms.'

'And what are they?' I asked.

'First, you go on taking the children to school every morning. I don't want our children growing up without a Dad.'

I ran the morning car pool. En route, I would collect Sasha Felix, daughter of Peter Felix and of his former wife, Teddie, one of the Beverley Sisters, a famous singing trio. Peter was now contentedly remarried to Helena. Sometimes, there were other children. I drove the girls to South Hampstead High School and Daniel to the Hall.

Daniel had started his school career at a local state school but had not learned too much, so with some reluctance, we decided to transfer him to the Hall, my old prep school at Swiss Cottage. South Hampstead was Mother's school – the place where she had been happiest in all her life. We knew that its standard of education was high. Getting the girls in was the problem.

I knew that I would be interviewed by the headmistress of the Junior School, whom I had learned was a lover of birds. So I mugged up on my ornithology. On entering her study, I admired the pictures of birds on the wall and said how pleased I was that wrens had returned to our garden that winter. 'Oh, you noticed!' she smiled, and the ice was broken. After we had talked about birds for a few minutes, Marion and later Laura were safely embedded into the school.

Those morning school rides with the children were joyful. I taught them songs and we sang our way through the traffic. Sasha, who later herself became a well-known singer, maintains that this was the start of her stage career. I loved those journeys and accepted Myra's first condition without any qualm.

'Agreed,' I said. 'So what's the other one?'

'That you won't seek or accept ministerial office.'

I did not have to consider that one either. I had no ambitions for office. 'Agreed,' I said.

'In that case,' said Myra, opening her arms, for a hug, 'let's do it together.'

The Party Agent was an experienced and shrewd man called George Billington. I spoke to him by phone and he said: 'Come to Party HQ on Belgrave Gate and we'll discuss it.' I went up by train and met George and the City Party Agent, Gordon Parker. We had pleasant chats and it was agreed that I would go onto the shortlist. Then off I went to see Lily Marriott. She chatted to me about tactics and then said: 'We're now going to make the rounds of the key people.'

The first was Bob Trewick of Westcotes Ward. He listened courteously enough but it was later reported back to me that he had said: 'The King may be gone, but that does not mean that we should accept the Prince.' Then the Revd Ken Middleton, who was one of the top figures in St Margaret's Ward. We got on fine and he invited me to their next Ward meeting.

Next, Abbey Ward – Ray and Betty Flint; yes, they would help. They were sure I would get the Abbey Ward votes and they would put me on their selection list. George Billington made sure that I was on the list for the New Parks selection. Westcotes Ward, I was told, was hopeless; forget it. I might pick up the odd vote from them at the selection meeting but they were very left-wing and unlikely to choose me.

I then consulted my much-loved childhood friend, Janet Setchfield. Her father had been Lord Mayor of Leicester at the time when mine was the local MP. Janet and I had grown up together. She told me not to waste my time with Bob Trewick but that Abbey Ward should be fine.

The Abbey Ward meeting was amazing. Like all good political events, it was well organised and it went splendidly for me. After the meeting, Betty and Ray Flint and 'Moo' Dawson and I danced arm-in-arm along the green. The St Margaret's Ward meeting was quiet, friendly and positive. The Westcotes Ward meeting was rowdy and I knew I had lost there. Western Park Ward did not even invite me to speak.

Sadly for me, Janet was in North Braunstone Ward, which at that time was just outside Leicester West. We did not then know that it would become part of my patch when the City seats were redistributed in 1971.

I reported back to Lewis Hawser and Charles Lawson. Neither was in the least surprised and both said that they would do their best to see that I retained my practice. At that time, the parliamentary salary was small and there was no way that the family and I could live off it. My clerk, Arthur Dorset, was much more direct. 'You go into the House, Sir,' he said, 'and your practice can't survive. Sir, you must think about it.' Arthur used the word 'Sir' almost as a curse.

About thirty-five people would be entitled to vote at the selection meeting. I phoned each of them in turn and, with few exceptions, I was well received. The meeting was in the Labour Hall in Belgrave Gate. There were thirty-one delegates plus the City Agent, Gordon Parker, who was in charge of procedure. The would-be candidates gathered in a small back room. Then we each gave our presentations and answered questions. I emphasised that I had been a member of the Party for some twenty years. That I had cut my political teeth at the Wimbledon election. That I had the time, the energy and the determination to serve all the people of Leicester North West and to work with them for the Party. I threw in as many local district names as I could. Mother had warned me that Leicester people are not demonstrative, so I was not surprised when my words received only the most modest rattle of applause. But it was dispiriting.

Next, a young man rose to his feet. 'Your father,' he said, 'stayed on as MP until he was seventy-six. Don't you think that that was much too old? And then he left, just in time for us to be forced to adopt you. That was wrong, wasn't it?' A few mutters of assent and of dissent.

I was furious. 'My father stood down because he was ill,' I said. 'As for age – there are some people who are young enough to give marvellous service when they're in their seventies – and others who are in their twenties and useless.' Cheers from a few who obviously disliked the questioner. Grumbles from others. Silence from most.

'Thank you,' said the Chair. I left the room and went across the road to the public telephone. I phoned Myra.

'Forget it, darling,' I said. 'I made a hash of it and it's hopeless.'

'Never mind,' she said. 'Anyway, you never know the result until it's announced.' Which was one of the few times that Myra quoted from my mother. They were both right. The election was by transferable vote. It was a secret ballot and the delegates marked the candidates from one to five. If nobody got a majority of first choices on the first round, then the bottom person would be knocked out and the second choices would be counted. And so on until someone had the majority.

To my total disbelief, I received sixteen votes on the first round and the rest fifteen between them. This time, they clapped me. Even old Arthur Reilly, from New Parks, who I knew had been against me, got up and said: 'Well, we've got you now. And we've got to win this seat for Labour and it won't be easy. So we'll all help, won't we, comrades?' Nearly all of them clapped.

I learned afterwards that George Billington had not voted for me on the first round. He became my Agent and, later, joint Agent with Janet. Our friendship was deep and we stood by each other in good times and in bad. But we did not let him forget that he was not one of the sixteen. 'Well, I voted for a hopeless candidate and would have voted for you on the second round,' he said, to everyone's amusement.

One of my competitors was a well-known broadcaster and Arabist, Keith Kyle. My friends were chortling about how he had ruined his chances. He was asked what he knew about Leicester and he said that he knew it very well. 'I've been in and out of people's drawing rooms for weeks,' he said. This was greeted by a chorus of laughter. Leicester people never did have 'drawing rooms'.

That weekend, the Crossbencher column in the *Sunday Express* carried a story which nearly everyone believed. It claimed that my father had stood down after the posters and pamphlets had been printed with 'Janner for

Labour'. The Party could not afford a reprint. Therefore they had no choice other than to adopt me! It was such a good tale that I never denied it and people believe it to this day. What the hell. I had been selected. The battle began and as Father's majority was only 7,807 and Labour was not doing well in the polls, we were set for a tough fight.

Much of my father's majority was his personal vote, built up over twenty-five years of energetic service to the City and to any of his constituents who needed help. My problem: to dip into this immense pool of goodwill, while establishing my own individuality. 'You must concentrate on bringing out your voters,' said Mother. 'If we get out the Labour people, we'll win. You have limited energy and resources, so you must use them where they will achieve the most effect.'

We did a preliminary canvass at some old people's bungalows in New Parks Estate, a huge area that had been a tank training ground. Father had successfully battled to get it reallocated for Council housing. I knocked at the first door and a white-haired lady emerged. 'Good morning, me duck,' she said, eyeing my large red rosette.

'I'm Janner, the Labour candidate,' I said. 'I'd be very grateful if you would please vote for me on election day.'

'Vote for you, Barney?' she replied. 'Of course I'll vote for you. I've voted for you for the past twenty-five years so why should I change now?' I thanked her – and learned my first lesson. Merge into father's shadow.

Myra and I moved into two rooms at the local Holiday Inn. We had decided not to make our home in Leicester. Myra did not want to shift out of London and away from her friends and family. The children were happily settled in schools. So the Holiday Inn became and would remain our Leicester base.

We started building our team. Most of the Party's inner circle rallied round, even if they would have preferred not to have had 'the Prince'. What mattered was to keep the seat for Labour. Much of election work is routine. Setting up the central committee room and the ward committee rooms. Pasting up the canvass cards. Drafting and preparing and printing the election address. The candidates and their agents must watch election expenses with an accountant's eagle eye. The candidate's personal living expenses apart, the permitted allowance is minimal. So they must count the pennies.

Out of some 100,000 people who lived in my patch, there were maybe half a dozen Jews. There were about five hundred in the city, including our friends Lea and Ronnie Benson and their family. They lent us a car. We fitted it up with posters, hired a loudspeaker and were off on our rounds. The art of street loudspeakering: keep the message very short. Speak slowly and clearly. 'This . . . is . . . Janner . . . your Labour candidate. It's two weeks . . . to polling day . . . please . . . vote . . . Labour . . . vote Labour . . . vote . . . Janner . . . Janner . . . for Labour . . . Labour . . . for Leicester North West.' Over and over and over again. Speak close to the microphone and do not shout or you will soon lose your voice.

If you are a sitting MP, you never mention your opponent's name and refuse to give your opponent any publicity by taking part in debates, whether in person or in the media. Your opponent does not exist. As a new arrival, your job is to get yourself known. So I called into the local paper, the *Leicester Mercury*, and got to know the top people.

Radio Leicester was the only local radio station until it was joined by a commercial station, Leicester Sound. My most triumphant feat with Radio Leicester came when, some years later, they invited me to the studio for an interview. I arrived on time but the interviewer did not show up. After half an hour's waiting, they allowed me to interview myself. I asked myself difficult questions and gave brilliant answers. When the interviewer eventually arrived, he simply dubbed in the questions in his own voice.

In 1970, though, my job was a simple one: to get across the message that, as a man in my own right, if they elected me I would continue the tradition of service set by my father.

George Billington looked after me. Lea Benson kept an eye on Myra. I enjoyed the canvassing; Myra hated it. She loathed the yapping and snapping of the dogs. You put a pamphlet in somebody's letter box and there's a roar and a thud as a huge animal heaves itself up against the door and tries to bite your fingers. You were lucky if the spring on the letter box did not chop off at least one finger tip. We had our laughs, though – like the time that an unwelcoming hound lifted up its leg and watered mine, showing me precisely how he felt.

Father's main bases in the constituency were the Working Men's Clubs. Theoretically, they were non-political. In practice, Labour people always came round to shake hands while the Tories and Liberals usually kept well away. Father's chest was now much better, so he came up to Leicester and took me around the clubs. The air was filled with cigarette smoke and the pungent smell of beer. I learned Father's trick of getting a pint of shandy and holding it in your left hand for the evening, leaving your right hand free to shake other people's.

'You know my son, Greville?' Father would enquire. 'He's the candidate now. You will vote for him, won't you?' Most of them stood up and said: 'Of course we will, Sir Barnett.' A few sat with their arms folded and said: 'No thank you'. I would then say: 'Well, you don't have to vote for me. But I'm going to be your MP and I'm going to look after you, so please shake hands.' Some did, some didn't. Then the show would start on the stage and we had to stop our rounds. Most people said to me: 'Glad to meet you. Good luck.' Others said: 'Don't know why you're bothering. You'll walk it.' I knew that I wouldn't. 'Please don't forget to vote,' I pleaded. 'Every vote counts. If I'm out by one vote and it's yours, you will feel bad, won't you?' Next would come bingo; absolute silence; another twenty minutes of sitting and waiting. Clubs and pubs . . . youth centres and communal centres . . . old people's homes . . . door to door, street by street . . . loudspeaker and personal. Encouraging and motivating your canvassers. And always with a sense of urgency which I felt that too few of my colleagues shared.

Election day, May 1970; reasonable weather. Round the polling stations we went, stopping the van at a decent distance and moving in to thank the people working at the polls and smiling at the voters. We were a great team. Our friends rallied round, whatever their politics. At that election and every one after it, Marianne Keats organised our polling day cars, and our children, family and friends turned out in force.

Father planted his homburg hat on his head and wound a scarf round his neck and was driven in state around the constituency. We would hear his Welsh voice ringing out across the rows of Victorian houses and the spaces of the great estates: 'Come out and vote, please. This is Barnett Janner. Please vote for Greville. Greville Janner for Labour now.' A coachload of supporters came for the day on the Saturday before the poll and friends by the carload on polling day. We were deeply grateful to them. They helped to bring out the vote and to keep up our morale.

The city at that time was divided into four seats. The ballot boxes for all four were collected and the votes counted at De Montfort Hall. Myra and I had supper and arrived at about 10.30 p.m. Some of the votes were already being sorted. Ward by ward, table by table, pile by pile. Ray Flint was sitting at one of the tables, looking anxious. 'It's going to be close,' he told us. As we watched the separated piles of Conservative and Labour votes mounting up almost equally, we knew he was right. There was no hope for the other parties: the Liberals and the National Democratic Party. But for my real opponents, the Conservatives, and for me, it was stress at its most extreme.

Soon after midnight, the town clerk called my opponents and myself and our agents to a table where they were sorting the votes that were doubtful. Crosses against the name of the Tory candidate . . . fine. 'Don't want that bastard' across the name of another . . . spoiled vote. On one memorable ballot paper, a disillusioned citizen had written: 'To hell with the lot of you.' Myra reminded me that in Australia, voting was compulsory. There, many unwilling voters expressed their feelings in that sort of way.

Then the Lord Mayor mounted the platform and announced the result: 'Greville Ewan Janner, Labour, 18,226 votes. S.J. Symington, Conservative, 15,584 votes . . .' Hooray! We were elated. Our troops cheered as I came forward to the microphone, thanked the administrators and staff for organising the election so efficiently; thanked my opponent for a clean and decent campaign, and wished him well; and then thanked my band of marvellous supporters – Myra, Father and Mother, Ruth and Philip – the family, the friends, the colleagues, the canvassers – and above all, my comrades in the Leicester North West Constituency Labour Party. They cheered and cheered and clapped and waved their arms in delight and hugged each other.

After my opponents had courteously congratulated me and thanked their teams, we came down from the platform and waited for the results from the other constituencies. Then, at the end of that long day, back to the Holiday Inn; Greville Janner, Member of Parliament for Leicester North West. I thanked my parents – and then Myra and I walked through the Holiday Inn, up to our room, hand-in-hand.

The next day was bliss. Myra and I made our triumphal tour in the battle bus. 'This is Janner – Greville Janner. Your Member of Parliament. Thank you. Thank you, St Matthew's . . . thank you in the club . . . thank you in Hawthorn Street . . . thank you, New Parks . . . thank you, Bateman Road. I am proud to serve you all. This is Janner – your Member of Parliament, at your service. Thank you.' We waved and most people waved back. They came to their doors and waved. They opened their windows and waved.

When someone shook a fist at us or told us to shove off, I would call out over the loudspeaker: 'Thank you, the gentleman in the tweed jacket on the crossing. Thank you for your support, sir. Thank you for your vote. This is Janner, thanking the man in the tweed jacket.' Inevitably, the man would shake his fist in fury. We laughed happily. Served him right, didn't it?

Now for Westminster.

ELEVEN

Constituency MP – Colleagues and Campaigns

Euphoria – there was no other word for it; joyful, spiritual, emotional uplift. I was walking into the parliament building in my own right, Greville Janner, grandson of four immigrants. I was thrilled.

I walked through the great Central Lobby, where I was to spend so many hours waiting for guests to arrive . . . through the Chamber, where I would be sworn in . . . through the corridors, the libraries, the eating and drinking places . . . out onto the Terrace, with its view across the Thames, to Lambeth Palace and St Thomas's Hospital, to the white buildings of the Greater London Council and the green roof of the Royal Festival Hall.

It was on the terrace that Father had introduced me to Winston Churchill. He was still Prime Minister but his handshake was weak. We met him again in one of the lifts, when he was no longer PM. 'Do you know my boy, Winston?' Father had asked, in his Welsh lilt. 'Pleased to meet you, young man,' the great man responded, with his famous growl. I was honoured to meet him.

On my first day in the Commons, I was approached in the lobby by a well-known Conservative, Bernard Braine, who later became Father of the House and then a peer. 'I've been a friend of your father's for many years,' he said. 'Political opponents but personal friends. That's what this place is about. I'm so pleased you're here.'

I thanked him. 'My father has told me that you are a wise and experienced politician,' I said. 'What advice have you got for a new boy with a marginal seat?'

He paused. 'Young man,' he said. 'You must never do good by stealth! You must build your personal vote and support and if your constituents do not know of your good deeds, they will wonder why they elected you.'

I knew that if I wanted to move out from under my father's shadow, I had to do many good deeds, and where appropriate, use the media to establish my credentials. But I never advertised a success in winning results for constituents without getting their agreement and confirming it in writing.

I also learned quickly how to deal with unpleasant mail. If it was racist or anti-Semitic muck, I passed it through to the Board of Deputies of British Jews, and if it was from someone who was obviously underprivileged, and wretched, I developed an adaptable but standard reply.

If a constituent wrote to me – as too many did – saying that I only cared for the immigrants and then setting out their own miseries, I would answer: 'Thank you for your letter. I am sure you did not intend it to be personally offensive, so I shall do my best to help you. I am at the service of all my constituents, whomever they may be and however they voted and whatever their origins. If you would be kind enough to come and see me at my next surgery, I will do all I can to get matters put right for you.' I then attached the surgery details. Almost always, I got a pleasant reply, thanking me and saying that no offence was intended.

Much of this I learned from my mother. She had always served as my father's driver, personal assistant, organiser and guide – to an extent that, especially as a youngster, I had resented. Myra and I had a different relationship. She was a home bird – wife and mother, friend and shopper.

It was Mother who taught me that 90 per cent of your constituency mail should be dealt with by standard letters, topped and tailed by hand and where necessary with a personal PS. Housing problems – refer them to the City Director of Housing. Social security – some to the local authority, others to the appropriate Minister. Family problems – to Citizens' Advice Bureau or solicitor. To many – 'Please do come and see me at my next surgery. Details attached.' All this I had set up before I was sworn in. Looking after the people of Leicester North West was my top concern; both because that was my deep interest and also because I knew that if I could not at least hold my personal vote, I would lose my seat.

Backbench Members of Parliament have two jobs, separate but interconnected. At Westminster, they are politicians . . . supporters of their parties . . . promoters and critics of legislation and of policy . . . members of committees: Select, Standing and All Party. In their constituencies, they are servants of their constituents. In that service, they have access to Ministers . . . power to raise constituents' problems at Question Time or in Early Day Motions . . . a whole array of parliamentary prods and procedures.

My first step as a Leicester MP was to visit the heads of all Council departments. One of them said to me: 'When I got a letter from your father, the alarm bells rang'. That's it – as an MP, you can press the alarm bell and cause a lot of trouble for anyone who treads on your constituents.

In 1970, Leicester was divided into four constituencies – Leicester South, with the veteran Tory, John Peel; Leicester North, with Tom (later Lord) Boardman; Leicester East, with former Labour Party Chairman, Tom Bradley; and Leicester North West – mine. On the whole, we worked well and happily together.

I sought Tom's Bradley's advice on how best to serve my constituents. He said: 'Remember that we are politicians, not social service workers.' I admired Tom greatly but never shared this view. As politicians, our top job is to look after those who elected us, irrespective of whether or not they voted for us. Morality apart, when the next election comes they will take their revenge – as, sadly, Tom Bradley's later did to him.

Immediately, I arranged 'surgeries'. My mother told me: 'You do not make them regular. If you have them every week and miss a week, you'll get complaints. But if you have them one week then miss one, then miss two, then have two weeks in a row or even two in a week, everyone will be pleased with you – especially if you move the surgeries around and have some at HQ and some in the wards'; wise advice, which I always followed.

George Billington agreed to be my agent. He collected others who knew the constituency to work with him. We found some lawyers to help me with the inevitable problems with landlords . . . stresses with neighbours or with the police . . . and a spectrum of other legal anxieties.

Even if a helper saw some of my constituents, they always came on for a word with me. I learned to deal with the queue swiftly, by listening carefully and by asking them to write down all the details for me, so that I could pass them to the appropriate director of the council department or to the Minister concerned. In cases where people had problems with writing, I would dictate their stories, immediately and in their presence, onto my portable dictating machine.

A young Greek called Pavlos Yeroulanos had driven me during the General Election. I had met him at our neighbour King Constantine's birthday party and he wanted to see British politics from the inside. He taught me enough Greek to call out greetings on my loudspeaker, as I passed the Cypriot fish and chip shop on the Narborough Road.

'*Yasu!*' I would cry, and wave to the Cypriots, who waved back enthusiastically. '*Efcharisto*', I responded. 'Thank you.'

One of the chippie merchants turned up at a surgery. 'Do you remember me?' he said. 'I am from the Cypriot fish and chip shop.'

'Of course I do,' I replied. 'How did you like it when I called out "*Yasu*" and "*Efcharisto*", when I passed your place in my election battle wagon?'

'We didn't like it at all,' he replied.

'Why not?' I asked.

'Because . . .' he said, pausing ominously . . . 'we are Turkish!'

To get myself known, I held area surgeries, preceded by loudspeakering. 'This is Janner . . . proud to be at your service . . . Surgery Saturday morning at the community centre . . . Come and meet me. Meet your MP.' Plus advertisements in the *Leicester Mercury*. My constituents heard the call and came to surgeries by the dozen. It was at one of these surgeries that I first met Jeff and Maureen Martin and their son Jimmy, a thalidomide child. The Jimmy Martin campaign presented me with my first parliamentary challenge – and victory. Jimmy Martin was ten years old. He was born with only one arm and no legs. He coped well, thanks to artificial limbs. But because he did not need to be looked after, twenty-four hours a day, his family were refused an attendance allowance. This, I believed, was scandalous. If the family had sat back and treated the lad as totally disabled . . . if Jimmy himself had not done everything possible to achieve normality, in spite of his disability . . . they would have had a full allowance. But because of his own courage and his parents' care, the Attendance Allowance Board ruled that he was not even entitled to a partial allowance.

In spite of an appeal brought at the request of the Chief National Insurance Commissioner, Jimmy's parents found that they alone had to carry the financial burden of bringing him up. They were penalised for encouraging him to walk and to attend a normal school and not confining him for life to a wheelchair or keeping him in a special hospital, as they were advised to do when he was born. This, then, was my first major campaign. To attack this monstrous discrimination. Colleagues, friends and I collected a million names on a petition in support of the family. I asked the then Minister of Health, Sir Keith Joseph, to see us. He regarded this as a political act on the part of a Labour MP and he refused. So I contacted the famous, legless air ace, Douglas Bader. I asked him to join me at the House of Commons on the day when I presented the petition. He agreed and on 22 January 1974, I presented the petition. Douglas Bader ensured that our battle received the impetus of national publicity and outrage.

The Guardian: 'Commons Fight For Jimmy . . .' *Daily Mirror*: 'Brave Jimmy's Bundle of Hope . . .' *Evening News*: 'Helping Hands for Legless Jimmy . . .' Photographs and headlines in the *Daily Telegraph*, *The Times*, the *Daily Express*, the *Daily Mail*. Eventual result? The Mobility Allowance, an alternative to 'Attendance', with – at least in cases like those of Jimmy Martin – a similar result. So we lost our legal battle on the attendance allowance, but we eventually achieved a proud success. This helped not only Jimmy and his family but, over the years, many thousands of others who successfully kept on the move, in spite of their disablement, and their families. These included Margaret Lancaster, my loyal audio typist, whose husband, John, was long disabled. She attached a note to this chapter when she typed the draft: 'Little did I think when I helped collect signatures for this petition for Jimmy, that we would also benefit from the Mobility Allowance (or Disability Living Allowance as it is now called) just a few years hence! Thank you!'

During the General Election campaign, I had noticed one morning that Jimmy Martin's mother, Maureen, was busy scrubbing the floor of our HQ. I said to Myra: 'Just look at that. Isn't she wonderful? There are not many people who will work to show their appreciation in that way.' Myra just looked at me. 'Are you blind?' she said. 'Don't you see anything?' I hadn't a clue what she was talking about. She told me later. Maureen had got attached to my agent, George Billington, and George to her. It was not too long before Maureen and George both divorced their spouses and married each other.

When he thought that a major local scandal was about to break around his marital infidelities, George came to see me and told me that he thought he should resign as my agent. 'Certainly not,' I said. 'Your private life is private and your business and not mine or anyone else's.'

George and I worked together until I left the Commons. By then, he had left the Council and now had no political work left. Not long after, he died.

As a Member of Parliament, the spotlight is always on you. The public may believe that you get special privileges from the law because you have the magic letters MP after your name, but that is far from correct. On the contrary – in most cases, ordinary folk would get the benefit of the doubt, but not an MP. Not altogether unreasonably – that is, for anyone other than the unfortunate accused. An MP's activities are scrutinised with special care; no one wants to be accused of 'letting him off' because he was important. Take, for instance, a distinguished and delightful Tory colleague, who was accused some years ago of the variety of theft which is easiest to allege and most difficult to disprove – shoplifting.

One of my early campaigns was to try to prevent people from being wrongly accused of theft from shops. The most honest of customers may carelessly or thoughtlessly walk out of shops with goods that they have not paid for, in their hands or handbags or with other shopping. My advice to all shoppers, in this world of cash and carry? If you have not paid for goods and they are not in a basket provided by the shop, then hold them over your head until you reach the pay desk. It may look stupid, but at least you will not be wrongfully charged with stealing.

In the mid-1980s, my colleague MP was charged with shoplifting, and the media descended on him. It was clear to me that this was a decent, honest man who had appeared dishonest because at the time of his alleged offence his mind was far from his body. So we went down to one of the interview rooms, below the Commons Chamber. I explained to him the rules of evidence and how the case would be conducted, and I took him through his evidence. To my delight, he was acquitted – and, some years later, he was rightly honoured with a knighthood.

In November 1983, Woolworths unsuccessfully prosecuted a woman pensioner for alleged shoplifting. The time had come to do battle, to try to induce retailers to recognise that some customers, especially some elderly or infirm women, do not pay for goods taken from self-service stores, not out of criminality but through sheer carelessness. In the Commons, Early Day Motions are powerful expressions of parliamentary opinion, especially when heavily supported. On 18 November 1983, I put one down, attacking Woolworths' pensioner prosecution. Sixty-seven MPs signed it.

On 17 January 1984, I introduced a Private Member's Bill, entitled the 'Theft From Shops Bill'. These Bills enable backbenchers to have ten minutes to make their points. They very seldom become law, but they achieve publicity and pressure. Mine required that all prosecutions for shop theft should be brought by the police, and not by shopkeepers. Its main purpose: 'To end the tragic, inefficient and awful system under which in Greater London and a few other areas, the police will not take prosecutions for what they choose to call petty theft. That leaves private people, especially those who run shops, to decide whether or not to prosecute – and to bring prosecutions when they have neither the resources nor the ability to make such decisions in the interests of justice or in a way that is fair to the people involved.' There was no opposition and the Bill obtained its first reading. Sadly, there was no parliamentary time for its second reading. So I put down a series of questions and at least I heard very swiftly that shops, including supermarkets and department stores, were taking more care.

Some of those who steal from shops are sick and need medical treatment. Others, like the late Lady Isobel Barnett, the once distinguished television star from Leicester, are afflicted souls, unable to resist the temptation to steal, even though they have not the least need for the goods taken or for their value. For the professionals – especially those who work in their own teams and are organised in gangs – I had, of course, no sympathy whatever.

My main opponent in this campaign turned out to be none other than the doughty, fiery, loveable Baroness Nora Phillips, mother of my ebullient MP friend, Gwyneth Dunwoody. Nora was the director of the Association for the Protection of Retailers, who were incensed at the allegation that they and their teams were much too ready to arrest and prosecute alleged shoplifters, with insufficient cause. I never believed that I would get the law changed, but the campaign did achieve its object. Since then, most stores are much more careful before prosecuting for shoplifting.

Politicians are a complex lot. Take the case of one of Britain's best-known political villains – Robert Maxwell. I saw only the good side of him. It was my efforts to extract Jews from Eastern Europe that brought me into contact with Maxwell. I found him a complex, difficult and flamboyant character – tough to deal with, and rarely on time, but a great and unique ally in my battles for those Jewish communities.

I was taking a parliamentary group to Czechoslovakia or Hungary, or to Romania or Bulgaria. I would phone him to seek his help and he would speak to me himself and tell me to fix an appointment. I would arrive at the Mirror Newspapers and be taken up to his boardroom. There I would wait. Suddenly, he would sweep in. 'And what do you want today, young man?' he would ask. I told him. I was going to Eastern Europe with some other MPs. I needed contacts, to help induce their governments to allow the remnants of their Jewish communities to leave and to live.

No problem. He was publishing the autobiographies of the President . . . his man was working in the capital . . . his people would meet us and help us. 'Anything else?'

'No. But thank you.'

'You're welcome. Thank you for what you're doing.' And out he marched.

Each time, he gave the appropriate instructions and his man or his people met us and helped us and introduced us and smoothed paths that would otherwise have been strewn with political boulders. So I invited him to dinners. Sometimes he would arrive, very late. Other times, he would send his likeable son, Ian – his representative on Jewish matters and occasions. When Maxwell's world collapsed, I was deeply shocked. We all knew that he was a buccaneer and an economic adventurer. What we did not realise was that when he got himself into a tight corner, his efforts to extract himself were ruthless and immoral.

On 5 November 1991, Maxwell was drowned at sea. Was he pushed overboard? Almost certainly not. Was he leaning over the edge when he had a heart-attack? Possible, but unlikely. Was his final corner so tight and his intelligence so clear that he knew that he would end up in court and in jail, in disgrace and in misery, and he jumped? Almost certainly, yes.

On 15 June, a series of MPs raised points of order about Maxwell's death. Michael Meacher talked of Maxwell 'dealing dishonestly with the pension fund monies'. He was followed by David Winnick, asking about the Maxwell pension fund . . . Dennis Skinner, referring to 'that crook Maxwell' . . . Ian McCartney accused the Government of 'keeping from the public gaze the intelligence information about Maxwell's fraudulent behaviour' . . . Then Jeremy Corbyn referred to possible government improprieties regarding the Maxwell pension fund. I listened in silence. Should I not argue that we should at least wait until we had the evidence before we condemned and convicted a man who is dead? Should we not express a word of sympathy for his long-suffering wife and family?

On the other hand, if as seemed likely, this man had robbed thousands of pensioners of their rights and in the attempt to save his own fortune, pillaged the poor and if he was a massive financial crook, stealing from the needy to enrich himself, then he did not deserve even a word of support. But what about his family? Surely I should say something. By the time I had finished debating with myself, the moment had passed. Was it discretion or cowardice that had caused me to miss the moment? Either way, the House had moved on to other business.

I got on well, personally, with most MPs. Alan Clark was an exception. Our non-relationship began when I received a complaint from Michael Marmur, a friend of my daughter Laura. At that time he was President of the Cambridge University Jewish Society and is now a rabbi and Dean of Jerusalem's Hebrew Union College. Clark had agreed to address a meeting of a Cambridge right-wing Tory organisation. His subject: 'Hitler – philosopher, statesman and wit'. Michael and his colleagues did not consider the title in the least witty. Would I please speak to Clark?

It was a weekend. Without the least expectation of results, I consulted *Who's Who*. Behold, there was the phone number of his castle. The butler answered and passed me on to Clark.

'What do you want?' he asked. I told him. The title of his talk was highly offensive.

'Rubbish,' he said. 'It's a joke.'

'Not for those of us whose families were killed on the orders of that philosophical, statesmanlike, witty person,' I replied.

'Well, what would you like me to do about it?'

'That's for you to decide, isn't it. But at least know that if you go ahead with the meeting, there'll be demonstrations and a lot of trouble.'

'Are you threatening me?' Clark asked.

'No. Simply informing you. If I didn't tell you and you were greeted by banners and demonstrators, you'd complain that I hadn't told you, wouldn't you?'

'I'll think about it,' he said.

I thanked him and that was that.

Clark cancelled the meeting. Some time later, on 12 March 1993, he gave an interview to London's *Evening Standard*, entitled, 'Indiscretions and Alan Clark'. It demurred that Clark 'wishes to answer the recurring allegations that he is anti-Semitic.' The accusation, it said, 'has been fuelled by his tolerance towards the right-wing historian David Irving, and more recently by his claims that Churchill would have done better to make peace in 1941.' Alan Clark: 'Just because I make jokes about Jews, people think I'm anti-Semitic . . . The Secretary of State I was most comfortable with was David Young. My favourite businessman is Arnold Weinstock. The contemporary of mine whom I admire most and who is a close personal friend is Jimmy Goldsmith. They are all Jews. If I was really anti-Semitic, I wouldn't be friends with them.' To which the writer commented: 'In fact, as the saying goes, many of his best friends are Jewish.' Then, Clark: 'Greville Janner says that I am anti-Semitic. But the reason I don't like him is not because he is Jewish but because I think he is a nasty little worm.'

After reading Clark's words, and after careful thought, I wrote to him. If he disliked Jews, I said, then there's nothing I could do about it. But as his dislike was reserved for me, and as we scarcely knew each other, I would be very pleased if he would join me for lunch or dinner. I received no reply. That, David (Lord) Young later told me, was uncharacteristic of him. Ah well.

I made a brief appearance in his diaries. I rarely interrupted colleagues' speeches, but one evening during Clark's inglorious ministerial career, the combination of his apparently excellent dinner and complete ignorance of his brief made the temptation to speak out too great.

In his ministerial speech, Clark read out a passage of a text. I suspected that he did not know what he was talking about, so I rose to interrupt him. He wrote: 'Up bobbed a teeny little fellow, Janner by name, a Labour lawyer who always wears a pink carnation in his buttonhole. He asked me what the last paragraph "meant". How the hell did I know what it meant? I smoothed away. He started bobbing up and down as, it seemed, did about fifteen people on the other side, plus I couldn't see how many of my own, on my side and behind me. This had the making of a disaster. Never mind. Heads down, bully and shove.'

Then Clare Short, dark-haired and serious with a lovely Brummy accent, went for him and the ultimate result was for him a bibulous catastrophe, which he well deserved.

Emmanuel Shinwell – or 'Manny' as everyone called him – was born in 1885 and died in 1986. On his hundredth birthday, I asked him: 'To what do you attribute your health and longevity?' 'Scotch whisky, my boy. I drink a glass every night before I go to sleep.'

Shortly after his death on 8 May 1986, I chaired a Memorial meeting for him in the House of Commons. It was a remarkable gathering, with politicians including the Prime Minister, Margaret Thatcher, Alec Douglas-Home, and Leader of the Opposition, Neil Kinnock. We mourned the passing of a great parliamentary character. Then there were readings by Prunella Scales and Richard Baker.

After the meeting, I congratulated Pru Scales on her reading and told her that I had represented her husband, Tim West, in his recent divorce proceedings. 'Sorry,' she said. 'You didn't. That was another barrister.' I wondered what had happened to my memory. A few days later, I received a letter from Pru, who apologised, saying that I did represent him in part of his divorce problems and suggesting that we met. We did, together with Myra, and Pru and Tim and their family became our lifelong friends.

For years, colleagues and I campaigned for the law to require all passenger cars to have seat belts in the front and the rear, and for drivers and passengers to be required to wear them. I helped lead that campaign. Some politicians regarded these requirements as a breach of people's freedom. One of the most vocal opponents was Norman Tebbitt. We were and remain political opponents, but I have much affection for him. On the seat belt issue, we had a memorable clash on a radio programme. He maintained that it was an essential part of the freedom of British people to decide whether or not they wore seat belts. In his view, there were already far too many laws and regulations and requirements imposed on our citizens. If people want to take risks, that's a matter for them.

That was not my view. Hundreds of drivers and passengers died each year in car crashes, many of whose lives would have been saved if they had been wearing seat belts. The Department of Transport estimated that back-seat passengers who did not wear seat belts were three times more likely to suffer death or serious injuries than passengers who were wearing a seat belt and some thirty front-seat passengers died each year because passengers in the back seat were not wearing their seat belts. So compulsory seat belt wearing would not only save the lives of passengers themselves but would prevent them from killing and injuring others. And anyway, even if people are free to kill or injure themselves, it is generally and rightly the public that has to pay for their medical treatments.

In 1983, our campaign succeeded. It became compulsory to wear seats belts in front seats, and as a result the Department of Transport estimates that at least 370 lives and 7,000 serious injuries are saved each year. People still must drive carefully and far too many still die and are injured on our roads, but far less than in the bad old days. Good.

In 1987, a child named Billy Walker died in my constituency. He had swallowed the top of a Bic pen and choked to death. I immediately put down an Early Day Motion* urging the Government to investigate why schools provided such pens with separate tops of the type that caused Billy's death. As a result of the publicity, Bic and other pen manufacturers who make pens with separate tops put holes into them, so that children who swallow the top will be able to breathe. And the Government introduced a Trading Standard, requiring the ventilation of pen caps intended for children up to fourteen years of age. Breach of those regulations became a criminal offence and local authority Trading Standards Officers had the power to remove unsafe products from the market and prosecute.

In spite of the new rules, early in 1995, another child died of choking on a pen top. I asked for a debate 'on the need to ban not merely unsafe pens for use in this country, but those that are imported from overseas, to ensure that there are no more unnecessary deaths of this nature'. The Minister, Tony Newton, referred to the recent regulations and standards requiring ventilation of pen tops for youngsters, and promised to draw my concerns 'to the attention of the President of the Board of Trade'. I believe that since then there have been no other needless deaths from children swallowing pen tops. That at least is the legacy of poor Billy Walker.

One of my longest journeys was to the Argentine, in 1992. Together with fellow MPs, James Clappison and John Wheeler, and guided by my PA, Jon Mendelsohn, our primary purpose was to pay our respects at the site of the Israel Embassy, which had been bombed with a loss of twenty-nine lives. As a gesture, their Government released half a dozen war crimes files for our

---

* Early Day Motions are expressions of House of Commons opinion, in the form of motions to be debated on an early day, which never arrives.

inspection, but the gesture was more cosmetic than real. The following year, the Jewish Community Centre was blown up. Eighty-five people were killed.

Unlike many of my Labour colleagues who regard Margaret Thatcher as the embodiment of evil, I have always had a soft spot for her. Politically, she was a doughty opponent. Personally, our relations were and remain surprisingly cordial. For instance, Margaret was once kind enough to invite me to an official tea at Number 10, to welcome President Mubarak of Egypt. In the receiving line, she introduced me to her guest as follows: 'Mr President, this is Greville Janner. He is a Socialist Member of Parliament. In other countries, I would have him locked up. But here, I invite him to tea!'

Most of my other official contacts with Margaret Thatcher were on behalf of the Jewish community. She was friendly, responsive and helpful, and undoubtedly pro-Jewish. At one time, she had a group of Jews – or at least, colleagues of Jewish origin – in her Cabinet. These included Malcolm Rifkind; and Nigel Lawson, who was MP for Blaby, the neighbouring seat to mine. As for Michael Howard, who had a better Jewish education than any of us, his biographer recently told me that my father had acted for Michael's father, in getting him naturalised. Each year, on the anniversary of the death of his father – his father's 'yahrzeit' – he conducts the service in a synagogue, in Hebrew.

It was David Wolfson (Lord Wolfson of Sunningdale) who told me how careful I had to be in addressing Margaret, when she was Prime Minister. As President of the Board of Deputies, I had led a delegation to bring her greetings. David was with her. The conversation was brisk, practical and friendly. Later, I asked David how he thought it had gone. 'Not bad,' he replied. 'But the PM said to me: "Greville called me Margaret! Fancy that. He didn't even know enough to call me Prime Minister!"' Well, I'd called her Margaret for over ten years . . . But from then on, while she remained Prime Minister, I called her by her title, not by her name.

Apart from that incident, Margaret Thatcher and I have got on very well, from her vantage point at the top of the political heap and mine not too far from the bottom.

Another time when I led a Board of Deputies delegation to Thatcher, to discuss Middle East matters, she suddenly said: 'I am very sorry, but I have been reminded that I must go. I have a meeting with Archbishop Makarios.'

I knew that Margaret had often attacked the Cypriot leader and accused him of wickedness. 'Why are you going to talk to that terrorist?' I enquired.

'Because, dear boy,' she replied, 'if you want to make peace, you must deal with terrorists.' So off she swept.

I often remembered this dictum when meeting Yasser Arafat. For years, I had regarded him as an enemy of the Jewish people. But in the rosy days of the Middle East Peace Process, I had many meetings with him. I remembered not only what Thatcher had said but also Nelson Mandela's reply to Myra, when she had asked how he could deal with the former advocates of apartheid, who had locked him up for so long. If you wish a bright future, you must look forward. You cannot just focus on the past (Chapter 27).

Thatcher's greatest and most lasting success as Prime Minister? Probably, her decision to allow council house tenants to buy their homes on very favourable terms. That won her party an untold number of votes. Leicester West electors told me time after time, as I canvassed them in the next election: 'Sorry, Janner, but we can't vote for you. After all, it is thanks to Thatcher that we now own our own house.'

Thatcher's greatest failure? She could not keep her own colleagues in line. Too often, she treated them and their views with disdain. Result: huge dissension in the Tory ranks – and some wonderful stories. One which I was assured at the time was true concerned her relationship with her most loyal, staunch and honourable ally, Willie Whitelaw. At the end of a bitter Cabinet dispute which she only won thanks to Whitelaw's heavy intervention on her side, she announced: 'Every Prime Minister needs a Willie!' Well, it was no secret that she was the best man in her Cabinet . . .

My favourite, though, is the apocryphal tale of how she allegedly tried to pacify her rebellious crew by hosting a dinner for them in a private room at the Savoy Hotel. The waiter approached her with the menu and enquired: 'What will you have for the main course, Prime Minister?'

'Roast beef. Medium rare,' she replied.

Waiter: 'And the vegetables?'

Thatcher: 'They'll have the same . . .'

Days after the Argentinians invaded the Falklands, I went to see Lord Goodman – Arnold Goodman, a wise, shrewd old solicitor. My purpose: to seek his advice and intervention to prevent an anti-Semitic play being put on at the National Theatre. First, though, we chatted about Margaret Thatcher. 'What do you think she's going to do about the Falklands?'

'Well,' he replied, 'she has two alternatives, hasn't she? She can either flick the whole incident off her shoulders'. He gave a great flick with his finger and thumb. 'Well it's a long way off . . . the place is mainly inhabited by sheep . . . Or she can thunder in, guns blazing, and make sure that she wins.' Which, of course, is precisely what she did. And for two elections, the Labour Party's divided and flabby views on defence were major issues.

My old Trinity Hall friend, Geoffrey Howe, was a main cause of Thatcher's downfall. He resigned from the Cabinet and, in accordance with tradition, explained his reasons in a speech in the Commons. A packed House heard him denounce the Prime Minister.

Michael Heseltine then challenged the Iron Lady for the leadership of their party. He lost to Thatcher, but his 152 votes made it clear that a powerful minority wanted change. Thatcher stepped down. In the second ballot, John Major was well ahead of Heseltine and Douglas Hurd, both of whom withdrew in his favour. Major would be the next Prime Minister.

The following week, Thatcher made her final appearance at Prime Minister's Question Time. I had drawn Question 4 in the lottery. I had prepared two questions for her, one adulatory and one critical. After a great series of songs of praise from other questioners, I decided to go for it. The House was completely packed. I was, as usual, terrified. I had placed myself in the back row between a couple of pals. As my turn grew closer, I became ever more frightened.

Speaker Weatherill: 'Mr Greville Janner.'

GJ: 'May I first thank the Rt Hon. Lady for the many courtesies which she has given over so many years to so many back-benchers.' (Labour MP Tony Banks – sotto voce: 'I don't remember any.')

'At the same time, however, I must say that my constituents are deeply concerned that she has left the place in such a shambles. Is she aware that they are desperately worried about the poll tax, the growing recession, the health service, the education system and the whole Tory shambles . . .?'

I had started in silence. My first attacks were greeted with silence. But gradually Labour cheers and 'hear, hears' had picked up to a nice crescendo, with the Tories shouting back. The Speaker called for order.

'Question, please,' he demanded.

GJ: 'Will the Prime Minister say who she thinks should share the blame for what is, after all, a Conservative mess?'

'Well,' she said, 'the Honourable Gentleman always was quite a good advocate. He could speak to any brief. And I don't believe that he believes a single word of that.'

The place erupted with laughter. The Tories waved their Order Papers in delight. And I was duly hand-bagged.

In the corridor afterwards, I passed Edwina Currie, talking to her Conservative colleague, Martin Brandon-Bravo. She said to me: 'You know, I can't understand your attacking Margaret the way you did, after everything that she has done for the Jews. You should have praised her.' 'Rubbish,' said Martin, himself a proud Jew. 'I'd have hit you if you'd done that!'

Then came letters from infuriated Jews, attacking me for attacking her. They didn't understand that this was politics and not at all personal. But Margaret did. I met her in the Lobby later that day and she said to me: 'Well, Greville, I was prepared for you. I thought you were going to be naughty . . . and I was right!'

I still show the clip of that incident, at the end of media training sessions. It does the troops good to see how *their* fierce tormentor was downed by the mighty Thatcher, with such a relaxed and well-prepared swipe. She left her throne with her head held high. I have always believed that we should stand down our nuclear strength if and only if others would do the same. This was at the time an unpopular view in my party, but not now. Then, Thatcher *meant* strength, *used* strength and *played* on strength as she hand-bagged her way through her unforgettable regime.

It was in the Spring of 2003 that I was chatting with Margaret, now Baroness Thatcher, in the Peers' Lobby. She talked about the Jewish community. I asked her whether she had ever been in a Jewish home on a Friday night. After all, she had been MP for an area with many Jewish constituents. To my surprise, she told me that she had not. 'I wonder whether you and Denis would do my family and me the honour of joining us in my home, for a traditional Friday night,' I asked her. 'We are the ones who would be honoured,' she replied. 'We'd love to.' We fixed a date and she and her husband arrived promptly and early, so as to meet my young grandchildren. To their delight, she talked and listened to each of them and signed books for them, Denis happily chatted to their parents, while quaffing his customary gin and tonic. They did not leave until after ten.

Too soon after, Denis died. It is always lonely at the top, but infinitely more so when you lose your partner in life. I retain my friendship with Margaret, but am sad at the family pressures, weighing so heavily upon her.

How come that this Tory leader is a friend of a Labour peer? As a colleague once told me: 'In our Parliament, the enemy is often behind you – on your side – and your allies on the benches opposite.' Very true. We do battle on issues of politics but we unite on common ground. And we do not choose our friends by their political parties. That is a mark of our sanity.

I am often asked: Why did you go into politics? There are many answers.

First: since childhood, I have been surrounded by political life and people. My parents talked politics and personalities, at table and in the car, at work and on holiday. So I grew up, accepting that politics was a part of life.

At Cambridge (Chapter 6), I was enthusiastically involved in the Labour Club and in the Union, achieving leadership in both. Being a Labour activist was part of life – stimulating and stressful, enjoyable and inevitable.

Second: chance, the last-minute invitation to fight the then hopeless seat of Wimbledon. And when I had sunk myself into the family necessity to earn a living and had regarded my political days as over, suddenly Father's illness . . . being offered the chance to fight his seat . . . and with Myra's conditional backing, falling for it. From then on, politics was the breath of my non-family life.

'Yes,' you may rightly say, 'but surely your political beliefs had some major part in your life's work?'

Indeed. But unlike some of my more intellectual colleagues, I have always been a man of action, rather than an intellectual. I believed that my job was to serve. Parliament became and remains a fantastic base for such service.

In Leicester, I identified with the needs and the problems, the stress and the joys of my constituents and of that great city. I automatically reacted to challenges, most of them not of my making. Like the impact of the influx of immigrants . . . the inadequacies of provisions for health and housing . . . and individual and unnecessary suffering, like that of Jimmy Martin. I identified with suffering and shared the hurt of individuals. I believed that my job was to make use of political access, to look after my constituents.

Of course, there is a lurking self-interest, both in that work and in its electoral impact. In 1983, mine was the first Labour seat north of London. I had built on the Janner reputation for service, created by my father. I still have a sticker on both sides of my diary, with a photo of young Janner and the slogan: 'Janner Cares'. I did. My constituents knew it.

Beyond the boundaries of the constituency MP, I embedded my energy into two main areas of political policy: employment and foreign affairs. I soon learned that in political life, if you do not specialise, then there is little to achieve. As Chairman of the Employment Committee, I had a taste of the power to motivate change (Chapter 14). And I relished Question Time, both to raise constituency issues, personal and communal, but also to prod and to probe on overseas concerns. My primary international interests were, and remain, the Middle East and Israel, India and the United States.

So my prime task in the Commons was to serve my constituents and ensure that they kept me at work. I was embedded into the work of what we call All Party groups, not least the British Israel Parliamentary Committee.

Above all, I was elected to serve as a Labour MP, which meant: loyalty to my party. If I had not and did not now agree with the vast bulk of its aims and objects, its policies and purposes, then I would leave it. But I do.

I hate poverty, inequality and injustice. While no party achieves perfection, if I did not believe that my party does more than any other to focus on and to achieve these results, then I could not support it. But I do.

So I was hugely fortunate to be elected into the Commons. And when I retired, some twenty-eight years later, I was, of course, deeply fortunate that Tony Blair rewarded my efforts by putting me into the House of Lords. It became and remains my respected political base. In Britain, being Lord Janner provides some status but nothing like the appreciation and access which I receive abroad. I have close friends who insist upon calling me 'my lord', because it gives *them* pleasure. And my peerage certainly provides kudos which will enable me to carry on with my work, at home and overseas, until either the body or the mind decides that I must retire. And as both of my parents kept at work until their late eighties, and as medicine has advanced since their days, I look forward to a long future of active political work. God willing!

TWELVE

Asian Citizens and British Diversity

By 1970, the influx of Indians into Leicester had begun. I was determined to serve them well and to become their friend. At Cambridge, I had learned that I felt completely at home in Indian company. I had become a member of the Indian Society, the Majlis. I had three special Indian pals: Milon Banerji, Jai Mukhi and Natwar Singh. They and their families became and remain close to me (Chapter 26).

I discovered that while Hindus have different gods to the Jews, their principles and way of life are remarkably similar to ours. Top priorities: home, children and their education and upbringing – and later, care of their elderly family. The home is the prime centre of their religious practices.

When I became MP for part of Leicester, India's then High Commissioner in Britain was Apa Pant, a tall, distinguished and eloquent figure. Soon after, he visited Leicester and local Asian leaders held a meeting for him in a hired hall. Apa Pant's message: you have decided to settle in Britain. If you wish to get the best for yourselves, for your children and grandchildren, then you must take part in British life including its politics. It is not enough to accumulate wealth and to achieve a high standard of living. If you do not serve the wider community, then you will not become part of it.

I then decided to hold my own meeting and to invite the Indian communities to attend. Most were Gujaratis – originating from a clump of villages near Ahmedabad, in Mahatma Gandhi's state of Gujarat. They were mostly Hindus, but there were some Sikhs from the Punjab and a scattering of Muslims from different parts of India. Many had escaped from persecution in the Uganda of Idi Amin.

The church hall was packed. I started the meeting by repeating the guidance of Apa Pant and offering to help them in any way I could to enter Leicester's political life. I told them of my connections with and love for India and my delight that they had added to the diversity and colour of Leicester's life.

Immediately, a tall young man got up, wearing a traditional Indian khaki dhoti, buttoned up to the neck. 'Mr Janner,' he announced, 'you have no right to lecture us on how we should live. You do not understand the problems we face. You have never been spat on because you are of a different colour. You have never been cursed on a bus or sworn at because of your accent. Mr Janner, go away.' He sat down. The room was silent and the silence was electric.

'You are wrong, sir,' I responded. 'I am a Jew and half my family were murdered by racists. Destroyed because of their race. Sadly, I am an expert in discrimination. I know far too much about it.

'So my job, ladies and gentlemen, is to work together with you, to make sure that you never suffer from racism as my family and I have done. We have the same enemies. We have the same friends. We have the same ideals. Now let's work together, shall we?' A voice from the hall shouted: 'He's right'. They stood and clapped and cheered. They invaded the stage and clapped me on the back.

From then on, they adopted me as one of their own and I worked with our Asian community, happily and without stress. Rightly, they regarded me as a friend and an ally, and I was proud to serve them, together with the rest of my constituents. Many of them became my friends and allies. Although even by 1992 only about 10 per cent of my constituents were Asian, they were the basis of my often tiny majority. It was not merely that 90 per cent of them voted for me, but that over 80 per cent of them voted – a far higher percentage than any other section of the community.

Many of them became and still are close personal friends. Like Sunil Gadhia, whose father was and remains a factory worker and his mother a home worker. He became the first Asian partner in Stephenson & Harwood, distinguished city solicitors, and is now its Chief Executive. One of his brothers is an IT consultant, the other an accountant. His family are as proud of them as my grandparents were when my Uncle Alf won a Rugger Blue at Cambridge and then when he and Uncle Henry and Uncle Edwin helped him to build the hugely successful family furnishing business. So I recognised so much of my own family history and of my own background in the traditions of my Asian constituents, and I was determined to battle against some of my indigenous constituents' dislike of the unlike.

As the Indian community grew, it started fitting into our Leicester scene. Thanks not only to the city's political leaders but also to its media and to its police and to the nature of the Asian community itself, we never had the racial combustion that afflicted and continues to afflict too many other cities. That said, the city's Asian population grew from almost nil in the 1960s to over one third by the 1990s. Many of their ways and customs were different from those of our indigenous people. The older generation of Asians did not find it easy to assimilate and to learn the English language.

In my constituency, Belgrave Road was a main thoroughfare and boundary. The streets on both sides gradually emptied of most of their white citizens. Belgrave Road itself acquired rows of excellent Asian stores, which soon became a magnet for Asian shoppers from other towns. And on the great Hindu festivals of Navrati and Diwali, not only were the temples filled but the street was bright with what for others were Christmas decorations.

By the mid-1970s, about 10 per cent of the pupils in one of my primary schools were Asian. I asked the head teacher, himself non-Asian, how he was coping. He replied: 'They have raised the level of intelligence in my school.'

You hit the resentment when you visited the working men's clubs. Curiously, they allowed black people in but excluded Asians – just as in some London areas with a large Afro-Caribbean population, similar clubs excluded blacks but welcomed Asian members. Time after time I recoiled from racist remarks. That racism was almost entirely directed at Asians and not at Jews. Anti-Semitic remarks were very rare. The constant stream of fascist or Nazi mail which reached my office came almost entirely from outside the city.

Our Asian citizens soon adapted. They reminded me of my own grandparents, who had to learn new languages and ways, and of Myra, who was also an immigrant. She came from Australia and the first time she saw snow from close up was when we were living at our first home in Northway and there was a snowstorm. She shouted with happy laughter as we built our first snowman and she sat on a sledge and ran it down the pavement.

The older generation of Asians were almost all diligent and good-natured people who made me welcome in their homes and temples. If you closed your eyes and listened to their children, you would not know that these youngsters were born anywhere other than in our city.

The City of Leicester survived the great slump of the 1930s, almost unharmed. My father had told me that Leicester never needed to worry because it produced the essentials of life. 'People can't do without shoes or clothing and that's what we make in our factories.'

Sadly, others – mainly in Asia – managed to manufacture footwear and hosiery and clothing much more cheaply than we could. Gradually, our key industries shrank in the face of imports, often of excellent quality but the products of underpaid labour.

Our Asian immigrants did much to save our Leicester economy. They brought in new ideas. They built up our wholesale and retail sectors. They heeded the words of High Commissioner Apa Pant and soon entered active political life. No political party could afford to ignore them. They were wooed by all. But even though Conservative Prime Minister Edward Heath was largely responsible for letting them into Britain, the allegiance of all but the most wealthy largely stayed with Labour.

Why did they choose Leicester when Idi Amin had made life intolerable for Asians in Uganda and life was becoming worse for others in Kenya and Malawi? The first Asian immigrants came to our city by chance and the rest, by recommendation. Like the Jews before them, they joined their extended families. When a cousin or an uncle, a brother or a grandparent arrived from Uganda, the rest of the family moved over and made room for them. Then they in their turn welcomed other generations.

In 1971, the Council took fright. It put an advert into newspapers in Kampala, Uganda's capital, saying that Leicester was full up and that emigrating Asians should look elsewhere.

Being highly intelligent people, the families of those who had already arrived in Leicester said to themselves and to each other: 'We'd better get moving or they'll close the doors.' The pace of immigration into our city increased, fast.

The *Leicester Mercury* and the local police were my allies in keeping the local National Front and other fascists at bay. In local elections in 1977, the National Front only missed gaining a seat in one of my great housing estates by a few votes. 'Enough,' I said to my Labour colleagues. We recognised that the estate was almost entirely white. They were afraid of people whom they had never met. The National Front seemed their natural ally. We must expose them.

I consulted the Board of Deputies. They had recently produced a powerful pamphlet, with the bold slogan on the front: 'The National Front is a Nazi Front'. We put one into every letter box on the estate. The local fascists cringed and never achieved the same level of votes again, anywhere in the city. Then one of those named in the pamphlet threatened to sue the Board of Deputies and its Vice President – me. A few weeks later, I took my distinguished businessman friend, Stanley (now Lord) Kalms, on a visit to Leicester Prison. As we drove up from London, I told him about the threat. I knew something of the costs of libel actions, not least the problems for successful defendants to claims brought by apparently impecunious plaintiffs. With Myra and three children to feed – and working as I always did on the basis that I used my parliamentary salary to promote my parliamentary business and had to live off my other earnings from writing and lecturing – I was worried. 'Forget it,' said Stanley. 'If you are sued, we'll have a whip round. Anyway, it's probably hot air. I'd be surprised if he sues.'

Stanley was right and we heard nothing further, but I have not forgotten his reassurance. That was only the first time that Stanley stood by me when times were actually or potentially tough. I was delighted when, in 2004, the Tories put him into the Lords, as a life peer.

MPs look after all their constituents, irrespective of their race, creed or colour. And most constituencies have their own special concerns and problems. It has not been easy for Leicester's indigenous population to absorb literally tens of thousands of neighbours from East Africa. Their customs and their background, their language and their religion – all were different. It was not merely dislike of the unlike but genuine fear by local people that their familiar city culture was ebbing away. The greater the deprivation, the greater the fear.

As Asians moved into an area, others tended to follow them and local people moved out. Not surprisingly, on the one hand our new citizens felt more comfortable in the company of their own and on the other, they felt the resentment of local people who felt uncomfortable in the new environment. At its simplest, many non-Asians disliked the smell of curry, invariably used by the newcomers for their cooking.

Again: the poorer the area, the greater the resentment. When Asians were housed on some of the council estates, neighbours made their lives a misery, not only so that they would move out, which they often did, but so that others would not follow them in. Conversely, the better off the area, the greater were the chances of both the existing population and the new arrivals learning how to co-exist happily.

My job was to serve all my constituents. That meant helping the local Leicester people to understand and to deal with the new influx and our new citizens to fit into and to join in serving our city. Not easy, but we did well.

In East London communities, nothing much has stayed still. When Father was MP for Whitechapel and St George's, the area had a large Jewish community. By the time that I became a voluntary manager at the Brady Club, of which Mother had been a youthful founder, our community was already shrinking, but there were still enough Jewish youngsters to pack the club and for me to run my then famous folk music group, the Brady Ramblers. Still, the Club's concert party was already singing: 'They're talking Hindustani where the *Mamaloshen* (Yiddish) used to be . . .' The Hindus, the Sikhs and the Muslims were moving into the East End and the Jews were moving out to north London. Community life is seldom static. In the City of Leicester, as in London's East End, it has been moving on fast. By the year 2010, over half Leicester's citizens will be of Asian origin – a higher percentage of people of overseas origin than any other city in Britain. Wow!

The key to accepted and sensible immigration can be summed up in one word – integration. You retain your pride in your own culture, customs, religion and traditions, but you adapt to the place where you have chosen to live.

Integration takes time. First generation immigrants in Leicester tended to club together, for security and their common language. Their children and grandchildren speak English and have merged into our society, not least in politics. To no small extent thanks to the local media, police and Members of Parliament and local councillors, there has been the minimum of racist attacks and ill-will and none of the riots that plague other cities with major immigrant communities.

I was proud to be part of this integration process, and to build into a city with very few Jews, our Jewish experience of true integration – keeping your own culture but contributing to that of the city and country of your choice. I salute Leicester's immigrant communities, as I knew them. And I pray that as the city evolves and changes, positive integration will continue. As the French put it, in a totally different context: '*Vive la différence!*' If you want to live in peace and goodwill, then you must accept and benefit from the differences between you. Which, you may say, is all very well – but perhaps not in the era of terrorism. On the contrary. The greater the threat, the more vital it becomes to work together with those of other faiths who are prepared to work with you.

In the then predominantly Hindu immigrant community of Leicester, the problem was not relating to others but to each other. The different castes and temples did not find it easy to seek out and to unite on their common ground. Multiply this problem nationally and you discover why Hindus and Sikhs have such limited national access, especially at government level.

The Muslims know better. They make sure that their voices are heard. They have formed councils and organisations, to provide them with voices which are heard by our national leaders. Of course, they are more likely to be consulted by the media than their Hindu or Sikh cousins, because – so sadly for them – so many of the terrorist miseries, both abroad and in the UK, are carried out by Muslim extremists, usually prepared to give up this life in the beliefs that they will have immediate and joyful access to the world hereafter. The vast majority of our British Muslim world is as anxious as all the rest of us to live normal lives, in peace with their neighbours. The tragedy is the tiny minority.

Now consider our British extremists, from right to left. While studying at Harvard, I heard Dwight Eisenhower proclaim: 'Decent people travel in the centre of the road. There's a gutter on each side.' Problems and hatreds against Jews come from both gutters. Often, they attack Israel, the Jewish State – and hence, the Jews. But today, while the far left seek links with the Muslim world, the far right regard attacks on Muslims as totally acceptable, especially in a country where too many terrorist roots have emerged from mosques and mullahs, and where Islamic extremists have been blamed by our police and other authorities for such unspeakable horrors as the bombs on tubes and buses.

In Leicester, the Muslim community is growing. Following the death of my parliamentary Labour colleague, Jim Marshall, a by-election was held in Leicester East. It was won by the Liberal Democrats, on a low poll and focusing on the Iraq war issue. Canvassing for our Labour man, Sir Peter Soulsby, I found that nearly every Muslim whom I approached said: 'I shall be voting for the Liberal Democrats.' As I knew from Leicester West, it is not the size of your community that matters at election time, but how many of them are prepared to use their votes. Happily, in the 2004 election which followed closely after, Peter won the seat. But the omens are clear.

I was part of the Arab Muslim world, during my stay in the Arab town of Sakhnin in Northern Israel (Chapter 24). People kept saying to me: '*Nahnu buni am*' – we are cousins. Jews and Muslims have much in common. The golden age of our Jewish people was not in the Christian world but in medieval, Muslim Spain. As a Muslim told me recently: 'We shall live or we shall die together.' I love life, and that is why I use whatever weight I have, to bring our communities together. It is also why I joined with Prince Hassan bin Talal of Jordan, in creating an international organisation of Muslim and Jewish political leaders, all over the world (Chapter 24). Its influence can only be for the good. *Inshallah*. God willing.

THIRTEEN

The War Crimes Campaign

In August 1948, I was serving as a War Crimes Investigator in Germany (Chapter 3). I was called in by my Commanding Officer, Peter Priestley, and told that the War Crimes Group was being packed up. I asked why, and he replied: 'I don't know. I can only suspect that they do not care any more, provided that these people are anti-Soviet.' I was shocked and furious and was determined that one day, however long it might take, I would work to recreate the battle against these evil criminals. It took over forty years.

In the early 1970s, I had visited the Australian War Crimes Unit in Canberra. Their Chief told me that they had some excellent records about Nazi atrocities. 'Did you lose any of your family in the Holocaust?' Indeed. 'Could you give me their names and the towns in which they lived?' I did. And a few minutes later, he returned with one file. It told the terrible story of a man called Chaim Katzin, a relative of my beloved Israeli cousin, Leah Katzin. He was severely disabled and walked with a limp. The Nazis had taken him out from his home and set their dogs on him. To escape them, he had climbed a tree and remained up in the branches until he was so exhausted that he fell down. The dogs then savaged him to death.

In October 1986, the Simon Wiesenthal Centre in Los Angeles gave the British Government a list of seventeen alleged war criminals residing in the UK. We knew that between 1945 and 1950, the Attlee Government had allowed some 90,000 displaced persons (DPs) into the UK to do manual work in the coal mines and elsewhere. The British authorities made little or no effort to enquire into the wartime records of these people. Instead, as the then Commonwealth Secretary, Philip Noel Baker, put it: 'We must dispose of the past'. So we set up the Parliamentary War Crimes Group in the late 1980s. Its Chairman was ex-Home Secretary, Merlyn Rees, and I was elected as the Group's Secretary.* My PA, Philip Rubenstein, was our Director. We were a forceful, formidable and articulate group.

We met Home Secretary, Douglas Hurd, and urged him to take action to track down the war criminals among these DPs. He was polite, but took no action. He promised to look into our concerns but nothing happened for months and we suspected that his civil servants had buried this potentially explosive issue, which would unleash some citizens' disgraceful past.

At the start, our British Jewish community was surprisingly divided on the war crimes issue. While the majority applauded our work, some believed that we should leave ill alone. Enough. The war and the Holocaust were over, some forty years ago. They believed that it would encourage anti-Semites to allege that the Jews were seeking revenge. Happily, the majority, and especially the new generation of Jewish young people who wanted to know what had happened in the past, overcame this timid over-sensitivity. As our campaign progressed, our Jewish community united behind it.

Still, it was the extraordinarily vigorous, vocal and outspoken non-Jewish support that eventually won our battle, combined as it was with the determination of some brave survivors. Like Kitty Hart, who had suffered in Auschwitz. She told me that she could not forget the face of the man who had tortured her for a year. Another survivor said: 'I forget the people whom I met yesterday, but I would not forget the face of the man who snatched my baby from me and threw her into a pit.'

Our next big break: Scottish Television employed a journalist called Bob Tomlinson, who was totally and passionately devoted to the exposure of one specific case – that of Antoninas Gecas, a 71-year-old retired mining engineer, living in a suburb of Edinburgh. Interviewed four years earlier, Gecas had admitted that he had been a member of a Lithuanian police battalion which had been involved in the mass murder of Jews. But he claimed that he took no part in the shootings. 'That's apparent,' he had said. 'I'm a Catholic.'

Then Channel 4 broadcast that remarkable and incontrovertible programme unveiling the criminal, murderous past of Gecas. The allegations: that he was personally involved in massacres of Jews. His reply:

---

* Other members included Peter Archer, Alex Carlile, Llin Golding, John Gorst, Elwyn Jones, Ivan Lawrence, Roy Mason, Stefan Terlezki and John Wheeler.

'I was only a distant onlooker.' But the TV evidence against him was powerful, and Scottish TV had also obtained a further list of thirty-four Nazis, now believed to be living in the UK. Our Committee returned to Home Secretary Hurd. He confirmed that at least six of the seventeen on the list were definitely alive and living in Britain, but said that there was 'nothing that could be done about them'. We did not agree. That was when our campaign lifted off.

Gecas then sued Scottish Television for defamation. Happily, he lost. The judge declared that he was satisfied that Gecas had 'participated in many operations involving the killing of innocent Soviet citizens, including Jews in particular, in Byelorussia . . . and in doing so committed war crimes against Soviet citizens, which included old men, women and children'.

It took nine years before the Lithuanian Government issued a warrant for the extradition of Gecas, in the same month that the Scottish Justice Minister sanctioned the start of proceedings against the murderer. Shortly after, the Minister announced that the warrant would not be served. Gecas was too ill. A few days later, Gecas died in an Edinburgh hospital, still a free man.

Our Committee published two reports. The first was historical, showing how the DPs had been allowed into the UK, without investigation of their potential Nazi past. The second was a legal report, by the Vice Chancellor of London University, Graham Zellick, and Peter Archer, former Solicitor General.

It took another year before the Government appointed an enquiry into war crimes. Its members, Sir Thomas Hetherington and William Chalmers, published their report in July 1989.

We had been sceptical of their research. We believed that they would produce a whitewash. We were delighted to be proved wrong. They examined seven cases in detail and found that in four of them there was sufficient evidence to warrant prosecution. They recommended a change in the law to allow such prosecution. And they concluded: 'The crimes committed are so monstrous that they cannot be condoned . . . To take no action would taint the United Kingdom with the slur of being a haven for war criminals.'

Until that moment, we had been stirring up the past, in the remote hope of action in the future. From that moment, our campaign lifted off into reality. We did not believe that the Government could, should or would resist our determination to push through war crimes legislation. In the mini-debate that followed Hurd's statement, the lines were drawn between our majority, demanding action, and the right-wing and vocal minority resisting it. To our delight, that minority included Sir John Stokes, who was renowned for his hilarious statement that 'there are not enough red-blooded Englishmen in the Cabinet'.

The Government was reshuffled. Douglas Hurd was replaced as Home Secretary by David Waddington. We were apprehensive when he arrived in the job, because he was believed to be a hanger and flogger, who was most unlikely to support our campaign. Again, we were wrong. He made this clear in his speech in the debate on the Hetherington Enquiry, on 12 December 1989. He said: 'Sometimes one is brought face to face with facts that cannot be buried and I do not believe that the Hetherington Report can just be interred. The terrible stories revealed in its pages and the evidence of foul deeds that is presented cannot be just put aside or ignored.' Hooray! We had a new and powerful ally.

That debate showed that we had many other articulate allies. The most moving moment came when Llin Golding told the House how, when she was only a child, her father, Ness Edwards, for twenty-one years MP for Caerphilly, returned home from the Buchenwald concentration camp, which he had visited with a parliamentary delegation.

'Father stood there, grey and drawn and said: "Do not touch me. I'm covered with lice. Everyone in the camps is covered with lice. We have been deloused many times, but I'm still covered with lice." He could not sleep for many weeks and he had nightmares for many years . . . He told us of what he had seen in the camp . . . of the hanging and gibbets. Human beings on hooks and hung from under their chins until they died. He told us that people in charge of the camp rather liked tattoos, and they skinned prisoners and used their skins to make lampshades. They discovered that when people died, their skin was given to shrinking too quickly, so they tried skinning them alive. My father showed me photographs of piles of bodies on carts.'

By then, nearly all of us were crying. This was the only time I have ever been reduced to tears in a parliamentary debate.

Llin was followed by Winston Churchill, grandson of our wartime leader, and by Peter Archer, both demanding action. The vote endorsing the need for legislation 'to permit the prosecution in this country for acts of murder or manslaughter or culpable homicide committed as war crimes in German or German Occupied Territory during the Second World War, of people who are now British citizens or resident here' was passed – by 340 votes to 123. We were on the way.

With the Commons voting almost three to one in favour of legislation, we did not believe that the House of Lords would reject it. They were old soldiers, with indelible memories of the miseries of war and the criminality of the Nazis and their regimes. Surely they would not try to block this effort to repair even a little of the criminality of the Nazi past. We were wrong.

During the Lords debate, our antagonists expressed many reasons to reject the Bill. Among those who joined in the chorus of demands to forgive and to forget or at least to let the murderers live or die in peace was Lord Shawcross, who had been a prosecutor at Nuremberg.* Lord (Gerry) Fitt said: 'In my native Northern Ireland, there are three thousand unsolved murders. I could not support the amendment which seems to say to a killer: "If you hide successfully for long enough, you will be safe." It seems that certain elements within this country are prepared to accept Britain as a haven for yesterday's terrorists.'

The result of the debate: In favour of the decision of the House of Commons: 74. Against: 207. Then we knew that we had a fierce fight on our parliamentary hands. Leader-writers in the next day's newspapers were as divided as Parliament. Nigella Lawson, daughter of Nigel (now Lord) Lawson and then Chancellor of the Exchequer, described the prosecution of the war criminals as a 'moral imperative'. She told me later that when her article appeared, she endured a torrent of 'disturbing letters from the mad anti-Semites, who seemed to see my column as just another arm of the world Jewish conspiracy'.

---

* Lords Callaghan, Grimond, Hailsham, Longford and Soper, and the Bishop of St Albans spoke against the Bill. Speakers in favour included my brother-in-law, Lord Morris of Kenwood, Lord Clinton Davis, Lord Arnold Goodman, former Chief Rabbi Lord Jakobovits, Lord Mason, George Thomas (Lord Tonypandy), and Lord Kagan, who declared himself to be the only peer who was himself a survivor of a concentration camp.

We then wondered whether the Government would use the Lords' decision as an excuse for dropping the legislation. We were hugely relieved when, early the next year, the Government introduced the War Crimes Bill. We knew that we had to pull public opinion in general and parliamentary support in particular onto our side. After Llin Golding's speech, we realised that the forty-fifth anniversary of the liberation of the Buchenwald concentration camp was fast approaching. With her brave and energetic support, we organized a Buchenwald exhibition in the Imperial War Museum, which afterwards was transferred for a week to a House of Commons exhibition hall. Then we called in the public support of colleagues from the legislatures of Australia, Canada and the United States. They had supported, helped and guided us over the past few years and had all passed laws to enable them to prosecute war criminals who had found refuge in their countries. We flew over officials from each of those countries for a one-day conference in the Palace of Westminster. They were all long-standing civil servants, highly credible. The press did us proud.

In March 1990, the Government introduced the War Crimes Bill into the Commons. Alex Carlile told of his mother's experiences in the ghettoes of Lvov and Warsaw. Strangely, former Prime Minister Edward Heath opposed the Bill, arguing that it was 'debatable' that alleged war criminals knew that they were in breach of any law. The House passed the Bill with a larger majority than in the previous debate. We won by 273 votes to 60. Then on the Bill went to the House of Lords.

At the end of their vigorous debate, the Lords threw out the Bill by 137 votes to 62. Because my father was a peer, I sat on the steps of the throne. On our way out, an attendant came up to my mother and myself and said: 'Mr Janner, you had no right to sit on the steps, you know.' I replied: 'But my father was a peer.' 'Your father is deceased, Mr Janner,' said the attendant. My mother looked at him and began to cry. It was a bad evening.

Next question: would the Government take the unique step of invoking the Parliament Act, to force through the legislation in the teeth of the Lords' rejection? To do so, they would have to reintroduce the Bill into the Commons and then return it to the Lords for a second time. When, as now seemed certain, the Bill was again rejected by the Lords, would the Government then invoke the Parliament Act? The media in general and the press in particular argued over an expected constitutional crisis. Our job: to make sure that the crisis was resolved in favour of this crucial law. Of course, we knew that there would not be many prosecutions under it, but it had huge symbolic value for us, for the survivors and for decency and justice.

A month or so later, the Government announced that it would reintroduce the Bill. Prime Minister Margaret Thatcher discreetly let it be known that she would not be bullied by the Lords – a decision which lifted her up in my estimation for ever. We convened a meeting in the Moses room of the House of Lords, addressed by Sir Thomas Hetherington. He was heckled by Lord Christopher Mayhew, a vigorous, vicious opponent both of the Bill and of the State of Israel. Sadly, while Hetherington was totally persuasive, the Lords were unpersuaded. They rejected the Bill for the second time. The Government invoked the Parliament Act, and the Bill automatically got the Royal Assent. We had won a great, unique and difficult battle.

While waiting for Royal Assent, the Government had set up a special War Crimes Unit, as part of the Metropolitan Police. Immediately after Royal Assent, it started work.

Why did colleagues and I press so hard for this legislation, when so few of these Nazi killers were still alive and at large and apparently immune to justice? There were three reasons.

First: for me, the process was as symbolic as it was real. At last, Britain, which had battled – at one time alone – against the Nazis, was determined to bring to justice at least some of those mass murderers who had found refuge in our land. We were ashamed that our postwar Government had allowed Britain to become a haven for Nazi murderers. At least now they would not sleep comfortably in their beds. At least we would have the possibility of justice, for however few.

Second: for the Jewish community, this campaign was crucial. Yes, it revived memories. But more important, especially for our younger generation, it brought new confidence and new allies.

Third: for me, it was the end of a trail which began with the horror of my work as a War Crimes Investigator. As a youngster, I had seen the aftermath of the atrocities and been shocked at the escape of the perpetrators. Now at least there would be some hope of some justice.

Only two men were prosecuted under the War Crimes Act: Andreas Sawoniuk and Szymon Serafinowicz. Sawoniuk was convicted on two counts of murder. He was sentenced to life imprisonment and died in jail. Serafinowicz was committed to trial in 1996 but, nine months later, an Old Bailey jury found him unfit to stand trial, due to his failing mental health.

Why, then, when so many war criminals had seeped into Britain, were so few of them prosecuted under our 1991 Act? The Metropolitan Police set up a special unit which investigated 367 cases. In nearly a third of them, the suspects were dead. In many others, they were too old or too senile to face interrogation. Twenty-five were clearly innocent. What of the rest? A distinguished author and expert, David Cesarani, wrote a book entitled *Justice Delayed: How Britain Became a Refuge for Nazi War Criminals*. In some cases, he said, it was decided that a prosecution was unlikely to succeed for lack of reliable credible evidence. In others, including that of a Latvian war crimes suspect called Konrad Kalejs, that 'lack of evidence was not unrelated to absence of political will'.

Whatever the prosecutions, at least some of these old Nazis who had so wrongly been given a refuge in our decent land may not have slept well in their beds. At least the land that had once stood alone against Hitler and his allies had made a gesture of intent, however late.

FOURTEEN

The Employment Committee

Chairing the Employment Select Committee was the peak of my Commons career – my most challenging, rewarding and generally enjoyable task. It enabled me to give service, both to the House and to my party, without breaking my promise to Myra that I would not look for or accept departmental office, and to make use of my rusting talents as a cross-examiner. Thanks to media coverage, I became a minor and temporary national celebrity.

In February 1982, I was appointed a member of the Committee. By arrangement between the parties, it was one of those committees in which the Tory majority elected a Labour Chairman; in this case, Ron Leighton, MP for Newham Northeast.

During the years leading up to the 1991 election, most of our hearings were unmemorable and generally of little interest to the media. The exception: the mammoth clash between two men of arrogant charisma, miners' leader Arthur Scargill and the Chairman of the Coal Board, Ian MacGregor.

I enjoyed cross-examining witnesses, a pastime that I had missed since I had given up work at the Bar. I especially remember battles with Norman (now Lord) Tebbitt, who was then Employment Secretary. They were fierce and fun. During one session, I was called to cross-examine very late. After we had finished, the Permanent Secretary, Tebbitt's top civil servant, came up to me, smiling. 'I thought you might like to see this,' he said, handing me a bit of paper. On it, Tebbitt had written: 'I'm bored. When is Janner coming on to bowl?'

When Tebbitt moved on from the job, I thanked him for his courtesies and especially for not taking cross-examinations personally. He replied: 'Of course I didn't. We had a very happy synergy, didn't we?' Indeed. Politics is an odd profession where you so often have a synergy with people with whom you profoundly disagree and none with people with whom you are ostensibly in full agreement.

Unfortunately, when Tom (now Lord) King took over as Employment Secretary, he took my cross-examinations personally. This I regretted and I later apologised to him if I had caused him personal offence when certainly none was intended. He accepted my words gracefully and we have since had a friendly if remote relationship.

Select Committees have little purpose unless they probe and question and search for truth and reality. That is their job, and it is for all witnesses to present their cases with honest clarity, and to accept that they are there to answer questions and not to be affronted by the persistence or tenacity or directness of those who ask them. They are making presentations and must prepare and present with care and with skill.

Soon after the 1991 election, I was approached by one of my Tory colleagues. He said: 'The Conservatives on the Employment Committee have decided that we want you as Chairman. We have had enough of Ronald. If I nominate you, will you stand?' I thanked him warmly and asked for a little time to think it over. On the one hand, I realised that I would love the job. I knew the law on employment and I enjoyed the politics. While Ron had always treated me with courtesy, I never warmed to him. More important, he did not use the Committee to achieve any useful impact on Tory Government policies.

I quietly asked around and it was clear that all my Labour colleagues, with the possible exception of Ken Eastham, would vote against me. But all the Tories would vote for me, and as there were six of them and five of us, and I would definitely vote for myself, I would win. But, my opposing a Labour colleague would cause ill-will.

I consulted my Chief Whip, Derek (now Lord) Foster. Under my leadership, he said, the Committee would have much greater impact. He told me how he had been elected Chairman of a Committee on his local council, thanks to Tory votes. Two weeks later, everyone had forgotten the origins of his success. 'I advise you to go for it,' he said.

I did. The meeting was tense. A Tory nominated me. Ron was in the Chair and he added: 'Are you prepared to stand, Mr Janner?'

I paused. 'Yes,' I said, firmly. He flinched.

Then one of our colleagues nominated Ron. 'Yes, I will stand,' he said.

The Clerk called out the names for the votes and I realised that there was a problem – Sebastian (now Lord) Coe was not there. Suddenly, he rushed in, just as the clerk was calling his name.

'Mr Coe,' said the Clerk. 'Yes,' said Seb. 'That's me.'

'No, Mr Coe, that's not the question,' said the Clerk. 'Are you in favour of Mr Leighton or Mr Janner as Chairman?'

'Mr Janner,' said Seb.

Then came Ken Eastham. 'I abstain,' he said.

All the Tories voted for me. Except for Ken's abstention, all the Labour votes were against me, but I was duly elected by seven votes to four.

Michael Portillo was then Employment Secretary. I paid a courtesy call on him, at the Employment Department. Knowing from experience that I would be far more likely to have a useful conversation if I was alone with the Minister, I suggested that we chat without the civil servants present. He readily agreed. He greeted me warmly and we sat comfortably in armchairs in his office. 'Congratulations,' he said. 'I am sure that we will find much common ground.' I thanked him. 'How is Myra?' he asked.

I told him that she was recovering from horrendous operations for cancer but was making good progress. I saw his eyes flick to one side. I soon found out why. One of his family had been afflicted with that awful disease, but happily had recovered.

We turned to business, and for half an hour discussed the work of the Committee and the cooperation which I hoped for and he assured me I would get from him and from his team. Recognising as we both did that my survival, like my appointment, depended on the backing of the Tory majority, it was clear that we must work on common ground and respect our differences. We parted and remain on excellent terms.

The following day, Myra received a very personal, four-page, hand-written letter from Michael. It was full of encouragement and of hope. We were both very moved. Myra said: 'Now there's a *mensch* – a real human being.' Quite a compliment for a politician! Since then, I have retained an affectionate regard for Michael. Of course, he was a determined and ambitious politician – and why not? If it is right and accepted for academics, lawyers and business people, trade unionists and shop-floor workers to be ambitious, why is it wrong for a politician? The fact that I did not seek or want high office was no reason why others should not do so, least of all Michael. And I was sad that he did not win the leadership of his Party – and even more so, that he has moved out of Parliament.

It was curious how much it meant to us that Michael's letter was hand-written. Tony Blair also wrote hand-written letters of encouragement to Myra. So did Gordon Brown. I mentioned this to a normally cynical colleague who said: 'Really good people always find time to do what is really important.'

In 1994, we learned that British Gas intended to cut earnings for thousands of its workers, but to give its Chief Executive, Cedric Brown, a 75 per cent pay rise. His salary would increase to £475,000 a year. Tony Blair, then Leader of the Opposition, asked Prime Minister John Major to confirm that Brown would earn more in a week than his staff earned in a year. The Prime Minister slammed down his documents on the Commons despatch box. 'One day you complain about the gas monopoly,' he said, 'and the next day you complain that British Gas faces competition and makes its own cloth cut accordingly.' The Employment Committee decided to call Brown to give evidence before us.

In January 1995, Cedric Brown appeared before the Committee. I attacked him for announcing plans to cut the pay of retail staff, to increase gas charges and to reduce showroom services, so soon after granting himself a 75 per cent pay rise. Was this not 'at the very least, highly insensitive and tactless?'

Brown: 'It could have been handled better.' Indeed. But he defended his pay, telling us that he had worked his way up in British Gas, starting at the bottom some forty years before, wielding a pick and shovel. If he were Chief Executive in an American gas company, in competition with British Gas, he would earn ten times as much. And anyway, he insisted, his salary had only been increased by 28 per cent. Angela Eagle attacked his earning £1,000 a day when his showroom staff were on £10,000 a year, and Ken Eastham described the pay rise as 'golden nuggets, not pennies from heaven'.

Cedric Brown was followed into the witness box by James Smith, Chief Executive of Eastern Electricity, whose annual pay had shot up from £62,000 when the company was in the public sector and was now nearly £250,000. Then Sir Desmond Pitcher, Chief Executive of Littlewoods, sought to justify his pay of £360,500 as Chairman of North West Water.

The following month, Sir Iain Vallance, Chairman of British Telecom, appeared before us. His annual salary was £663,000.

Then the Tory press descended on me. If these guys were 'fat cats', what about the Labour MP, Greville Janner QC? A *Daily Express* columnist had said that he had a 'sneaking regard' for my 'energy and enterprise' – but 'with his speaking fees, his consultancy fees, his director fees, his legal fees, his income from writing, his parliamentary salary and allowances, the MP for Leicester West is not short of a bob or two . . . His dedication in maximising his own income does not prevent his adopting an aggressive holier than thou approach when grilling bosses of the privatised utilities in his capacity as Chairman of the Commons Employment Select Committee . . .'

They later ran a centre-page spread, headed: 'Rich MP who grills the "greedy bosses".' The caption to one picture read: 'Millionaire Greville Janner leads the outcry at privatised industries' excesses'. There were pictures of my wedding, our flat and our family. The *Daily Telegraph*, the *Guardian*, *The Times*, the *Daily Mail* and the rest, they all weighed in. *The Times* published a splendid cartoon of a laughing me, wearing my barrister's robes and holding a document headed: 'J'accuse', with Mr Brown in the dock. The original hangs proudly in my home.

I discovered that British Gas were employing a team of PR people to bash me. Each time she saw a piece about my alleged wealth, Myra would chuckle and say: 'I wish . . . I wish . . .' or sometimes: 'Where have you hidden it? I'm your wife, I'm entitled to my share, aren't I?' At that time, Stanley (now Lord) Kalms was on the board of British Gas. I asked him for his view on his company's attacks on me. 'Enjoy, enjoy, Greville,' he replied. 'We've made you famous!' Meanwhile, sixteen Tories put down an emergency Commons motion, alleging that I had a 'conflict of interests', because of my place on the Board and Remuneration Committee of Ladbroke's, whose Chairman earned more than Cedric Brown.

Robert Kilroy-Silk attacked me in the *Daily Express*. He described me as the 'most wimpish man I knew in the Commons. I had never met anyone so afraid of his own shadow, so anxious to please, so desperate to be loved. We called him Grovel Janner.' My reaction: as far as the personal insult is concerned, I treated it with contempt. In my view, my job as Chairman of the Select Committee was to get at the truth. And I vowed that I would not be changing my style because of Kilroy-Silk's criticism. Until then, he and I had got on fine – since then, we have had no contact, and his influence has happily evaporated.

Meanwhile, the *Financial Times* reported that I was 'facing removal' from the Chair of the Committee. Would the majority on the Committee now boot me out? My Labour colleagues threatened to walk out if I was forced to leave the Chair, but the key to my survival came when my Tory friend, Iain Mills, bravely but firmly announced that he would not vote for my dismissal, so that the Tories would not have a majority.

Result: as the *Daily Telegraph* put it, we 'failed to agree on curbs for "fat cats"'. But we did come to some unanimous conclusions. Directors should not be given contracts lasting more than twelve months without advance approval from shareholders; stock exchange listing requirements should be given legal backing by amendment to the Companies Act; and institutions should use their votes at shareholder meetings, and not simply hand them over to directors to use at their discretion, as the board of British Gas had done.

At the end of 1995, the Government announced its decision to abolish the Department of Employment. This I attacked as a 'blazing scandal', carried out by the Tories 'in a bid to cover up the true unemployment figures'. Soon after, the Department of Employment vanished, and our Committee along with it.

FIFTEEN

Making a Living

Public life is great, but no way to earn a living. Anyway, both my parents taught me that you should serve both Britain and its Jewish community because you wish to and not for financial gain. Which is fine, provided that you can find the money somewhere else. When Myra and I married, we had little money, but we needed plenty to live off. My grandfather, Joseph, provided us with an extra chance to earn.

After the war, Joseph and Henrietta lived in a high, service flat, in Park Lane's Grosvenor House. Grandma had suffered a stroke and needed day and night nursing – and entertainment. In those days, young and high-class hookers used to sell their services to passers-by in Park Lane. Grandma's main recreation was to sit at the window with her watch and count the minutes from the moment when a passing motorist picked up a girl, until the moment when she returned to her pitch. She was paralysed down one side and could scarcely speak. When I told her that I was engaged to Myra, she pronounced slowly but clearly: 'I wish her luck!'

Joseph and Henrietta – who referred to each other fondly as 'Yoshke' and 'Etka' respectively – cared for each other deeply. Grandpa continued to fuss over Grandma, even after he himself contracted stomach cancer.

Under the taxation laws of the time, a gift given at least five years before death was received tax free. Grandpa was determined that a Trust that he had set up for the family with £5,000 for each of his grandchildren would reach them in full. He hung on to life until that five-year date had passed, and then he faded away. Grandma followed him, five years later. Mother ensured that even at the end her mother had oxygen and they tried to keep her alive. I asked Mother: 'Why?' She replied: 'While she's still living, you never know . . . she may recover. Once she's gone, that's it.' After Grandma died, Mother said to Ruth and to me: 'I feel like an orphan'. For the family, the flat in Park Lane had been a magnet and a gathering ground. With that generation gone, we were all one step nearer our own end.

What to do, then, with Grandpa's £5,000? Our very close friends, Martin and Cynthia Clore, were themselves looking for an investment. We decided to pool our resources and become equal partners in a launderette business. By combining part of the names of Cynthia and Myra, we formed a mighty company, Thiara Ltd, with a capital of £100. We believed that launderettes were one business that required little supervision and where profits were certain and risks minimal. We were wrong.

The market was controlled by the Bendix company and we consulted them for openings. We ended up with two, the first in New Addington and the second in Margate. New Addington is a reasonably accessible suburb of Croydon in South London, and our families both had holiday homes on the South Coast, not far from Margate.

I attended a training course for prospective owners, set up by Bendix. We equipped our shop and appointed staff, happily believing that the money would flow in. When the winter arrived, we discovered that locals called New Addington 'Little Siberia'. It was a great council housing estate and many of the tenants had no clothes-washing facilities of their own, but it was so cold in New Addington that they preferred to take the bus into Croydon for their laundry needs.

We knew that the bulk of the Margate trade would be in the summer and believed that we would spend enough time down there to supervise adequately. In fact, our supervision was inadequate, and so was the summer trade. From May until September, business boomed. Then the holidaymakers returned home and the business died.

We were lucky enough to sell off both businesses without much loss. And we had learned two key business lessons. My sagacious friend, Stanley (now Lord) Kalms, proclaimed the first: 'There are only three things that matter about retail business: position, position and position. Yours were wrong.' The second: you must not go into a business unless you understand it and are prepared to spend the time to keep a close eye on it.

I once asked Martin's renowned and multi-millionaire uncle, Charles Clore, how he managed to make such a success of so many diverse businesses, when obviously he could not know each one in depth. He replied: 'When you know how to run one business, you know the lot. It doesn't matter if you're selling shoes or machinery, it's the organisation that you must understand. You can employ experts to deal with the particular product. But if you don't know business, then you have no business to be in one.'

So Martin continued with his skilled work as a solicitor and Myra and Cynthia with their happy tasks as housewives. As my earnings at the bar did not cover my family expenses, I tried my hand at writing. That career began with a retail journal called *Furnishing World*. I had been telling my cousin and friend, Edmund Cohen, that I was not earning enough as a barrister. He said: 'Why don't you write about the law, then?'

'For whom?'

'I'll introduce you to the editor of the leading furniture journal.'

The editor, who rejoiced in the name of Mr Batty, agreed that I should write a weekly legal column, provided that it combined law with readability and fun. So I invented a whole cast, with nonsensical names. The owner of the mythical store was called Nitcha. The store itself: Good Furnitcha. Nitcha was always in legal trouble – sacking someone unfairly or wrongfully . . . putting the wrong price tag on a table or chair . . . dealing with landlords who wanted to turf him out . . . coping with threats of nuisance action from neighbours, disturbed by the noise of his delivery van or with claims from employees, injured at work. Other leading characters included Sir Dan Chair. The puns and jokes were appalling, but the series was a success, and it earned me some money, which I badly needed.

Just as Charles Clore could adapt his methods to shoes, socks or Selfridges, so I found that I could adapt my pieces for almost any other trade or business. For instance, I invented Mrs Henrietta Negg for *Poultry Farmer and Packer* and she and her family helped to provide food for mine for many years. Other papers wanted straight questions and answers. *Drapers Record* started receiving legal queries from BW in Edgware or Concerned Haberdasher in Hoxton – all of which were from me. Naturally, I provided them with wise answers, written in layman's language. The great Lord Denning once told an audience: 'So I asked myself the question . . . We judges always ask ourselves questions because in that way we know that we will always get swift and intelligent answers!' So I asked myself the questions – and I answered them, courteously and well. But the newspaper added a disclaimer of liability, in case anyone followed advice which turned out to be incorrect.

I wrote or adapted pieces for journals as far apart as *Waste Trade World* and *Menswear*. The fees paid by each were low, but I was happy to accept them provided that they agreed that I could adapt pieces to any journal that was not in competition with them. The total payments added up nicely.

I wrote my first piece for *Furnishing World* in longhand. My secretary typed it out for me. Then came the marvellous world of the dictating machine. I dictated an article; again, my secretary typed it; I corrected it if necessary and I kept an extra copy, to adapt for other journals. With the help of the wonderful and patient Pat Garner and Margaret Lancaster, I made a good living from these articles. But as a practising barrister, I was not allowed to advertise. So my articles all appeared under pen names. The first and most used: Ewan Mitchell – my middle name and Daniel's. Then Laurance Marne – Laura and Marion. And many others.

It was also Ewan Mitchell who wrote my first books. *Farming and the Law* – the law as it affected farmers in their everyday life and work. It was published by Farming Press in 1962. The best pages were the elegant and hilarious illustrations by Thelwell. Then came *The Businessman's Lawyer* – largely a combination of articles I had written for *Business*. Under varying titles, including *The Businessman's Lawyer and Legal Lexicon*, the book ran into many editions. Then some fifty books on business law, most of them compiled from articles in my journals. It was much later that I wrote my now happily standard work on presentational and media skills: *Janner's Complete Speechmaker*, which has reached its seventh edition. In the main, I was glad to be cloaked in anonymity and to collect the fees for the articles and the advances and royalties for the books. I wanted to make my name at the Bar and in politics.

My first literary agent had been a tall, willowy, suave and charming woman named Ursula Winant. When I decided to turn my hand to novel writing, I mapped out my first epic. Topic: Death and Politics. Title: Candidate for Death. The first chapter – a masterly innovation, revealing the murderer. Summary of the rest of the book – tracing back the extraordinary circumstances. I sent the magnum opus in embryo to the sainted Ursula. She replied: 'My dear Greville, the title is excellent!' There ended my career as a novelist and I just kept on churning out those good,

The General Election, 1931, with
Mum and Dad.

Whitechapel, canvassing for Dad.

Training for the hundred yards at Bishop's College School, 1944.

National Service with the Royal Artillery, 1946.

Myra, presented at court, 1953.

Sir Barnett (left), Elsie and Greville
Janner, Buckingham Palace, 1961.

Father's honorary doctorate, Leeds University, 1957 – with him and my sister, Ruth.

With Father and Daniel, Leicester, 1964.

With Myra and our children, 1970.

Queen's Counsel, 1971.

With President of Egypt, Anwar Sadat, 1979.

With Israel's president, Chaim Herzog.

Israel – our first grandchild, with my mother and Daniel, 1986.

Myra and me in Barbados, 1987.

Meeting Pope John Paul II in Rome, 1989.

With Nelson Mandela and Walter Sisulu, 1990.

Leicester – Election victory,
1993, with Myra and Laura.

Myra, 1994.

It's magic – Leicester, 1995.

Israel, 1996, with Shimon and Sonia Peres.

Introduced into the House of
Lords, 1997.

With the then Archbishop of
Canterbury, George Carey, 2001.

Israel Rally, Trafalgar Square, 2002.

Daniel Janner QC and family, 2002.

My sister Ruth, her late husband Philip and their family.

Our family cruise, 2003.

With the Queen and the Duke of Edinburgh at the Commonwealth Jewish Council reception, 2003.

Speaking at a House of Lords reception, 2003.

Speaking at the United Nations, 2005.

Marion, 2006.

Laura, David and children,
Portugal, 2006.

My House of Lords crest.

solid books on employment and business law and, above all, on presentational skills.

I once watched a famous author on television, explaining his technique. 'I don't write books,' he said. 'Books write themselves. I write a chapter when the spirit moves me. Then, when it moves me some more, I slot them together. Behold, the book!' Since then, I have learned from great novelists and storytellers – including Israel's Amos Oz, whose family I was privileged to join when Laura married his brother David – that they hide themselves away for weeks or even months, in spiritual purdah. But for me, the chapter-by-chapter method is the only way to create a book, in intervals between other activities. The book writes itself.

Every time a book goes to press, I am satisfied with it. When I re-read it, a year or two later, I am not satisfied. So back it goes to the drawing board, preparing for its next public exposure.

Why did I leave the Bar? Because once I was elected to Parliament, clients kept phoning my Chambers asking for me, and my Senior Clerk, Arthur Dorset, would reply: 'He's out.'

'When will he be back? When can I see him?'

'So sorry, but we don't know. He's in Parliament now . . .'

My practice lasted long enough for me to 'take Silk' – to be appointed a Queen's Counsel. In those days, if you were an MP and had not any visible criminal connections, taking Silk was rarely a problem. But making a living at the Bar most certainly was.

So in the early 1970s, when I had Myra and the children to feed, clothe and house, and not enough coming in from my writing, I was stuck. Then, as so often happens in life, chance stepped in. The director of the London Brick Company, whom I had once represented in court, asked me whether I would talk to their senior executives about changes in employment law. Suddenly, I had to become an expert in the subject about which I knew little, and an expert I duly became.

I had already learned that most experts cannot write layman's English. They cannot explain the law in a way that human beings can understand. I now discovered that the same applied to lecturers. London Brick were pleased with my effort and called me back, and there began my career as a teacher of employment law.

The following year, Paul Secher – my then assistant, who became my business partner and remains my great friend – came into our Orchard Street office. He had found a message on our voicemail from a very senior executive in a particularly distinguished professional firm. The message concluded: 'I have just been made senior partner and I'm going to have to make a lot of speeches. I have been reading your book on speechmaking and was wondering whether you would give me some training.'

With much trepidation and prodded forward by Paul, I accepted the invitation. We booked a hotel room and hired in video equipment and an operator. We were in business and for two days, we put our client through his paces. The man was clearly brilliant and incisive of mind and of speech. We immediately knew why he had been appointed to his top job. But he wore tinted spectacles and slid forward in his chair until his chin all but rested on the table. He looked like a mafia chief. So we sat him back, head up, chin up, voice up. We showed him how to structure and to make a presentation. We recorded it and played it back to him. He questioned criticism but once he accepted it, he adapted his style and his approach. Two days later, he was so pleased with his own transformation that he decided to inflict us on all his partners, two at a time.

This association was the first of many with a series of other renowned professional organisations and major public companies. For instance, we worked with MFI's formidable, ex-policeman chief, Derek Hunt. He feared and disliked cross-examination, so I put him through the mangle and after I had tied him into an impossible knot, he paused. He looked me straight in the eyes, and he quietly exploded: 'You bastard!' At which we all collapsed with laughter – and I showed him how not to let himself be twisted into a corner.

My valued friend, Peter Mandelson, now a European Commissioner, is a highly intelligent and focused political organiser. We showed him some techniques, and from then on, whenever possible, he sat in and helped with sessions with Labour colleagues. I concentrated on the skills and he on the substance and when it came to election time, we put batches of our Labour team through their paces.

Learning presentational skills used to be a secret, suspect project. You hid your inadequacy. You were expected to study economics or business management, computer skills or the fine arts of your expected area of expertise. But presentational skills? Those should come naturally. Running a presentational skills coaching operation sometimes felt a little like living off the proceeds of crime – or, worse, training the criminals. To alter your speaking style was to change your natural, God-given way of presenting yourself and your case. You were becoming a conman and we were your teachers in deceit.

True, it was fairly common knowledge that Margaret Thatcher had sought and accepted training. She was known to have spent forty-five minutes in the Chamber, with the doors locked on her trainer and herself, while she learned how to put on her spectacles and take them off, when performing at Question Time. Margaret was and is a pro. In a remarkable *Woman's Hour* interview, while she was still Prime Minister, she spotlighted a major problem for all presenters and speechmakers. Nerves.

Interviewer, Sonia Beesley: 'Prime Minister, do you suffer from nerves?'

Thatcher: 'Yes. And I don't know any Minister who doesn't. I am nervous. How long have I been Prime Minister? About seven and a half years. I'm nervous every time I get up to make a major speech. I'm nervous every time I go into the House of Commons. Every time I go in, I think, "Now look, love. Keep calm. Concentrate." And so as I get up, yes, one is desperately nervous.

'Believe you me, if I go to Wimbledon or I go to the Cup Final, I know exactly how these people feel when they walk out onto the pitch or onto the court. Nervous . . . frightened to death until the game starts and then they lose themselves in the game. And that's the only way to do it.'

Top rules for nerve control then? Concentration and expectation.

In the Commons, I often sat beside that remarkable, Oscar-winning actress, Glenda Jackson. One Tuesday, we each had a question to ask the Prime Minister. 'Scared?' I enquired, gently. 'Of course,' she replied.

'Were you scared before you went on stage?'

'The only time I was worried,' she replied, 'was when I was not scared.'

Sebastian (now Lord) Coe was a great international track star and remains a wise and generous friend. I asked him: 'Before a race, were you nervous?'

'Yes. Certainly.'

'So what did you do about it?'

'My father was a farmer and he taught me that what matters is to get the hay in the barn. You harvest the hay, bale the hay and get it into the barn and then you can relax for the winter. And so it is with running. If you are properly trained and fit and prepared, then you've got the hay in the barn and you can relax.'

Concentration, expectation and preparation. Plus relaxation, and you are ready for the winter.

Happily, if gradually, presentational skills training has become accepted as a necessity, not as a form of trickery. It should teach you to make the most and the best of your own personality and talent and style. Both message and messenger remain intact but the messenger should come over with authority, charm and dignity while the message loses nothing in the process.

It was Peter Mandelson who paid the most joyful and kindly tribute to my presentational skills training. He spoke at my seventieth birthday party, in the Palace of Westminster. 'There was only one secret weapon in our Labour Party's General Election campaign. And it is time for me to unveil – Greville! He played an extraordinary role.

'I unleashed Greville on the Shadow Cabinet. My God! The first one staggered out of the room. I'd gone off to do some work. I thought I could safely leave him in Greville's hands, but the chap came out pale, drawn, mumbling . . .

'Greville sits in front of his victim and gets two pieces of card. On one piece he writes "SLOW" and he puts it behind one of the lenses of his spectacles and up against his forehead. He then gets another piece of paper and he writes "DOWN" and puts it behind the other lens. So there you have Greville, with his glasses and two bits of paper behind the lenses, announcing: SLOW DOWN.

'"Right, we'll start again . . ." Greville peers across. His victim is terrified and starts . . . speaking . . . slowly . . . Can you imagine?

'So we send them all off with a video tape of their performance. And that chap – every time I hear him on the radio – I can only think of one thing: Greville sitting across the table with SLOW DOWN behind his lenses. And do you know – it worked!'

In 1986, Leslie Benson joined Paul and me. JS Associates became JSB – that is: Janner, Secher, Benson. Paul is thoughtful, cautious and capable:

a lawyer by training and by instinct. Leslie is an energetic entrepreneur. The two complement each other – and both are the most reliable, honest and hard-working partners that anyone could hope for.

Together, we built the business. Then, in 1997, I sold to them the bulk of my majority holding and they have continued to build what was and is rightfully regarded as a reliable, well-run and honest business. They honour their obligations, legal and moral – not least to me. I am proud of them. In 2003, they bought the remainder of my shares – and I retired from JSB.

Parliament . . . the law . . . speechmaking and presentation . . . training and teaching and translating complex concepts into layman's language. . . . Communicating with people at every level. Each strand was weaving into a life of leadership with a firm and contented home and family base; I was gradually becoming equipped to fight the battles which were and remain at the core of my beliefs.

Cyril Stein was the boss of Ladbroke's, one of Britain's top gaming companies. He was also an activist, leader and funder of the Campaign for the Release of Jews in the Soviet Union – a preoccupation which I shared with him (Chapter 22). Early in 1986, I received an invitation to come to see him at the Ladbroke's office, and I presumed that he wanted to discuss our shared concern. Instead, and totally to my surprise, he invited me to join Ladbroke's board, as a non-executive director.

'That's very kind of you. But why me?' I asked, completely taken aback.

'Because you have three qualities that are vital for non-executive directors – integrity, intelligence and independence of mind.'

'Thank you. But I've no experience of the running of any vast business.'

'You work in one – Parliament. Anyway, we've enough people on our board who know how to run a company. Your contribution will be different.'

Indeed. I would be the only lawyer; the only politician; and the only specialist in training and in the law on health and safety.

At that time, I was involved in the anti-apartheid movement. 'Do you do business with South Africa?' I asked. 'No,' he replied. 'We do not.' 'Or in competition with the public sector?' 'No.' Good. I could not have served on the board of a company which did either.

I asked him what the time commitment would be and he told me: 'There's about ten board meetings a year. But there'll be some special meetings and events in between.'

The pay? More than my total parliamentary salary and no expenses involved. I requested and he readily agreed to give me time to think it over.

Back in the Commons, I approached my Chief Whip, Michael Cocks, and told him of the offer and asked him whether it would be acceptable for a Labour MP to be on the board of one of the country's top companies? 'What do you think?' I asked.

Michael smiled at me. 'Think?' he said. 'There's nothing to think about. Grab it, my boy, before they change their mind! It's about time some of our people knew what was going on in major companies.'

I told Mother. She reminded me of the travails that Cyril and Ladbroke's had both gone through, when they had lost their casino licences. 'Just make sure that they are respectable,' she said. 'They are not just getting your good brain, but also your good name.'

I ran it by Myra and she told me that she thought I should be certified if I did not agree. And was it not especially remarkable of Cyril to invite me onto his board, when I was on the Left in both British and Jewish politics and he was well on the Right in both?

So I sought a meeting with the redoubtable Sir Kenneth Cork, former Lord Mayor of London and an accountant with an unassailable good name and, above all, a long-term non-executive Ladbroke's director. We hit it off at once, and I decided that, with his careful eye on the company, it was and would remain entirely respectable. This I confirmed with some respected neutral business friends. In spite of Mother's doubts and reservations, I did 'grab it'. I accepted, with no formal contract, just a brief letter from Cyril, welcoming me to the Board; confirming my salary; and saying that I should contact him whenever I wished.

At that time, gaming apart, Ladbroke's had a small, three-star hotel operation. Cyril promised to introduce me to both sides of the business and I soon spent two days with him, visiting hotels and betting shops. He was a hands-on Chairman and Chief Executive, with an eye for detail. Walking around one hotel, I asked Cyril how he would judge whether or not it was well managed. 'Look for three things,' he replied. 'First: how you are received when you arrive. Does the doorkeeper smile and welcome you back? Do the people at the reception desk smile and welcome you? Second: Is the place clean?' He pointed to dirt in corners. 'Third – go to the staff toilets and staff canteen. If they are spotlessly clean, then you can relax. If either is scruffy or dirty, you've got a problem.'

We all received papers and documents, several days before board meetings. We were expected to read and to absorb them. To absorb, you must understand. To understand, you must grasp the terminology. At the meetings themselves, they talked in millions and in words that were a foreign language to me. So I made sure that I sat beside Keith Edelman, one of the youngest and brightest of our colleagues. He quietly and patiently translated for me.

The rest of the team were all clever and good-natured and when I carried out Cyril's wishes and asked questions, they never laughed at me, even though the answers to the questions must have often been patently obvious to them.

Cyril himself was the absolute model of courtesy. When I asked a question, he thanked me and answered it, and when I spoke to him privately afterwards, he thanked me for bringing reality into the boardroom. He told me that the trouble with boards of major companies is that they tend to see everything from their own financial angle and not necessarily as their decisions would be viewed by the outside world. We always had lunch at the end of our meetings and then Cyril himself would escort me out.

Triumphs during my time with the company? The purchase of Texas Homecare, which Keith Edelman then ran. Above all, the acquisition of Hilton International, achieved at the end of long and stressful negotiations and confirmed at a board meeting which extended far into a vivid and unforgettable night.

Cyril commanded loyalty, from people as diverse as the soft-spoken Peter George, who succeeded him as Chief Executive, and from Kenneth Cork. His main failure: to delegate and motivate some of the outstanding people who worked with him and who left us too soon. John Jarvis – hotelier; Keith Edelman – Mothercare and now, Chief Executive of Arsenal Football Club; and David Michels – who rescued the Stakis Hotel Group and then returned to Ladbroke's to run the Hilton Hotels and then to become Chief Executive, in place of Peter George.

In 1995, Cyril himself was forced out and I suspected that my time to go would soon arrive. John Jackson became Chairman. He was good-natured and genial, clever and an excellent manager of people, a lawyer and an industrialist. He told me that I should serve another twelve months and then make way for new blood. I was sorry to go. It was a privilege to serve that great company and under Cyril Stein's leadership and with a group of such remarkable colleagues. I learned and earned much and greatly enjoyed an important chapter in my life.

One morning, early in 1973, I was telephoned by David Kessler. He was Chairman of the *Jewish Chronicle* (JC), the prime newspaper of the British Jewish community, and he and his family were its majority shareholders. He would like to meet me as soon as possible. That afternoon, I joined him for tea in his office. 'How would you like to join our board?' he enquired. 'We'd like some bright, new life and a touch of the political.'

'A Labour MP?' I queried.

'Why not?' he replied. 'We've all got our faults, haven't we?'

He told me that the board met about once every month, over lunch, in his office. The pay was modest, but the directors sat at one centre of our communal life and it was immensely interesting. 'Yes, please,' I replied, with a broad smile and without hesitation. 'I am very honoured.'

The board meetings were fascinating. There were inside stories – could or should they be put on the outside? Communal rivalries and internal battles – would it be appropriate, fair or newsworthy, to publish? Who was threatening to sue the JC and for what and why? And, of course, accounts and business concerns.

I learned much and was sorry when, in 1979, shortly after I was elected President of the Board of Deputies, our able editor, Geoffrey Paul, told me that I should resign from my JC position. In his view, there were bound to be conflicts of interest. The President of the Board of Deputies is the elected leader of our community and the JC, as the voice of British Jewry, must be free to attack him, as and when it wishes. Of course, I did as he asked. I had learned much, enjoyed myself greatly and was sorry to go.

So, one way or another, and all my adult life, I have succeeded in earning my living. But the main source of Myra's and my security during her last years and my survival until now was Myra's horrendous extravagance in the size of her required family home. We lived for over twenty-one years in our large and splendid Hampstead Garden Suburb house and by the time we decided to move to our final flat, we had built up mighty debts. By then, though, property prices had soared and from the proceeds of the sale of our detached and glorious home, I was able to pay off all our debts and have enough left over to buy the freehold of a flat with a garden and a view, not far away. That's what we Jews call '*mazel*' – good luck.*

* For a great example of her methods, see Chapter 29.

SIXTEEN

From Commons to Lords

In June 1992, I fought my last election. I was defending a majority of 1,201. To my delight, I won by 3,978. I was back at work.

Two years later, Myra was diagnosed with cancer and I soon decided to leave the Commons. Her surgeon, Adam Lewis, had said to us: 'I am virtually certain that I have got rid of it – all of it.' We hung onto that phrase like a lifebelt in a stormy sea. We clutched it, repeated it, to ourselves and to each other. I decided to retire primarily because we believed that Myra would recover fully from her mighty operation and return to normal life. So let's enjoy what's left of it.

Second reason: I had always looked forward to my constituency 'surgeries'. I took pride and pleasure in the service I gave to my constituents and regarded that service, both for individuals and for the City of Leicester, as a central pillar of my political life. After a quarter of a century, I was beginning to tire of the work. When I realised that I was hoping there would be very few people at a surgery and not, as I had always wanted, a large crowd, I knew that the time had come to move on. I might be appointed a peer. That would be splendid, but anyway, I had to leave the Commons.

When I told Myra, she said: 'That's your decision, darling. As for the Lords, you can try for it but don't count on it. But whatever happens, you've got to be out of *this* house by half past eight in the morning!' Her priority was to see that our house was tidied and that I would not be in the way during that crucial process.

I consulted my friend, Peter Mandelson. I told him that I did not want to leave politics but that after a quarter of a century as an MP and with the dreadful possibility of a recurrence of Myra's illness hovering over us, I would like to go 'upstairs', to the Lords.

'You'll have to talk to Tony,' he said. 'I'll ask him.' He did.

A week later, I was walking towards the door of Tony Blair's office at the Commons when Peter emerged. 'What have you been up to?' I asked him.

'I've just been reminding Tony of the reason for your visit,' he smiled. I thanked him. He is not only a brilliant man but the most kind and thoughtful of friends.

I knocked and entered. Tony was sitting in his shirtsleeves, on the couch. 'How's Myra?' he asked.

'Thank God, she seems to have recovered.'

'She's had a terrible time, hasn't she?'

'Yes. She certainly has, and she sends you her love.'

'Please give her mine. I'm so glad that she's feeling better. Now, I understand you want to go to the Lords.'

'Yes please.'

Tony smiled. 'I shall do my best to get you there,' he said. 'It's not just that I'm fond of you, which I am. It's not just that you've helped me a lot, which you have. It's because you deserve it. But I can't give any guarantees. If we win the election, there should not be a problem.'

I thanked him. We chatted about Cherie and the children and the election and his plans and hopes and prospects. As I left, Tony sent his love to Myra. 'Tell her that I'll do all I can,' he said. When I returned home, I told Myra just that. 'Wonderful,' she said. 'But don't count on it.'

I travelled up to Leicester and told my friends, Janet Setchfield, George Billington and Ray and Betty Flint, that I had decided to retire from the Commons. I had worked with them for over a quarter of a century, but they all understood. Each in turn said: 'How about the House of Lords?' I replied. 'Who knows? That would be wonderful.' 'Myra would love it,' each said. 'You both deserve it.'

One evening in early December 1996, when Myra was literally dying, one of my Whips phoned me. 'The 10 o'clock vote tonight is terribly important. We think that it will be very close. There could be one vote in it. Please will you come into the House for us?' I told Myra. 'Go,' she said. 'I'll be fine. But come back as soon as you can.'

I arrived at the Commons in time to vote. We lost by a sizeable margin and it was clear that I should not have left Myra. I was nobbled by a Whip in the Lobby. 'Hang on a bit, please. We expect there'll be another vote, probably in about twenty minutes.'

'No, I won't,' I replied. 'You know my wife is desperately ill . . .' I stormed away and passed my Conservative 'pair', John Marshall.

'How's Myra?' he asked.

'Terrible,' I replied.

'You don't look too good yourself,' John responded.

'I am furious,' I replied. I told him that the Whips had ordered me to stay on but I was not going to.

'You go, and give Myra my love,' said John. 'If there are any more votes, I'll pair with you. I shall not vote and I shall tell them why.' I have never forgotten his kindness.

Then the battle for the Leicester West succession began. Eventually, Patricia Hewitt was selected as my successor and my old colleague and valued friend, Willie Bach, whom she had narrowly defeated, was later elevated to the House of Lords and became for some years an important minister. I was delighted to join Roy Hattersley in introducing him into the House, when he took the oath.

So I finished my work in Leicester. During the General Election, I did precisely what both Patricia and I thought would be best for her – keeping away until election eve, so that she would establish her own name and position, which she did with great success. For over fifty years, 'Janner' and 'Labour' had been synonymous in our area. Now the curtain had come down and our family had left the Leicester stage.

Myra died in December 1996 (Chapter 29). Labour won the national election in May 1997. It was a great victory for Labour. My daughter Marion joined me, first at a reception at the BBC and then for the mighty Labour bash at the Royal Festival Hall. We watched on television as the tower of Tory seats collapsed. We cheered and we rejoiced. Then I paused to share in what I knew would be a huge upset for many of my defeated Conservative friends – people with whom I had shared common ground and many who had supported me, in tough and in good times alike, such as Michael Latham, Ivan Lawrence, John Marshall, Michael Portillo and David Sumberg. I knew how anguished those friends would be. What would they now do? There's a classic Westminster saying: 'There is nothing as ex as an ex-MP.'

Outside and behind the barricades we went, to welcome Tony and Cherie, helicoptering down from the North. Tony made his gloriously happy and triumphant speech and Marion and I cheered and clapped and laughed. Then the great pair descended from the rostrum and walked by the crowds behind the barriers, shaking hands and waving. They spotted us. They came straight over. Cherie put her arms around me and said: 'Oh, how I wish Myra were here tonight.' I wanted to cry. I embraced them both and wished them all the luck and health and success in the world.

As for my elevation to the Lords, all was silent. There were rumours about people, but no sound about me. What to do? I had a word with Peter Mandelson, who said he would keep an eye on it, and one day I had an appointment with my old friend and the new Chancellor of the Exchequer, Gordon Brown. The subject: the need for him to authorise the payment from the Exchequer of funds for the restitution of monies confiscated by the Custodian of Enemy Property from victims of the Nazis (Chapter 20). Gordon greeted me warmly. 'At last we're in office. I suppose you'll be going to the Lords?'

'I hope so,' I said, 'but who knows?'

'Hasn't Tony said that he's going to do it?' asked Gordon. I stayed silent.

'I'll have a word with him about it,' said Gordon.

I thanked him but said that I would not like Tony to think that I was canvassing for the job. He replied with a knowing look. 'I have a special relationship with Tony and can talk to him about anything.' So much for the constant and continuing allegations of permanent ill-will between Tony and Gordon. I thanked him – for that and for his assurance that, within practical limits, he would help with the cause of the survivors of the Nazi brutalities.

Soon after, I appeared on the Labour Government's first list of new peers. To say that I was and remain eternally grateful is a massive understatement. After Myra's death, I was lonely in our home. The Lords provided me with a new and warm refuge and a base for my political and public life.

So I became a Lord but my Myra did not live to become a Lady. Alas! Some call the House of Lords 'life after death'. For me it has been just that. A new political life, after Myra's death.

My first job – to choose an appropriate name. I attended at the office of Garter King of Arms, or 'Garter' as peers refer to him. 'Well, by what name do you wish to be known?' he asked me.

'How about "Lord Janner"?' I asked.

'Sorry,' he replied. 'That was your father's name. You must be Lord Janner of . . .'

'All right, Garter,' I replied, cheekily. 'I will be "Lord Janner of . . ."'

'No, no, no,' said Garter, shaking his head. 'You must be Lord Janner of somewhere . . .'

'Very well,' I replied. 'Then I will be "Lord Janner of Somewhere".'

Garter looked at me and shook his head. 'You know perfectly well what I mean,' he said. 'You must choose a place.'

I did. I chose Braunstone, which was the most underprivileged area and estate in my constituency, where I had spent the most time with those who needed help the most.

Garter nodded. 'Lord Janner of Braunstone, it will be,' he said, smiling. It is a name which I remain proud to bear.

On 30 October 1997, my brother-in-law, Philip Morris, and my respected friend and founder chairman of the Parliamentary War Crimes Group, Merlyn Rees, led me into the Chamber. At that time, we still carried the old-fashioned, tricorn black hats, which we doffed in unison on signals from Garter. I took the oath and emerged from the Chamber into the joyful and excited arms of my family. Only Myra was missing and painfully missed.

Since then, the House of Lords has been my second home. I was immensely lonely, on my own in our Hampstead flat. In the Lords, I found good company, warm friendships and a place where family and friends, from home and abroad, enjoy being entertained. Politically, it became the centre of my work. With my communal and personal office just ten minutes' walk away, alongside the Strutton Ground market, the Lords brought me back into the Palace of Westminster, for which I was and remain deeply grateful.

I am often asked whether I miss the Commons and my constituency. Yes, it was more fun attending Prime Minister's Questions in the Commons Chamber than watching it from the Gallery. But otherwise, no. Each day that I arrive, I appreciate my good fortune, not least the absence of that permanent cloud of electoral uncertainty that hangs over MPs. Yes, I miss my Leicester colleagues, and I much enjoyed my constituency work, but after twenty-seven years of service in 'the other place', I look back with pleasure and forward with deep gratitude for my good fortune. Following the wise advice of Shimon Peres, in this life you must always look forward, focus on the future, look where you are going and remember where you have been.

Inside the Lords, I continue my active support for the Labour Party, and use parliamentary procedures and access for my key causes. These continue to range from human rights to road safety, from communal relations to coping with crime and with smoking. Overseas issues – the Middle East and the Commonwealth, of course, and whatever else is topical.

It is my work overseas that has benefited most from my place in the Lords. Yes, it is useful for my foreign affairs battles, but more important is the remarkable access which being a peer gives us, especially abroad. We are 'peerless' because we are peers. The title opens the doors of parliaments and of palaces. It is a vast honour to serve in the House of Lords, and one that I deeply cherish and appreciate.

When I drive into the Lords at the start of a working day, I often think of when my mother was in hospital, fighting her terminal illness. One day, she said to me: 'I want a favour. Please will you get me into your car and drive me to Parliament?' She struggled into the passenger seat and we drove to Westminster. In through Black Rod's garden, along the internal road and out through the Commons exit and New Palace Yard. Mother was silent until, as we approached the exit, she said quietly: 'I love this place. It has been my second home. I only wish I could have been here in my own right . . .' – to which she did not add, 'and not only as your father's driver, secretary and PA.' I am so proud and lucky that the House of Lords has become a home for me, in my own right.

It was in the summer of 1997 that I joined Daniel and Caroline and their children at Florida's Disneyworld. One evening, we were sitting by the road, waiting for the evening parade, and we chatted with an American family alongside us. 'Where are you from?' I asked. 'Utah,' the father replied.

'Are you Mormons?' I enquired.

'What's a Mormon?' six-year-old Phoebe interjected.

'We believe in the Lord . . . we love the Lord . . . we pray to the Lord . . .' the man replied.

'Oh,' Phoebe exclaimed. 'That's interesting. My grandpa is a lord!'

The man looked shocked at this blasphemy but smiled wanly when we explained. The Lord Janner and his family were doubled up with mirth. Praise the Lord!

SEVENTEEN

Honours and the Royals

Many of my parliamentary colleagues regard the honours system as the epitome of outdated snobbery. Knights and Lords . . . Members, Officers and Commanders of the Order of the British Empire – an Empire which, of course, does not exist . . . marks of chivalry, long dead. All these, they say, should go. I see their point of view, but I do not agree with it. It gives huge pleasure to good citizens, most of whom have made significant contributions to our decent society, and the honours impose no financial cost on the nation. They crown the lives of servants of others, like Myra's Uncle and Aunt, Chief Rabbi Israel Brodie, and his wife, Fanny (Chapter 8).

Hereditary titles are different. As an ungenerous colleague put it when most of the hereditaries lost their voting rights: 'Why should they have parliamentary privileges because one of their ancestors slept with King Charles the First?' I voted for the removal of most hereditaries from the Lords. It was unreasonable and wrong that, after British voters had, by a huge majority, elected a Labour Government, Tories in the Lords could veto Commons legislation. That said, I was ashamed at the way that the hereditaries were cleared out. Just a letter from the Leader of the House, asking them to remove their goods and chattels. Even my brother-in-law, Philip, was wounded. True, he seldom attended, especially since he had contracted a disabling illness, but a word of kindly appreciation would have cost nothing.

How, then, can I as an opponent of hereditary titles and honours support the continuation of our monarchy? The answer is simple – because it works well and has, in the main, done so over centuries. We are lucky that Queen Elizabeth is a professional of the very highest order. Over many years, I have often watched her at work and especially enjoyed her unexpectedly acute sense of humour.

My first contacts with the Queen were both at a distance and formal. Backbench MPs are invited to Royal Garden Parties at Buckingham Palace, so Myra and I enjoyed our annual stroll around the great lawns, celebrity spotting and sipping iced coffee. We caught glimpses of the Queen, the Duke of Edinburgh and other members of the Royal Family, as they passed through lines of smiling, adoring and hand-shaking guests, many of them from far-off lands in exotic costumes, and others in glorious hats and gowns from local couturiers.

In July 1981, I led a group of leaders of our British Jewish community to Buckingham Palace, to present a Loyal Address to Her Majesty on the forthcoming marriage of Prince Charles. I expressed our community's good wishes to the Prince and to Lady Diana Spencer for a joyful future. None of us could foresee the grim sadness to come for that fine, delightful and bright but tragically incompatible young couple.

On my birthday, 11 July 1989, Myra and I were joined by Marion and a friend of hers for a Buckingham Palace Garden Party. That friend was the star of the party – Alice Ashdown, aged almost 99, and sitting cosily in a wheelchair. Alice had been in long-term psychiatric hospitals for at least 80 years. No one knew why. Maybe she was as deaf then as she was when old, so that they 'put her away' because they thought that she was 'mental'. Marion's job was to take people like Alice out of institutions and rehabilitate them into the community. A visit to the Royal Garden Party was part of that difficult process.

About a week before, Marion had asked me whether I could arrange for Alice to be introduced to the Queen. A ridiculous idea, of course, but what the hell. I telephoned the Lord Chamberlain's Office and spoke to an official. Well, it was rather late and a bit unusual, wasn't it? But why not wheel Alice along to the left-hand lane, where the Queen would be coming. People would let the wheelchair through to the front and Alice could at least see Her Majesty. What's more, the official would have a word with the boys on duty and perhaps I could fix something when I got there.

On the 11th, at 3.30 p.m. sharp, Alice arrived with Marion by car at the House of Commons, Members' Entrance, her wheelchair in the boot. She wore a tasteful flowered frock and a floppy hat. So off we drove to the Palace, Marion and Alice, Myra and me. Out with the wheelchair at the entrance and into the courtyard, where two guardsmen wheeled Alice as far as the lawn, then across to the Queen's lane.

The official was right. The crowd parted to allow Alice through, but by then I had learned the sad truth. Alice would not see the Queen. Why? Because even though Alice was wearing very thick spectacles, she could only make out shapes. We would somehow have to bring the Queen to her.

By good fortune, I found myself standing next to my close and respected friend, David (now Lord) Hunt, then a Tory Whip. 'What are you up to, Greville?' he asked.

'I've been told that I should speak to one of you lot and ask whether you would be kind enough to present Alice to the Queen.'

'I can't do that. But I'll tell you what, I'll introduce you to that courtier up there. That burly chap, with the paper in his hand at the top of the steps. He not only decides whom to introduce, but actually does the introducing.' So we climbed the steps to that mighty man in the grey morning coat. He listened courteously. 'Tell me, Mr Janner,' he said. 'What is exceptional about this lady?'

'Absolutely nothing,' I replied. 'She is nearly ninety-nine years old. She has been in a home for about eighty years. She has never had a really happy day, and this is the greatest occasion in her life. But otherwise, she is a very ordinary citizen.'

'Around here, Mr Janner,' said the courtier, 'she is exceptional. I will have her presented to the Queen. Please go down into the lane and you will get instructions.'

Not believing our good fortune, down I went. Marion chortled with delight. She put her mouth beside Alice's ear and cried out: 'Alice. You'll be meeting the Queen.'

'Oh, good!' said Alice.

One of the retinue introduced us to Marie Goossens, the harpist, and her family. She was to be presented first. 'Then you, Mr Janner. And then you'll introduce your daughter and Alice.'

Within moments, Her Majesty arrived, cool in a dress of mauve. 'Alice!' Marion shouted into the ancient ear. 'The Queen's coming!' The crowd laughed.

In due course, I was presented. 'Greville Janner, Your Majesty. Member of Parliament for Leicester West.' I bowed, turned and introduced Marion to the Queen. 'And this is Alice Ashdown, Your Majesty. Next week, she'll be ninety-nine.'

The Queen smiled and inclined her head and held out her gloved hand to Alice. Marion put Alice's hand into it and yelled in her ear: 'Alice! You're shaking hands with the Queen!'

'Oh, good!' said Alice. 'Hello, Queen.'

The Queen made polite conversation. 'Where does Miss Ashdown live?' she asked. Marion told her.

'I suppose that she'll be going back home from here. I wonder what she'll say.'

'She'll say she's been at Buckingham Palace meeting the Queen, Your Majesty,' Marion replied. 'And everyone where she lives will tell her that she's gone out of her mind!'

By this time, the crowd was enchanted, listening and laughing attentively. Her Majesty nodded. We had a brief discussion about wheelchair access to the Palace and the fact that its provision is eventually, at least, a form of enlightened self-interest. Then Her Majesty said goodbye to Alice. Marion yelled in Alice's ear: 'The Queen's leaving, Alice!'

'Oh, I am sorry,' said Alice. 'Goodbye, Queen.'

'Goodbye,' said Her Majesty. And she was gone. The crowd grinned and clapped.

For the next hour, we wheeled Alice around the grounds. She was the sensation of the day. We introduced her to a pair of nuns, because she was a fervent Catholic; to police chiefs and to magistrates; to Members of Parliament and to peers. 'Very nice,' said Alice. 'I am so happy.'

We passed the bands and strolled across the lawns and we made our way out. Marion asked: 'Would you like to go through the Palace, Alice?'

'Yes, I would.' So we asked the guardsmen at the foot of the steps to carry her up in her wheelchair.

'Sorry, sir,' they said. 'No wheelchairs allowed in the Palace.'

'Do you want to walk, Alice?' asked Marion.

'Yes. I want to see the Palace.'

So Myra wheeled the chair around to the side of the Palace stairs and left it there. Marion and I each took one of Alice's arms. Up the steps, with Marion providing a running commentary which was certainly overheard by most of the remaining five thousand guests.

'We're going up the steps . . . There's two more steps to go, Alice . . . Now we're in the Palace. It's a huge room. Lots of people. Porcelain in showcases on the walls. The ceiling is gold and scarlet . . . It's very big and wonderful, Alice.'

'Oh, good. I am happy.'

Then down the central steps. 'That's right, Alice. Down the first step. Now another. Now another.' Then came the most hilarious moment of the day. Marion lost her footing and started falling. 'Shit!' she cried out as she grabbed Alice for support. The crowd around us collapsed with laughter and cheered us down the remaining steps. I found the wheelchair at the side of the Palace and wheeled it back for Alice. And while the great, the famous and the wealthy, the mighty and the majestic moved off in their limousines, Marion wheeled Alice out of the Palace. No one was happier or prouder that day than we were.

On another occasion, the Queen and Prince Philip were guests of the Board of Deputies at a reception, which I hosted as its President, at St James's Palace. I thanked them for honouring us and apologised for the crush. I hope Her Majesty did not mind the pressure from people, so anxious to get a glimpse of her. 'Are these occasions a great strain?' I asked.

'Not at all, Mr Janner,' the Queen smiled. 'You see, I so seldom have to introduce myself!'

I then asked the Queen what it felt like to wear the Royal Crown of State when she opened Parliament. She replied: 'Well, how would you like to walk and then to stand and read in public, with the equivalent of a seven-pound salmon on your head?' For me, it would have been seven pounds of books – for Myra, the same weight in food – but for those who fish, weight is gauged by what hangs at the end of a rod.

In November 1997, I represented the Commonwealth Jewish Council, a non-governmental organisation (NGO), at a Commonwealth Heads of Government Meeting (CHOGM), in Edinburgh. The Queen hosted a reception at Holyrood House. When I was presented to Her Majesty, I said: 'Ma'am, I have two matters for which I would like to thank you.'

She inclined her head. 'Oh, yes?'

'The first is that when you recently visited India, you were kind enough to go to the ancient synagogue in Cochin.'

'Oh, it was fascinating.'

'Second, Ma'am – not long ago, I received a letter from Prime Minister Tony Blair. He said that he was minded to appoint me as a life peer, should Your Majesty approve. Your Majesty did approve, and I am very grateful.'

Without hesitation, the Queen smiled and replied: 'Oh, Lord Janner – nowadays, one has not got much option, has one!'

We all laughed and the guests around us chortled with delight as Her Majesty moved on, serene and smiling, to greet Nelson Mandela and a group of other leaders of the new South Africa.

In 1986, King Juan Carlos of Spain paid a state visit to Britain and Myra and I were invited to the reception in his honour at the Spanish Embassy. There we met Princess Diana, who was looking especially glamorous but who, press gossip claimed, was having unhappy rows with her mother-in-law, the Queen. She asked Myra where she came from.

'Australia, Ma'am,' Myra replied.

'Oh,' said the Princess, nodding. 'Do you have family who are still there?'

'Yes,' said Myra. 'My mother still lives in Melbourne.'

Princess Diana looked at me and smiled. 'Oh, lucky you,' she said.

We all laughed. Obviously, mother-in-law relations at Buckingham Palace were indeed not at their best, but I did not share her disdain for either hers or mine.

PART FOUR

The Jewish World

EIGHTEEN

Communal Leadership

The ill-informed refer to 'the Jews' as if we were a homogeneous entity. We most certainly are not. Religiously, politically and in almost every other way, we are a hugely varied family. There are those of us, for instance, who have no relationship with our community in life but who still wish to join us in death in a Jewish cemetery. Then there are people born of Jewish mothers but not of Jewish fathers, whom Jewish laws regard as part of our community. They may or may not identify, wholly or at all. At the other end of our communal scale are those whose lives are not far removed from their ancestors in the ghettos of Europe – in custom, in tradition and most visibly, in dress.

All my life, I have belonged to the United Synagogue, which is in the centre of our organised, religious bodies. So has my son, Daniel, and his family. For over half a century, I belonged to a synagogue near to my Hampstead home, to which I paid a substantial annual membership fee. In 2004, I realised that I very seldom attended my synagogue. Sometimes, I would go with Daniel and his family to their place of worship and sometimes with my rabbi daughter Laura to hers. So I sent my synagogue my annual subscription, together with a letter of resignation explaining why this would be my last year of membership. I received a reply, not from the synagogue, but from an administrator at the cemetery where Myra is buried in our double grave. The writer informed me that if I did not retain my membership in the United Synagogue, they would not be able to bury me in their cemetery. I was incredulous, and wrote a brief letter to my friend, Peter Sheldon, then President of that organisation. If I am not allowed to be buried in the grave alongside Myra, I enquired, who would they propose to put beside my wonderful wife?

Peter replied immediately and with horror. Of course, he did not know of the system and would change it. Of course, there would never be a question of keeping me from joining Myra, although hopefully not too soon. He then arranged for me to pay a 'non-attending subscription' to the synagogue which would be used for the upkeep of our still joint grave. That will be a considerable relief to Myra, if her spirit knows the compassionate kindness of the United Synagogue, and certainly it was to me.

At the end of the argumentative day, there are three prime leadership realities in our Jewish community. First, the Board of Deputies; second, the Chief Rabbi and his religious cohorts; and third, people like myself are who regarded and treated as voices for our communal concerns.

Whether or not the Board is under able and respected leadership as it is at present, with Henry Grunwald QC at its head, it is always regarded by the government and the media as the official, lay voice of our community. Or, to use the language of our enemies, it is the modern British equivalent to the medieval, non-existent Elders of Zion.

I have been close to a series of Chief Rabbis. Israel Brodie, Myra's uncle; Lord Jakobovits; and now Sir Jonathan Sacks. The Chief Rabbi's is not an easy job. But happily, we have been blessed with fine men to do it.

My communal involvement, and voice as a non-religious communal leader, is also not easy. One of my family described it as 'an inherited disease'. But it is a lifetime's habit and I believe that because of my roots of service outside the community, especially in Leicester and in Parliament, I can often act as a bridge in both political and religious circles.

Any leader of Britain's Jewish community must face a series of realities, some excellent, some not. As a start, we should be proud of the contribution that we are able to make to the life of the United Kingdom, not least through our own origins, backgrounds and faith. Whether in professions such as mine – the law or politics – or in science or the arts, commerce or industry, we can be proud of the contribution of our Jewish community. Above all, though, most British Jews are fully, positively and constructively integrated into the life of our country. Yes, we take a pride and an interest in Israel, the Jewish State. Yes, we focus especially on issues that caused the obliteration of so many of our families in Europe, not least on the growth of racism, whether aimed at Jews or other British minorities. And we communally shuddered at offensive comments made to a Jewish journalist by London's mayor, Ken Livingstone. I had long enjoyed a happy relationship with the mayor, but when I wrote a personal letter to him suggesting that he apologise for remarks that had so deeply offended our Jewish community, sadly I received no reply.

That said, most British Jews enjoy their working and leisure lives, never having to endure an anti-Semitic word against them. And what right have I to complain of attacks, with my proud Jewish head high above the political parapet? My parents taught me that we are deeply privileged and fortunate to live, to work and to serve in Britain. They were right – and long may they so remain. One mighty bulwark for our communal safety is the Community Security Trust (CST). It provides remarkable and unique security to our Jewish community and is trusted by all who know it, most crucially by the police and other authorities. In tough and dangerous times, it is crucial to our safety and a model of its kind.

Unfortunately, our UK Jewish community is under threat – from the political extremes of both Far Left and Right . . . from the National Front and other successors to Hitler's and Mosley's Nazis . . . and from Islamist extremists. Of course, in this world of suicide bombers, there is no guarantee of safety for anyone, least of all for politicians like me. Indeed, a very senior police officer told me that the three most dangerous places in this land are the Palace of Westminster, Buckingham Palace and Canary Wharf. CST is our communal barrier against extremist terror and anti-Semitism.

CST provides security at hundreds of synagogues and Jewish schools across the country and at major events, like the great rally to support the people of Israel in Trafalgar Square, in June 2002, under our slogan: 'Yes to peace – No to terror'. I was proud to give a rousing kick-off from the great plinth, and extremely grateful that the CST and the police worked together to provide for our safety and security and to keep the small group of shouting anti-Israel demonstrators at a safe distance from our peaceful event. More constant, though, are the less obvious threats and dangers to our schools and our synagogues, to our organisations and our institutions, in their daily work. With its full-time professional staff and highly trained volunteers, the CST provides a remarkable bulwark for our community. Its key to success is its respect for the law and for those whose job is law enforcement.

The creator, guide and leader of the CST is an extraordinary man, Gerald Ronson. A lifetime fighter against Fascism, he created the mighty Heron business, moving from cars and petrol stations to properties and developments. He has built a fine CST team, many of whom have worked with him for many years and become his close friends.

Ronson's great fortune has long been his wife, the beautiful, statuesque and loyal Gail. In 2004, she was rewarded for her work for the Covent Garden Opera House and Jewish Care. She is now Dame Gail. Gerald has the respect of the business world and of our Jewish community, and has continued to build up both the CST and its relationship with the Metropolitan and other police forces.

My most joyful memory of the Ronsons came when Gail invited me to join a group of friends for an evening of opera at Covent Garden. Among the guests were Scotland Yard's then Chief Commissioner, Sir John (now Lord) Stevens and his wife.

At the end of the performance, which Gerald endured with some impatience but the rest of us greatly enjoyed, Gail asked whether we would like to go backstage, when the audience had left. Indeed we would. About ten minutes later, the great curtain rose and the stage, like the auditorium, was empty and on stage we went. John Stevens said to me: 'You know, I've always wanted to sing on the stage of Covent Garden.'

'Well, why don't you?' I asked. 'I'll join you . . .'

'What would we sing?' the Commissioner enquired.

'How about Gilbert and Sullivan's "A Policeman's Lot Is Not a Happy One"?' I suggested. He agreed. Then came the only operatic moment in my uncultured life. The two of us entertained our hosts and fellow guests with the most unmelodious and hilarious rendering which has ever emerged from that great stage.

In October 2004, the Commonwealth Jewish Council presented our Annual Award to Gerald and Gail. We spoke of their dedication to public service, their generosity to projects, organisations and causes and their friendship to so many of us. What was left unsaid was what we were all thinking – that no other couple has ever emerged from adversity with such courage and success. He and Gail are a remarkable example of how courage and family support can overcome adversity and misery, however cruel.

There are probably half a million Jewish people in the UK, so why do official figures report less than 300,000? Because the rest do not identify as

Jews. They neither belong to synagogues nor to Jewish clubs or organisations and nor do they enter their religion as Jewish on census forms. Some four thousand Jews were thrown out of England by King Edward I in 1292. Oliver Cromwell allowed us back, but the community remained small until the end of the nineteenth century, when immigrants such as my grandparents boarded boats heading for Britain.

I am often asked how many Jews there are in the Houses of Parliament. In the Commons, maybe a dozen take an active or passive interest in Jewish life, and certainly more in the Lords, but there are many others in both Houses who exercise their right to keep apart.

Lionel Rothschild was the first Jewish MP. Elected in 1847, he refused to take his oath of allegiance on the New Testament, so he was forbidden to take his seat. It was not until a Private Member's Bill was passed in 1858, largely through the energetic efforts of Sir John Russell, that he proudly took his oath on the Old Hebrew Bible – as I did, thinking of him, in 1970.

The representative body of our Jewish community, the Board of Deputies of British Jews, was founded in 1760. Most of the years from 1835 to 1874, it was presided over by the famous Sir Moses Montefiore, friend of Queen Victoria and brave champion of Jewish rights. He travelled to Palestine and beyond, seeking fair treatment for his Jewish people. Ever since, the Board has been recognised as the lay voice of the British Jewish community and its elected President as the lay leader of that community. Equally, however great the religious divisions within our community, the outside world regards the Chief Rabbi as its religious spokesman. The effectiveness of both offices certainly depends to an extent on the personality, energy and stature of their occupants, but each office carries its own credibility.

The Jewish people is minute. After Nazi destruction of 6 million, today there are only some 12 million of us left in the world. When you consider that the population of China is 1.3 billion and that of the world is 6.3 billion, people wonder why so few Jews can make so much noise. Certainly we are an active lot, in general giving proud and good service to the countries in which we live. Some say that nations get the Jews they deserve. Sadly, as Jews in so many lands have learned over many centuries, they do not always get the nations they deserve.

So how have we survived at all? What is the essence of our strength? Our religion, our traditions and our families, but also the power that others believe us to possess. The Board of Deputies has long and rightly been a British basis for that belief. The Board, and similar organisations in other lands, are regarded as the repositories of Jewish political strength and energy. The truth is not the reality but what others believe it to be. I have always known the importance of prestigious organisational notepaper. Whether for a business or a charity; for the Board of Deputies or the Commonwealth Jewish Council; for the Holocaust Educational Trust or the Inter-Parliamentary Council Against Antisemitism – the notepaper counts. It is the root of the perceived reality.

Members of the Board are elected by those synagogues and other Jewish bodies that wish to participate in its work – and, happily, that means most of our organised community. Through ancient anomaly, three Australian communities were also represented – Wellington, Perth, and Myra's city and my original Board constituency, Melbourne. My father was the Board's President from 1955 to 1964, a task that he relished. I followed him in 1973. I regarded my election as a mighty honour and, at the age of forty-five, I was the Board's second youngest President in its long history.

As the Board's President, and as a Member of Parliament, I had a double platform. I made sure that my dual role in no way interfered with my service to my constituents or to the Labour Party, whether in Leicester or at Westminster. Far from resenting my dual role, my Leicester colleagues were proud of it (Chaper 11). Somehow, I managed to combine my parliamentary, constituency and Board work, largely thanks to our staff and to my colleagues. My job, as I saw it, was to direct, guide and energise, and to delegate wherever both reasonable and possible.

The Board and our community were heavily involved in the campaign for freedom of Soviet Jews. We were concerned with the good name and fair understanding of the Jewish State, especially in and by the media. And as the representative body of the British Jewish community, representation of our communal interests was the Board's prime responsibility. There were battles over our right to *shehita*, the Jewish method of animal slaughter. We believe that it is as humane as any other. Its opponents disagree. To boost communal morale, we organised the first and only Festival of British Jewry, with major communal events all over

Britain. Our monthly Sunday morning meetings were lively and well attended.

A distant relative called Arnold Morris complained to me that there was no memorial, no monument, no public place where Jewish people could come together to remember the victims of the Holocaust. Why, he asked, do we not try to get permission to erect such a memorial in Hyde Park or Kensington Gardens?

'The Board has no money,' I told him. 'Who would pay for it?'

'I would,' Arnold replied, smiling. 'But we would need a committee to organise it. In my view, every committee should have an odd number of people on it, and three is too many.' So the work would be done by him, but we needed permission to erect the first memorial in a royal park. I would seek the consent of the Minister for the Environment with responsibility for the parks, Michael Heseltine. I made an appointment to see him.

Heseltine received me in his office, sitting in his shirtsleeves behind his desk. 'Tell me about it,' he demanded. I did.

'What will happen,' he asked, 'if your memorial is defaced? What if people draw graffiti over it?'

'We'd clean it off, as soon as possible.'

'How about resulting press and publicity?'

'We'd avoid it like the plague. In my experience, publicity would simply encourage other vandals.'

The Minister sat back in his chair and smiled. 'OK,' he said. 'On that basis, you can have it.' Which we did, and you will find it, behind clumps of trees and bushes, near London's Wellington Barracks. Thank you, Michael.

My main problem? Doing my two jobs, parliamentary and Board of Deputies, while as always giving priority to Myra and the children. It was not easy, but because I could do much of my administrative work at home in the evenings, or into the nights, I managed.

My major communal calamity came towards the end of my term of office. In December 1980, Prince Charles and Princess Diana were our guests of honour at a dinner at Hampton Court Palace, to celebrate the Board's 220th anniversary. Our finances were weak and this was our chance to put them onto a sound basis. Reluctantly, I decided that the only way to do it was to have a very expensive preliminary dinner for those guests who would pay a high price. The rest would have a buffet meal in another part of the Palace. After the special dinner was over, Myra and I would escort the royals to meet our colleagues, their spouses, partners and guests.

I deeply disliked this division of my colleagues and friends into those who could and those who could not afford to make a major donation in return for dinner with our guests. But I decided that the future of the Board depended on our raising a substantial sum that evening and that this was the only way to do it.

The evening started well enough. The Prince and Princess were charming and relaxed. They chatted cordially to our colleagues and guests. During dessert, I got my first hint of disaster. One of our staff came in and whispered in the ear of our Director, Hayim Pinner, who came over and whispered in mine. There was not enough food for our standing dinner guests. They were furious. If we did not come quickly, there could be a walk-out or a riot.

Imagine – several hundred Jews come to dinner and there's not enough food to go round! I told Prince Charles and Princess Diana, who expressed their sympathy for my plight. Prince Charles said: 'Come on, Mr President. Let's go.' So he and the Princess and I left the remaining guests to enjoy their coffee and headed for the throng. The staircase was steep and the Princess, looking gorgeous in her sheath dress, was holding tightly to the banister. 'May I take your arm, Ma'am?' I asked. 'Be my guest,' she replied. At the foot of the steps, we plunged into the 50 per cent hungry crowd. The only appropriate words for the situation were in Yiddish: '*Oy vay!*' Happily, our royal guests took the jostling throng in good part. My foodless colleagues treated them with due courtesy, reserving their ire for the President.

Whose fault was it that so many people went home, royalled, fireworked but hungry? In my view, the fault was irrelevant. The responsibility was mine, and at the next Sunday plenary session of the Board, I apologised, took the blame and asked the Deputies to look at the positive side of what had in all other respects been a grand and great occasion.

My presidency ended in 1985. I resolved that I would take an active part in the Board's work only if and when my successors wished me to. As Harold Macmillan once said: 'When the final curtain falls, the wise actor leaves the stage.' Well, that stage anyway. One exception to my self-denying ordinance resulted from the saga of the Richard Burton manuscript. Sir Richard Burton was a famous nineteenth-century explorer. He was also a raging anti-Semite who, towards the end of that century, served as British Consul in Damascus, Syria. On his return to England, he penned an attempted justification of the blood libel accusations against the Jews. They had indeed (he said) murdered a priest called Father Tomaso and used his blood for Passover rituals.

When Burton died, his family placed his manuscript in the care of the Board of Deputies. When I became its President, I was shown the document, which had been locked up in a safe. I understood that Burton's family did not want his good name blackened by proof of his racism but equally felt it wrong to destroy the manuscript. They believed that the representative body of British Jewry would be a safe repository for it, and would ensure that its contents would remain unpublished. During my presidency, my fellow officers and I honoured their wishes and refused access even to Jewish scholars. The document was not for viewing.

In June 2001, I received a phone call from the BBC *Newsnight* programme. 'Did you know,' they enquired, 'that the Richard Burton manuscript is coming up for auction at Christie's, next Wednesday?' I certainly did not. Apparently, Christie's had told the Board that they expected that it would probably sell for £250,000 and possibly even more. As the Board needed money to buy new premises, they had put the document on sale. An official concerned with communal security had advised the Board that the document was so ancient that it would not create a problem if it were sold and published, so into auction it was going, with a reserve of £150,000.

I was outraged. As I had carefully avoided criticising my successors at the Board of Deputies, I at first said no to *Newsnight*'s invitation, but the next day, the programme planners phoned again. They read out a long statement by a Board official, extracts of which they were proposing to broadcast. 'All right,' I said. 'I'll comment on it for you.' And I expressed my view, on their programme, that for the Board to put this anti-Semitic document on sale was a grotesque error. In my view happily, the bids for the document did not reach its reserve price and it is now back in the Board's safe.

NINETEEN

Worlds Apart and Together

It was 17 June 1982. The Israeli–Lebanese campaigns and catastrophes were at their awful height and British Jews were learning how British Sikhs must have felt after the assassination of Prime Minister Indira Gandhi. I had drawn number three in the ballot for questions to the Prime Minister. In the lobby, I had met Ted (later, Lord) Short, former Deputy Leader of the Parliamentary Labour Party and then still President of the Labour Friends of Israel. 'Terrible, isn't it?' he said. I knew that on this occasion he was referring to the Lebanon and not to the Government. 'Appalling,' I replied. 'Well,' he said, 'this is one of those times when you keep your head down and let the waves roll over you. You can climb back on your feet when the storm subsides.'

I would not use my question to challenge or even to enquire about the policy of Her Majesty's Government in the Middle East. No. Unemployment was rampant and the City of Leicester was no longer the second most prosperous in Europe. Instead, we had been struck down by the misery of jobless people. If you were useful and skilled, you should have few problems. But God help you if you were unskilled or not especially bright or both. He had better help you, because the Government would not. Ergo: a question to Mrs Thatcher on unemployment.

'Mr Greville Janner,' the Speaker of the House, George Thomas, sang out in his wonderful Welsh voice. The House hushed, presumably awaiting my two-sentence presentation of Israel's case.

'Will the Right Honourable Lady,' I asked, 'find time today to consider the problems of . . .' pause – 'the unemployed . . .' – the interruptions and shouts began – 'in the City of Leicester . . .'

To my shocked amazement, the place broke out into bedlam from Arabists behind me but mainly from their bellowing allies on the Tory Government benches. They were shouting at me: 'Begin . . . Zionist . . .

Beirut . . .' A small knot of Tories below the gangway were even waving order papers at me. I knew what they meant. I was a splendid target and the fact that I had opposed the political philosophies and most of the military exercises of Menachem Begin since my youth was totally irrelevant, as was my political and personal attachment to Shimon Peres and to Israel's Labour Opposition. I was the open symbol of Jewry. They attacked me with unrivalled savagery. After noisy chaos which to me seemed to last minutes but which was no more than a few tortured seconds, the marvellous Speaker, George Thomas, intervened.

'The Honourable Gentleman,' he intoned, 'is entitled to be heard' . . . and so I was.

Question Time over and feeling slightly sick, I was strolling towards the Members' entrance when one of the loudest of the screaming mob approached me. He was and is, of course, a very nice gentleman so I shall let him roast in anonymity.

'Greville, old boy,' he said. 'Have you got a minute?'

I stood still and waited.

'I suppose you know, old boy, why we were shouting at you in the Chamber?' he asked.

'Of course I do,' I replied. 'You don't like bloody Jews.'

'Oh, not at all, old boy,' he said. 'But you can't come here and talk about unemployment when your lot are killing innocent people in Beirut!'

I enjoyed telling him with icy self-composure, which to my surprise I found easy to assume, just where he could go and just how I proposed to say whatever I saw fit in this great parliament to which I had been elected to speak on behalf of the citizens of Leicester, which I had been doing for many years and intended to go on doing just so long as they were good enough to continue to elect me. I had the impression from the man's somewhat patronising smile that he was taken aback that I had felt offended.

I remembered this incident, many years later, a few days before the outbreak of the Iraq war. I was walking down a corridor in the Lords when a venerable Baroness approached me, waving her forefinger at her Jewish victim. 'Well,' she said, 'we've dealt with Saddam Hussein.'

I waited.

'And you can't go on persecuting the Palestinians for ever, you know.'

'I'm not persecuting anybody,' I replied, coolly.

'You know what I mean,' she said.

'Yes, I know precisely what you mean,' I replied, and continued on my way. I have not spoken to her since.

When I was promoting the War Crimes Bill in the Commons, I referred in my speech to the awful fact that half my family had been locked up in a synagogue in Lithuania and burned to death. At which my Conservative friend, Martin Brandon-Bravo, overheard one of his colleagues saying: 'They burned the wrong half.'

Still, I have not often faced anti-Jewish racism in Parliament. Partly because most colleagues in Parliament are decent and despise racism and partly because it is not generally acceptable to show it.

These incidents encapsulate and illustrate one aspect of my role, inherited from my father, as a political spokesman for Britain's proud and disparate Jewish community. That role was official as well as personal during my six years as President of the Board of Deputies of British Jews, the community's mini-parliament. I have enjoyed most of the panorama of Jewish leadership. I have especially appreciated the respectful, kindly and thoroughly courteous way in which so many leaders in authority, national and local, have helped me in my battles for tolerance and equality and against racism and bigotry.

World leaders have displayed the same generosity of both spirit and time. I salute the memory of President Anwar Sadat of Egypt and Prime Minister Indira Gandhi of India and I record, where I can properly do so without breach of confidence, my precious meetings with them (Chapters 24 and 26) and with other leaders, with whom differences are happily still decided by dispute, discussion and debate and not concluded by bomb or bullet.

Whether I am received as a Member of Parliament or as a fellow Socialist or as a Jewish leader, it matters not. Human beings are not divisible into their separate fields of activity. I thank those at home and abroad who have been so very kind to me and to my family and, in happier times, to my wife. I salute those who have given us what I once heard US Presidential candidate Adlai Stevenson describe to an election meeting as: 'That most valuable of human assets . . . the only one that is totally irreplaceable . . . time!'

To wish to be rid of me and mine on grounds of political difference may be unkind, or even show a lack of political balance, but it is at least proper. I regard any decent leadership as anti-racist and my determined and persistent efforts in the Jewish world have always been, first – to ensure that Jewish communities understand that an attack on any other ethnic, religious or racial minority is an attack on our own and must be treated accordingly; and second – to invite other minority groups to take the same view in reverse. Parties and nations that erode or remove the freedom of any of their minority citizens are unlikely to retain it for anyone else.

Pastor Niemuller is my hero and his words are my guide. You battle for the rights and for the dignity of others because that is a moral duty but you also recognise that if races or religions or minorities other than your own are engulfed by hatred, your turn will come.

Early in November 2002, the then Archbishop of Canterbury, George Carey, asked me to visit him in Lambeth Palace. When I arrived, he smiled at me benignly: 'I cease being Archbishop of Canterbury, next month,' he said. 'I shall be introduced into the Lords, in my own right. I wonder whether you would do me the honour of being one of my two introducers,' he asked. 'The other is Brian Griffiths.' I was stunned. Brian is a distinguished Conservative Anglican. That George Carey would ask me, as a Labour peer of the Jewish faith, was remarkable, unique and wonderful. 'The honour would be mine,' I replied.

On the eve of that great event, Tony and Cherie Blair hosted the Carey family and the two Introducers to a happy dinner at Number Ten. For far from the first time, I marvelled at the way in which the Prime Minister could block off and cast away his deep anxieties, this time about the probable war in Iraq.

At 2.15 p.m. on the introduction day, George Carey, Brian Griffiths and I donned our scarlet and ermine robes. As the Junior Introducer, I followed Garter King of Arms into the Chamber, with George and Brian in stately train behind me. Immediately, there was a rustle of whispers around the Chamber. Peers were smiling and obviously surprised that I, a Jew, was leading into the House of Lords the man who until so recently was head of the Anglican Church. George read out the oaths. All of us made the ritual bows, in a ceremony considerably shortened since my Introduction. We then marched out through the Royal Gallery into the Queen's Robing Room, for photographs.

Later that day, several colleagues expressed their pleasure at George's 'ecumenical gesture'. One of them told me: 'When I saw you leading in the Archbishop of Canterbury, I thought to myself, "Now, that's very odd!". Then I said to myself: "No, it's not. After all, our Lord was a Jew, wasn't he?"'

Then I was approached by my old Conservative Commons friend, now an experienced Baroness, Sally Oppenheim Barnes. 'When you came into the Chamber, leading George Carey,' she said, 'I heard the man in the row behind me saying to his neighbour: "Who's that, introducing the Archbishop?" "Oh, just some Jew," the neighbour replied.' She identified the two men to me, but I will not shame them, much as they deserve it. Still, it was a wondrous, joyous occasion and I was proud of this remarkable land, where 'just some Jew' can introduce a great leader of the national religion into the Upper House of its Parliament.

Lately, much of my anti-racist work has inevitably moved into relations with Muslims in Britain and abroad. There is a mosque in Leicester and I always got on well with its leaders. Our Muslim community was comparatively small, but as in many parts of Britain, it has been expanding rapidly. Local minor problems have spun off into deep concerns, especially since the tragedy of the Twin Towers and the aftermath of 11 September 2001, and more lately, since the hideous suicide bombings on our London underground and buses and the airport and aircraft anxieties.

Not surprisingly, the Muslim world has looked for ways to counter the attacks upon it. At its most grotesque and evil, that response has blamed 'the Jews' for 9/11, alleging that Jews were warned to get out of the Twin Towers before they were bombed – not an approach that commended itself to the families of those hundreds of Jewish people who died in that epic misery. Then there is the anti-Semitic attempted linkage between 9/11 and the conflict between Israel and the Palestinians. Too often, I have been told that 'if it were not for the way the Jews are persecuting the Palestinians, none of this would have happened'. The killers of 9/11 (they say) were suicide bombers and whether suicide bombers attack in the US or in Israel or in the UK, they are all people who are determined to give up their lives for a cause, and who are motivated by the hopeless squalor of their lives and those of their families. And who causes that? The Jews, of course.

The problem in dealing with this obscenity is that people believe it because they have to find a scapegoat. I recognise, of course, that anti-Muslim racism is an evil which we must not allow to grow and that if, for instance, our local Nazis and Fascists wax fat on hatred of Islam, we Jews are next. Happily, this is well recognised by the Jewish community. The converse equally applies. If the Muslim world helps to increase anti-Jewish racism today, then tomorrow it will be their turn.

So I work with Muslim colleagues, wherever possible, and I pay special tribute to my courageous and distinguished friends and colleagues, Sir Gulam Noon and Dr Khalid Hameed who have played such a positive and helpful role in the new Coexistence Trust. I meet with Muslim leaders, at home and abroad, and I travel the Muslim world, in the quest for understanding and for peace, and surprisingly often, at their leaders' invitation.

As a youngster, I read a pamphlet entitled 'Jews are News'. I asked myself – why? We are the People of the Book – 'chosen', perhaps, to suffer, ultimately and uniquely in the gas chambers and incinerators of the Holocaust. In modern times, it perhaps goes back to that celebrated forgery, 'The Protocols of the Learned Elders of Zion', which led to pogroms and murders in Eastern Europe. No, we did not plot the downfall of anyone, but the myth of the powerful Elders continues. On the one hand, it paved the road to Auschwitz. On the other, it provides us with hope for survival in the future and of exercising strength for a better world for others who may learn from our tragedies.

My old and valued Indian friend, Natwar Singh, is a Congress Party leader who was his nation's Minister of External Affairs. His gracious and brilliant wife, Hem, is a daughter of the Maharajah of Patiala. One day, when I was visiting their home in New Delhi, Natwar asked me: 'How many Jews are there in India?'

'How many do you think there are?' I replied.

'Well,' he said, thoughtfully. 'We have about a billion people in our country. Maybe there are only a million Jews?'

When I told him that there were five thousand, he refused to believe me.* After all, there had been a Jewish general and a Jewish admiral in modern India. How could that be possible, from such a tiny community?

In February 2000, I called on the President of Kenya, Daniel Arup Moi, in his London hotel suite. I told him how honoured I was to meet him, both previously in Nairobi and now in Britain. He replied: 'The honour is mine. I know that you and the Jewish people have great influence – and my country and I now need it.'

Obviously, neither our real nor our perceived influence saved some half of our Jewish people from destruction. So how have we survived? Some escaped from Eastern Europe, to avoid service in the Tsar's Army or so as not to be murdered in pogroms. Others simply sought a better life in the United States or Canada, or Australia or Britain. Then there's care for each other. Family, friends and the rest of our Jewish people. Wherever we are free to serve others, we do so. We have an acute sense of service to the wider communities in which we live. Sometimes, as in Britain, this leads to a large measure of acceptance and security; sometimes, as in pre-war Germany, that very sense of security breeds complacency which leads to death.

Then there are others, who are especially dear to us. Most obviously, the Righteous Among the Nations – individuals like Raoul Wallenberg who saved Jews and other Nazi victims, sometimes at the cost of their own lives. All my political life has been enriched by friendship with a mass of fellow politicians from all parties who are allies of mine and of the Jewish people. Many of their names appear in this book. There are dozens of others whom I salute with affection and appreciation. It is these people who protect us against a constant sense of insecurity. Henry Kissinger once remarked: 'I know that I'm paranoid, but that don't mean I ain't got enemies!' We do have enemies, but happily we also have many friends.

Family life and education help our survival, together, for some of us, with the warm coating and comfort of religious belief. In the postwar Belsen Jewish Displaced Persons Camp, I found that many of the happiest people in that dread and hopeless place were those who created a religious cocoon

---

* See Chapter 26, on my relationships with India, and with its leaders, not least with Natwar Singh MP.

around their individual and communal lives. Jews are cultural, tribal people – non-religious but still identifying members of our community. Why? Partly, I suppose, because we know that however much we unidentify, Nazis will still consign us to the gas chambers because of our birth, and partly because identification with our culture is an inherited ailment.

Our sense of humour has been a major source of our survival. The basic rule for jokes and humour is to aim it at yourself. You will then offend no one else. With rare and beloved exceptions, such as my late friend, Bob Monkhouse, we Jews do not like others making fun of us. That is a privilege which we extend to ourselves in full measure and is displayed, at its most hilarious extreme, by Sasha Baron-Cohen's Ali G. Often with self-deprecating pathos, humour lights our way through life and sometimes even brightens the tunnels that lead to death.

Throughout my parliamentary career, I have been regarded by friends and enemies alike – rightly, I hope – as a resonant voice for the Jewish people and the Jewish State. I regard it as a proud role, handed down by my father. In Parliament, my approach was and remains simple. Israel has plenty of enemies who are delighted to attack its government and its people, right or wrong. As I had decided not to share the dangers of life with the Israelis and as they were and indeed remain the sole vibrant and turbulent democracy in the area, it was for them to choose their government and for me to seek to explain their view. Not to defend what I believe to be wrong, but to ensure that Israel's viewpoint is fairly and clearly heard.

Whether in China or Peru, in nearby Europe or far-off Polynesia, I always found stories about the Jews and Israel in their media, and scarcely a Foreign Office question time goes by without parliamentary battles over the Middle East. For me, the most formidable and memorable came on 9 June 1981. Israel had – in my view, absolutely rightly – bombed and destroyed Iraq's nuclear plant. At Prime Minister's Question Time, I asked: 'Would not Iraq have had a nuclear weapon potential that it would have used against Israel?'

Uproar. The bearded former Shakespearean actor, Andrew Faulds, who sat immediately behind me, boomed out his usual denunciation of Israel and of me, this time adding in a very loud voice that Israel has a nuclear potential and had not signed the anti-nuclear treaty. There were disapproving shouts and mutters at me from all over the Chamber. For what seemed like minutes but was in fact maybe twenty seconds, I stood, waiting for enough quiet to complete my question. Then Speaker George Thomas rose. 'Order', he cried out. 'Order. The honourable and learned gentleman must be allowed to put his question.'

I continued: 'Does the Prime Minister not feel a certain sense of relief that the Iraqi regime will not have nuclear weapon potential for some further time to come?' Again, shouts of 'Rubbish' and 'No'. And from Andrew Faulds: 'Go back to Tel Aviv.'

Prime Minister Thatcher: 'Had there been an attack on Israel of the kind there has just been on Iraq, I should totally and utterly have condemned it. I, therefore, totally and utterly condemn the attack on Iraq.'

Sir Hugh Fraser, a doughty Conservative ally of Israel, then added his voice to mine: 'Although she condemns the use of force, does my Right Honourable Friend recall that over the past year, many Honourable Members have drawn attention to the danger and threat to peace of the previous French Government's export to Iraq of enhanced uranium? Although not condoning the use of force, will the Foreign Secretary take the opportunity to prevent, as Sir Anthony Eden did, the sale of offensive weapons to an area that is already vastly over-supplied with such weapons?' The Prime Minister agreed that 'we should be very careful over the countries to which we supply such uranium'.

As I was leaving the Chamber, trembling with emotion, a Tory MP whom I did not know said to me: 'Well, Greville, I thoroughly disagree with you, but I do admire your courage.'

Over the years, I had to meet many attacks on *shehita* – the Jewish form of religious slaughter of animals. Since the Muslim population of Britain burgeoned, the anti-*shehita* lobby has usually started with attacks on the Muslim method of slaughter – *halal*. *Shehita* and *halal* are not the same, but their opponents and enemies generally are. So far, their opponents have failed, not least through the efforts of Sir Ivan Lawrence, then MP for Burton-on-Trent. A member of the reform (non-orthodox) Jewish community and representative of a reform congregation on the Board of Deputies, he was a staunch, warm and courageous ally and friend. Along with other Conservative allies, he proved the truth of the old parliamentary maxim that you have many friends before you on the other side of the House and that too many of your enemies sit behind you, on your own.

In 1985, the Farm Animal Welfare Council sought to introduce legislation to ban *shehita* and *halal*. As I walked into the 'No' lobby, I was assailed by that doughty Tory warrior and great ally on this and other causes important to the Jewish community, Julian Amery. 'Why are you looking so worried, my dear boy?' he asked. 'We're not going to lose this one, you know.'

'What makes you so sure?'

'It's very simple, my boy. There are far more Muslims and Jews with votes than there are cows!' Which is, I suppose, one definition of human democracy.

The Jewish vote as such does not exist. We are a contentious, argumentative and politically divided people. True, when it comes to survival and to the basic rights of Jews, we unite, but when it comes to British politics, we enjoy our differences. Like their fellow citizens, Jewish people vote in what they regard as their own interests, only one of which is their interest as Jews. When Jewish voters consider that the interests of the nation and the pro-Jewish sentiments of one of the parties and especially those of its leader coincide, then they will probably vote for it. Margaret Thatcher was perceived as a great friend of the Jewish people, which she was and is, and during the Thatcher era, the mass of our Jewish community voted Tory.

One evening, Myra and I were at a Jewish charity dinner. A man pulled up a chair and sat uninvited between us. Thrusting his chin forward, he announced to me: 'I have no use for your Labour lot. They are no good.' I responded to this aggression with silent dignity. 'Mind you,' he continued, 'the Tories are no good either. I say, it's a plague on both your houses.' Myra looked round at him. 'You know what, sir,' she said quietly. 'When the plague comes to our house, I shall invite you in.' She glared at him. He got up, pulled his chair away and left.

If, then, there is no Jewish vote as such, why are political leaders of all parties so concerned about the political loyalties of Jewish voters? First and mainly, because so many non-Jews have an inflated perception of our strength. Second: there are a number of constituencies where Jewish voters are concentrated and, especially where the seats are marginal, their votes can swing the result in either direction. Third: there are many British Jews with influence. Influence, through the respect of others for their views. Influence, through their commercial, professional or industrial weight. And influence through their qualities of dignity and wit, leadership and moral example.

For the sake of Jewish rights, we must be grateful for that influence. Anyone who underestimates that influence reduces its weight. Like all others, we are entitled to use our strength for those causes which we believe to be politically right and these certainly include such essentials as the battle against anti-Semitic racism and for the survival and security of the Jewish State; against resurgent Nazism or Fascism, wherever it may be found; and for the restitution of assets to the victims of Nazism and Fascism throughout the world.

Nahum Goldmann, founder of World Jewish Congress (WJC), was a great leader. But he and I had one major area of profound disagreement. He believed that in order to do the best for the Jews of the Soviet Union, we should wherever possible avoid conflict with its Government. I did not.

At a WJC meeting in Geneva, where Goldmann lived, he denounced me as the player in the Jewish orchestra who kept striking discordant notes. 'We play the violins and the cellos,' he said. 'Janner blows the horn.' So Myra and I were especially pleased when Goldmann accepted an invitation to dinner at our home, on one of his fleeting visits to the UK. He was on his way to the US, after a visit to his friend, Marshal Tito of Yugoslavia. I asked him: 'How do you become friends with people like Tito? You are, after all, the leader of a comparatively small organisation and he is boss of a nation.'

'You must get to know them as human beings,' Goldmann replied. 'Always talk to them first about whatever interests them. In Tito's case, it's ballet and sailing. Only then should you turn to your own concerns and interests.' I then repeated my question: 'But why should Tito talk to you at all? Does he not know how few Jews there are in the world?'

'Of course he does,' Goldmann replied. 'But happily for us – and like so many other leaders with whom we have to deal on behalf of our people in peril – he over-emphasises our strength and influence. Thank God for that, otherwise we would have very little of either!'

Nahum Goldmann had created the WJC which had and still has remarkable, top-level access – which gives it the influence that it needs in order to have the power to achieve results on behalf of those whom it serves. Which, in its turn means the less well-off and less powerful and influential . . . people of all religions. I remain happy to be a WJC vice-president and to work with its remarkable leaders.

There are two reasons why I have run into little anti-Semitism in my public life. One is that everyone knows that I am Jewish, so I seldom endure personal attacks. The second: overt anti-Semitism is rarely acceptable in Britain. Most British people accept you for what you are, whatever your race or religion.

When I fell for Myra, I knew that if we married we would have a kosher house, but I wondered how we would cope with her Sabbath observance and absolute, Chief-Rabbi's-niece compliance with the strict rules of our religion. I need not have worried. One Saturday, during our engagement, I was ill in bed. Myra was looking after me. She brought me the traditional Jewish blood transfusion – hot chicken soup. She had heated it herself. '*Pikuakh nefesh*,' she said, smiling. In our religion, the 'saving of a soul' has priority over all.

So we too kept a kosher house and had joyful Friday nights. Like Father, I held surgeries in my constituency on Saturday mornings, but my colleagues and constituents understood that Friday evenings were sacred and that I would only be around on Fridays in emergencies or elections.

Leicester has a small Jewish community with a small and pleasant synagogue. But nearly all the few hundred local Jews live in the south of the city. There were not more than half a dozen in Leicester West, but in twenty-seven years of service, openly Fascist rantings apart, I encountered anti-Semitism only half a dozen times. Once, going round a Working Men's Club, shaking hands and listening to problems, a man folded his arms and said: 'No thank you. I don't shake hands with Jews.' I remember the occasion because of its remarkable rarity.

The positive side was extraordinary. It was summed up when I was invited to stand as President of the Board of Deputies of British Jews – to become British Jewry's elected lay leader. 'What do you think?' I asked my Agent, George Billington. He replied: 'If you did not serve your Jewish people, Greville, we would not respect you.' Like my father before me, I served my constituents with persistent energy and concern. Provided I did that, they accepted without question or hesitation that I should also serve my Jewish community. Mutual respect. Once again I thought of Father. He always said that it was a privilege to live and to serve in Britain as a whole and in Leicester in particular. He was right.

Sir Isaiah Berlin told me a revolting story, illustrating the feelings of those who believe that Jewish people are really foreigners. Nicholas Ridley was a Cabinet Minister and a colleague of Sir Keith Joseph who was Jewish. The two of them had had a row. 'I can't understand Keith behaving like that,' Ridley said to Sir Isaiah. 'We've always treated him as if he were one of us.' Ridley's mother was a great friend both of Myra and me and of the Jewish people and she was 'one of us'. She often spent Friday nights with us at our home. She amazed our children by her massive consumption of whisky. They affectionately called her 'Lady Wigley'.

The story is told of Henry Kissinger, then US Secretary of State, being received in audience by Saudi King Faisal. He approached the mighty throne, with white-robed guards on either side, scimitars raised in salute. He bowed.

'Secretary of State,' proclaimed the King. 'I welcome you, not as a Jew but as a great human being.'

Kissinger bowed. 'Your Majesty,' he said, solemnly. 'Many Jews are human beings.'

My son Daniel and I were once received by the then Crown Prince of Bahrain, who later became the Emir. During the course of our conversation, my origins emerged. 'Mr Janner,' said the Prince, 'I did not know you were Jewish.'

'In that case, Your Royal Highness,' I said, 'I'd better go!'

'No, no, no.' said the Prince. 'You are very welcome!' And very welcome he and the Bahrainis made us.

Happily, at least for our British Jewish community, our country remains one of Europe's least racist lands. France is turning nasty, and so are the Netherlands and Belgium. Even Denmark, that former bastion of decency, is suffering from the rebirth of Fascist evils. So why is this happening and how can we best defend and counter-attack against it?

Origins vary. Le Pen and his ilk move in from the Far Right, focusing on immigrants and the traditional dislike of the unlike. The Far Left is little better, too often using the Israel–Palestine miseries as their base for attacks on the Jewish State and thence on the Jews. As for our new Muslim arrivals, some seek to deflect the pressures against them onto other potentially vulnerable targets, usually local Jewish people.

In Britain, we are fortunate. While there are no Jewish people in the top ranks of the Labour Government, its leaders – not least, both Tony Blair and Gordon Brown – are mighty opponents of racism and valued friends of the Jewish community and of mine. There can scarcely be allegations of top-level anti-Semitism in the parliamentary Conservative Party, with Michael Howard, Oliver Letwin, Malcolm Rifkind and Maurice Saatchi among its leaders. And while Liberal Democrats are too often too ready to attack the Jewish State, right or wrong, there is much goodwill among their political ranks, and some fine Jewish people.

My father used to tell me that you cannot always see or hear anti-Semitism, but you can usually smell it. Occasionally, I catch some whiffs of it, but happily, most of our politicians take and treat you on your merits, your personality and your goodwill towards them. They do not judge you by your religion, your race or colour or national origins.

As with Jews, so with colleagues who are Muslims, Hindus or Sikhs, or non-white. Most colleagues will accept them as they are and for what they are. All that said, some problems have grown, sadly along with the size of our British Muslim community, now well over one and a half million souls. There are perhaps half a million British Jews, of whom some 60 per cent identify with our community. We are a long-established and vocal lot, but few realise that in today's Britain there are some 1.3 million Hindus and Sikhs. While Jews and Muslims have loud and representative communal voices, those of the Hindus and Sikhs have usually been divided and largely unheard. Not surprisingly, many Muslims identify with their co-religionists in Kashmir and the Middle East. Fair enough, provided that they do not allow these issues to spill over into personal ill-will against those who disagree with them, in this land of their choice.

How, then, can we deal with these inter-communal challenges? As the French proclaim, in a different context: '*Vive la différence!*' We should be happy that Britain has become varied in its people and in its culture. We should know and respect our differences, but concentrate together on areas of mutual concern, knowing that we have many of the same enemies.

Since childhood, I have hated racism. From my initiation into the sight and smell of anti-Jewish racism at Bishop's College School, through the emotional trauma of the Belsen concentration and displaced persons' camps. I have fought against racism, from the War Crimes Group to the War Crimes Act . . . from work in Leicester, to welcome and integrate our new Hindu, Sikh and Muslim citizens from East Africa and India, to the Maimonides Foundation and now to the Political Council for Coexistence, I join in the constant battle to foster good relations between Jews and our Muslim neighbours, whatever the miseries or conflicts of the Middle East. From the Nazi Gold Conference to the Holocaust Educational Trust and efforts to provide at least a measure of restitution for victims of the Holocaust, the battle against racism and anti-Semitism has been and remains at the core and centre of my life and work.

On 11 September 2001 the world changed. Some 7,000 totally innocent human beings were smashed to death. Everyone agreed – this time, the world would never be the same again. Or would it?

On 7 July 2005, it was London's turn for Islamic terrorist attacks. Four suicide bombers murdered fifty-two Londoners, travelling on the tube or by bus. New York . . . Bali . . . Madrid . . . and now London. Where next?

How could and should those of us who work together with the Muslim world deal with this new scene? By telling the truth. Set out simply, it is this: First: that their terrorists who murder non-combatant civilians or who use terror to achieve their ends are unacceptable in decent society, whomever the victim may be.

Second: that, happily, Jewish communities of the world were not sighing with false relief and saying – or even thinking – 'thank God it's the Muslims who are getting blamed for once and not us'. We know too well that the Nazis, Fascists and other right-wing extremists who muster strength by attacking Muslims today will be after us tomorrow.

And third: that the Muslim world should learn from our experience and understand that if they try to blame the Jews, that may perhaps earn them a temporary respite from attack. But we Muslims and Jews have the same enemies. If anti-Semitic propaganda brings political strength to the foes of the Jews, the Muslim minority will be next. So we must each teach our own communities that we are Abrahamic cousins and that if we allow our enemies to divide us, that will lead to disaster for both our communities.

I have long worked on the principle that whether or not we like diversity – and I do – it is here in Britain to stay. I have tried to convince my Muslim colleagues that we either live together or we die together. If the Nazis in the British National Party or anywhere else win power on the back of attacks on the Muslim community, then we Jews know that we are next. Equally, British Muslims must recognise that if our Jewish community is destroyed, whether by the Nazis or anyone else, then they are next. We have common and dangerous enemies in this land. Yes, there will always be differences between us, perhaps about Kashmir but more likely on the Middle East. So let us focus on our common ground – and there is plenty of it.

One of the enduring leaders of our Jewish world was the remarkable Moses Ben Maimon, universally known either as Maimonides or as 'Rambam'. Born in Cordoba in Spain, his family took flight and eventually settled in Fez, Morocco. From there, they travelled to the Holy Land and on to Egypt, where Maimonides was not simply a spiritual leader of the Jewish people, but a physician to the mighty. So when colleagues and I decided to set up a base and structure for the Jewish community to create and to work on common ground with those Muslims who wished to achieve the same, whether in Britain or abroad, we called the organisation 'The Maimonides Foundation'. Together with the late Rabbi Hugo Gryn, Dr Richard Stone, and other concerned colleagues, and led and organised by the redoubtable Douglas Krikler, we registered our organisation as a charity. On the one hand, Maimonides created the British base for the rescue of Jews from the Yemen (Chapter 25); on the other, it became a focus of relationships with the Muslim community.

I gladly accepted the role of President of the Foundation and David Khalili, a world-renowned collector of Islamic art, became our Chairman and chief funder and fundraiser. We hosted lectures, arranged for visits of Muslims to synagogues and of Jews to mosques and even organised an annual football match between mixed teams of Muslim and Jewish youngsters at the Arsenal stadium.

From a Jewish organisation seeking and promoting relations with the Muslim world, we were transformed in 2000 into a Muslim–Jewish organisation. Dr Khalili felt, with some justification, that my interests were more political than cultural. He suggested that I resign as President, and that our energetic colleague, Dr Stone, should do the same. Before long, we both did as he asked. That said, the purpose and the focus of Maimonides was and remains extremely important, bringing Muslims and Jews together, in a land and a world where too often we have been drawn fiercely apart.

Since 9/11, it has become increasingly difficult to find Muslim colleagues in the Palace of Westminster who are prepared to work openly and vocally for our joint communal interests and together with us. For instance, my respected friend Lord Nazir Ahmed and I made two major visits together. We travelled first to Israel in 2000, where we talked to top leaders; to Jordan, for discussions with King Abdullah and Prince Hassan; and then to Palestine, for a meeting with Yasser Arafat. In 2001, we travelled again to Israel, where Nazir became the second Muslim leader ever to address an Executive of World Jewish Congress – the first was Prince Hassan of Jordan. Then we visited the Gulf. Since 9/11, Nazir and I have remained good friends, but he has not felt it appropriate or perhaps safe to make similar journeys together.

My relations with the Hindu world began with my journeys to India (Chapter 26), and with my work with my Asian constituents in Leicester (Chapter 12). I have always felt a symbiosis between our religions and our communities. But unlike British Muslims, our Hindu and Sikh communities have not, at least until recently, come together to promote their interests and their causes. Yes, they do boast some members of both Houses of Parliament, but as communities, they have not created a political force for themselves. There are some 1.2 million of them in Britain, only about half a million less than our Muslim community, but they are seldom heard. Happily, my respected friend who was Leader of the Liberal Democrat Party, Lord Navnit Dholakia, and colleagues have now created a central Hindu political body. They need it, and the Board of Deputies could and should be their model.

So, in this great and diverse country, it is vital that we all live and work together. We must recognise that as minorities, we are deeply privileged to live in Britain – not least when you see the level of ill-will that is growing in so many continental European countries – but we must not take tolerance and mutual respect for granted. We must ensure that our communities walk and work in the centre of the road and with each other. Separately, the danger will be great.

In the autumn of 2005, a neighbour phoned me in my office. She told me that a fairly bulky object had arrived at our building, and it was ticking and clicking. She and other neighbours had called the police. Meanwhile, they had put the packet in the outside flowerbed. I offered to return home immediately but she said that this was totally unnecessary and she would keep me in touch.

A couple of hours later, my neighbour phoned again. All was OK. Yes, the police had arrived in strength. So had ambulances and fire engines. The whole area had been cordoned off. Eventually, the bomb squad had arrived and opened the packet. It contained a small radio, adorned with a large pair of red metal lips. These objects had been clicking. A highly orthodox local synagogue called Aish had sent this weird object, with its best wishes for the current High Holy Days. The police had tried to contact them, but because of the festival season, they had not replied.

This was not my first contact with Aish. Some time ago, a vandal had set light to part of their premises and I had attended with other communal leaders, to express my dismay and sympathy. A few days later, their rabbi had asked to see me and I invited him to the House of Lords. I took him upstairs to a quiet room and asked him what I could do for him. He responded by telling me that, as a Jewish leader, I should follow Jewish religious practices. I should say the required prayers in the morning and attend synagogue . . . and so on and so on. I stood up and thanked him for taking the trouble to visit me and escorted him out of the House of Lords.

I have told this tale to colleagues and friends in the Jewish community and without exception they have described the rabbi's conduct as 'chutzpah' – the traditional Yiddish word for 'bloody cheek'. I agree. But the man was doing what he regarded as his holy duty, in seeking to bring this distinguished sinner into the fold of righteousness.

TWENTY

Nazi Gold and Looted Art

In September 1996, World Jewish Congress in New York sent me a copy of a letter from the Swiss Legation in Washington DC. Dated 1946, it alleged that the USA, Britain and the USSR had agreed to a secret deal over Nazi Gold, known as 'Operation Safe Haven'. It showed that British Intelligence knew that the Nazis had transferred gold looted from their victims to Switzerland, to pay for armaments, food and other necessities for their war effort. I immediately wrote to Foreign Secretary, Malcolm Rifkind, and to Defence Secretary, Michael Portillo. I asked what we knew of this alleged secret deal. Malcolm wrote back saying, 'None of the Intelligence Services is aware of having such information.' I sent him a copy of the letter, which clearly indicated that he had been misinformed by his civil servants. To his credit, he immediately set up an enquiry into the allegation.

The Foreign Office researched Government archives, and produced a 23-page Memorandum which suggested that at least $500 million – now worth £4.6 billion – remained in Swiss banks at the end of the war. It then held a press conference, to reveal the contents of their research. We decided to hold our own, at the headquarters of the Holocaust Educational Trust, an hour later. To our happy surprise, nearly a hundred journalists and broadcasters turned up from all over the world. Cameras clicked and the Swiss balloon soared into the media.

'The Swiss had $500m in Nazi Gold and returned $60m' – *Daily Telegraph*; 'We will open up the books on Nazi gold, promised the Swiss' – *Daily Mail*; 'UK Report claims gold in Swiss banks was looted' – *Wall Street Journal*; 'Swiss asked: "Where is that stolen gold?"' – *Independent*; 'Swiss told to repay £4.6 billion Nazi gold' – *The Times*; 'Shame of the Swiss' – *Guardian*; 'The goods of evil – did Switzerland's bankers profit from the tragedy of the Nazi Holocaust' – *Time Magazine* – cover.

My key first target then – the Swiss. My key co-conspirator – David Hunt, a Tory MP, once a very senior member of John Major's Cabinet, a joyful, humorous companion and a brilliant and loyal colleague. Together, we attacked the Swiss banks. Together, we visited Switzerland and met many of their leaders. By March 1997, they had agreed to our call for an International Meeting on Nazi Gold.

While all this was going on, Myra's dreadful illness was taking an ever firmer grip. The family and I tried hard never to leave her alone. She accepted that I needed to get on with my work. Eventually I decided I should do so, both for its own sake and because by keeping active outside our home, I could cope better emotionally with what neither of us wanted to accept was inevitable. Since her death, it has been my work, my family and my friends that have kept my spirit burning.

I ran my idea for an international conference on the Nazi looted gold by Foreign Secretary Malcolm Rifkind. I knew that he was proud of his Jewish ancestry. Indeed, I had enjoyed breakfast with him shortly before and asked him how he got his name. He told me that his great-grandparents lived in Russia, where the males in each family were called up for service into the Tsar's army. The only exceptions: sons who were the sole support of widowed mothers. So, in the early nineteenth century, an ancestor was adopted by a local widow, whose name was Rivka – Rebecca, in English – and he became known as '*Rivka's kind*' – Rivka's child. Or, for short, Rifkind.* Sadly, I could not persuade the great-grandson to agree to host the Nazi Gold Conference. After considering my request with his customary and courteous thoughtfulness, he said: 'It's too near to the election. We must wait and see who will then be in government. This is not the right time to make a decision or an announcement.'

So I asked Robin Cook, then our Shadow Foreign Secretary, to chat with me after Question Time. We went into the Members' tearoom and he sat back and looked at me. 'Well, Greville,' he said. 'What can I do for you?' I told him. He then submitted me to a ten-minute cross-examination with such questions as:

---

* For the origin of my surname, see Chapter 1.

'Where will it be held?'

I suggested: 'Lancaster House.'

'Who will pay?'

'Well, I hope the individual governments, but otherwise ours.'

'How much will it cost?'

'I don't know, but in the grand order of life and of government, and especially with the huge issues involved, not too much.'

'Who would come?'

'Everyone concerned, I hope. It would put Britain in the centre of a most honourable human rights project.'

At the end, Robin said: 'All right, Greville. If we win the election, I'll do it.' We did – and he did. I was very grateful – and very sad when in the summer of 2005 he suddenly died.

Most nations concerned readily agreed to take part. There were three exceptions – Russia, Lithuania and the Vatican. I was invited to see the Russian Ambassador, Yuri Fokhine, whom I later learned to like and appreciate. 'I suppose you're after the art which we captured from the Germans at the end of the war?' he enquired. 'Well, we shall keep it. It's spoils of war. They devastated our land and we are entitled to the art we rescued.'

'I don't disagree about the bulk of the artefacts,' I said. 'If they belonged to the Nazis, please do keep them. But not if they belonged to victims whom the Nazis murdered. That is stolen property and you should return it wherever possible to its true owners or to their heirs or to the Jewish people or to a victims' organisation.'

Eventually, Russia did decide to be represented at the Conference, and in a later meeting Ambassador Fokhine told me that they were now prepared to return Nazi looted art, provided that they had the funds for research and could trace the owners or their heirs. This began another long trail for justice, a search which still continues.

Then there were the Lithuanians. I received a message that they were not going to attend the Conference. I telephoned their embassy. Their ambassador was away so I spoke to his chargé – his number two. No, they did not intend to attend. 'Oh, I do understand,' I said. 'Indeed, I understand all too well. Most of my own family were murdered in Lithuania, many of them by Lithuanians. Local people rounded up some of my family, together with other local Jews, and locked them in a wooden synagogue and set light to it. Others they murdered and buried in mass graves. Not one survived. So I do understand why your nation does not wish to attend.

'Anyway, it's a free world and whether you wish to attend is up to you, but as I am a convenor of the Conference, I am sure that you will not mind if I explain to the delegates why your country prefers to stay silent and away.' Silence from the chargé. Then he said: 'Please don't announce anything until I have spoken to the ambassador. He is back this evening.'

The next day, I received a telephone call. The ambassador would like to see me. Within the hour, he appeared at the House of Commons. Over a cup of coffee, he thanked me for making my position so plain, and he assured me that his country would be represented. They were.

Third was the Vatican. Then and now, maintaining whatever silence they deemed possible. We pushed, courteously but firmly. Eventually, they agreed to be represented by two distinguished priests, but on the basis that they would be observers only and would say nothing. They came, they saw and they remained silent.

Robin Cook hosted the Conference in the dignified elegance of Lancaster House. Unlike many such gatherings, this one had content, and like all the best conferences, the corridors were filled with useful networking. Before departing, delegates agreed to accept the invitation of the United States for a follow-up conference in Washington. When the idea first surfaced, the Americans had wanted the first conference in Washington. Colleagues and I convinced them that it should be in Europe, the scene of the tragedies which led to Nazi crimes and where much of the loot still remained. Washington was next.

Meanwhile, we kept up the pressure on the Swiss. *The Times* ran a first leader, headed: 'Tainted gold – Switzerland behaviour is unworthy of a democracy'. That pressure was increased by the Washington Conference on looted art, insurance policies and other assets. On the opening day, President Bill Clinton announced a new Presidential Advisory Commission on Holocaust Assets, chaired by Edgar Bronfman, President of World Jewish Congress. Art historians and insurance groups agreed to further action; and I launched for the first time our proposal for a Day of

Remembrance, which later became in Britain Holocaust Memorial Day, on 27 January.

I then turned my attention to the Bank of England. Its board finally admitted that they did hold two gold bars, each with a swastika on it. They had been found in a bank in Munich and were shipped to Britain in 1996 for safe keeping. Value, about £155,000. They let me into the vaults, to prove the ultimate truth – a photograph with me holding the bars, which was widely published in the next day's press.

Then the real battle began, on three fronts – Nazi Gold, mainly in Switzerland; bank accounts belonging to Nazi victims, appropriated by British authorities; and looted art. After years of struggle, the first two processes have almost ended, but the battle for the art works continues.

After Switzerland, we began a series of journeys to European capitals. We met top leaders in Portugal, who denied any connection with Nazi Gold. As we had no adequate proof, that trail led us nowhere. In Spain, we met King Juan Carlos, who was very supportive, but again we achieved no practical results. In Belgium and in France we were warmly received, and we bolstered the efforts of their own Nazi Gold Commissions. Austria had set up its own Commission, but we were not surprised that some of our hosts ran the line that they were the first victims of German Nazis. In each of these capitals, we met Jewish community leaders and offered them our encouragement and help. We consulted with our UK ambassadors, some of whom were pleased to see us. And we met national leaders, and encouraged them to support efforts in their lands to provide decent, honourable restitution for those who had suffered at the hands of their wartime predecessors.

Finally, and in many ways, our worst and greatest failure: the Vatican. World Jewish Congress had tipped us off that during the war, priests and monasteries had not only saved many hundreds of Jewish lives by giving refuge to escapees from the Nazis, but they had also received and kept in the vaults of their churches and cathedrals many valuable paintings and other works of art, brought to them by the refugees. None had been returned to their owners or to their families after the end of the war.

The then head of the Roman Catholic Church in Britain, Cardinal Basil Hume, lived and worked in Archbishop's House, near to my parents' home. He received me in his office and when I told him the problem, he said: 'You must go to the Vatican. I will speak to them and arrange it.' He lifted his telephone, made the arrangements and a week later David Hunt and I were on our way to Rome, accompanied by the then director of the Holocaust Educational Trust, Janice Lopatkin. There, we swept into a Cardinal's Residence, and were courteously received by his Eminence, who simply said that he would 'look into it' – but we heard nothing further, so we suspected that he had avoided looking very far.

Our British ambassador to the Vatican received us in his elegant residence and commiserated with us. He suggested that we wait and see whether there were any results and if there were none, that we should return. Some months later, we did. Again, we were courteously received but got no results. This time it was the Cardinal who was in charge of relations with the Jewish people and communities throughout the world who nodded his understanding but left us suspecting that he would do nothing. He lived up to our expectations.

We urged the Vatican authorities to follow the example of all democratic and decent authorities and to open up its archives, after fifty years. At first, they blankly refused. Eventually, under pressure from WJC, they agreed to open them but only to the beginning of the Second World War. These took us nowhere, but we have not stopped the pressure. One day, we shall succeed.

One land of eventual good news – Britain. As one survivor told me: 'Thanks very much for attacking the Swiss. You're absolutely right. But what about Nazi victims who put their savings into bank accounts in Britain to prevent the Nazis from getting hold of them? Britain stood alone against the Nazis and won the war, but why did it appropriate our assets as if they had belonged to Nazis?' Why, indeed? I received letters, claiming and demanding repayment of pre-war accounts in the UK, which our government had appropriated in 1946 under powers contained in the Trading with the Enemy Act, 1939. The victims were right and we started a campaign for justice.

We urged the Government to set up a special Commission of Enquiry to investigate claims by survivors or their families, for confiscated bank accounts. Civil servants at both the Department of Trade and Industry and the Foreign Office advised against it. I know this for certain because

I received a plain brown envelope which contained a copy of a confidential Memorandum to Ministers, recommending refusal of our request and saying that they needed to 'handle Lord Janner' with special care. Indeed!

I immediately had a series of private conversations with Peter Mandelson and other Cabinet Ministers. In March 1998, to the joy and relief of us all, Secretary of State for Trade and Industry Margaret Beckett announced that the Government had decided to set up an Enquiry. I went to see Chancellor Gordon Brown. To my delight and without hesitation, he accepted that assets belonging to Holocaust victims should not have been classified as enemy property and appropriated along with Nazi bank accounts. Where survivors or their heirs could prove ownership, their assets should be repaid. He agreed to set aside the necessary funding. To my surprise and joy, the Government swiftly set up the Enquiry Commission and appointed as Chair my old friend and former activist in the Parliamentary Committee for the Release of Soviet Jewry, Lord Peter Archer.

Over the years, the Commission received over a thousand claims. One third were successful and over £14 million was paid out. Some residual claims remain. With all the problems created by the passage of time, Peter Archer and his team made valiant and honourable efforts to ensure that the maximum justice was done.

Why, then, were we so successful in so many of our efforts, but failed with the Vatican and others? We won in Britain, partly because of the sheer decency and understanding of our allies – in particular, Chancellor Gordon Brown and Lord Peter Archer. But also because our research and our understanding of the background and issues were so powerful that, as Peter Mandelson made plain to his civil servants, failure to do what was right would have caused a nasty outcry. It was primarily thanks to Robin Cook that Britain hosted the first Nazi Gold Conference, which in its turn led to the establishment of the Nazi Persecution Fund. The Swiss eventually made at least some compensation to Holocaust victims, largely due to the international outcry created by World Jewish Congress, with my team alongside. But, most sadly, the Vatican authorities continue to refuse to open up their archives to independent researchers, or to pay any compensation to the families of murdered victims whose paintings or other valuables were and no doubt still are on the walls or in the vaults of their monasteries and churches.

It was clear that the theft of victims' assets was international. The worst thieves were the Swiss. The Nazis had paid them with gold bars for armaments, tungsten and other supplies required for their war effort against us. The Nazis had stolen most of these from the national banks of occupied countries, but some included gold extracted from the teeth of Jewish and other victims, on their way to death in gas chambers and crematoria. American lawyers, WJC and individual victims and their families had already started action and outcry in the United States. We raised vibrant voices in Britain and Europe, attacking the outrageous way in which the Swiss had cashed in on this international misery. The press was on our side and after the first outburst of publicity, the Swiss television broadcast a confrontation between myself and a Swiss MP, Nils de Dardel, who turned out to be our brave ally and supporter, with two of his Swiss colleagues who sought to defend their nation's benefit from Nazi invasions and atrocities.

David Hunt, Janice and I then visited Switzerland. I discovered that I was a national figure of hate. While their future President Ruth Dreyfus, Nils de Dardel and some other honourable Swiss colleagues did all they could to help, we were greeted with cold courtesy by President Flavio Cotti and other leaders.

Back home, our media continued to finger the Swiss as financial criminals, unwilling to pay compensation and, still less, to apologise. Why not? After all, their nation was not short of money and none of the leaders we met had been responsible for their ignoble wartime fraud.

WJC weighed in, with strident voice. David Hunt and I used parliamentary and governmental pressure, and eventually, the Swiss caved in. Their government set up a fund of $200 million for Holocaust survivors. Swiss commercial banks agreed to pay Holocaust survivors and their relatives more than $1.25 billion, over the next three years, in response to claims that they had withheld millions of dollars since the Second World War.

In 1996, the World Jewish Restitution Organization (WJRO), the WJC and the Swiss bankers' organisation set up a Commission, under the chairmanship of Paul Volker, to conduct an 'investigative audit' of dormant Swiss bank accounts that may have been held by Nazi victims. It found 54,000 accounts probably linked to such victims. While the Commission agreed that there was 'no evidence of systematic destruction of victims' accounts' nor 'organized discrimination' against them, it found that the bank showed 'a general lack of diligence – even active resistance – in response to private and official enquiries'. Paul Volker declared that he saw no reason to revise the $1.25 billion settlement that the two largest banks had reached with victims.

We met Volker, and expressed our great appreciation for his efforts. We had the impression that he was pleased to have achieved the results he had in the current rough circumstances, in which not all Swiss were totally in support of his efforts or ours. Meanwhile, the Swiss government itself had set up a Historical Commission under the chairmanship of Professor Bergier. From the professional, intellectual and academic viewpoint, he did a good job. But it had little interest for us, in our search for compensation.

As the classic joke goes: 'The Austrians are the finest diplomats in the world. They have convinced the world that Hitler was a German and Beethoven an Austrian.' The Nazis had no need to conquer Austria. Hitler was welcomed to Vienna and addressed a huge, cheering mob from the balcony of the Hofburg Palace. Thousands of wildly supportive followers raised their right arms in the Nazi salute.

In 2003, I addressed an official luncheon in that same palace. When I reminded my listeners of its horrendous history, my Austrian hosts were not pleased. My first visit to Vienna had been in 1970. The Soviet Union had closed down a transit camp, which housed Jewish Russians, en route to new lives in Israel. Austria's Chancellor was then a non-practising, non-admitting Jew called Bruno Kreisky. To my surprise and delight, he opened a new transit camp for the escapees – commonly called 'refuseniks' – in the Austrian town of Schönau. Shortly after, I travelled to Vienna to thank him, both officially and personally, for this lifesaving act.

'Chancellor,' I said to him, 'I cannot tell you how much I and my colleagues involved in the Soviet Jewry movement appreciate your humanitarian goodwill in opening the Schönau camp.'

'I was pleased to do this,' Kreisky responded. Then he paused. 'After all,' he said. Long pause. 'I am . . .' I thought that, at last, he was going to say that he was Jewish. But no. 'I, too,' he repeated, 'am a citizen of a persecuted nation. We Austrians know what it means to be a persecuted people.' Well. No matter. He had kept our refuseniks' escape route open and we were all very grateful to him.

Since then, I have visited Austria many times, usually following advice from their helpful ambassadors in London. Before the war, there were 300,000 Austrian Jews. Today there are only some 7,000. I have helped their leaders to advance their efforts to obtain fair compensation for Austrian Holocaust victims. Most recently, in November 2004, David Hunt and I travelled together to Vienna to try to induce the Leopold Foundation to release a most valuable painting, *Häuser am Meer*, by Schiele. In 1940, the Nazis had confiscated this famous work from a family of survivors, now living in the UK. They sold it in a notorious auction and it later came into the possession of the Leopold Foundation.

Now, if this painting were in a gallery owned by Austrian local or governmental authorities, Austrian legislation would have allowed restitution to the owners. Instead, even though half of the directors of the Leopold Foundation are appointed by the state and half by the Leopold family, it is a 'private' collection. Result: the Austrian restitution law does not apply in this case. So we were trying to induce the gallery voluntarily to do what is honourable, decent and compassionate. We failed. The Austrians should amend their law to require the return of these stolen goods to the family to whom they belong.

So much, then, for the realities of this remarkable and sometimes surprisingly successful campaign. For years, it held a passionate grip on my public life. Yes, it was good that we had done all in our power to track down Nazis in Britain, sadly unmasking too few and usually too late. But we had not done nearly enough to help survivors or their heirs and families. To some extent, the reason for the delay was theirs. Most had wanted to block off the unspeakable tragedies of their lives. Yes, many of them lived in poverty and would be grateful for their property. But most did not want to reopen those unspeakable wounds. Now, at least and at last we could bring some sustenance and help to the victims, most of whom needed it so desperately. Our success exceeded our expectations but we had hoped for far more. The battle continues, especially with the Vatican. We shall not give up.

My hero, Nobel Peace Prize winner Eli Wiesel, once said: 'Returning stolen assets will not bring back the life of even one of the Nazis' victims. But the money is a symbol. It is part of the story.' The story continues – and our part in it remains to try to provide help to as many Nazi victims and their families as possible. We could do at least a little to help at least a few of the survivors to obtain at least a modicum of justice.

We were less involved in claims by survivors and their families against insurers. Eventually, an organisation rejoicing in the name of ICHEIC (International Commission on Holocaust Era Insurance Claims) was set up, with the distinguished US diplomat Lawrence Eagleburger at its head. We assess the measure of its success by the sad fact that out of some 90,000 applicants, only about 3,500 have received offers.

In London in 2001, Michael Newman, a former colleague at the Holocaust Educational Trust (HET), set up the Central Office for Holocaust Claims. It still provides free advice and assistance to Holocaust victims and their heirs on all Holocaust era restitution and compensation. So, quietly and in the background, our efforts for survivors continue.

How, then, could we use our experience to teach others? In 1988, our solution emerged: the Holocaust Educational Trust – an organisation whose sole purpose would be to show our citizens and especially our youngsters what happened when racism replaced diversity and when mass murder took over a nation and its satellites. The Nazis and their accomplices destroyed the lives of six million Jews and tens of thousands of gays, travellers and disabled people, democrats and political opponents. It was not enough to say 'never again'. We had to act. And who more appropriate to initiate that action than myself – a man who had lost almost his entire family on the continent of Europe at the hands of the Nazis; who had suffered and learned from the survivors in Belsen and worked in the Kinderheim; and who had not done nearly enough to turn past nightmares into permanent hope? I had a job to do and HET would be its vehicle.

We must educate young people, in their schools and universities, through lectures and especially through visits to the dread horrors of Auschwitz-Birkenau. So we made up a cadre of Holocaust survivors, brave and ready to tell their stories in schools and institutions. We took on staff to teach and to train. And we built up a team of colleagues, both professional and amateur, to head and to guide our work, led by our President, Stephen Rubin, and our Treasurer, Paul Philips, and our fine team of professionals.

Then came the extraordinary good news. Two colleague MPs, Ian Austin and Tom Watson, talked to Chancellor Gordon Brown and persuaded him that the time had come when every senior school in Britain should be helped and enabled to send two students to visit, to feel and to understand the horrors of Auschwitz. The Chancellor announced that the Government would contribute £1.5 million for each of the next three years towards this project, which would be organised by our Trust. And the balance we would have to find, from contributions to fares paid by the young people, or whatever. For colleagues and for me, this is a dream. Literally thousands of young people would see and feel the nightmare of racist mass murder. As this book goes to press, HET is creating the structure for a mighty project of true education. Thank you Ian Austin, Tom Watson and especially Gordon Brown.

The campaign to win at least a measure of justice, however belated, for survivors or their descendants was for years a powerful incentive in my life, both public and private. The public effort was energetic, powerful and obvious. Without the help of the media, we would not have succeeded. Unless it had been a thoroughly extraordinary venture, the media would not have been interested. It was a public issue, in Britain, the United States and much of Europe.

In a strange way, the campaign helped me to cope with Myra's illness. Literally and metaphorically, it took my mind off her suffering and enabled me to inject at least apparent normality into both our lives. I could not have helped her more if I had quit my work. And the battle for at least some justice for those who suffered directly or indirectly from Nazi atrocities was vigorous and valiant. I salute Lord David Hunt, Lord Peter Archer and all our allies and colleagues in that epic effort.

In December 1998, the United States Government hosted the Washington Conference on Holocaust Era Assets, in Washington DC. Representatives from over forty countries came to the capital for the conference. The US Secretary of State Madeleine Albright made an emotional plea for an international consensus on victims' assets, especially on looted art and unpaid insurance. She told us of her Czech Jewish grandparents, murdered in the Holocaust. 'I think of the blood in my family veins,' she said. 'Does it matter what kind of blood it is? It shouldn't. But it mattered to Hitler and that is why it matters to us all. That is why six million Jews were murdered.

The struggle to reveal and to deal with the full truth surrounding the handling of Holocaust era assets is wrenching, but also cathartic. Only by knowing and being honest about the past can we gain peace in the present and confidence in the future.'

I was delighted to report to the conference that our British Government was now committed to repaying hundreds of Holocaust victims for the millions of pounds of their assets, confiscated during and after the Second World War. The assets which the UK had formally agreed to repay belonged to Holocaust victims from countries such as Bulgaria, the Czech Republic, Hungary and Romania, which were held to be allied with the Nazis. I reported that the Holocaust Educational Trust had already identified some 300 claimants, now living in Eastern Europe, Israel and the Argentine, who would be allowed to claim their property 'with reasonable proof' of their ownership. As always with conferences, the most useful work was done behind the scenes. We nudged and pushed and encouraged representatives of countries to bring at least a modicum of financial justice to their citizens who had suffered from their own pre-war countries' wartime plundering.

The move towards compensation and justice created by the Nazi Gold Conferences in London and Washington has now been almost completed. Originally, Chancellor Gordon Brown had agreed to pay out a maximum of £2 million. By the end of 2005, the total distributed was £20 million. It was an honourable finale to disgraceful and dishonourable acts.

TWENTY-ONE

Murders, Massacres and Mass Graves – Auschwitz and the Baltics

Mass graves are impersonal, unreal and unimaginable. So are 6 million dead people. When you hear of Anne Frank, one child with a diary, she is comprehensible. We can identify with her. How many people were murdered in the twin tragedies of New York's World Trade Center and Washington's Pentagon? Thousands. Of course, we remember the visions of the planes slamming into the buildings and the buildings crumbling away like sandcastles. But we identify with the woman on the plane, phoning home and saying, 'I love you. Goodbye.'

It was during the chilling winter of 1978 that Myra and I first landed in Warsaw. We were sheltered and fed at the British Embassy. There was no food in the restaurants. From a pre-war Jewish population of some 400,000, there were now only a few hundred Jews left in Poland's capital. But that did not prevent the press and sometimes the government from blaming 'the Jews' for shortages of food and fuel which were making Polish life so wretched. The fact that there were so few local Jews left alive was the direct result of their slaughter in concentration camps in Poland, but that in no way reduced the virulence of the anti-Semitic attacks.

The community had its own organisation and a building which included a theatre. We watched a performance in Yiddish of *Tevye der Milchiger* – the musical version of the famous Shalom Aleichem novel, *Tevye the Milkman*.* All the cast but one were non-Jews. The leader of the community, Szimon Szurmiej, was also the head of the theatre. He had not only survived the Holocaust but later the rigours of the Communist regime.

---

* The story became world famous when it emerged as the basis for the musical *Fiddler on the Roof*.

He brought another dozen or so communal figures to meet me. We chatted in Yiddish.

I asked: 'Have you a rabbi?'

Reply: 'No. But then we can "*daven*" – pray – on our own. We don't need a rabbi.'

GJ: 'Have you a "*shohet*" – a kosher slaughterer?'

Reply: 'No. But then we don't need one. There's no meat.'

GJ: 'What about a "*mohel*" – a circumciser?'

Reply: 'No.' Then, very sadly: 'But that doesn't matter either. There are no little Jewish boys . . .' Most of the community were dead. The remnant were old and dying.

Szimon took me to Auschwitz. The official in charge welcomed us and asked for my family names. He checked the camp lists. 'When people arrived here, they were put through the selection. We have no records of those who went directly to the gas chambers. Our lists include only those whom they considered well enough for slave labour. There seem to be none of your family.'

We walked under that most grim of all arches, with its cynical words 'ARBEIT MACHT FREI' – work makes you free. That was where the camp orchestra was forced to play, as the prisoners were marched out to their slave labour. Then the barrack blocks. The exhibition – a room with relics of death behind glass, with one especially grim showcase, filled with hair cut from the heads of murdered women and girls. Others contain sad possessions of political prisoners, travellers and disabled people, homosexuals, but mostly Jews. More window rooms, with piles of victims' pathetic attaché cases, spectacles, false teeth, hair brushes, artificial limbs. Then the gallows where the Russian liberators had hanged the camp commandant.

Out we went to the area known as 'Kanada', where prisoners' property was sorted, sifted and sold. I took a green, rusting teaspoon from a pile of decaying cutlery.*

We were shown the original incinerators, used until 1943 when the adjoining Birkenau death camp became the site of the mass killing. Birkenau – lines of wooden and brick huts, with wooden bunks, each for four inmates. Open latrines – holes in cement slabs. We walked along the

---

* The spoon is in the Holocaust Memorial Collection, London.

pathway of death. SS guards had found their way slippery, so they ground up victims' bones, mixed them with ashes and spread them on the paths. The place was a desert.

When I returned to Warsaw and to Auschwitz in April 1998, with a group from the Board of Deputies of British Jews, we were led by that redoubtable survivor, Ben Helfgott. He had come to Britain on a Kindertransport – a train full of child refugees. I first met him in 1950, when he was an Olympic champion weightlifter. We were both members of the British team at the Maccabiah games – the Jewish Olympics. Now, on the coach, he led us to the village where he had lived before the war, and to his home. He showed us the holes on the doorpost, where the *mezuzah* had been – the cylinder containing words of God, fixed to the doorpost of every Jewish house. Since then, I have always looked for signs of past mezuzahs. In what had been the Jewish area of Cairo, a former resident had shown me where he had buried his mezuzah in the wall and covered it up, so that rioters would not recognise his home as Jewish.

My third visit to Auschwitz was in 2001. Israel Singer, of World Jewish Congress, roped me in as one of the leaders of the 'March of the Living'. Over five thousand young people, mainly from Israel, the United States and Canada, marching from Auschwitz to Birkenau, on Yom Hashoa – the Day of Remembrance of the Holocaust. Teenagers, all wearing the same light blue zipped jackets, embossed with the symbol of the March of the Living . . . all come to learn, to feel and to try to comprehend that unspeakable tragedy.

The youngsters lit candles in the crematoria. They sang Hebrew songs. The Nazis had killed millions, but the Jewish people had somehow survived. '*Am Yisrael Chai*' – the people of Israel live. The ceremony itself was not good. A series of speeches, too many and too long. Some were in Hebrew. The worst was by Israel's elderly and ailing President, Ezer Weizmann. The Polish President, Krazniewski, spoke in Polish with translation into English. Most of the young Israelis understood only Hebrew and English.

There had been a one-hour wait before the start of the two hours of speeches. I marvelled at the stoic silence of the young people. At the end, the chairman called out: 'Lord Greville Janner of Great Britain's Parliament will light the first beacon of memory'. I was followed by the Comptroller of New York, Alan Hevesi, and half a dozen more. Then a guide took us through the camp and showed us where and how he himself had lived, as an emaciated victim.

We visited the old Jewish quarter of Krakow. One synagogue was still in use but the rest were museums. We walked through a graveyard, undesecrated, with ancient tombstones with Hebrew writing. With me were my bright young PA, Mitchell Coen, and my lanky, kindly Canadian cousin, Alexander Lyons. Both were soaked in emotion. Neither commented.

Auschwitz-Birkenau is the ugliest, most evil place on God's earth. Two weeks before, I had attended a libel action brought by Holocaust denier and history twister, David Irving, who was triumphantly demolished by writer Deborah Lipstadt. Irving had proclaimed that there were no gas chambers at Auschwitz and that people had 'only' died of disease and starvation. How good that the court had destroyed his case.

For the thousands of young visitors that day, Auschwitz changed from history to reality. Together, we wept. Never again, we resolved. Never again, if we could help it, to anyone.

Litvaks are Jews from the Baltic, mainly from Lithuania and Latvia. My family are Litvaks, and proud of it. We are modest people, but we Litvaks simply know that we are the best! Those of my family who remained behind in the Baltic are all dead. Every Rudaizky and Natansohn and Vitumjaner and Zwick who had not escaped was murdered.

In January 1992, I gathered together a group of parliamentary colleagues and Myra and I set off with them on a pilgrimage to Latvia and Lithuania. En route, we stopped in Stockholm where we were joined by former Swedish Deputy Prime Minister Per Ahlmark, a great friend of the Jewish people. Among those who joined us from the UK were Tory MP David Sumberg and his wife, Carolyn. Our shepherd was my then PA, Jon Mendelsohn. First stop: Latvia's capital, Riga, home of grandma Henrietta and her family. Just a few thousand Jews, most of them émigrés from Russia. The only relic of our family was a listing of the Riga Natansohn shop in a 1925 street directory which we found in the small Jewish museum in the former ghetto. Riga's Jews had been marched out of town and into woodlands where they were murdered and buried in deep pits. We made our pilgrimage to the mass graves in Rumbola and recited the traditional Jewish memorial kaddish prayer, and we wept.

Then to Lithuania. Here we were met by the young and cheerful Emanuel Zingeris, the only Jewish Member of its Parliament. He took us to our small, bleak and modest hotel in central Vilnius. 'I'm sorry, but there's no heating,' he said. 'We have a fuel crisis.' There could have been a food crisis too, judging by the menu. That night, we were truly frozen. Not even extra underwear and sweaters held off the cold. Myra decided that the Lithuanians wanted us to share their lot. I checked that the Sumbergs were coping and found that Carolyn had piled her luggage on top of her blankets and had snuggled underneath, shivering. By midnight, we were still awake. The phone rang. It was Zingeris. 'Please come downstairs. I've something for you.' He had purloined three small electric heaters from their Parliament building. We were to be warm again!

The next day, we were collected by car and taken to the Parliament to see President Lansbergis. We kept on our overcoats, in his unheated office. I told him that his name was not Lansbergis but Icebergis, a transformation which luckily he found vastly amusing.

Then to the mass graves – the Sumbergs to those of their family, and Myra and I to the Rudaizky villages. First, to Ritover (now Rietavas), where they had herded Jews into a synagogue and set light to it and burned all of them to death. Another wooden synagogue remained intact. It is now a storeroom and locked. On the village green there is one memorial stone only, for a murdered rabbi. After the war, his remains were taken to Israel and reburied. The murderers had marched the survivors of our Ritover family to the outskirts of the nearby town of Tels, where they killed them and threw them into mass graves. We made our pilgrimage to those graves but we were too numb inside and too cold outside to weep.

Then to Plungyan, now Plungye. There we found only one Jew, a small, leathery character called Josef Bunka. He had survived by joining the Soviet Army and he had become a hero of the Soviet Union and proudly showed us his jacket, both sides of its chest brightly covered with rows of medals. He made his modest living as a sculptor in wood. He told us that because there was no ghetto in Plungye, the Germans and their local collaborators had herded the Jews into the synagogue and kept them there for a fortnight. They were starved and were even forbidden to throw out their dead.

Local people had driven their Jewish neighbours, including many of my family, from youngsters to the very old – nearly two thousand of them – out into the woods on the outskirts of town and then murdered and buried them. There were two large mass graves and one small one. Bunka told us that a brave and decent local priest had thought he could at least save the lives of fifty Jewish girls by baptising them. But the killers did not care and murdered them too, so whether or not they were Jewish or Christian in the eyes of the Lord, they were just as dead as their parents and grandparents, their cousins and brothers. The children were all buried in the small grave. Bunka and some friends had carved trunks of trees into massive, weeping human figures. We choked – and said kaddish.

We walked back to the road, in total silence. I was thinking: how can we prevent this from happening again to Jews? God bless Israel. At least there is one place in the world where Jews have a right to go, if they are not wanted in the country where they live. Bunka brought us back to reality by telling us that local people who had joined in the murder of their Jewish neighbours had then helped themselves to their homes and possessions and were deeply satisfied with their day's work.

Bunka took us to the synagogue. Downstairs, a jumble sale of old clothes on rails and trestle tables, but the ladies' gallery had been turned into a museum, and a notice stated that this was by courtesy of our distinguished British actor, Sir Anthony Sher. His family, like mine, had either emigrated from Plungyan or remained there and been slaughtered. In the museum, there were photographs of our '*shtetl*', our family village. The *shtetl* was gone and the villagers were dead.

Chaim, our guide, took us to Kaunas, formerly Kovna, and to an area called Fort Number Nine, with its mass graves and huge monument, and a building with prison cells, where the Nazis locked up their victims. One room is a museum. On its wall I found a photograph of a group of Jewish men, sitting by a table. Second from the right was my disabled and murdered cousin, Chaim Katzin.

In the autumn of 2000, I returned to Lithuania for a conference on Nazi Looted Art. We stayed at a hotel, on the outskirts of Vilnius and owned by my friend, Ben Brahms. He had come to Britain from Lithuania as a young man and now lives with his family in Hampstead. Our guide, Chaim, first took us to Lucknik – now Luocke. It is an overgrown country village with maybe a thousand inhabitants and not one Jew. In the days of my Janner grandparents, it was more than half Jewish.

We walked out of the town and into the woodlands and there was the mass grave. Neatly kept but with fenceposts obviously at one time holding metal chain railings. 'Stolen,' Chaim shrugged. 'Melted down.' We said kaddish and returned to the village. An old man hobbled by. I wondered whether he was one of the people who had murdered my father's family, or watched other people doing the killing. We walked around the old Jewish graveyard, with decent gates but only broken gravestones. I looked for inscriptions which might bear family names, but found none.

On to Ritover – Rietavas – for another look at the Cohen family's old house and at the graveyard. Then, back to Plungye, where Josef Bunka was waiting for us. He took us to the old synagogue. It was locked and Tony Sher's museum had been moved to a small office. Then to the mass graves and kaddish and Bunka's carved trees. Again, no signposts from the main road and without Bunka or Chaim, we would not have found them.

It was then that I decided that we must start a campaign to mark the location of the graves before they disappear into the landscape, as no doubt most of the locals would wish. Back at the hotel, we asked Ben Brahms. He agreed. 'But now let's have dinner,' he said. 'The restaurant's full, so let's go to the nightclub.' We started eating, then the lights went down and a spotlight shone on a pole in the centre of the dance floor. Leaning to and fro was a glamorous dancer, a stripper. For half an hour, we gazed at three lithe and lovely maidens, removing their scanty clothes before our eyes. The contrast between the mass graves and the strip dancing was indescribable . . . surreal and grotesque.

So how could I induce the Lithuanians to allow the marking of these graves? I sought the advice of our remarkable, outspoken and energetic ambassador to Lithuania, Christopher Robbins. He listened quietly while I recounted the sad saga of the unmarked graves. At the end, he simply said: 'You are right. Let's do it. I'll help you.' Which he did, and without his help and that of his successors, Jeremy Hill and Colin Roberts, it could not have happened.

The trail began at the top. I met President Adamkus at the reception he hosted for delegates for our Nazi Looted Art Conference. Would his government agree, please, to the signposting of the sites? 'Of course,' he said. 'We will do it.' 'Thank you, Mr President,' I said. 'I will write to you and confirm.' 'No need,' he said. 'We will do it.' I am sure he meant it at the time, but nothing happened. It took Ambassador Robbins to get the consent of the Department of Culture and to set up a competition for designs for the markers.

From Lithuania to Latvia and a happy and useful meeting with its delightful woman president, Mrs Vaira Vike-Freiberga. She agreed to a similar signposting project for her country and to be president of the project. My Latvian grandmother, Henrietta, would have been pleased with our efforts. Her family were all murdered and buried either at Rombola, which we had visited on our first journey to the country, or in Bikernieke, to which we made a pilgrimage this time, and where a German charity had paid for the site to be paved and landscaped.

There was plenty of work to be done. We were first told that there were some twenty mass graves in that grim land but they have now discovered nearly two hundred. Sol Bukinholz, the distinguished economic adviser to the President, took charge of the project in Latvia.

We visited Estonia and its Jewish community of some 3,000 souls. They told us that the local and German Nazis had murdered over 10,000 victims in that small land, most of whom had been cremated and their ashes scattered. So there are only six mass graves. We visited the ones at Kaleir-Liiva and Kluga, both concealed in lush forests and sand dunes. The entrances to two of them were already marked with granite stones. We have helped the community to mark the others.

In the autumn of 2004, our Lithuanian mass graves project was complete, largely thanks to our ambassadors in Vilnius. They had taken on an extremely bright young Lithuanian graduate called Rita Dargyte as the administrator and given her office space in the Embassy. Many of my family and descendants of other victims had contributed to the cost of the project, and our ambassadors provided Rita with a small car, in which she drove literally thousands of miles up and down that grim country, in search of the graves and for consultations with contractors and municipalities.

On our first day, our guide, Chaim, took us to the mass graves at Lucknik, Plungyan, Ritover and Tels. The next morning he led us to a tiny village of some twenty ramshackle farmhouses and a church. To reach the village, Chaim steered our minibus off the roads and onto dusty, brown dirt tracks. We stopped outside the church and Chaim said to me: 'This is the village of Vitumjan, from which you got your surname.' 'How do you know?' I asked. Chaim brought over the only human being we saw in the village, a middle-aged woman, in raincoat and headscarf. She held up her identity document. 'Look,' said Chaim, pointing to a page. 'Place of residence – Vitumjan. Your grandfather was only known by his Hebrew names, until he left this place and took the name Vitumjaner – the man from Vitumjan.' He showed me a copy of a document from 1892, recording the name: 'Voytimianer Ovsey – four family members, shopkeepers'. The fact that the script and the spelling were different did not matter. I had tracked down my roots and they were sunk into the soil of this country hamlet.

'Your grandfather', Chaim continued, 'moved from this village to Silale, the small town just up the road from here. Then he went to Kaunas – that's Kovna. There, his Lithuanian trail ran out.' He must have found his way to the coast and onto a boat that landed in Barry, South Wales, where he dropped the 'Vitum' and so they and the generations that followed acquired the proud name of Janner.

I walked off on my own, to absorb my history and its roots. There were trees by the roadside, loaded with ripe apples. I collected a bag of them, so that the great grandchildren and the great-great-grandchildren of Ovsey Voytimianer, later Joseph Janner, would get their taste of the vanished past.

In Vilnius, I was received by Prime Minister Algirdas Brazauskas. He promised that he would keep up the pressure on the municipalities to preserve the mass graves and their memorial markings and signposts, an undertaking which he repeated when he addressed the Holocaust Memorial Day gathering at the memorial by the five mass graves at Paneriai. In all three Baltic countries, the governments and municipalities have now undertaken to maintain these sites, so that at least people like our family and other relatives of victims slaughtered by the Nazis can pay our respects. We all felt so helpless in the wake of this untold carnage, but at least we have done a little to preserve the memory of the murdered. Maybe the paths to the mass graves will mark a road for today's young people to be aware that dictatorship and racism lead the ways to mass murder.

I was asked by a senior journalist on the *Jewish Chronicle*, my distinguished friend Jenni Frazer, what I regarded as the ultimate importance of our project. I replied: 'The victims were people like us, families like mine. Now we must ensure that such tragedies never happen again, to human beings of any race.' In a *JC* editorial headed, 'People Like Us', the then editor Ned Temko repeated my quote and praised our 'painstaking, four year effort' and our ceremony by the mass grave in the forest which 'marked the restoration of a dignity, respect, recognition for the tens of thousands of Holocaust victims whose remains lie in 202 mass graves now suitably signposted and cared for.'

We cannot bring our Baltic relatives back to life, but at least we respect and preserve their memory. And thank you, our beloved grandparents, for getting out of there, or the Nazis would have put an end to all of our family.

One morning, in March 2002, I was told that President Valdus Adamkus of Lithuania would be in the Palace of Westminster that afternoon. He would be especially pleased if I would meet him in one of the Commons Committee Rooms. Of course, I agreed.

I arrived and was greeted by the President and his entourage, who had been on an official visit to London. The President congratulated me on the work that I had done in his country and, to my absolute amazement, asked me if I would accept a major Lithuanian honour and become a Commander of the Order of the Lithuanian Grand Duke Gediminas. He told me that Gediminas was one of their great national heroes and that the award in his name was given only to those who had performed outstanding service for his country. This (he said) I had done by piloting the mass graves project in Lithuania, which was now firmly in place. I briefly wondered whether my murdered relatives would have approved of my accepting a Lithuanian award, but decided that, on balance, they would have felt it appropriate. So the President hung the ribbon and medal of the Order around my neck. We had a ceremonial hug and handshake, and I acquired my only foreign award.

Later, I received two sets of information. First, I was officially informed that I am entitled to wear the Order of the Grand Duke on official British occasions when those attending wear medals and Orders. Second, a colleague gently pointed out to me that the notification of the Order indicated that mine was 'third class'! But never mind. He had been informed by the Lithuanian Embassy that the first two classes can only be awarded to Lithuanian citizens. Ah, well.

Early in January 2005, I received a remarkable phone call from the Foreign and Commonwealth Office. Would I be prepared to represent and to speak on behalf of the United Kingdom, at the United Nations commemoration of the liberation of Auschwitz, on Monday, 24 January? And how! The Foreign Office would cover my return fare and two days in the hotel.

I telephoned my daughter Laura. 'So who's coming with you, Dad?' she enquired.

'My PA, of course.'

'No one else?'

'No. Who else do you think should come?'

'You must be joking! You think that you're going to New York to speak to the United Nations and that we're not coming with you?'

So the five of them and I flew together to New York on the Friday and had a sensational weekend. On the Monday, we walked into the UN building. I sat with the British delegation, in the centre of that great arena, and my family in the front row of the visitors' gallery.

After all these years of public speaking, I am still terrified of a major presentation. When the United Kingdom name was called, I somehow reached and mounted the rostrum without dropping my speech. As always, immediately I started speaking my fear fell away, and I enjoyed that incredible experience. When I finished, I looked up. My three grandchildren were leaping up and down, waving their arms and cheering. What a moment! I soon found out that the man who had put me forward for that remarkable honour was the Minister for Europe, Denis MacShane. I was mortified when, a few months later, he was moved out of his job.

The sixtieth commemoration of the liberation of Auschwitz was on 27 January. I flew out to that awful place the day before, on an official aircraft together with Prince Edward, Foreign Minister Jack Straw and other leaders. The day was a huge event, with a vast array of international political leaders and literally thousands of Holocaust survivors. It was freezing cold and we needed all of our winter coats and scarves, hats and gloves. We wondered how any of the inmates had survived, in that grim climate. There were speeches, choirs and prayers. Moving, yes – but I was not torn apart by the most evil place on the face of the earth, as I had been on previous visits. It was a huge arena, a massive stage and a remarkable occasion. But when you walk on your own past the lines of wooden huts or pause before the showcases with victims' hair and children's clothing and cases, that is when you weep. Still, it was an appropriate and dignified occasion.

On 17 April 1945, British troops liberated the awful Belsen concentration camp – the only one, in fact, where the inmates were freed by our troops. I discovered that on the 60th anniversary of that day, our Ambassador to Germany and a retiring junior minister would lay wreaths. No one else. I went beserk. I spoke to the Lord Chancellor, Charles Falconer, and he agreed that if invited, he would most certainly wish to attend. Next, Attorney General Lord Peter Goldsmith. No, he had not been invited but he would certainly want to be there. Then I met the Minister of Defence, Geoff Hoon, at a major Jewish charity dinner. I told him of the problem and he said: 'Just leave it to me.'

A short time later, I was told that the Duke and Duchess of Gloucester were leading the British delegation to the 60th anniversary Belsen commemoration. They would be flying over with a group of distinguished leaders in a royal plane. Would I join them? Indeed. We flew over the night before and I stayed in the officers' mess. I found it hilarious that senior officers were calling me Sir. I told them that when I used to come to Belsen, 58 years ago, I was Gunner Janner of the Royal Artillery and had to salute officers, so thank you for treating me as an equal!

The next morning, we walked into the concentration camp, with its mass graves and simple memorials. The royals laid the wreath. I joined the Jewish survivors in chanting our traditional prayer for the dead: '*Yisgadal veyisgedash shamei rabo* . . .' I stood and sobbed, as I had done in the same place and for the same reason, fifty-eight years before. The mass graves and the weeping mourners and then those children in the Kinderheim . . . death and hope. Belsen had become and remains a kernel of my life.

PART FIVE

One World

Most mentally well-balanced people travel for one of two reasons – either for business, because they need to move so as to make a living, or to relax, by lakes or on beaches or mountains. I am very lucky. My business and my pleasure are combined. Politics are the business of my public life and serving my Jewish communities is an essential of my soul. So I am hugely fortunate that I can serve both my nation and my communities, not only in the UK but throughout much of our world.

Younger folk take aircraft travel for granted. One day you can be in London and twenty-four hours later at the far end of the globe. When Myra first travelled from Australia to London, it took her six weeks. A journey from London to the European continent meant a day on train and ferry. Now, it often takes longer waiting for an aircraft at an airport than it does for the flight.

All of which is good, until you realise that it is not only people who can be propelled with the speed of sound but also missiles with nuclear warheads. As a result, we live in one world in which each day brings not only a growing potential for peace but also terrifying prospects for future wars.

It has long been my good fortune to work not only for my Leicester constituents and in both Houses of Parliament, but also in lands and with people far apart. I hope that the stories of my travel, from east to west and north to south and in so many parts of our one world, will put both problems and pleasures into focus.

TWENTY-TWO

Soviets and Satellites

By 1970, when I entered Parliament, there were some one and a half million Soviet citizens who declared themselves to be Jewish and probably as many who did not. No one knew for sure. The only certainty was that, with a few exceptions for 'reunification of families', they were not allowed to emigrate to Israel.

The battle for the release of Soviet Jewry had begun in the 1960s and my father was a leading activist. In the 1970s, both Myra and I became deeply embedded in the campaign for their freedom. We worked at home, by telephone; from the streets, through demonstrations; and in public and in Parliament, through questions and deputations, correspondence and broadcasts. We laboured together with our transatlantic colleagues, in the USA and Canada, and with activists throughout Europe and the non-Communist world.

Myra was a passionate member of a group of mainly Jewish women who campaigned specifically and symbolically for Raiza Palatnik, whom the Soviets imprisoned in June 1971. Her crime: 'slandering the Soviet Union'. For two years, she suffered brutality and neglect, in insanitary cells, with prostitutes and bed bugs as cellmates. Then, after a hunger strike, she was moved to a Siberian Labour Camp where she had a heart-attack. She was thirty-five years old – hence the Women's Campaign for Soviet Jewry called themselves 'The 35s'. They were a fearsome, determined, firmly focused group of devoted women.

In Parliament, we set up 'The Parliamentary Committee for the Release of Soviet Jewry', headed by Patrick Cormack, Hugh Dykes and Tim Sainsbury, with myself as Secretary. We put down motions, attacking the refusal of the Soviets to release named individuals – including the Slepak family, and the famous professors, Mark Azbel, Benjamin Levich and Alexander Voronel. We had meetings with Prime Ministers Heath, Wilson, Callaghan and Thatcher.

We took every opportunity to lobby personally the Soviet Ambassador of the day and any visiting Soviet luminaries whom we could accost.

In March 1975, Alexander Shelepen, former boss of the KGB and then head of their so-called trade unions, visited Britain. I organised a Commons Early Day Motion saying that he 'would not be a welcome guest'. The 35s set up a mass demonstration and a march to the Soviet Embassy. We were later told that our 'welcome' to our unwelcome guest contributed towards his downfall.

The Board of Deputies organised a mass rally in Speaker's Corner in Hyde Park. By then, my father was in his eighties. After the speeches, we moved off in a march to the Embassy in Kensington. I said to Father: 'Are you going to be able to walk this distance?' He replied, memorably, 'What's the matter, son? Do you want a piggyback?'

In October 1976, Boris Ponomariev, a senior member of the Central Committee for the Communist Party in the USSR and head of their International Department, arrived in the UK as leader of a delegation. Colleagues and I organised appropriate questions and a spectacular follow-up. The Soviet guests were in the Gallery when Peter Blaker alleged that Ponomariev had worked closely with Stalin and was 'an accessory to the slaughter of millions of his countrymen and had played a prominent part in organising the invasion of Czechoslovakia.' His 'present objective is to mastermind the destruction of our own liberty'. So why was he received by the Prime Minister?

Prime Minister James Callaghan: 'Insulting words do not make for good relations between us and a powerful country of great importance to the future of Western Europe . . .' Then he quoted Churchill: 'Jaw, jaw, jaw is better than war, war, war.' The well-known left winger, Eric Heffer, tried to put the matter 'in perspective' – which went down badly. Margaret Thatcher, Leader of the Opposition, attacked the 'propaganda use that would be made of this visit in every Iron Curtain country in the world'.

Then came my turn: 'Will my Rt Hon. Friend accept that there are many of us here who think that the argument as to whether these people should be here is sterile, because they are here? We believe that the occasion should not be one to abuse them but to condemn their abuse of the minorities in the Soviet Union and, in particular, the imprisonment of Jewish people last week as a prelude to this visit.'

Callaghan: 'Both my predecessor* and I have used opportunities available to us to make our attitude known on the questions that particularly concern my honourable friend. I shall continue to do so.'

Thatcher: 'Does the Prime Minister think that soft soothing words will have any effect whatsoever on their regime?'

Callaghan accused Thatcher of 'misunderstanding the situation. Representations to the Soviet Union on these matters,' he said, 'are best conducted privately and they have had an impact, as is known both to Mr Janner and to others and we shall continue to make them their way.'

At the end of Question Time, Tory MP Nicholas Ridley raised a point of order. 'In view of the presence in the Chamber of a man who holds this free parliament in contempt, I beg to move, that Strangers do withdraw.' In other words: Let's clear the Gallery and get rid of the unwanted Russian. By prearrangement with Nick Ridley, I raised a point of order during the division. By tradition, to do so you must cover your head and remain seated. There was always a top hat in the Chamber for that purpose. For symbolic reasons I did not use it. Instead, I put on my black skullcap, my '*yarmulka*'. Seated, I said: 'On a point of order, Mr Speaker. In view of the fact that most Honourable Members will wish these particular guests to see . . .'

Speaker George Thomas: 'Order. The honourable and learned gentleman must have his head covered.'

Janner: 'It is covered, Mr Speaker. I carry this skullcap with me for such occasions'. I held up my '*yarmulka*'. The Speaker smiled, and I continued. 'In view of the fact that most Honourable Members, on reflection, would feel it right that our guests should see how the democratic process works and hear our protests at their behaviour, may I ask the Honourable Member for Cirencester and Tewkesbury [Mr Ridley] to reconsider the matter?'

Mr Speaker: 'That is not a point of order for me, as the honourable and learned gentleman knows.'

Ian Gough then pointed out that at 'the first sign of fury' from Nick Ridley, Ponomariev and his crew had left the Commons Gallery. Would it not be appropriate to call off the division? The Speaker had no power to do so, so the House divided, Ayes 80, Noes 192. We had made our point in true and rare parliamentary fashion.

---

* Harold Wilson.

After dinner every Friday evening, Myra and I gathered together with our guests, around a telephone with a loudspeaker. The 35s and other Soviet Jewry Groups had allocated 'refuseniks'* to different activists. Slepak was at the top of our pile. Vladimir Slepak and his family lived in Moscow. Their thirteen-year-old son, Leonid, was not allowed a barmitzvah, so we held one by telephone. We recorded his sung portion of the Torah and we put it onto a gramophone record which we reproduced and distributed as a weapon in the fight for their release.

Eventually, the Slepaks were shipped off to what they described in a letter to me as 'a village among endless Mongolian Steppe'. In winter, the frost reached –50°C. 'If it is not difficult for you, please enclose with your letters photos, postcards and views of Israel,' they wrote. Israel was their hope.

Then there was academician Benjamin Levich and his family. He was a distinguished scientist who was forbidden to teach. And in far-off Saratov in south-east Russia lived the Kogans, to whom we spoke every Friday night for over two years, if and when the Soviet telephone operators put us through to them. We knew that our calls were recorded because on one occasion after our call the telephone rang in the Kogan household. They lifted their receiver and heard a replay of our 1½-hour conversation.

All our contacts wanted these calls or we would not have made them. They believed that when the authorities knew that a Member of the British Parliament was keeping an affectionate watch over them, their suffering would be modified and that they would eventually be released, as all of them eventually were. Many became my friends – including the Kogans, and especially their son, who is now Dr Ariel Cohen of the US Heritage Foundation. He came to Britain as guest of our Parliamentary Committee and addressed audiences of Soviet Jewry activists and their allies, all over Britain.

Anatoly Sharansky, imprisoned hero of the Soviet Jewry movement, later known as Natan Sharansky, became and remains a distinguished Israeli leader. For him, we prepared two major pressures. First, we put down an Early Day Motion. Dozens of colleagues joined us in expressing their 'revulsion and that of the British people at the trials of Anatoly Sharansky

---

* Russians who had been refused permission to leave the Soviet Union for Israel.

and Alexander Ginsberg and the suppression of human rights in the Soviet Union' and calling upon Her Majesty's Government to take appropriate action. Then we acquired a large Bible, which we dedicated to Sharansky and which hundreds of parliamentarians signed, calling for his release. We then asked every distinguished Russian who came our way to present it to Sharansky, who by then was in prison. If they had been intelligent, they would have taken it from us and binned it. Instead, as we expected, they all refused. We were proud to present it ourselves to Sharansky when he eventually arrived in Israel.

So the campaign continued, year after year, reaching its climax when Mikhail Gorbachev visited Parliament as General Secretary of the Soviet Communist Party. I nobbled him when he was passing through the Central Lobby. I asked him in English whether he would arrange for the release of Slepak, Sharansky and others and allow those Jews who wished to go to Israel. His interpreter translated. Gorbachev shrugged and shook his head and marched on. I did not remind him of this on his later visits to Parliament, when I joined in saluting him as a former Soviet leader who had brought freedom to his people, including those Jews who wished to leave for Israel. Meanwhile, we brought over other former refuseniks, to talk to parliamentary and other groups. These included Eli Gurfel, who came as part of a delegation led by Prime Minister Begin. Eli returned for lecture tours and he became and remains my close friend.

Our campaign had two major effects. The first, of course, was its success in prising open the doors of the Soviet Union, so that those of its citizens who wished to leave for whatever reason and to whichever destination were free to do so. The other was that our own communities had learned how to energise and organise, and how to conduct a united campaign against a formidable adversary. We and our allies had won against a massive superpower. We had shown the world that the Soviet propaganda epic that theirs was a happy and harmonious land was rubbish. In our own small way, we helped achieve the downfall of that cruel regime.

Many of our activist colleagues visited the Soviet Union and the refuseniks in their homes. The Soviets refused visas to Myra and to me. So I learned some basic Russian and used it for my telephone calls. One key phrase: '*Ya tozhe refusnik!*' – I am also a refusenik. I identified with my friends.

In November 1989, Myra and I were finally given visas to visit the Soviet Union. We travelled together with Peggy (later Dame) Fenner MP. We visited our great heroes, Andrei Sakharov and his brave wife, Elena Bonner. They lived in a bare, book-lined apartment in central Moscow, grim and grey and sparsely furnished. We talked to them through an interpreter. Then we walked to the largest synagogue in Moscow. Russian Jews had crowded there on the Jewish High Holy Days, whatever the risks of arrest. We took with us a picture of our daughter Marion in the synagogue gallery, on a school visit many years before. It was strange to be welcomed there and courteously shown around, especially as we were accompanied by very bright young Russian Jewish students.

From the synagogue to the Yeshiva, on the outskirts of town – the last and only centre of Jewish learning in a city with over a million Jews. The authorities were proposing to close it and Chief Rabbi Pinkus Goldschmidt, who later became personal assistant to the media mogul Vladimir Goussinsky, had asked for our help. We hired a small bus for the journey to the outskirts of the city. Rabbi Goldschmidt greeted us warmly and told us of their anxious concerns. Presuming that the place was bugged, I walked around each room announcing loudly: 'If they force this place to be closed, there'll be an international outcry – and I shall lead it. And I'm coming back in a couple of weeks, to see whether they've carried out their threat.' Happily, they never did.

When we returned to our bus, it was gone. 'If you'd have given the driver some cigarettes, he'd have stayed,' said one of our young friends. 'Well, we'll have to go by train.' We walked over to the railway station and climbed into the next train. Suddenly, we realised that we were in a tunnel, travelling deeper and deeper into the earth. We emerged at what our hosts told us was the deepest underground station in the world. Myra, who was terrified of escalators, was shaking. 'I'm sure there's a lift,' I said. But there was none. We arrived at the foot of the first of a series of mighty escalators and Myra groaned: 'I can't do it. I can't do it.' 'Sorry, you must,' I said. 'Otherwise we'll spend the rest of our lives down here. Close your eyes and walk with me.' Six of us surrounded her and whisked her onto the escalator. We were all around her. She was totally protected, but she was still shaking. Off the first escalator and onto the second . . . then the third . . . and then above ground again. 'Thank God,' she said.

We had brought a wreath of red poppies with us from London and we placed it by the tomb of the Unknown Soldier. We were not sorry to leave that grim city.

On 4 October 1999, I was back in Moscow. Sadly, Myra had died and never visited Russia in its freedom. My friend, Henry Strage, and I were warmly received by Uri Fokhine, formerly Russia's Ambassador to London. We visited the Central Synagogue and met Chief Rabbi Goldschmidt, who thanked me for helping keep his seminary open. He told us that there were now officially some 400,000 to half a million Jews in Russia and there were probably nearer 700,000. If you included those with one Jewish parent, up to 1.3 million. Fifteen synagogues were now operating in Moscow and seven Jewish day schools, plus the Jewish University of Moscow. Russian Jewry was free. There was still anti-Semitism, but it was a new Russian Jewish world.

I returned again in May 2001 for the opening ceremony of the Moscow Synagogue, with its magnificent, refurbished dome. A Jewish choir was singing Hebrew and Israeli songs on an outdoor stage, at the end of the street. I remembered my refusenik friends, standing lonely outside that same synagogue, on the High Holy Days, in constant danger of arrest. I remembered our battle for the release of Soviet Jewry. I listened to the Hebrew songs and to the Jewish music. I thought of Myra and the 35s, and I wept. I reached for my mobile phone and spoke to our Chief Rabbi, Jonathan Sacks, and let him listen to the music. I had been a refusenik. Now, with all their difficulties and problems, the Jews of the former Soviet Union were free. Hallelujah!

In June 1978, Romania's tough dictator, Nikolai Ceaucescu, visited London together with his formidable wife. I met them at a reception at the Romanian Embassy, where I was introduced as a Member of Parliament who was a leader of Britain's Jewish community. I thanked him for the freedom that he gave to Romania's Jews, to live and to practise their religion or to emigrate if they wished, and I told him how much I would appreciate the chance to discuss this and other matters with him. Could I perhaps pay a visit to Bucharest and meet him in his own capital?

'You would be very welcome,' he said. 'Please fix the date with my ambassador.' Which I did, just a few weeks later. He confirmed that his

President would be very glad to welcome both my wife and myself and our daughter, Laura. So we bought our tickets, and Myra started packing our bags.

The day before our departure, I received a message. Would I be kind enough to call at the embassy to see the ambassador? I did, and to my astonishment he said to me: 'It is not a convenient time for the President to see you. Would you mind postponing the visit?' I told him that I would mind very much and while I would be very sorry not to meet President Ceaucescu, I had made arrangements with Romania's Chief Rabbi Moses Rosen to be received by Romania's Jewish communities in Bucharest and in the provinces. The ambassador shrugged and said: 'Very well. But the President will not be able to see you.'

When we arrived in Bucharest, we were met by the British Ambassador. He indicated that we should discuss the matter at the embassy. He did not want anyone else to hear our conversation. 'The sun shines here,' Myra nodded to me – which was our code for saying that we were being bugged.

At the embassy, the ambassador led me into a room with a second chamber inside it. It had a table and chairs but was otherwise bare. 'This was built by our own people,' said His Excellency. 'You can talk in here without worrying. But not anywhere else in this country.' He told me that Ceaucescu had discovered that I was not only a notorious international Zionist, but especially unpopular with the Soviets for my leadership of the Soviet Jewry movement. Ceaucescu was due shortly to meet Soviet leaders at a Black Sea resort and he was not prepared to wreck such goodwill as existed between him and them for the sake of a meeting with me. I was astonished and impressed by my own perceived importance and readily accepted that I would not meet the President. 'So what have they arranged?' I asked.

'You will be received by a Minister, here in Bucharest,' he said. 'Unfortunately, it will be a very junior one. Then you will go to the famous resort of Poianna Brasov, up in the mountains. There you will be met by Chief Rabbi Rosen, who will take you later to meet your Jewish communities. Sorry we can't arrange anything else official, but that's it.'

So it came to pass that after a totally useless chat with an insignificantly junior acolyte of the Romanian dictator, Myra and I took our well-packed luggage into an official car and were whisked up into the mountains. There, in a hotel which was by Eastern European standards of the time excellent, we were met by the brilliant, brave and bearded Chief Rabbi and by his well-matched and equally over-nourished wife.

Rosen suggested that we go for a walk. We strolled onto a woodland park by a lake, with bare tree trunks emerging starkly from its depths. I asked him in Yiddish: '*Kenmir reden yetst?*' 'Can we talk now?' 'Shortly,' he replied.

Then I asked him in Hebrew: '*Shomim otanu?*' Do they hear us?

'*Min hashamayim,*' he replied, pointing upwards. From the heavens . . .

A few minutes later, we sat on a hillock by a noisy stream and he told me the story of his disappearing community. Aided by the Israelis and by the poverty of the Romanian people, they were gradually flying the Jews out of their bleak land and quietly taking them to Israel. Soon, he told me, there would only be old Jewish people left. 'I am the only religious leader in the world,' he said proudly, 'who spends much of his time depleting the size of his flock.'

Israel had made deals with the Romanian Government. They were buying the lives of Jews. Ceaucescu's regime was not only Stalinist but also corrupt. That said, unlike the Soviets, they had good relations with their Jews. Indeed, the Chief Rabbi was a member of the Romanian Parliament. Symbolic, perhaps – but no rabbi could be a member of the Supreme Soviet.

Before the war there were about 757,000 Jews in Romania – by its end perhaps only 300,000. Most of the others had been transported to concentration camps and murdered. Neighbouring Bulgaria had protected its Jewish community, but not the Romanians. 'And today? Perhaps five thousand,' he said, 'and most of them in old people's homes. I'll introduce you to them. But first, we will go back to Bucharest and you will join us in our Great Synagogue on Friday night. I will ask you to address the congregation. Please speak to them in the Yiddish language.' I said that I would be honoured, and I remembered the words of the Jewish leader in Prague, who had invited me to speak in their famous Altneu Shul: 'Please remember that every word you get wrong may mean a year in prison for me.'

We met mainly old people – 'the youngsters go away and do not return,' the rabbi told us. We visited ancient wooden synagogues and homes, reminiscent of *Fiddler on the Roof*. We were treated with courtesy throughout, which meant being accompanied by a government escort car, theoretically for our own safety and distinction, but in reality as eyes and ears upon us. Rosen was respectfully received. He was, I presumed, a useful financial asset to the regime.

What could we do to help? The Chief Rabbi shrugged. 'Just understand my position,' he told me, quietly. 'Too many Jews believe that I am the friend and the pawn of my President. Well, if I did not remain friends with him, our Jews would be like those in the Soviet Union. We would not be free to stay or free to leave, free to pray in our synagogues or free to serve the Romanian people.'

When we left the country, Rosen said: 'Please come back. It is very good for us that our leaders know that we are important to our Jews outside. And why not bring some of your parliamentary colleagues with you next time?'

In February 1980, it became clear that my efforts on behalf of the Jews of Romania had attracted the attention of our British security services. I received a letter from the Ministry of Defence, from an 'Officer in Charge' who believed that I might be able to assist his Department and asking me to meet an appropriate officer and to keep the arrangement for the meeting strictly confidential. We met. I explained. And that, happily, was the end of the matter.

Myra and I returned to Romania in October 1990, with a delegation of Members of Parliament.* The great scandal of the day was the way Romania treated its orphans – many of whom in reality had parents who did not care for or about them. Emma Nicholson MP and her Booker Prize sponsor husband, Michael Caine, took us to an orphanage. It was like a prison – window bars and bare walls and beds packed side by side into dank dormitories. The place stank. We were revolted. Myra told me that I should do some magic and try to bring some pleasure to those hideously wretched youngsters. So I did. Bouncy balls appearing from behind ears. Youngsters crying out with pleasure as we tossed the tiny, coloured objects to an audience hungry for entertainment, whose lives were sad and with neither affection nor joy.

---

* Others in our delegation were MPs Nigel Griffiths, John McFall and David Sumberg and his wife, Carolyn; Jon Mendelsohn, Clerk to the Committee; and my PA, Bryony Rudkin.

It was a hot summer's day when we were received for lunch by the British Ambassador at his Residence. I hung my jacket on a hook by the toilet. In the middle of the meal, I headed for the loo. To my horror, I saw one of the white-coated waiters putting his hand inside my jacket pocket and taking out my passport and inspecting it. 'What are you up to?' I snapped at him and grabbed my passport and jacket out of his hands. He shrugged and walked away.

I went over to the Ambassador and told him what had happened. 'Par for the course, old boy,' he said. 'Everything you do or say in this country is monitored.' Call it 'sunshine' or '*min hashamayim*' – they were watching and listening. We were not sorry to leave that land.

My first visit to Czechoslovakia was in grim Communist times. It was the winter of 1987 and its people were as unsmiling as the statues on the famous Charles Bridge. Jewish survivors were few and mostly old. I was taken by car on a chilly journey down to Bratislava, in Slovakia. Again, a small, poor community, operating out of an office in a dilapidated block. I asked them whether it was true that the Nazis had hidden the treasures that they stole from the country's synagogues in the basement of the local castle. 'Probably,' they told us. 'But we'll never find out.' We never did.

In 1989, the Soviets moved out and in February 1992, I was back in Prague. My old friends, Peter and Helena Felix, had decided to return to their family city, and to celebrate the barmitzvah of their son, Mark, in the glorious Altneu Shul. The Nazis did not destroy the oldest synagogue in Europe because they wanted to show tourists where the Jews who had infested Europe used to pray.

So Myra and I and Jon Mendelsohn flew to Prague, where we found that its people were smiling. The synagogue nestles in a hollow, because when it was built in the fourteenth century, no synagogue was allowed to be higher than any church. For us, it was a joyful and warm return to this frozen but free and glorious city.

Raoul Wallenberg belonged to one of Sweden's richest families, who regarded his pro-Jewish attitudes and actions as odd in the extreme. In 1940, he joined the staff of the Swedish Embassy in Budapest, and set about saving the lives of Hungary's Jews. He took Jews off trains heading for Auschwitz. He distributed Swedish 'Certificates of Protection'. He employed 300 Jews in his department. He initiated the establishment of the 'international ghetto'. He provided Swedish protection for thousands of Jews and even managed to take some 500 prisoners off a convoy of trucks carrying food and clothing, distributing medicines to the dying and food and clothing to the marchers himself. By his efforts, he saved at least 10,000 Hungarian Jews from extermination.

In 1945, Russian troops drove the Nazis out of Hungary. Wallenberg begged the Soviets for food for his rescued Jewish victims. Instead, they took him into custody and he disappeared. I joined campaigns in the 1970s, demanding his release by the Soviets, but we could never prove where he was and it is now certain that he died in Soviet bondage. He remains one of my great heroes.

In the summer of 2003 I travelled to Budapest where my respected friend, US Congressman Tom Lantos, celebrated his seventy-fifth birthday. Wallenberg had saved his life and now he brought together his family and friends, in the city of his birth. He was acclaimed by Hungary's leaders. I had first met Tom in Washington, together with his incredible Mormon wife, Annette. Their two daughters had decided that they would replace at least some of the family murdered by the Nazis. Between them, they have nineteen children, all of whom were present at this wonderful occasion. The family were greeted by all of Hungary's top leaders and my PA Mitchell Coen and I enjoyed both the official ceremonies and the family coach trips which followed, visiting many of Hungary's glorious lakes and castles.

The 2,600th anniversary celebrations of Georgia's first Jewish settlement was in September 1998. At the suggestion of my former refusenik friend, Ariel Kogan (now Cohen), its government invited me to attend. The ceremonies themselves were in the capital, Tbilisi. There were dinners, attended by national leaders, including President Eduard Chevardnadze. The country's Jewish community – some 10,000 souls – held a celebration service in their synagogue. Then we headed off by car to Gori, the birthplace of Stalin.

We passed the wooden house where Stalin was born, protected by an overhead cover, and then entered the museum built in his memory. Its only other visitors were a couple from New York. The high point of the day was our reception by the Patriarch and his four colleagues in their cathedral residence. They were seated in a throned row – impressive men, each with a long white beard and white mitre. The Patriarch spoke first, through an interpreter: 'Why do you British not recognise the mighty memory of Josef Stalin? Without him, you would have lost the war and your Jewish people in Britain would have been wiped out, along with the rest.'

I agreed. 'Yes, for his wartime role, we salute his memory.'

'There is a monument to him outside this building. Why is there none in London, if he saved your capital city from destruction? None in your parliament. None in your palaces. None in your Trafalgar Square.' I nodded and decided that I would not mention the Gulag or Siberia.

Then his colleagues joined in. I kept silent and nodded and agreed. Whenever I could pay tribute to his part in our wartime alliance, I did so. The session ended in peace and goodwill and we left Stalin's birthplace without regret for his death.

Myra and I were delighted when King Constantine and Queen Anne Marie of the Hellenes moved into the house next to us. We soon became good friends both with them and with their children. We were only sad that they could not return to their country, to give the service to their people that they so eagerly wished. Meanwhile, we enjoyed their company, and getting to know some of their family, including especially Crown Prince Alexander and Princess Katherine of Yugoslavia.

Yugoslavia has now been carved up into largely ethnic components. Since Alexander and Katherine were welcomed back to Belgrade, the capital of Serbia, they have twice welcomed me to stay with them in their Palace. Theirs is a world of incredible contrasts – a palatial home but days spent in the grim service of their people, some 40 per cent of whom are unemployed including about 350,000 refugees from Croatia, Bosnia and Kosovo. In November 2004, we visited refugee camps and centres; a huge 'travellers' encampment, near the centre of the capital; hospitals and clinics, where they presented desperately needed modern equipment, bought with funding raised at charity dinners, organised for our remarkable hosts, in many parts of the Western world; and several children's homes. Everywhere, the royals were greeted with affectionate appreciation. They keep a polite distance from politics, serving their entire nation with vast energy and unremitting tact.

Our hosts took us out to the provincial town of Subotica, where we were received by its elected leaders in their lavishly decorated town hall. We visited a hospital, a primary school and the synagogue, which was once beautiful, but is now a sad shell. Only some 230 Jewish citizens still live in the town, most of them over the age of sixty-five. They have Sabbath and festival prayers in the small side room. As in so many European cities, their Jewish community is dying of old age.

On my second visit, in 2005, the young, bright, optimistic and focused Belgrade rabbi came to the Palace and told us of his community's needs and hopes. Then our hosts took me to the city's central mosque, serving its Muslim citizens, about 150,000 of them. Some months before, radical vandals had set fire to its library and destroyed part of their prayer hall. The ancient, bearded and robed Imam, and his 34-year-old son, told us of the problems they were facing from local extremists. Like us, they were looking for common ground. The rabbi was helping them to find it – he was their first visitor, after the bombing of the mosque. The arson attack could so easily have been the synagogue or the Jewish community offices, just across the road. Their corner of our one world is not easy to live in. Perhaps the most extraordinary aspect of that anti-Muslim terrorist horror was that no one had set about tracking down the arsonist criminals. Certainly, there would have been the same lack of action had those evil people set light to the synagogue. What could we do to help?

My third visit to Belgrade in the spring of 2005 was joyful. It was Crown Prince Alexander's unique celebration of his sixtieth birthday. Feasts and fireworks, concerts and speeches, but above all a sense of family, spread across this vast gathering. Mighty leaders – from Sweden, its King and Queen . . . from South Africa, F.W. de Klerk . . . royals and parliamentarians, family and friends. A well-deserved tribute to a remarkable man and to his wonderfully energetic and supportive wife. As I listened to the Belgrade Symphony Orchestra, playing in the grounds of the old city castle, I sat thinking. Yes, there are times to weep and be sad, but there are also times to rejoice and be happy. There is too much tragedy in our lives. Most of the guests were with their husbands or wives and I was on my own. Those are times when I ache for Myra.

The Soviet Union and its satellites were grim and awful lands. There is still far too much poverty, misery and hardship. But there are times for joy and laughter. Times to be grateful that the Soviet regime and those of its satellites have gone. Today there is hope. So I enjoyed the music and the fireworks. It was what we Jews call a '*simha*' – and what a royal delight and privilege it was for me to be part of that remarkable event. Hooray!

That autumn, I travelled to Jordan. There I met my old friend, Prince Hassan. After a long discussion, we agreed that today the Muslim and the Jewish worlds are both at grave risk; that where there are attacks on either, such as that on the mosque in Belgrade, we both need a top-level, political voice, with access to leaders who can and should take action; and that our two communities must work together. I asked him to become President of a new Muslim–Jewish organisation and he said: 'Only if you will be Joint President with me.' So we founded the Political Council for Coexistence,* and started bringing in senior politicians, from all over the world. From Jordan and Palestine to Britain and Israel, from Morocco to the USA, from France to Egypt and Tunisia. We now have over forty nations represented on our Council. Our Executive Committee is in London, and we work, usually quietly, in many parts of the world, where Islamophobia and anti-Semitism are growing and serious problems.

Eastern Europe, then, was for many years a major focus of my parliamentary work. One week in Romania and the next in Hungary, one in Moscow and the next in Bucharest. It was a non-stop, passionate campaign to help the Jewish communities of actual or former communist lands to emerge – physically, if they wished, but otherwise at least to remain with the freedom to practise their religion. I have always enjoyed energetic support and encouragement from parliamentary colleagues of all faiths; from Jewish communities and leaders from many lands; and from individuals, who silently and privately funded our organisations and efforts.

What, then, did I learn from these remarkable visits to our Jewish communities? First, Jewish people and their organisations are generally highly resilient. Yes, we have our differences about religious practices, but we know that these are not a concern of our enemies. When Hitler and his

---

* Now known as the Coexistence Trust.

cohorts sent Jews to their death in Auschwitz, he did not care whether or not they practised their religion. If they were Jews, then they must die.

Second: if we Jews who were fortunate and survived the Holocaust wish for our children and grandchildren to have the freedom to live where they wish, then we must battle against anti-Semitism, wherever we find it. In great and decent countries like Britain, we are free to live and to serve, within the law and the customs of our land. Others are not so fortunate. We must do all we can to preserve our liberties and to serve others – especially other minority communities.

Third: Holocaust victims had nowhere to go . . . no place on this vast earth where they were entitled to be received and accepted. No Jewish State. So thank God and a blessing on Arthur Balfour and all others who helped create and build the State of Israel. In our decent world, Jewish people can live in almost any land, in equality and freedom. But if for any reason they prefer to live in a Jewish State, good luck to them. I often ask myself how many Jewish people, including my own murdered family in the Baltics, would be alive today if Israel had existed then.

I have had the great fortune to be born and to live in a free land, where liberty of choice is the right of all. We take it for granted in Britain, which is a mistake. So, fourth and finally: we must not only remember for our own sake but educate our children and our grandchildren, our colleagues and our friends, in the fragility of our freedom and democracy. It is good that we commemorated the sixtieth anniversary of the liberation of Auschwitz and of Bergen-Belsen. Yes, it is right to repeat the wisdom of that great Nazi hunter, Simon Wiesenthal: 'Know your enemies and cultivate your friends.' There are too many enemies of freedom and decency in our world, but joyfully, there are far more friends. For those who have helped me and my family in our lives – and, indeed, who continue to do so – I am deeply grateful. The darkness of the past is in deep contrast with the sunlight of today. But we must never take a decent, clean and peaceful future for granted.

TWENTY-THREE

Israel

Until 1948, a Jewish State had been a glorious dream. For me, as a youngster living in a Zionist home with parents constantly crying out for a national home for the Jews, it was an unreality, until the grim and searing realities of postwar Belsen turned it into a vital and obvious necessity (Chapter 4). And then, on 17 May 1948, the people of Israel achieved the realisation of that dream, with its President, Chaim Weizmann, its Prime Minister, David Ben Gurion, and its Foreign Minister, my parents' old friend, Moshe Sharett, among its first leaders and heroes. On the Day of Independence, friends and I danced the hora, in Trafalgar Square. At last . . . at last . . . Never again . . . never again for a Jewish people with no land that would welcome them.

I once asked Sharett when he visited our home: 'Why do so many British people prefer the Arabs to the Jews?' He replied: 'Romanticism, Greville. When they go to visit an Arab sheikh, he entertains them in his tent. He feeds them exotic foods. He takes them outside, to see fabulous feats of horse riding. But when they visit Jews, their hosts give them cups of tea and show them their family photograph albums!' He might have added that this preference of many diplomats comes from their Foreign Office training. There is, after all, only one tiny Jewish country, and we have British embassies in twenty-five Arab and Muslim lands.

In June 1950, my sister Ruth and I travelled to Marseilles and boarded the Israeli ship *Kedma*, en route to Israel. There we visited our cousin Leah Katzin and her son Ronnie, and youngsters from the Belsen Kinderheim, most of them in peaceful children's or youth villages, in the then flourishing 'kibbutz' communal farms and settlements.

I had won a place in the British team for the International Jewish Olympiad, known as the Maccabiah. My sporting career collapsed when I twisted my ankle, training on a rough, sandy track at Kibbutz Ein Harod, but I joined the opening parade, around the stadium in Ramat Gan. Suddenly, a voice in the front of the crowd yelled, 'Gavriel . . . Gavriel . . . Greville . . . Gavriel . . .' It was my friend, Shlomo Hornung, the teacher from the Belsen school. 'Shlomo . . . Shlomo . . .' I yelled back, waving furiously. OK, so it wasn't very professional, but who cared?

I had learned to speak Hebrew, at least enough to make myself reasonably well understood in the children's villages. My most memorable moment came when I needed a towel. I asked the young woman in charge of the group whether she could give me '*agavet*'. She collapsed with laughter. 'He wants *agavet*,' she chortled. 'He wants me to give him *agavet* . . .' Within hours, I was known on the kibbutz as the Englishman who wanted the girl to give him venereal disease! A towel is '*magevet*', and I had left off the first letter. Ah well . . . that's how you learn . . .

Ruth and I visited the British kibbutz, Kfar Hanasi, where we shared a tent, with no mosquito netting. We were covered with bites from head to toe, and I contracted the dread disease, '*shilshul*', the Israeli equivalent of India's Delhi Belly or Egypt's Pharaoh's Revenge. Ruth kept me going by lugging my rucksack as well as hers, a '*mitzva*' (or good deed) of which she sometimes reminds me, even today.

We visited Nazareth and the Church of the Nativity. We drank tea on the pavement, outside an Arab barber's shop. Two men were standing beside a tall, handsome camel. They asked what we were doing in Israel and I said we were brother and sister and visiting friends. 'Ah, this lady is your sister,' one of them smiled. 'Now, I am looking for a wife. Your sister is extremely good looking. Would you sell her to me?' I asked him what he would be prepared to pay and he replied: 'Maybe ten camels?' I told him I thought that was a ridiculously low price and he went up to fifty. To Ruth's relief, I declined to sell. After all, I would not want to take a camel with me to carry my rucksack. They then offered me £1,000 in cash and I turned that down too. Not nearly enough.

I travelled to a very left-wing kibbutz called Merhavia, to visit brother and sister waifs, from Belsen. The head of the children's village told me that they had a fourteen-year-old English boy there, whose parents had separated. He was immensely lonely and would I please spare time to see him. I did, of course. His name was Michael Adler. He was born in Czechoslovakia. His parents had sent him off to Britain, to save him from the Nazis. He was given shelter and adopted by an Anglican minister and his wife. By a miracle, his parents had both survived the war and had traced him to Scotland and they had brought him back to Israel. He is now Professor Michael Adler of Columbia University and he has become a lifelong friend of all my family.

In another children's village I found Yehoshua Taler. He and his brother, Aharon, had been on the Jewish refugee ship, *Exodus*, which Bevin had so cruelly returned to Germany. The Talers had been placed in the Belsen Kinderheim. I saw the director of the village. 'Yehoshua will be so very pleased to see you. He is terribly lonely. He said to me this morning: "Today, *I* have a visitor." You are the first to come to see him since he arrived here, two years ago.' I then found his brother, Aharon. A quiet lad, he was in a different village. Later, when serving in Israel's army, he and friends went swimming offshore. He was sucked down by a freak wave and drowned. Alas, for him and for the lonely Yehoshua, who kept in contact with us until his sudden death in 2006.

My ultimate joys though, were the visits to 'my children' from the Belsen Kinderheim. In Kibbutz Afek, just north of Haifa, I found Bronya, who had been in charge of the Kinderheim group which I had adopted. She and her new husband collected us in a horse-drawn cart at the entrance to the settlement. Boaz, who used to be Bruno, awaited us, with his refound sister. Ruth and I travelled to several other children's villages. We ate with the youngsters in the communal dining rooms . . . we played with them in the fields . . . we slept in the visitors' huts or tents . . .

In Jerusalem, we visited Moshe Sharett and his wife, Nehama. They entertained us to dinner. She did the cooking and he waited at table. I asked him how Israel was going to cope financially, when so many people told me that its unstinting absorption of immigrants and the building of its new land meant that it was economically bust. He told me this story:

A Jewish man in South Wales had long run a modest but successful retail clothing business. His son came to help him, during a college vacation. After a month, he said to his father: 'Dad, I've seen the accounts and the company is bankrupt.'

'My boy,' the father replied. 'My boy, I have been in business here for many years. I am trusted and respected and my credit is good. You come here and in two weeks, you have made me bankrupt.'

Sharett smiled at me. 'You get the point, Greville?'

'There's no way I could miss it, Sir.'

'Well, we are not going to go bust. Our Jewish people and those who wish us luck and success will not let us down. It will be a hard battle. Why don't you join us?' I told him that I would give it much thought.

The following summer I was back, and this time I stayed with the Sharetts, in their home. Over dinner, the great man asked me, in Hebrew: 'Have you come to settle?' I replied by asking him what I would do if I lived in Israel.

'What about going onto a kibbutz?'

'No, I'm afraid not. I find agricultural work deeply boring.'

'What about the Foreign Service, then?'

'That is certainly possible. But how would I set about it?'

Sharett fixed a meeting with Walther Eytan, Director of their Foreign Service, who listened to me and then shook his head. 'I'm sorry,' he said. 'Today, we are looking for *sabras*.' I knew that native-born Israelis call themselves *sabras* – the fruit of cactus plants – because they are prickly on the outside but soft and sweet within.

I reported back to Sharett and he grunted: 'What *chutzpah*! Eytan is not a *sabra*.' Well, it may have been cheeky, but it was final. Which at least pleased my parents, who were delighted when I returned home.

So I never settled in Israel. Instead, I got immersed into my legal studies. To my surprise and to my parents' pleasure, I got a good result in my Bar Finals (Chapter 7) and I set about earning a living. But my links with Israel remained and grew with the years. I decided that I would remain in London, working in political life but seeking to build bridges between Britain and the Jewish State.

On the wall facing my comfortable chair in my working office hangs a large, head-and-shoulders portrait of my hero – David Ben Gurion. Israel's founder Prime Minister, he strode through life, his bald scalp ringed by a halo of white hair. He spoke his mind and usually that of his people and certainly of his Labour Party. I met this historical giant many times, first with my father and then often in Israel and in Britain.

In 1957, BG (as my family and friends and most Israelis called him) agreed to be guest of honour at a reception in the residence of Israel's

London Ambassador, hosted by 'The Bridge in Britain'. Colleagues and I had founded the organisation to create a link between Britain and Israel. We brought young Israelis to spend time with families in Britain and sent young Britons to Israel, to work on kibbutzim and to see and feel the still young Jewish State. The then famous writer and soldier, Colonel Robert Henriques, was our President. We were a happy group of enthusiastic volunteers – and with Ben Gurion as our guest, we would now be able to raise some much-needed money.

BG arrived late. He had been combing bookshops in Charing Cross Road. I started the meeting by telling him how welcome he was. '*You* would be welcome if you came to live in Israel,' he interrupted. 'Why don't you?'

'I am married and working in London,' I replied. 'But I do often visit Israel.'

'That's not enough,' he said, shaking his head. 'You are a proud Jew, are you not?'

'Indeed.'

'Then why don't you live in the Jewish State?'

'Prime Minister, I am also a proud Briton,' I said. 'Anyway,' I tried to continue, 'you, Sir, are a great hero to us all.'

'I don't need your praise,' said the Prime Minister. 'I need your support in my work.'

'You certainly have that, Prime Minister,' I said. 'That's what "The Bridge in Britain" is all about.'

'Well, that's fine insofar as it goes,' said BG. 'But it doesn't go far enough. You must send your Jewish people to Israel, so that they can help us in our difficult task of building our Jewish State.' I gave up.

'Prime Minister, please do tell us whatever you wish – but know how honoured we are to welcome you.' We all clapped. He looked around and said: 'So if you're honoured to meet me, why don't we meet in Jerusalem? Why are we meeting here?'

Yes, he had a mischievous twinkle in his eye and he knew perfectly well what he was doing to me. And when he had finished telling us about Israel's triumphs, tasks and troubles, he turned round to me and said: 'Mr Janner, you are a fine man. You would be much finer if you came and worked and served in the new State of Israel.'

For most of us who remember the world with no Jewish State, Israel remains a miracle. For me, with memories of Belsen and its thousands of survivors with no home and with my children of the Kinderheim on Friday evenings, singing of the land of their hope . . . of my home in my childhood, with my father bravely preaching, to all who would listen and many who would not, that it was a massive injustice to the Jewish people that there was no Jewish state. Mosley and his Nazis joined Hitler's chorus of anti-Semitic filth and, unlike all other peoples, there was no land where any Jew who wished was entitled to live. Yes, for us Israel was and remains a miracle. Our grandchildren – yes, and even our children – do not remember, that time after tragic time, Israel's neighbours tried to destroy it. I remember Israel's War of Independence. Invaded from all sides by vastly superior numbers, its small but brave people fought back. Their country survived but too many of them were killed. Then they endured all those horrific wars . . . the Six Day War, the Yom Kippur War, and the second Gulf War. Today, it is too easy to forget how bitter were the battles, how eager its neighbours to destroy it, even with the war against Hizbollah raging as I write.

God bless the memory of President Anwar Sadat and of King Hussein, who created Israel's peace with Egypt and with Jordan. I knew and respected them both. There is still peace with Morocco and with Tunisia. 'Why, then, are there no diplomatic relations when the leaders of both countries would wish them?' I asked a Tunisian leader and he replied: 'The street, Lord Janner . . . the street . . .' Incited and spurred on by the intifada and by the anti-Israel – and sadly, often anti-Jewish – rhetoric of too much of Arab television, too many ordinary people on the streets hate Israel.

I first met Arafat at Rajiv Gandhi's funeral. Knowing how many leaders of new and independent lands had emerged out of terrorism, I decided that I should keep contact with the man and perhaps help a little towards peace, as a non-Israeli but a proud Jewish catalyst. So I met him often, in Britain and in the Middle East, in the United States and once, most memorably, in Oslo. It was in 1994 and Myra was recovering from treatment for her hideous cancer. It was a moment of deep hope, when Yitshak Rabin, Shimon Peres and Yasser Arafat were together to receive the Nobel Prize for Peace.

Myra loved both Shimon and Sonia Peres and it was for them that she struggled onto the aircraft and across to Norway. She was too ill to join them and the rest of us at the evening celebration dinner, but she did, with much reluctance, agree to meet Arafat in his suite. He greeted us cordially and afterwards, Myra said: 'Well, you never know. He just might make peace I suppose.'

I talked to Rabin in his room. 'What do you think of Arafat?' I asked him.

'Never mind what I think of the man,' he replied. 'That doesn't matter. Unless, God forbid, he is murdered, we will have to deal with him for the next fifteen years.' Alas, it was Rabin himself who was assassinated, by one of his own people – like Rajiv and Indira Gandhi and Anwar Sadat.

Shimon Peres is my guru and my admired friend. A man of huge intellect and stringent wit, he reminds me of Adlai Stevenson – just too brilliant to be appreciated by the ordinary voter. As, to my astonishment, the Americans voted for Eisenhower (Chapter 6), so Peres was never voted Prime Minister. He assumed that office twice, first in 1984 as head of a national unity government and again in 1995, in the wake of Rabin's death. But he was not re-elected, after a pre-election, vicious Palestinian suicide bomber attack, which caused havoc in Jerusalem. Sadly, Israel's voters did not believe that he would protect them from terrorists. So they elected Benjamin Netanyahu in his place.

On 27 April 2002, UN officials accompanied my PA, Mitchell Coen, and me to the tragic town of Jenin. Like the rest of the world, we had read reports that the Israelis had invaded this refugee camp and 'massacred' thousands of Palestinians, including hundreds of women and children. A few days before, the Israeli army had moved out and the UN had driven in. We would be the first Jewish people to visit, after the Israelis left.

Wearing blue UN flak jackets and helmets, we set off from Jerusalem in a two-car convoy, with UN flags flying. Two and a half hours later, we drove through Jenin City and up to the refugee camp, home to some 13,000 registered refugees. We pulled up outside a boys' school, used by UNRWA* as a distribution centre. A youngster who was playing with a piece of metal

---

* United Nations Relief and Works Agency for Palestine Refugees in the Near East.

piping in the shape of a gun pointed it at us. On the perimeter walls of the school were posters of the '*Shahids*', the suicide 'martyrs'. A group of young boys approached us, looking grim and threatening. I took bouncy balls from my pocket and did magic for the lads. The ice broke and they relaxed and laughed. A security officer asked a twelve-year-old what he wanted to do when he grew up. 'To be a *Shahid*,' the boy replied.

Then to a girls' school, the HQ for Aid Agencies, with the same poster of a '*Shahid*' on the wall. UN officials briefed us on the situation. According to their latest assessments, there were fifty-four Palestinians confirmed dead, and some eighty missing who could be in detention or hospital or have run away or died. No, definitely not the reported thousands. Eight hundred families had been displaced, but UNRWA had a 'good grip' on the humanitarian situation – food, water and medical and hospital requirements.

We walked out of the building and into the ruins of the battle. Our UN guide told us that the camp had indeed been a centre for Palestinian 'fighters' or 'terrorists', depending on your point of view. The Israelis had bulldozed some ten per cent of the area and in the process some twenty-four of their troops had died. It was a grim and nasty battle, but certainly not a massacre of Palestinian refugees as most of the world media had reported.

There were '*Shahid*' posters everywhere, together with graffiti, sprayed in red paint. 'Israeli soldiers are cowards'; 'Palestine is for Palestinians'; 'Sharon – this will be your grave'.

Outer walls of houses had been sliced off. Families were still living in some of the open rooms. Children ran about, many with wooden guns over their backs. One approached Mitchell with a home-made dagger and muttered words in Arabic which ended with '*Yahud*' – Jew. The official told me that he was saying 'Death to the Jews'.

The UN man suggested that we meet the Mayor of Jenin, which we would gladly have done. He refused to meet us.

We walked silently through the ruins, the UN man and myself in the front and Mitchell behind us. When Mitchell frowns he looks grim and fierce and I enjoyed his protection. We now knew for certain there had been no massacre in Jenin, but we were glad to leave in safety.

The next day, we talked to senior Israeli officers, who told us that the Israel Defence Forces (IDF) had entered the camp to capture terrorists and to find the laboratories used to manufacture explosive devices. Jenin, they said, was the base for terrorists including engineers and planners. The Israeli soldiers were chosen because they were level-headed and experienced reservists.

Our hosts described Jenin as a well-prepared terrorist camp. But why, I asked, did they bulldoze the place? Because there was a vast array of booby traps, including pipe bombs and refrigerators. The terrorists had booby-trapped buildings and dug tunnels between houses so that they could freely move between them. There were slots cut into the walls of houses to offer sheltered firing positions, and booby traps everywhere. 'Our rules of engagement were clear – we must only shoot at armed men.' The officers agreed with UN reports of ambulances being used to ferry terrorists out of Jenin. 'We offered water, medicine and blood for the inhabitants,' they told us. 'But the Palestinians refused to accept Jewish blood and even when we offered to send in Jordanian blood, this was refused.' Why did Palestinians themselves not drive in to deliver aid? 'For fear of booby traps.'

Out of Jenin, our job was to let the world know what had and what had not happened within it – the truth of the terrorist base and the lie of the massacre. We put out press releases. I did interviews and broadcasts, but sadly, the myth of the massacre lives on and outside Israel, the USA and the Jewish world, is almost universally believed.

In the summer of 2003, my PA Edward Lewin and I travelled to Jordan, to the West Bank and on to Israel. In Amman, I was welcomed by my old and respected friend, Prince (formerly Crown Prince) Hassan, who had for many years kept to his determination on the path of peace and whom I appreciate greatly. No throne for him now, but still striving towards peace. Then a meeting with King Abdullah, discussing ways in which World Jewish Congress might find common ground with him and other Arab leaders, to bring our worlds even a little closer together.

Then to Ramallah, for meetings with Palestinian leaders. They expressed differing views on how, if and when the Peace Process might advance. They deeply resented the suffering of their people. And we discussed how Palestinian terrorism and Israeli occupation might both end and which was the chicken and which the egg. And, of course, they were concerned over what they called 'the wall' and Israelis describe as the 'security fence'.

The British Consul, John Jenkins, was our shepherd, and he drove us on to Jerusalem and along the security barrier. In East Jerusalem, the wall was high, ugly and sad. We chatted with local Arabs, whose homes were on one side of the barrier and whose work on the other. For them, it made life a misery. Then we talked to my Jerusalem family and to others who disliked the barrier, but whose concerns centred on the lives of their children and their grandchildren, endangered by suicide bombers. Before the building of the wall, terrorists moved across freely and there was no way to stop the murders. Now, the intrusions across the barrier had almost ceased.

The next day, an Israeli officer took us along the barrier, in his jeep. 'Yes,' he agreed, 'it is nasty. But it can be swiftly dismantled when we have peace.' How sad that the Israelis need to build barriers, to protect their children. 'Let's pray that the time will come when all barriers between us fall,' said the officer.

Father had fought all his life for a Jewish State – first, for its creation and then for its strength and democratic survival and Mother, of course, was always at his side. After his death, she was determined that Israel would recognise his services to the Jewish State and to the Jewish people in some permanent and recognisable form.

'They should name a town after him, dear', she told me.

'So how do we get that?'

'Well, you know Begin. When you are in Israel, ask to see him. He was very fond of Dad and I'm sure he'll do it if he can.'

Menachem Begin was a right-winger and Father was on the left. Begin was once the head of the Irgun Zvei Leumi; Father regarded the Irgun as a terrorist organisation and he supported David Ben Gurion, Golda Meir and especially his friend, Moshe Sharett, and their organisations – the Haganah and later, Israel's Labour Party. So why would Begin wish to pay tribute to the memory of his opponent?

On 2 July 1946, the Irgun had exploded a bomb in Jerusalem's King David Hotel, then the site of the British Army headquarters. Ninety-one of our troops had died and forty-five were injured. Begin had always firmly and vehemently claimed that he had given prior warning so that people could leave – a claim that the British authorities equally firmly denied.

Many years later, a former British colonel who had served in Palestine at the time contacted Father and told him that Begin had been telling the truth. Father announced this in a speech in Parliament. From then on, Begin regarded him as a brave friend. So on my next visit to Israel, I asked for an appointment with Prime Minister Begin, which he immediately and gladly granted. We met in his office, and he told me how much he appreciated my father and the work that he had done. He was so very sorry to hear the news of his passing, and how was my mother coping? I thanked him and told him that mother was doing well.

'And what can I do for you, young Janner?' he asked.

'My mother feels that Father's lifetime of work for the Zionist cause should be recognised in Israel.'

'I agree. What is there in this country that is named after him?'

'Nothing.'

'Then we must name an important street or building in his name.'

'Thank you. But Mother does not believe that anything other than a town would be worthy of his memory.'

'A town? We don't name towns after people any more. Anyway, we couldn't name a town "Janner", could we? It's not Hebrew.'

I produced a brainwave. 'Janner, Prime Minister, is "*Gan Ner*" – in Hebrew, "Garden of Light". Now, a garden of light in memory of Father would be wonderfully appropriate, would it not?'

'*Gan Ner . . . Gan Ner . . .* Ah, that's good. I agree,' said the Prime Minister. 'We must find a new town and name it *Gan Ner*. Now, there's one we are just starting to build . . .' He named a place on the West Bank.

'I am so sorry, Prime Minister,' I replied. 'Whilst my father was very fond of you, Mother says that he would turn in his grave if a town on the other side of the Green Line was named after him.' The Green Line was the internationally accepted, permanent border of Israel.

'That's a pity,' said the Prime Minister. 'Never mind. We'll look for somewhere appropriate and I'll be in touch.'

Mother had set up the Barnett Janner Trust, to provide funding for a village, named after Father, and she had flown over to Israel, to meet 'Garinim' – groups of people planning to create new settlements. But when she heard that Begin's government had offered a place outside the Green Line, she was incandescent with rage.

Happily, Begin came up with a village on the foothills of Mount Gilboa. A new settlement of mainly North African Jews, its homes were privately owned, neat and red roofed, perched on a hillside with glorious views across the valley. With that, Father's spirit would be well pleased.

Mother and Ruth, Laura and I attended the opening ceremony. The family's honoured friend, Shimon Peres, declared the village formally opened. Mother drew herself up to her full four foot ten inches. She threw her chest out and her head back and, in Hebrew and in English, proclaimed the pride and appreciation of all the Janners.

Gan Ner continues to grow and to flourish. It is the home of some 900 families, most of them still of North African origin. It boasts in its library a modest museum, with artefacts from the lives and careers of Barnett and Elsie Janner. It is indeed a garden of light, and an intimate link with my family to the tiny Jewish State, which Father had done so much to help create and support.

Ariel Sharon was a right-winger, but he pulled Israeli settlers and troops out of Gaza. So was Begin, who made peace with Sadat and took Israel's army out of Sinai. Both were elected by the only democracy in the Middle East. As I used to say during the eighteen years of Britain's Tory rule: the trouble with democracy is that it often elects the wrong people, but it's still the world's best political system.

As with Britain, so with Israel. When working on behalf of the Jewish world, my job has always been to deal with issues; to seek and to work on the common ground; and to use my experience, my knowledge and my access to promote understanding and, above all, to save lives. This has never meant hiding differences. I once flew to Israel for the day to confront Begin about what I regarded as his total mishandling of a disagreement with our British Government. He listened with courtesy and on reflection, he agreed that I was right. He told me that I should apologise quietly on his behalf to the Minister concerned, which I gladly did on my return home, and the issue was settled.

Israel and its neighbours need peace, above all. Over the years there have been many glimpses of possible settlements between Israel and the Palestinians, never more than those at Camp David, in 2000. With Ehud Barak anxious to achieve results before Israel's elections and Arafat apparently in the mood for reconciliation, President Bill Clinton led the parties away from war. Sadly, Arafat rejected the proposals and instead of returning to the negotiating table with alternatives, he started the intifada. Barak and the Labour Party were sunk. Sharon and his Likud-led coalition came into power.

As with Begin, so with Sharon. He always received me with friendly courtesy. Yes, we had our disagreements, as in 2003, when I met him in his office with a World Jewish Congress delegation. I told him how much harm Israel caused to its own image through its appalling PR, not least in Britain. He responded with an extraordinary tirade about how many Jewish lives would have been saved before, during and after the Second World War if Britain had allowed Jewish refugees to enter Palestine.

In the Spring of 2004, I accompanied my Conservative MP friend, James Clappison, and Elliot Conway, Director of the Parliamentary Committee Against Antisemitism, on a journey to Paris. We met leaders of the Jewish community, who described their current problems with varying degrees of anxiety. Then we visited a suburban, orthodox Jewish boys' school, which some months before had been attacked with fire bombs. The Headmaster brought some youngsters into his study to meet us and they described how they had been attacked and vilified as Jews, by young thugs, most of them clearly of North African origin. Now many of the lads wear baseball caps instead of their traditional skullcaps because they are afraid of anti-Semitic attacks on streets or buses.

We went into a classroom with twenty-five thirteen to fourteen-year-olds. I asked them three questions, in my best French.

'How many of you have been attacked on streets or buses?' All of them.

'How many of you have been called, "*sale Juif*" . . . dirty Jew . . . by those who have attacked you?' All but two.

'How many of you believe that you and your family will have to leave France before long, because of anti-Semitic attacks?' Again, all but two.

So when, just a few weeks later, Sharon said publicly that in his view French Jews should leave their native land and settle in Israel, I was not surprised. It was scarcely tactful or helpful, but it was well intended. On the BBC Radio 4 *Today* programme, I explained Sharon's view. Yes, he had seen this sort of misery before and yes, he believed that the only way that

French Jews could avoid the misery was to settle in Israel. Was it wise for him to speak his mind in that way? No. It would not help his dealings with the French Government. Then I told the story of the French school.

I continued to meet Arafat until the year 2000. We discussed the path to peace and he was always cautiously optimistic. He said: 'We should succeed.' And in letters, he assured me of his 'true commitment to the process of peace'. Of course, there would be arguments and discussions, compromise and concessions, and these continued until the grim year of 2000.

President Clinton brought Arafat together with Israel's Prime Minister Barak in Camp David. The world believed that they were moving towards understanding, hope and peace. This hope was symbolised in the famous photograph of a smiling Barak pushing an apparently happy Arafat towards Clinton, who was awaiting them in a doorway. Later, all three of them autographed a copy of the photograph for me.

Major Arab leaders such as President Mubarak of Egypt and King Fahad of Saudi Arabia encouraged Arafat to build a brighter future for his people by following the trail of promise. But he responded with the horrific violence of the suicide bombers. Hope for peace died while he lived on. In November 2004, Arafat died. He was the leader of lost opportunities. '*Ma'alesh*', as the Arabs say – too bad. While he lived, there was no hope of peace. Now, at least, Israel and Palestine might look forward with glimmers of hope.

Ethiopian Jews are black Africans, of the ancient Jewish faith. Peasants, villagers and relics of pre-history, they are accepted as Jews with Old Testament roots, but untouched by the wisdom and practice, interpretation and reinterpretation, of the past two thousand years by rabbis and sages. In November 1984, Myra and I watched 230 of them land at Israel's Ben Gurion Airport. We had travelled there with Shimon Peres, who was then Prime Minister, and with Efraim Halevy, who later became head of Mossad, Israel's Secret Service. It was Halevy's team who had risked their lives to rescue these extraordinary people, from a starving land.

By 1984, there were already some 7,000 Ethiopian Jews in Israel. Most had arrived during the previous twelve months, by perilous routes. Another

18,000 or so were encamped in the Sudan and probably 7,000 more still remained in Ethiopia. Many were old and infirm. When civil war broke out in Ethiopia, thousands streamed across the borders. Jews joined them. When they arrived in the Sudan, Israelis – all of whom spoke the Ethiopian language of Amarik – did their brilliant best to feed them, to sort them, and above all, to get them out. Onto the buses they went and off to Khartoum. Arrangements were complex and the flights had to be legal. So out they flew with appropriate visas to a friendly European country and then on to Israel.

Myra and I were now to have the great privilege of witnessing this modern exodus. We were excited, as our convoy moved through the dusk, to the airport. 'There she is.' Twin lights in the distance, hovering towards us. Runway lights switched on, then the great plane landed. Efraim said: 'Come.' Myra and I mounted the rear gangway. The plane was filled with silent people. A child smiled. Heads turned towards us with mild curiosity.

We left the plane. An ambulance was at the foot of the front steps. A baby had been born on board. A doctor told us that this had created no trouble and that nobody had really noticed. 'Natural childbirth is no problem for them.' Then buses drew up and down the steps came our Ethiopian brother Jews. The first was a solemn man, dressed in khaki shirt and torn trousers. He knelt on the concrete runway, put down his head and kissed the soil of the Holy Land. We were deeply moved. Here was the ultimate purpose and joy of Israel, with all its problems and blemishes. Jewish lives saved. Efraim said: 'They don't know of Israel. Only of Jerusalem. They have arrived in the Holy City.'

Old men with legs thin as sticks . . . women with cloths twisted about their heads . . . the mother of a three-day-old child, now in the ambulance and suckling her baby. Many stopped and kissed the soil. A woman in a printed cloth dress rose up and lifted her hands to the sky, then fell back onto her knees, kissing the tarmac. The doctor told us that a couple had malaria. A boy with white teeth and black, curly hair smiled at us. The rest just looked bewildered. Onto the buses and away. 'That's it. It's all over,' said Efraim. 'God willing, another lot in a couple of days.' '*Im Yirtseh Hashem*,' said an aide, in Hebrew. 'God willing.'

A few days later, we visited the new arrivals in the absorption centre at Kiryat Arba, in Hebron. A social worker told us some of their problems. Toilets unknown and the flush a miracle so they must learn how to use them. Gas cookers – how do they light? They were rubbing stones together to create a spark, same as they did at home – but *inside* the buildings. How do you put out a fire? You blow, of course. So you must explain that that is no way to put out a gas cooker. Language – they speak their local dialect. 'Luckily, they are very intelligent people who pick up language and ideas with great speed . . .' For them, the light switch was yet another miracle. They queued up to switch it on and off, quietly and in turn, so as to create the marvel for themselves.

How do you explain radio and television to people who have no experience of either? A social worker congratulated a woman who had arrived with eight sons. 'I wonder why I have four children and they are all daughters?' she had asked the woman with sons. The mother of men replied: 'Well, I suppose it's because we do it on the floor and you do it on a bed!'

The ragged tribe whom we had met had already been transformed by the simple expedients of baths and the changing of rags into blue tracksuits with white stripes, and with white trainers on their feet. They were now a race of Olympic smilers. I made my contribution to unreality by producing magic bouncy balls. Magic remains a universal language. They crowded round me, laughing with delight.

So how could the Israelis document their new citizens? In ancient times, each had a first name and was the son or daughter of . . . . Thus: Michael son of Solomon. So he was known in Ethiopia as Michael Solomon. But *his* son would be Jonathan Michael . . . Solution: go back to the last head of the family who had died and take his first name as the family's surname, thereby giving honour to him and a name for the family. They had no concept of time so nobody had a birthday or knew how old he or she was. They traced back dates by events and guessed their ages.

What then of their childhood marriages? Israel's primary schools did not take married pupils. That and other problems stretched forward from their strict religious practices and beliefs. They had brought nothing much else with them. No jewellery, no rings, no bracelets; nothing but their rags – and their history. Efraim had said as we met them: 'You now see history. It has taken a long time to produce it, like this.' Indeed. Like the rescues I had seen, when I was a youngster in the DP Camp in Bergen-Belsen. Hope for the otherwise hopeless. Life for those who had been dead – or almost dead.

Then I remembered the horrific discovery which my friend, Sir Martin Gilbert, had made among Churchill's Cabinet papers. In 1939, World Jewish Congress had applied to the British Cabinet for permission to save the lives of some Jewish children, bringing out trainloads of them from Poland to the UK. Request refused. The Cabinet notes read: 'Each child removed from Poland would reduce *pro tanto* the problem faced by the Germans in feeding the Polish population.' *Pro tanto*, Israel is a mighty lifesaver.

In November 2004, three Israelis from Ethiopia came to Britain, as guests of our United Jewish Israel Appeal (UJIA). Our British Israel Parliamentary Group welcomed them to the Palace of Westminster. They spoke of their experiences, which were many and moving. But to all of us, the key moment came when the bright young woman told us the following tale, in perfect English: 'We were taken from the aircraft to an absorption centre. I explained that I needed the lavatory and they showed me into a small room. When I had finished, I tried to get out, but could not open the door. Then I saw that a young woman was standing in front of me. I asked her how I could open the door. Then I realized that I was talking to a picture of myself. It was a mirror – the first one that I had ever seen.'

For many, Israel is a reflection of the ancient past. For others, like our Ethiopian friends, it is a very new world.

El Al is Israel's national airline. When its passenger planes landed on its ancient soil, its Jewish passengers used to sing their joy: '*Haveinu Shalom Aleichem*' – we bring peace unto you. At last, there was somewhere in the world where our Jewish people had the right to land and to stay, if and for so long as they wish. At last . . .

Even today, after over half a century, I land at the airport named after the wonderful David Ben Gurion with an uplift of spirit. Yes, it is a normal country, with all the failings of a vibrant democracy – the only one in that part of the world. Yes, there is too much of what the Bible describes as 'chaos and confusion'. But I am one of the generation that remembers that when the Nazis were wiping out millions, because of their Jewish roots and branches, there was nowhere in the world where they would be welcomed, as of right.

In most languages other than Hebrew, when you drink wine and make a toast, you say: 'Good health'. But not in Hebrew. We Jews say: '*L'chaim*' – to life. Others may call for good health because they take life for granted. We Jews still do not. But at least there is one free land where Jews are welcome. They have a right to life, which we who live in free lands take for granted. If Israel had existed in Nazi days, how many Jewish lives would have been saved? How many of my murdered family would have survived? Then, they had nowhere to go . . . nowhere that would be happy to receive them . . . nowhere to preserve their lives. When I land in Israel, I raise my glass and say: '*L'chaim*'. I am proud and fortunate to live and to serve in Britain. But I salute the Jewish State and all who helped to bring it to life. '*L'chaim*' indeed. To life!

TWENTY-FOUR

The Arab and Muslim Worlds

One day, *inshallah* . . . please God, Arabs and Israelis will live together in peace. For years, I have done my best to advance that cause. I have visited most Arab lands where they have been prepared to make me welcome. On the whole, it has been a worthwhile process. As my hosts in the Israeli–Arab town of Sakhnin in the Galilee keep telling me: '*Nahnu bani am*' – we are cousins. So we should be friends. It is an approach which is as intelligent and happy and refreshing as it is sadly surprising in a world in which Arabs and Jews too often are presumed to be enemies. My son-in-law, David, used to work in Israel with Arab communities. He found me the Shadi guest house in Sakhnin, run by Abdullah and Fawzieh Halayle. Even in the summer of 1997, they had very few guests.

When I left them, they loaded me down with gifts, from olive oil to traditional Arab coffee buns. Abdullah tried to prevent me from paying for my stay. He told me that I was family. Then I wrote a book about the road to peace, entitled *One Hand Alone Cannot Clap*, in which I summed up my hopes: 'The people of Sakhnin, like the vast majority of their Jewish fellow citizens, want a peaceful life. To go shopping, without fear of being bombed. To travel in buses, without fear of being blown up. To travel and to live not only in democratic but also personal bodily freedom. The greater the hope in the past, the more depressing the disillusion as the peace process falters.'

There is nothing new about fear and disillusion for Israel's Arab and Jewish citizens alike. There was plenty during and after the Six Day War . . . after Sabra and Shatila . . . the assassinations in buses and shopping centres . . . the murder of Yitzhak Rabin. Israelis – Arab and Jewish – want to live in decent peace.

I wish them and the world the conversations and the compromises, mutual respect and understanding, without which no peace is possible.

I wish peace, to my friends in Sakhnin and to all who dwell in the State of Israel. Call it *shalom* or *salaam* – the words and their meaning are the same.

Some of my Israeli friends and relatives thought that I had gone out of my mind to stay in an Arab town. Many British friends called it either pleasantly mad or perhaps just a little eccentric. In reality, though, it was safer in the Arab town than on its neighbourhood roads, with so many dangerous drivers. Anyway, if you want peace, you must travel along the roads that lead to it, and there is no point in travelling alone.

The Arabs have an ancient proverb: 'I and my brother against my cousin . . . I and my cousin against the stranger . . .' I have always believed that Muslims and Jews were cousins, and have never forgotten that 'the Golden Age' for Jews in Spain was under Muslim rule. But as with all families, we must work hard to preserve, advance and enjoy the relationship.

There are now over one and a half million Muslims in Britain. Whether their origins were in Pakistan or Bangladesh, in India or the Arab world, most adhere proudly to their religion.

There are about half a million UK Jews (Chapter 19). Outside the UK, the imbalance within the Abrahamic brotherhood is vastly greater. In post-Holocaust days, there may be some 15 million people of Jewish faith or origin. There are probably at least 600 million Muslims. As part of my education and work, and out of sheer fascination and pleasure, I have enjoyed the hospitality of visits to many Muslim lands. Everywhere, I have been received with courtesy and warmth.

I first knew Egypt from our Passover ceremonies. We Jews identify with our ancestors. We read in the Hagadah, the book that records our people's Egyptian history, 'We were slaves to Pharaoh in Egypt . . . I was led to freedom to the Promised Land.' And we were commanded to say 'we' and 'I', and not 'they' and 'he'. Since then, Egypt has retained an extraordinary fascination for me, which was sharpened by my remarkable visit in 1979, together with my daughter Marion. In Cairo, we visited the Karaite synagogue, a community founded around AD 800, which now had only about twenty members. Their President took us into their office and opened a creaking door of an ancient safe. It was crammed with documents. One of them was the most ancient complete Jewish manuscript Bible, the Ben Asher Codex, written in the ninth century and reputedly used by the famous Moses Maimonides himself. They told us that the only other copy was in Leningrad but was incomplete.

The Codex was in a shocking state of preservation. Our hosts could not open the pages fully for us. They simply lifted some pages, to show us the writing, on gazelle skin. It was literally falling to bits. Other ancient documents were in an equally appalling condition. Many were wormeaten. 'You will be seeing President Sadat?' our hosts enquired. 'Then please seek his permission to take the Codex out of the country to have it restored. It could then be exhibited, but returned to Egypt.'

After waiting for a week which we spent on a glorious Nile cruise, Marion and I received our summons to meet the President. We were to visit him in his home in the village of Mit Abul Kom. Sadat was much taller than I had expected. He was dressed in a simple grey coat with a wide collar, buttoned at the neck with no tie. He spoke perfect English and throughout our conversation, he was unaccompanied. Marion sat in the background. When I admired the garden, he said: 'This is where I get my peace. I have planted every tree here myself. Even that one . . .' He pointed to a palm tree. 'It was given to me by that crazy man Gadaffi . . .' He told me that he was writing a new book entitled *In Search of Peace*. It would tell of his journey to Jerusalem and of his brave and remarkable meeting with Prime Minister Menahem Begin. He described politics as 'the art of the impossible' and I told him that for us it was impossible that we were here, talking to him.

Sadat was very optimistic about the peace process. He kept referring to 'my dear friend Menahem . . . a very strong enemy and now a very strong friend . . . I shall urge him not to stop in the middle of the road. He must make real peace and not just with Egypt. We can do that.' We talked for nearly four hours, our conversation ranging from peace in the Middle East to the problems of the Arab States, from handling Arafat and Gaza and the West Bank to the Saudis and the Syrians, the Christians, the Muslims and the Jews.

'I have one great dream,' he told me. 'I want to create a building on Mount Sinai. There will be one doorway, leading to three places for prayer, one Christian, one Muslim, one Jewish. The Christians tell me that there would have to be three, for their three traditions. I said: No! The Muslims told me there would have to be two for our two traditions. I said: No! The Jews said that they would have to have two – for Sephardim and

Ashkenazim. I said: No! I want unity. There will be one mosque, one synagogue and one church. There is only one God. I want unity. And there I shall also have my tomb.'

I hoped that he would not occupy that tomb until he reached at least the age of 120. He laughed and told me that many Israelis had blessed him with the hope that he should live to the age of Abraham. I told him about the Karaite synagogue and the books in the safe and of the marvellous Codex and of their urgent need for repair. Yes, he said, we could take them out of Egypt if that was necessary to put them into proper order. But provided that they were returned to Egypt afterwards.

At six on the following Saturday morning, we returned to the Karaite synagogue. We found the President of the community, Eli Musouda, with two women but no one else. The service was almost Muslim in style, kneeling and placing the forehead on the ground . . . standing and holding arms outstretched while saying the Shema, the central prayer . . . and with no shoes on the feet. I told them how delighted I was that the President had agreed to our taking the Codex with us, to have it restored, exhibited and then returned to Egypt. Musouda replied: 'We have to have a committee meeting about this. It will not be easy. People will not agree.' I told him that we had to leave the following day and he said: 'It will not be possible to release the Codex by then.' So we left without the Codex. On 6 October 1981, while reviewing a Cairo military parade commemorating the Arab–Israeli war, Sadat was assassinated by Muslim extremists. I mourned him deeply.

I returned to Cairo in 1986 and again saw Eli Musouda. He told us that only about sixteen people remained in the community. 'What can I do to help you?' I asked. 'We would like to get the Ben Asher Codex out,' he replied. I reminded him that I had made arrangements with Sadat on my last visit but that they could not get the consent of their committee. 'No problem now,' said Musouda. 'I am the committee!' I told him that I would be glad to raise the matter with President Hosni Mubarak, assuming that I could see him. The British Ambassador would be with me and we would ask for the book to be restored at the British Museum. I would seek this not as a concession to Israel but in my role as a Vice President of the World Jewish Congress. Musouda agreed. 'But the book must be accompanied at all times by one of us.' 'Fine,' I said. 'If I get permission, we'll fly together and you will have the book with you.' He agreed. All we now needed was approval from President Mubarak.

On 8 January 1986, accompanied by our British Ambassador, Sir Alan Urwick, I was most courteously received by President Hosni Mubarak at his Rouba Palace. As Mubarak is still in office, most of this conversation remains confidential, but I did ask him for permission to take the Ben Asher Codex away to be restored and then returned. Mubarak replied: 'I do not know anything about it. I would have to look into it. It would have to be approved by a committee or I will be in trouble with the opposition.'

I reminded him that a camel is a horse created by a committee. 'By the time you have your camel, the Codex will simply die. There will be no treasure for Egypt and none for the Jewish people.'

'Can it not be restored in Egypt?'

'I'm not an expert,' I replied, 'but I am told that there are neither the resources nor the top capability here. The best in the world are in the British Museum and we can find the funds for it. It will be restored, exhibited and then returned to Egypt. It will be in the custody of World Jewish Congress.'

Mubarak: 'I'll have to look into it.'

GJ: 'Can I write to you about it?'

Mubarak: 'Of course.'

GJ: 'Perhaps someone will keep my Ambassador in touch?'

Mubarak: 'No need for the Ambassador. We will let you know.' But we never heard. I wrote, but without response. I hope that the Codex is somewhere safe. Who knows?

Since 1995, when I first visited Egypt with Douglas Krikler as my guide and interpreter, I have always been fascinated by that ancient land and civilisation. It is good that it remains at peace with Israel, but sad that the peace is cool, both above and below the surface. The two countries have much to offer to each other and hopefully one day there will be real friendship. *Inshallah*.

Jordan holds a major key to Middle Eastern peace. In 1994, Myra, Laura and I were in Israel and Prince Hassan, then Crown Prince, invited us to visit Amman, where he would host a dinner for us and fix an audience with King Hussein. Myra did not want to come. She was afraid. Laura did. Between us, we convinced Myra that she ought to give it a try and she finally agreed. We were accompanied as usual by our doughty colleague, Douglas Krikler. The result was a delight.

Amman is a modern city, but one where Douglas knew cafés where he could join young company in smoking a hubble-bubble pipe and in exchanging ideas and information. Politically, we were received with warmth and at top level. Clearly, our hosts felt that perhaps we might help steady the tightrope along which they were both committed and determined to walk – a rope bridge between the Arab world and Israel – and, as always, with an eye on 'the street'.

Our function with Crown Prince Hassan was, like the Prince himself, delightful. Then we were most cordially received by King Hussein. We discussed the Middle East and Jordan's place in it . . . how the small kingdom was coping with its vast proportion of Palestinian citizens . . . and how Britain might provide more, much-needed aid and assistance.

Since then, I have often returned to Amman and have always been received with courtesy, appreciative and appreciated. In December 2003, I travelled to Jordan, to the West Bank and to Israel, accompanied by my PA, Edward Lewin. Before meeting Jordan's leaders, we were taken to Petra, that most splendid of ancient civilizations, to enjoy its glories. Our talks with Jordan's leaders were, as always, constructive.

Morocco was Myra territory. Rabat, the capital, was excellent for her sumptuous rugs, but above all, she loved Marrakesh and that most luxurious of hotels, the Mamounia. For me, it was the networking that mattered. Meetings with ministers and an audience with the King, sessions with Jewish leaders and pilgrimages to the tombs and towns of ancient rabbis and sages. For Myra, it was much simpler. Shopping and fun, love and laughter. We shared each other's pleasures in an Arab land which we both found pulsating with interest and with friendliness.

The leading Jewish personality? André Azoulay, adviser to monarchs and to the mighty and a proud Jew who briefed us and welcomed us warmly to his home. We believed that his community was safe – unless, of course, the mobs rose again in the streets.

It was on a visit with a Board of Deputies delegation that we took part in an ancient Jewish religious celebration, called a '*hiloula*'. We visited the shrine of the saintly Rabbi Yahya, on the Jewish festival of Lag Baomer, with the mainly Jewish guests kissing his tombstone and enjoying the music and the six-course kosher meal under the huge awning.

In 2003, at the urging of my friend, Mohammed Belmahi, Morocco's charming and energetic Ambassador to the UK, I agreed to return to Morocco. He arranged for me to meet powerful politicians and, of course, Morocco's Jewish community. I would travel together with my PA, Edward Lewin. Two days before we were due to leave, terrorists planted bombs in Casablanca, damaging a number of Jewish buildings, including the community's central club. Edward and I had decided that we would carry on with our journey, to show solidarity both with our political hosts and with the Jewish community. It was not to be. First, the Government said: 'Not a good time to come. Please postpone.' Then communal leaders telephoned: 'Your visit would draw attention to our community. You must postpone.' So we did.

Happily, the invitation was renewed and in the late summer of 2004, I returned to Morocco with my new PA, Terry Newman. We were guests of the President of their Parliament, M. Abdelwahed Radi, one of the country's most distinguished and powerful personalities. He organised meetings for me with his country's leading politicians of all parties, and I called on my old friend, André Azoulay, who remains senior adviser to the King.

Why was I made so welcome by so many of Morocco's leading politicians? Probably because they saw me as a Jewish leader, who had a warm relationship with much of the Muslim world and who made no secret of his affection for and connections with the Jewish State. Sadly, Morocco's official contacts with Israel had disappeared, since the start of the intifada. But they were pleased that through me they were retaining an acceptable and, they believed, important contact with the Jewish world.

From Rabat and the nation's leaders we were taken to Casablanca and its Jewish community. Less than 5,000 left, but living in freedom and without fear. The community is shrinking mainly because when its youngsters finish school, many doubt the excellence of local universities so they head off to French-speaking colleges, either in France itself or in French Canada. Some do not return and some of their families join them overseas.

Meanwhile, the community flourishes. We were taken to their Old People's Home and to a Community Clinic, open to all. Then we were shown a synagogue and, to our delight, found that a thirteen-year-old lad was celebrating his barmitzvah – his Jewish confirmation. We were immediately invited not only to join them at lunch in the synagogue hall, which we did, but to the parents' house that evening, for their barmitzvah party. We were at home. A marquee in the garden and lashes of excellent food, but above all, the chance to sit and chat and learn how this Jewish community in an Arab land continued to live in freedom and goodwill. I wish there were many others like it.

Tunisia is a small but apparently well-governed, largely contented land. On a series of visits, I have always found its people and leaders warm and welcoming. But I was told again that when roused, 'the street' can be dangerous. These Arab lands are not democracies whose rulers must respect the wishes of the voters but that does not mean that they can ignore the feelings of their people, stirred up as they so often are by the recorded cries of the extremist Mullahs and the Imams, or, as is the case in all Arab lands, by fierce and provocative visions and attacks on Israel from media across the Arab world. Yes, the leaders want peace and trade and goodwill with the Jewish State and often nurtured a deep dislike and distrust for Arafat. But if they cannot keep 'the street' under reasonable control, then their jobs and even their lives could be in danger.

The Tunisian island of Djerba is one of my favourite places. It is less than an hour's flight from Tunis and is the home of an ancient and fascinating Jewish community, in villages and synagogues and community schools, in peace and in harmony with their Arab neighbours. Each year, they welcome pilgrims to the town of Ghriba, to commemorate and sustain ancient and wonderful Jewish customs, with songs and with dance, with prayers and with preaching. They provide a unique, wonderful and all too small link between the Arab and the Jewish worlds – tiny, fragile and very precious.

I last visited Djerba in 2005, when my PA, Terry Newman, and I were seeking support for the newly created Political Council for Coexistence.

After some useful days in Tunis, bringing national leaders into our project, we flew over to Djerba. I was again astonished and enthralled by the way that its ancient Jewish community has preserved its customs and its traditions on this Muslim island. It was not surprising that on Saturday all the synagogues were full of prayer and song. But it was in the home of the community's president that we understood the depth of their traditions. A daughter in her early twenties told us how much she would like us to return in a fortnight's time, to attend her wedding.

'I'm so sorry, but we'll not be able to do that,' I said. 'How about introducing us to your future husband, today?' She shook her head. 'I'm sorry,' she replied, 'that's not possible.'

'Why not?' I enquired.

'Because we have a custom that after you get engaged, you have no contact with your future partner until the wedding ceremony itself. My fiancé lives just up the street, but I have not been allowed to see or to talk to him for the past three years.' Now, there's an incredibly stressful custom for young people!

In 1995, accompanied by Douglas Krikler, I visited Jordan and Tunisia, this time together with my son, Daniel. We were, as always, received with courtesy and kindness. Then we travelled on to Saudi Arabia, on a semi-official visit. We were not given ordinary visas and were, theoretically at least, the guest of our UK Ambassador. Unlike in every other Arab country, we were refused access to their leaders, although two Junior Ministers were brave enough to receive us, but in their homes and not in their offices. We met a number of British expatriates. Most told us that they were contented in their work and life, but their wives were not. Saudi women are veiled and all females are much restricted. The most serious irritation for foreign women? That they are not permitted to drive cars. A company director told us the probably apocryphal tale of a sign in a rear window of a car: 'Convicted shoplifter. No hand signals!' We were surprised by the modernity of the streets and buildings in the capital, Riyadh. We were welcomed to the home of a Saudi family whom we had met on the aircraft but we declined an invitation to witness the beheading of a convicted murderer in Justice Square, even though we were promised seats in the front row.

It was a surprising, fascinating and unique visit. We learned much, but achieved little.

Finally, Azerbaijan. In the autumn of 2002, I accepted an invitation from its Government to visit Baku as its guest. That visit taught me that any generalisation about 'Muslim countries' is necessarily inaccurate. Azerbaijan is a Muslim country. Yes, it has major problems with Armenians to the north, but none with the 35,000 Jews in its midst. I heard on all sides that there had never been a recorded incident of anti-Semitism in the history of that ancient community, whether among those who live in the capital or others who dwell in the hills. I visited the synagogue which was under reconstruction. Then I was the guest of the Mullah in Baku's main mosque. He brought together leaders of all the communities, Muslim, Christian and Jewish. They received me warmly and we chatted on our common ground. The Mullah told me that he and the mosque were making a substantial contribution towards the cost of rebuilding the Baku synagogue. Goodwill at its best. Our communities can still live together in happy harmony.

I returned in 2003, together with my parliamentary colleagues, Lord Parry Mitchell and Linda Perham MP. We were guests of honour at a remarkable event – the official opening of the first Jewish school in that or any other Muslim country. Together with leaders of their government and of the Jewish community, we congratulated the highly orthodox Lubavitch rabbi in charge and, of course, I entertained the pupils with magic. It was an extraordinary and excellent occasion. The great good fortune of Azerbaijan, both literally and metaphorically, lies in its oil reserves. We met with British Petroleum (BP) executives, viewing the offshore oil rigs from afar. We were proud to be guests in that remarkable land.

Out of the burning of the mosque in Belgrade by local extremists has emerged the Political Council for Coexistence. No one had tracked down and prosecuted the criminals who tried to destroy that Muslim centre, nor had its community been helped to re-establish its religious base. With the encouragement of our hosts, Crown Prince Alexander and Princess Katherine, my PA Terry Newman and I travelled to Jordan to discuss how the Muslim and Jewish communities of the world could find common ground and battle together against both Islamophobia and anti-Semitism, so sadly growing greatly in so many parts of the world. The result: the Political Council for Coexistence. (See page 331 for the tragedy of the murder of our Director, Alan Senitt.)

Since then, the Council has attracted Muslim and Jewish leaders from over twenty countries, including Israel's Prime Minister, Ehud Olmert and Deputy Prime Minister, Shimon Peres. Our members in Morocco include André Azoulay, the leading Jewish personality in the Arab world. But perhaps our most remarkable moments came on our visit to Egypt.

We were warmly received by leaders of the country's Parliament, and the chairmen of the Foreign Affairs Committees of both houses of its Parliament most willingly joined us. But while Dr Tantawi, the Grand Imam of the famous Al Azhar mosque, cried out with his praise of our effort, sadly he decided that he would not join the ranks of our distinguished patrons.

That said, we are proud of our distinguished members from so many lands – we have created a potentially vital link between the Arab and Muslim universe on the one hand and the comparatively tiny and vulnerable but potentially influential Jewish world on the other. May we succeed. *Inshallah and im yirtseh Hashem* – God willing, in any language.

TWENTY-FIVE

The Yemen

In 1991, there were some 1,500 Jews in the Yemen. Now there are less than 400. I am proud of my involvement in this small but epic exodus from that unique and fascinating land.

In the summer of 1991, I received a phone call from a friend in the Israeli Prime Minister's Office. He told me that the most powerful sheikh in the Yemen, Abdullah al Ahmar, who effectively then and now rules the north of his country, was visiting London and staying at the Holiday Inn, Swiss Cottage. Would I please see him and discuss whether the Yemenis would allow its Jews to leave their country, for Israel or elsewhere.

'What makes you think that he'll see me?' I asked.

'He will,' my friend answered simply.

On 14 September 1991, I went to the hotel, where Sheikh al Ahmar's son, Hamid, the fourth oldest of his nineteen children, came down to greet me. He told me that his father would be coming in a few days and that he would like to meet me and had suggested that I visit the Yemen. No, his father did not speak English. They would bring an interpreter.

About a week later, I was back at the hotel. This time, Hamid took me up to a top-floor suite and introduced me to his father. The Sheikh appeared to be in his mid-fifties. He had a black, pointed beard and a fine moustache, and was dressed in Western clothes. His eyes were sparkling and friendly and he welcomed me most warmly: '*Salaam aleikum . . .*' '*Aleikum asalaam,*' I replied in my first and, at that time, about my only words in Arabic. We shook hands and moved to a private room and a Yemeni diplomat acted as our interpreter.

GJ: It is very kind of you to see me. Your son, Hamid, was good enough to invite me to visit the Yemen.

Sheikh: You will be welcome.

GJ: I would like to bring another Member of Parliament with me.

Sheikh: Will he be Jewish?

GJ: The man I have in mind is not Jewish. He is a Christian Conservative.

Sheikh: That will be good. It will be nicer.

We then agreed that I would bring others with me, including an Arab-speaking professor. 'Anyone you like,' said the Sheikh.

GJ: Would I be able to visit my Jewish community?

Sheikh: Of course. Most of them belong to my tribe.

I wondered what he meant by the word 'belong'.

Sheikh: There are very few Jews left and they do not all live together.

I knew that many Jews from the city of Aden in the South of Yemen had left following the establishment of Israel in 1948. My father had been the key organiser of that exodus.

GJ: I know. About fifteen hundred remain, I understand, and they are nearly all under your much appreciated protection.

Sheikh: That's about right. They are my people, the same as all others. I do not agree that all Jewish people should live in one place, in Palestine . . .

GJ: I agree. And no one should be forced to live anywhere. I am a British Member of Parliament and I will always live here, but my daughter decided she wanted to live in Israel. I presume that you would have no objection to those of your people who want to join their relatives in Jerusalem doing so?

Sheikh: No, but there are problems. We should talk about them when you visit my country.

GJ: Thank you. I would like to come as your guest, but not to remain as a hostage. Would it be safe for me?

Sheikh: Of course. Anyone who comes to my country as my guest is safe. But we will have some very tough and full discussions. We will talk about everything. I also want you to meet Government Ministers and others to discuss these problems . . . You should come for a week.

I explained that an election was on its way.

Sheikh: I shall pray that you will be elected.

GJ: So shall I. But my majority is very tiny indeed.

Sheikh: I shall pray even harder for you!

I promised to learn Arabic; we chatted on for a few minutes; and we parted with a warm handshake.

Next step: to the Foreign Office; the officials told me that I needed an invitation from the Yemen Government as well as from the Sheikh. This I achieved with the help of the Yemeni Embassy. And during the following Christmas recess, I led a delegation to the Yemen – parliamentary colleagues Peter Archer, Martin Brandon-Bravo and John Marshall; Nessim Dawoud, a distinguished Sephardi academic, who would act as our interpreter; and my PA, Jon Mendelsohn.

We were met and briefed at the airport by our Ambassador, Mark Marshall. He remembered me from a House of Commons meeting with Foreign Office officials, when he had said: 'Our policy is . . .' and paused, and I had said: 'Ah, so we have a policy!' He told us that nearly all Yemeni men carry guns as well as curved daggers, but while there is shooting, it is always between local people, and we would not get involved in that. All our meetings had been arranged but we should remember that on Thursdays, everything closes early and the men start to chew '*qut*' – a local, narcotic leaf, which the Ambassador disliked.

My key meeting was with Yemen's Foreign Minister, a tiny, bald and brilliant man with smiling eyes. Highly educated, with a postgraduate degree in agriculture from Yale, Dr Abdul Karim Al-Iryani greeted us warmly. He told us that he did not want Yemen to lose its Jewish community, which had been there since the time of King Solomon and the Queen of Sheba, but that he did recognise their problems. The Yemen allows travel for its citizens, but it was illegal to go to Israel. He hoped that this restriction would soon end, and that Yemeni Jews in Israel would return to visit their former homeland.

We discussed Yemen's evolution towards democracy and its potential role as a catalyst in the Middle East peace process: 'Yemen,' he said, in his perfect English 'has always believed that peace must come and each side must settle for a solution which will not be 100 per cent of what it wants. There must be a compromise.' By the time we left, I felt that we had a friend in this man, and that if all was done discreetly, he would ensure that Jewish citizens had the same right to travel from the Yemen as any others.

That Friday evening, we visited the Jewish community, on the outskirts of the capital, Sana'a. We found them in two-storey mud buildings. Although they were totally conformist in their own religious practices and observed all the rules of the Sabbath, they did not object to our car journey to meet them. A family entertained us in their simple home. Alcohol was forbidden, so there was no kosher wine for the blessing. They made do with a fiery, locally made drink that burned like vodka. They cooked chicken over an open, charcoal brazier. They chanted blessings and songs and made us welcome. In their ancient tradition, women ate separately from the men, but served them their meal. We ate sitting cross-legged on the mud floor.

I was amazed at how much at home I felt, in these totally strange surroundings. My new friends drew me into their family, Sabbath warmth. Our traditions were different, but we shared the same ancient history. The next morning, we drove to the village to attend their Sabbath service. Men and boys were sitting on cushions around the walls. There were no women in the room. Young boys chanted each verse, in high-pitched, oriental rhythm and the men responded. They kept their ancient Torah scroll in a mud cupboard on the top of the stairs and, as they told us, removed it each day to read the required portion of the Law. When they came to the reading of the Law, we made the blessings. They listened, smiling with curiosity, as we chanted in our Western, Ashkenazi tunes.

We noticed that while the men wore the standard local dress – white robes and turbans – there were two differences in their appearance from their non-Jewish neighbours. First, they all had the long, side curls of highly orthodox Jews. We were told that they were required by Yemeni law not to hide the side curls, which marked them as Jews. To do so was a serious offence. Second: while every other Yemeni man carried a curved dagger (his 'jambiya'), the Jews were not permitted to do so.

What, then, was the status of the Jews? It was clear that they were not equal to other citizens, but they were protected by the local rulers and if anyone else attacked or molested 'their Jews', those rulers regarded it as an attack on their property and would retaliate.

Later that day, we visited the Jews in the town of Raida. The arrangements made for our reception by Sheikh Abdullah's son Yakhya went wrong. So the Ambassador found a man in the market (the 'Suq'), who told us: 'The Jew Salim lives in the white house over there . . .' He pointed to a large house with a locked outer gate and metal doors.

I knocked and a face which later turned out to be that of Salim appeared in a small window up above. '*Sabbat . . .! Sabbat . . .!*' he cried. It's the

Sabbath day. Between Nessim and myself, we managed to persuade him to come down to the door and that we were Jews who wanted to meet them. I spoke to him in Hebrew, which he did not understand. In desperation, I recited the prayer for the dead – the *Kadish*. He smiled and let us in, and led us up a flight of stone steps to the first floor. In a large, well-appointed room, a group of men were sitting around the walls on cushions and blankets. Apart from one man with a small, red fez, all were in local dress. They rose to greet us. A bearded man with a white '*galibaya*' robe told us that his name was Samekh Kadi, and that his father was a communal leader and his uncle was Chief Rabbi of the Yemen. He said that the sheikhs take great pride in their Jews but treat them like pets. The community had no leaders and he had been trying to create schools for them. They showed us their small synagogue and study room, leading from the courtyard, with half a dozen tables and three or four books and about fifteen youngsters, sitting and learning.

Then back to the Ambassador's residence and meetings and discussions with him and with the American Ambassador. We concluded that Mark Marshall was well disposed towards Israel.

Sunday started with the most memorable and nearly catastrophic sightseeing of my life. We visited the Great Rift – that strange and wonderful place where the earth and mountains and rock are sliced away and the view stretches down uninterrupted to the Red Sea, far below. Martin and I travelled with the Ambassador in his Range Rover, with the driver Mohammed at the wheel. Our colleagues followed in other embassy cars. The sun was shining but it had been raining. The road was coated with a thin layer of mud, so we drove slowly. Suddenly, the Range Rover slid – from one side of the road to the other. Mohammed tugged at the wheel. But the vehicle gently and quietly and inevitably and almost gracefully slid to the right, over the side of the Great Rift – and down onto a broad ledge. We drove up the ledge and back onto the road. Our party's car behind us had stopped. Our colleagues were standing on the road, horrified. The Ambassador clambered out of the Range Rover. 'You don't have to be good in this world,' he said. 'Just lucky.' Indeed. We had seen enough of the Great Rift.

The next day, our host took us to the arms market in the northern desert near the border with Saudi Arabia. You could buy rifles or machine guns, revolvers or *jambiyas*. Business was brisk and every bargain the result of a lengthy, traditional shouting match. On the way back, the Ambassador told us that about 65 per cent of males and 95 per cent of females are illiterate. Yemen's top export is tobacco and their top customer, Rothmans.

Our most surreal and remarkable occasion? An official lunch, hosted by Sheikh Abdullah in his palace. Our cars drove into the courtyard, lined with spectacular-looking people – the Sheikh's own bodyguard militia. Shoes off and into a large room, with cushions around the walls. We walked around shaking hands and saying '*Asalamu Aleikum*' and telling people who we were.

Most of the dignitaries were clad in white robes and turbans, with their curved *jambiya* daggers at their waists. We joined them, sitting on cushions with our backs to the wall. The Sheikh's children came in, one by one – Zadek; and Hamid, whom I had met in London. He was wearing Western clothes and embraced me and then left, because he was studying for exams. Then in came his son-in-law and two little girls, followed by a youngster, about twelve years old. The Ambassador told me that he was the Sheikh's son. I signalled to the lad to come towards me and I held out a red bouncy ball. '*Shoof*,' I said. 'Look . . .' And I tossed the red ball into my other hand and back again, this time emerging bright yellow. The boy's eyes opened wide and he let out a mighty scream. The tribesmen shot to their feet, clutching their unsheathed daggers, their eyes blazing at me. '*Ana sahar*,' I shouted. I am a magician. One of the tribesman turned to the others and said: '*Hoo'a sahar*', and to my deep relief, they all burst out laughing and returned their daggers to their sheaths. *Al Hamdulillah!* Thank God for that . . .

The Sheikh emerged and everyone stood up. I introduced my colleagues. 'Well, have you visited your Jews?' he asked me.

'Yes, thank you,' I replied. 'It was both interesting and enjoyable.'

A man who turned out to be the Chairman of the Yemen Parliament Complaints Committee intervened, very sharply: 'They are not his people. They are Yemenis.'

GJ: 'They are also my people because they are my cousins. I am a Jewish leader and these people are of the same religion as I am and when I visited them we said the same prayers. They are cousins in God.'

I asked how many Jews there were in the Yemen.

Chairman: 'Why are you only interested in the Jews? Why are you not interested in the Yemen?'

GJ: 'We are very interested in your great country and have spent much time in it.'

The Ambassador later told me that, between his taunts, he had winked at various people. He was winding me up – very successfully.

There were sheikhs from the regions where the Jews lived. Our Jewish acquaintance, Kadi, was introduced to the Sheikh and seemed terrified. The guests looked like North-West Frontier brigands, complete with turbans, wild beards and daggers. There was a group from a banking meeting, most of them wearing Western clothes and of Jordanian or Palestinian origin. Our party chatted to the Finance Minister of the Yemen and to other important business and government folk.

The Sheikh then accompanied me through the front door, along the courtyard, up steps, past an empty swimming pool and into a second house, for our meal. It was a banquet. They had slaughtered nine sheep for the occasion. The food included huge tubs of bread, soaked in honey; great chunks of sheep, carved from the carcasses; huge pots of boiled mutton; a plate of mixed vegetables in front of each of us; plates of salad; and by curious and prosaic contrast, plastic glasses and water in plastic bottles.

The Sheikh sat opposite me and a bank manager acted as interpreter. Our group were provided with spoons but most of the eating was by hand. We each had large chunks of '*khubz*' bread. The Sheikh honoured me by constantly dipping bits of *khubz* into different delicacies and handing them across the table to me. I had to eat them. Then he tore bits of mutton off the carcass and offered them to me. 'You must taste this – it's delicious.' It would, of course, have been discourteous to decline, and it was delicious. We talked little and ate much.

Then we picked up our shoes, washed our hands under a tap and photographed youngsters spraying guests' hands with perfume. The Sheikh took the canister from the child and personally sprayed my hands – an honour reserved for me as his principal guest. Then upstairs to a *qut* party, in a room with one of the finest and largest Chinese carpets I had ever seen.

The Sheikh sat at the centre of the back wall, facing the window. A small table in front of him held a telephone. I sat on his right. Servants arrived with huge bundles of *qut* – sheaves of what appeared to be privet hedge. They tore off bits and offered one to each of us, to chew. I tried and then secretly packed my right cheek with paper tissues. When it was well packed and looked large, I got many approving glances from our hosts. The *qut* tasted horrible. Then servants brought in two huge hookahs, each with black cords at the end of its small wooden mouthpiece. The guests passed these from mouth to mouth, but the Ambassador quietly warned us not to use them. 'Spectacular,' he whispered, 'but a primary source of TB.'

I needed to use the telephone, so I sat down alongside the low table. I screamed and the room fell silent. I had sat on an uncovered part of the telephone cord and received a vigorous electric shock. When the other guests realised what had happened, they all laughed. I decided to give up on the phoning.

Then the Sheikh and I were joined by the Ambassador, who thanked him for making everything possible. I said how honoured and happy we were to have visited the Jewish communities and how much they loved and respected him.

'Would you honour me, Your Excellency, by allowing me to speak to you if any question arises in the future concerning your Jewish community?'

'With pleasure,' he replied, and gave me both his own and his son Himya's telephone numbers in Sana'a.

Then they passed an incense burner around and we waved the smoke into our nostrils with our hands. The Sheikh peeled off some of the choicest leaves from the *qut* plant and handed them to me to chew and I ceremonially placed a few in my mouth. My tormentor, the Chairman, finally told me that 'Jews here have no problems' and 'I cannot see why it is a problem if a Jewish girl wants to go off with a Muslim man'. His colleagues smiled at me, sympathetically.

It was clear from our conversations with both the Foreign Minister and the Sheikh that we could now help Jews to leave the country. There were people in Israel, in the United States and in Britain with whom we could work, but we needed a worker for ourselves. It was then that Jon Mendelsohn told me about his friend, Douglas Krikler, who would shortly return with his wife from Africa, where they had been enjoying a long honeymoon. Douglas spoke perfect Arabic. I met, liked, respected and engaged him. We were in business.

First, we formed the British Yemen Cultural Society. With the cooperation and happy help of the Yemeni Embassy, we nurtured our links with Sana'a. Then we created the Maimonides Foundation, named after Moses Maimonides, a thirteenth-century sage who was born in Spain and then moved to North Africa and on to become personal physician to the Wazir of Egypt. Maimonides was a great scholar, whose celebrated letters included a number to the community in the Yemen. We would foster relations between Muslims and Jews, in Britain and abroad, never forgetting those in Yemen.

Douglas Krikler had a degree in Arabic from Leeds University and from Cairo's University of Ein Shams. Jon told me that he was ideal for the Yemen job because he was bright, discreet and determined and got on well with every variety of mankind and, of course, spoke excellent Arabic. Jon was right. Douglas started work for and with us and at once, and like Jon himself, he became and remains an indispensable friend and anchor.

Our British Yemen Cultural Society at once liaised closely with the Yemen Ambassador and Embassy. Douglas then began a series of visits to the Yemen – to its Jewish communities, in Sana'a, Sa'ada and Raida . . . to its government and other authorities . . . all designed primarily to help those Jews who wished to emigrate. We worked together with American and Israeli charities, organisations and individuals, but our main problems came not from the Yemeni authorities, but from a highly orthodox and extreme Jewish religious sect, the followers of a rabbi known as the Satmarer Rebbe. They tried to persuade the Yemeni Jews that they should not go to Israel because (these extremists alleged) if they did, they would not be permitted to follow the tenets of their religion. They should either stay where they were or, if they wished, join their rabbi's followers in New York.

Slowly, Yemeni Jews emerged, some of them passing through London. They could not travel directly from the Yemen to Israel, so we provided them with a staging post. At one time, we rented a house in Hampstead, which they used as a temporary base, and they created a minor sensation in the Lauderdale Road Synagogue when we walked them there one Sabbath morning. The whole operation was, at the time, very secret. So we took the Jewish press into our confidence – which they honoured.

In 1998, I led a group from the Maimonides Foundation back to the Yemen. It included my sister, Ruth, who had acted as solicitor for Jews from Aden,* with Douglas Krikler as our mentor and guide. We spent our days in Sa'ana and in Raida. There had been some kidnappings on the roads and we were advised to stay in the vicinity.

We had cordial official meetings with both my friend, Dr Al-Iryani, and with the mighty Sheikh Abdullah Al Ahmar, and we met some of the remnants of our Yemeni Jewish community. We found them sad, poor and totally under the influence and command of the Satmarers. We joined them in their Sabbath prayer, but were advised that the hygiene standards in their homes were deplorable and that we should not accept their hospitality.

We returned home, glad to have had at least some part in the transfer of over a thousand Yemeni Jewish souls to new life and hope in the modern world.

Generations of Israeli Jews of Yemeni origin have already made considerable impact by their contribution to the life of their chosen country. They have adapted remarkably swiftly to their new, Israeli world. Culturally, they have leaped over the centuries. An Israeli leader described them to me as 'wonderful material'. Myra and I visited many of them in their immigration centres. I salute these remarkable folk and those wise and good Yemeni leaders who quietly and generously allowed them to leave the land of the Queen of Sheba, and to find new lives in the land of King Solomon. As for the representatives of the ultra-orthodox Jewish followers of the Satmarer Rebbe, who persuaded the sad remnants to remain, I despise them, deeply.

So what did we learn from our visit to that unique and ancient land? To me, it was the contrast between ancient and modern. Here were people living in much the same way as their ancestors and ours, in biblical times – their homes, their foods, their customs and their ways of life scarcely changed.

---

* Other colleagues: Sidney Assor, Denise Cattan, Naomi Gryn and Linda and Robert Yentob.

Where else in today's world could you find such people, for whom ancient custom and habit are at the centre of their way of life . . . such buildings of sand and of stone . . . such warmth and such wisdom, but such potential dangers? Where else is there a market where camels circle around the well and raise drinking water to the surface? I salute my cultured friend, their former Foreign Minister, Dr Al-Iryani. But never in my life have I come closer to death, than on that terrifying and spectacular journey, on the slimy surface of the road above the Great Rift.

TWENTY-SIX

India and Beyond

For me, India has long been and remains both a land of vast fascination and a major focus of my political life. My affection for India has its roots in my first visit in 1967, with Myra and the children. My political connections were bound up with my service and attachment to the ever-growing Indian community within the City of Leicester. And as a Jewish leader, I worked for years to induce the leaders of the world's most populous democracy to normalise relations with the tiny Jewish democracy in Israel. Result: decades of involvement with a country and people whom I admire and respect.

My love affair with India began when I was a student in Cambridge. I felt wholly at ease with Indian colleagues and in their Majlis Society. Then, in 1967, I borrowed £5,000 from my friendly Barclays Bank manager and for the first time took Myra back to see her family in Australia.

En route, we paused in India. In Bombay, we were deeply shocked at the hideous horrors of the hutments, stretching and stinking from the airport to the outskirts of the city itself. Poverty, overcrowding, families defecating by the side of the road. In New Delhi, we visited friends and temples, monuments and the site of Mahatma Gandhi's cremation. We rushed out of a meal at Delhi's Ashoka Hotel, to watch a wedding parade. Richly caparisoned and painted elephants, with howdahs. The young couple were dressed in glorious and colourful robes and surrounded by crowds of happy, laughing, waving family and friends . . . We inhaled the colour, the sun and the excitement but we hated the poverty – Myra especially. It was many years before I could entice her back to India.

In 1976, I returned alone, with varied agendas. The most important was to try to meet Indira Gandhi, who had recently been released from the prison where she had been locked up, after the failure of her Emergency Rule. The British High Commissioner had arranged for me to visit that gaol. To my amazement, I saw none of the overcrowding that I had expected. I was later told that whichever part of the prison I visited, the prisoners had been temporarily shifted out, so that the place appeared decent and well run.

I contacted Mrs Gandhi and to my delight, she invited me to tea at her Willingdon Crescent home. She greeted me warmly and as we started chatting, I heard children's voices, laughing and shouting. 'My grandchildren,' said Mrs Gandhi. 'Would you like to meet them?' 'I certainly would,' I replied. In came grandson Rahul, aged about twelve, and his sister Priyanka, about ten. That marked the end of our political chat. I entertained the youngsters with magic and with games while their adoring grandmother looked on, entranced and delighted. I soon learned that her two absorbing interests in life were her country and her grandchildren and not necessarily in that order. After about an hour, the Prime Minister enquired whether I would like to stay for dinner with the family. I told her it would be an honour, which I later learned that it certainly was, because her dinners at home were very private.

Among the dinner guests was Mrs Gandhi's daughter-in-law, Maneka. Her husband, Sanjay, had recently died when his private plane crashed. To this day, no one knows the cause of that tragedy. The conversation was unforgettable. Maneka started by attacking Israel and asking me what I thought of the Palestine Liberation Organisation – the PLO. 'They are freedom fighters, aren't they?' she said.

'Just like the Naxalites,' I replied, referring to Indian insurgents whom they all regarded as terrorists. Mrs Gandhi nodded in agreement. Then Priyanka enquired: 'What do you think of the Government of India?' I told her that I regarded it as a miracle that anyone could govern her huge country. 'Margaret Thatcher's UK,' I said, 'with only 55 million people and far fewer problems, is not governed properly at all!' Mrs Gandhi smiled. But what a question from a child. Clearly, Priyanka would have a remarkable political future.

From then on, Mrs Gandhi treated me as a family friend. Later, she got on even better with Myra. Both of them spoke their minds and respected others who did the same. When Myra first met Indira Gandhi, she asked the great lady what sort of life she led and Mrs Gandhi gave her an idea of her weekly routines.

'Do you ever take a holiday?' Myra asked her.

'Of course I do,' said Mrs Gandhi.

'When was your last one, then, Prime Minister?'

'Last weekend. I went to my home in the hills.'

'Did you take your work with you, Prime Minister?'

'Of course I did,' Mrs Gandhi proclaimed.

'That, Prime Minister,' said Myra, 'was precisely what I was worrying about. You can't go on like this . . .'

Mrs Gandhi replied softly. 'I have no alternative, Mrs Janner,' she said.

On India's Independence Day, the celebration parade was held in the magnificent Red Fort. I was given one seat in a stand but told that I could bring with me a child under the age of ten. My Cambridge friend Jai Mukhi's younger son, Kamal, known as Bhai, joined me and we tried unsuccessfully to flag down a taxi. Finally, in desperation, we took a bicycle rickshaw, which attracted amazed looks as we drew up at the official diplomatic gate, alongside the magnificent limousines. Indira Gandhi, dressed in a white sari, inspected her troops. The small, upright, dignified woman was dwarfed by her men. After the ceremony, we were driven to the High Commission and then back home in the High Commissioner's white Rolls-Royce.

Jai Mukhi put his elder son, Deepak, in charge of escorting me around the capital. We visited Hindu temples and climbed the steps of the huge mosque. We strolled through the bazaars and were then driven to the Kutub Minar, that great pillar of copper. You stood with your back against it and tried to get your hands to meet behind you. If you succeeded, then you would have good fortune. We both failed.

That evening, the British High Commissioner held a reception at his home. It was there that I first met Swaraj Paul, a successful Indian industrialist who had settled in the UK. He was a friend of Indira Gandhi and I met him again several times, with her. To my delight, he is now a colleague in the House of Lords.

Then to the Punjab with an attractive, sari-clad woman guide, supplied by courtesy of the Indian Government. We were descending the steep steps of a temple when she stumbled and I thought she was falling. I took her arm and held her up. She shook me off. 'No thank you,' she said. Even in emergency, we must keep our decent distance.

We stopped in Jullunder, for the Festival of Janmashtami. That evening, a spectacular music group played on a platform in the central square. One drummer was amazing, his fingers flying across three tambours. At the end of one of the numbers, I caught his attention – not difficult as I was the only non-Asian in the audience. I gave him the thumbs up sign, with both hands. He turned to his friends, pointing at me, laughing. My guide quietly informed me that in that part of the world, I had given the English equivalent to the reverse V-for-victory sign. Sign language is not universal.

One evening back in Delhi, I visited that great Indian freedom fighter, Krishna Menon, whom I had first heard speaking in Cambridge at the Majlis Society. I found him terminally ill. I sat by his bed and we chatted. I asked him: 'If you were Prime Minister in India today, what would you do?' He replied: 'I would commit suicide.'

In Bombay, I visited the Israel Consul in his home and office, high in a tower block. The Indian government refused to have normal diplomatic relations with the Jewish State, but allowed a consul in Bombay to deal with visas. The windows of the apartment were armour-plated and guards sat outside his door. He took me into his study and raised the volume of the radio on the table and turned on the taps in the basin. He said to me in Hebrew: 'They listen to everything . . .' Then, very softly, we talked about India's policy towards Israel and the views of its leaders; of my belief that the two countries had so much to offer to each other; and of my hope that, before too long, relations would be normalised. Meanwhile, he must patiently battle on to keep his spirit alive.

On Christmas Day of the following year, I again arrived in Bombay, this time together with my daughter Marion. There, a social worker took us to visit the horrendous hutments at Kamala Nagar and at an encampment running down to the sea. We choked at the total lack of amenities and at the squalor and poverty. We visited a school with 3,000 children and totally inadequate accommodation, but as we walked around the hutments, we were greeted with smiling welcomes. Courteous, charming and proud people, coping with extraordinary grace with lives of unspeakable deprivation.

On Wednesday 30 October 1984, our friend Indira Gandhi was murdered. She was shot dead, outside her home, by three of her Sikh bodyguards. The

assassins' purpose? To rid India of its Hindu leader, whom they believed
had done grave injustice to the Sikh people of their native Punjab. I heard
the news while I was shaving in my bathroom. It was an unforgettable
moment – like the vision of the twin towers of the World Trade Center,
collapsing into dust. I wept. I had loved the woman, for her open friendship
to both Myra and myself and because she had so often given us the rare
privilege of sharing the privacy of her home, with her and with her family.
And I had loved her friendly and treasured letters. Two days after her
death, I received the last one. I was walking towards the House of
Commons when one of my staff ran up and handed it to me. I choked.

Mrs Gandhi thanked me first for sending a packet of toys for her
grandchildren, on their festival of Diwali. Then she continued:
'I understand your dilemma (in Leicester) with regard to the differences
which have arisen between the Hindus and Sikhs – Diwali and other issues.
You can imagine how much more complicated it is for us here. The worst is
the mischievous rumour-mongering which spreads bitterness! I hope your
constituents arranged a pleasant Diwali for you. With all good wishes to
you both . . .'

I still miss her.

Days after that dreadful murder, I found a pile of notes which I had made
after my meetings with Mrs Gandhi. It was clear that she was not going to
change India's policy towards Israel, even if the Jewish State came to terms
with some other Arab states. Only if it was accepted by all of them, would
India accept full diplomatic relations. 'We cannot afford to change our
foreign policy towards the Arab States . . . We have well over sixty million
Muslims here . . . If Pakistan got the chance to create dissension among
them, it would certainly do so . . . The Arabs could interrupt the flow of oil
and that would be disastrous.' Still, she said, she had resisted pressure to
close down the Israel Consulate in Bombay and would continue to do so.

I had discussed Israel with most of India's Prime Ministers, including
Morarji Desai. I visited him in January 1979 and we had a long conversation. He said that he wished friendship with Israel but, as he had told
its leaders, 'you cannot keep hold of territory acquired' and he had delivered
a lengthy homily on 'the conquest' and said that India had never behaved in
that way in all its history. Like Mrs Gandhi, he said that there would have to

be 'comprehensive peace' before there could be normal relations between Israel and India.

Why did these two leaders not recognise the potential and mutually useful relationship between their great and huge democracy and that of the small Jewish State? I decided that it was because both sought to retain India's primacy within the non-aligned nations and believed that recognition would be too unpopular among their non-aligned partners.

Indira Gandhi told me that Desai had once said that whenever women got into power, they became evil, and had instanced her, Golda Meir of Israel and Mrs Bandaranaike of Sri Lanka. He was prepared to make an exception for Mrs Thatcher. He believed that if Mrs Gandhi was returned to power, there would be no more elections in India. He was wrong, of course, but the continuation of her personal political power and of her dynasty remains both a present reality and a major prospect for the future.

Mrs Gandhi was the daughter of the great Pandit Nehru, father of her nation. I once asked her about her relationship with Nehru. She told Marion and me that she and her father had enjoyed a happy friendship and that she 'totally accepted the result of being his daughter'. When her mother died, she was a student. Nehru had travelled around Britain and she had accompanied him. Mrs Gandhi then turned to Marion and smiled and asked me a rhetorical question: 'Do you not like having your daughter with you? Is it not a natural thing to do?'

Well, it did seem natural that after her death her son, Rajiv, should succeed her. He was a former airline pilot and a totally different personality from his mother. I had always found him soft-spoken, courteous and self-effacing. Overnight, he needed to become a political giant – leader of the largest democracy and the second most populous nation on earth. His friends all wished him well.

Unlike the divorced Mrs Gandhi, Rajiv had the support of his partner – his wife, Sonia. Her strength was her quiet, determined authority, her dignified charm and the Gandhi name. Her problem: she was born in Italy and Italian was her mother tongue. She had to convince the Indian people that she was one of them. We had come to know and to appreciate both their children. Their son, Rahul, was a pleasant, intelligent and sensitive lad, who was not happy in school. Priyanka had already shown herself to be both argumentative and brilliant.

Rajiv survived, both in life and in office, for only five years. On 31 May 1991, I was travelling to Leicester by car. My assistant, Manoj Jasani, was driving. We were shaken and shocked to hear the announcement that Rajiv had been assassinated. 'You should go to the funeral,' said Manoj. I telephoned the Indian High Commissioner and he agreed. We turned the car around and that evening I was en route to Delhi.

Early the next day, I joined the queue of mourners, paying their respects to a Prime Minister who, like his mother, had been murdered by fanatics. They had blown his body apart. All that was visible under the robes that covered him were his feet.

I learned in Delhi how much business is quietly done by world leaders at the funerals of their colleagues. Among the mourners at Rajiv Gandhi's farewell were Prince Charles; Douglas Hurd, then Foreign Secretary; Neil Kinnock, Leader of the Opposition; Edward Heath and David Steel. We met after the funeral, at our High Commissioner's residence. Among the foreign dignitaries, most of whom I also met, were US Vice President Dan Quayle; the Prime Ministers of Pakistan and Bangladesh; and Benazir Bhutto, former Prime Minister of Pakistan, whom I later knew well, when she was in exile in London.

We were taken in official cars to the site of the cremation. There were literally millions in the crowd – a pulsating and colourful crowd of Indians of every creed and race and colour. I found myself at the front, near to the funeral pyre. Representatives of all the Indian religions were taking turns to chant funeral dirges. Suddenly I was riveted – it was the voice of the young man who conducted the services in the Delhi synagogue, singing the traditional Hebrew prayer for the dead, '*el molei rahamim*'. Only 5,000 Jews among over a billion people but a precious and treasured community which had enjoyed 2,000 peaceful years in mighty India, and now honoured by taking a moving and visible part in their Prime Minister's farewell.

The duty of pouring '*ghi*' – melted butter – over the corpse, rested on Rajiv's son, Rahul. I thought of how this lad had joined his parents in greeting us at their home on our most recent visit. Now he was a man saying farewell to his assassinated father, with silent dignity. As the flames rose, we all wept. What a tragic family. First his uncle, Sanjay . . . then his grandmother . . . now his father. Who next?

To me, India's refusal to enjoy a normal relationship with Israel was understandable but both sad and unacceptable. I had used every opportunity to press for change. Mrs Gandhi had, I believe, accepted that in spite of the difference in size and population, the two countries could do much for each other. She was especially interested in Israel's expertise in desert technology. Too much of India is covered by waterless, cropless sand and rock. Yes, we must normalise relations, but she always had a reason for delay. If you want a reason and you are Prime Minister, you can surely find one.

After Indira Gandhi's death, Morarji Desai took over. Like so many of my Leicester Asians, he came from the State of Gujarat and I regarded myself as an adopted, Jewish Gujarati. Mr Desai listened carefully to my representations and nodded but did nothing. Nor did Charan Singh, Prime Minister from 1979 to 1980. He was a caretaker PM, who would not take chances if he could avoid them.

Then Rajiv ruled from 1985 to 1989. I urged him to take the initiative. Again, he listened courteously but preferred to leave ill alone. After Rajiv's assassination, V.P. Singh enjoyed a brief reign – from December 1989 until November 1990 – followed by Chandra Shekhar, who lasted until June 1991. I met both but made no progress. Then came the elderly P.V. Narasimha Rao, Prime Minister from 1991 to 1996.

On my visit to Delhi in 1992, the British High Commissioner told me that the PM wished to see me. I went straight over to his office, where he greeted me warmly. 'I have good news for you, Mr Janner,' he said, smiling. 'I have decided that the time has come to normalise relations with the State of Israel. I came to this decision late last night and I knew you had been pressing for it and were coming to see me, so I thought I should tell you at once. Perhaps my predecessors could not do it because they were too young, but I am an old man and I know that normal relations with Israel will be good for my country.' So it was done and announced and some Arab ambassadors to India protested briefly. Very briefly.

Since then, my relationship with India and its leaders, with my Indian friends from Cambridge and beyond, and with its Jewish community, have remained firm and mellow, and I have had special kindness from Lalit Suri, now a member of the Upper House, the Raja Saba, and from his wife, Jyoti, and from Vipin and Greta Khanna and from their families; and especially from my Cambridge friends, Milon Banerji, Jai Mukhi and Natwar Singh, and their families

During the 2003 Christmas recess, I travelled to India, together with Maureen Gold, Director of the Commonwealth Jewish Council and my kind and gifted personal secretary, who was herself born in Bombay, now known as Mumbai. In New Delhi, we were entertained to lunch by my old colleague and friend Natwar Singh, and his enchanting wife, Hem. Natwar was foreign policy adviser to Sonia Gandhi, then Leader of the Opposition. 'What chances have you lot got to win the next General Election?' I asked. 'Absolutely none,' Natwar and Hem agreed. After all, the economy was doing very well and most people were better off than before.

So much for political predictions. In 2004, the Congress Party, headed by Sonia Gandhi, swept to a narrow victory over Morarji Desai and L.K. Advani's BJP. Yes, most people in the towns were doing better, but not the majority of country folk. There was too much hunger and unemployment and the disillusioned and the dispossessed removed their government.

Natwar Singh phoned me. 'I am now the Minister for External Affairs and Milon Banerji is Attorney General. Your parliamentary recess is coming up soon. Why don't you come and see us? You will by my guest in New Delhi.' So in August 2004, to the capital I flew, and the new Foreign Minister and his wife were my generous hosts.

I visited their Parliament, as guest of Speaker Chatterjee, who told me that he had sat in the gallery of the Cambridge Union watching me, when I was President. A Communist, he lives in the Speaker's marvellous residence, where he held a tea party for me and my Cambridge pals, Natwar, Milon and Jai, the distinguished lawyer.

On India's Independence Day, I was Natwar's guest at the President's reception, in the garden of his residence. Natwar took me into the marquee, where he introduced me to Prime Minister Shri Atal Behari Vajpayee, and the PM and I had a private discussion, on India's relations with the State of Israel. Sonia Gandhi greeted me warmly. She had refused the job of Prime Minister, possibly because her family remembered too well the tragic assassinations of her mother-in-law and her husband, and possibly because of her Italian origins.

I was entertained to dinner, by the Singhs, the Mukhis and, on my last evening, by my old friend and former Deputy Prime Minister, L.K. Advani. Together, we all relaxed and discussed the joys and problems of our troubled world. For Mother India, these include the poverty of so many of its people . . . its lingering caste system . . . its conflicts with its Pakistani neighbours . . . and varieties of racist and religious unrest, involving not only disputes with Hindus and Muslims, but also with Christians. That said, for me India remains filled with happy memories of the past; with fascination and friendships in the present; and with great hope for the future. It is a mighty democracy, haunted by the ghosts of murdered Gandhis; anguished by the dire poverty of so many of its people; but lifted up for me by the picturesque variety and friendliness of its inhabitants, and by the hospitality, the warmth and the wisdom of my friends. *Jai Hind!* God bless India.

In the spring of 2000, I visited China, together with my cousin, Edmund Cohen and his cousin, Cynthia Hipps. We were accompanied and guided by my former enchanting volunteer, Poppy Sebag-Montefiore, who was then studying Chinese at a local university. The Chinese Ambassador to the UK arranged for us to be sponsored by the appropriate Chinese foreign affairs organisation, which introduced us to a number of their leaders. We visited world wonders – in or near Beijing, the Forbidden City, the Great Wall of China and the Emperors' Summer Palace – in Xian, the buried terracotta warriors – and in Shanghai, a city bristling with mighty skyscrapers. A different world into which Myra and I had dipped, on a week's visit from Hong Kong, in 1980. Then it was bleak and there were no Jews and people stared at our occidental features. Not any more.

Our most remarkable moment? In a Chinese primary school, where all the pupils were identically dressed in white shirts and blue trousers or skirts. They put on a concert of Chinese music for us and then I was required to 'say a few words' to the pupils and teachers, which Poppy translated into Chinese. They all beamed and clapped. We then visited a hospital where men and women lay alongside one another in a huge ward, each receiving acupuncture. They lay in silence, with needles sticking out of various parts of their anatomies.

Even in China, we found Jews – about 600 out of a total Chinese population of some 1.3 billion. In Beijing, we were entertained by Israel's formidable Ambassador, Ora Namir, who had brought together a group of about thirty Jews from the Beijing community. They had recently enjoyed a Passover Seder service with some 300 of them. Mainly American, but a few Brits. Part of the expat world. Poppy had attended a Seder service in Beijing and said it was pretty chaotic.

In Shanghai, we met a rabbi, Shalom Greenberg, from the Lubavitch sect. He was in his mid-twenties with a warm smile, twinkling eyes and a small child constantly dangling and jumping from his hands. His flock were nearly all business expat families and all of us enjoyed his wife's kosher cooking. But few joined in the '*benshing*' – the grace after meals, in Hebrew.

After the Sabbath lunch, we walked down the eight flights of stairs and off to the restored Ohel Rachel Synagogue. That morning, we had visited the other refurbished, former synagogue – the Ohel Moshe. Our guide was an 81-year-old ancient Chinese, who had lived in the ghetto and who knew all the history of the Jewish community and had been with Jews so long that, unlike all other Chinese we met, he illustrated his every sentence with vigorous gestures of the arm and hand.

The Ohel Rachel is much larger. In honour of a visit by President Clinton, it had been changed back from a 'warehouse' which the Japanese had used as a stable during the war, into what clearly had once been a fine place of prayer. On three recent occasions, the community had received permission to hold these services. 'Maybe, one day,' said the Rabbi, 'the process of openness and reconciliation and the immense friendliness of the Chinese to our Jewish culture, which they rightly regard as similar to their own in so many ways, may lead to our being able to use the Shul, as and when we wish.' I promised to do what I could in the most tactful way, to promote that process.

The Chinese kept telling me that we Jews are a clever people. If we had been so clever, I asked myself, would we have lost 6 million of our people? Would we be so anxious about the treatment of Jews and the advance of anti-Semitism in France and in Russia and in so many other lands? I just wished that our Jews were as secure and as contented in all the world as they are in India and beyond.

TWENTY-SEVEN

South Africa and the Durban Conference

How great and wonderful, yet how sad is South Africa. The inter-linked miseries of dire poverty and uncontrollable crime fill much of the lives of its citizens with fear. On my many visits to that most beautiful of lands, I have met no family which has not itself suffered from a murder or has not endured the killing of a friend or of someone in a friend's family.

I have become close to a fine Johannesburg family, Denese and Irwin Schneider and their children. En route to Durban on my 2001 visit, my PA Mitchell Coen and I stayed at their home in a smart, residential suburb. Like almost all South African middle-class homes, it is surrounded by high brick walls, topped with barbed wire. You enter through a gate operated from within by people with a security camera view of the outside. Denese told us that three times in the past year, she had been 'hijacked' – forced out of her car by thieves who stole it. She was lucky to be alive.

Irwin and his daughter, Nicky, had suffered the most. Three men armed with machine guns came up to them as their car approached the entrance to their home. 'Get out,' they were told. 'We're going to kill you. Up against that wall. Move and we kill you.' The bandits took the car but did not kill them, which was all that mattered. It is scarcely surprising that many whites are leaving their country; especially youngsters who go abroad to study and do not return.

In Durban, we stayed with our friends, Arnold and Rosemary Zulman. They live in a white, American colonial-style building, set in a glorious tropical garden. Three of their four children are overseas, two in the US and one in Britain. They were brave fighters against apartheid and during that battle they provided a haven for Chief Mangasutu Buthelezi, leader of the Zulus. In life, it is those whom you help in their adversity who appreciate you most. Buthelezi, or 'Gacha' as they call him, is their lifelong friend. They introduced him to me when I came to Durban for the

Commonwealth Heads of Government Meeting (CHOGM) in 1999. He gave us a rundown of his view on the current situation in his country. Its underlying theme: grim but hopeful, tough but improving.

I remembered the days when he and Nelson Mandela were bitter adversaries. Arnold had told us how, in February 1994, he had brought them together. He booked three hotel suites in Durban, one for each of them and a third where they could meet in privacy and where the Chief could get his complaints off his chest, with only Mandela knowing about them. Result: the two men resolved enough of their differences to work together in and for a united South Africa. As with Sadat and Begin, they came to like each other and brought peace to their land.

Myra and I first met Nelson Mandela in March 1990, soon after he was released from Robben Island prison. As President of the Board of Deputies, I had refused to visit the apartheid state, and some of the South African Jewish community had attacked me for that refusal. I told them that if any of them were imprisoned and they needed my presence, I would be on the next plane, but that I would not add even an iota of credibility to apartheid by visiting their country during that evil regime.

A brave Jewish woman leader of what was known as 'The Struggle' against apartheid, Jill Marcus, took us to the African National Congress (ANC) headquarters in Johannesburg. We were greeted by the grizzled veteran fighter, Walter Sisulu, and a few minutes later, Mandela joined us. He was tall and dignified, warm and welcoming. After the opening pleasantries, Myra said to him, with her Australian directness: 'Mr Mandela, I do not understand you.'

'Why not, Madam?' Mandela responded.

'These people,' she said. 'These people,' she repeated, with disgust, 'they kept you locked up for twenty-nine years. Eighteen years in Robben Island. How can you talk to them?'

'Madam,' the great man replied, 'if you want a bright future, you cannot keep your focus on the darkness of the past.'

Wow! What an amazing human being, I thought. South Africa was very fortunate to have him as a leader. My other friends in South Africa, most of whom were activists in the days of the Struggle, include Helen Suzman, once the only white Member of Parliament who struck out constantly and bravely against the apartheid regime.

I have met President Thabo Mbeki several times. He is a man of courage and of intellect. His problem: that he follows after the incomparable Nelson Mandela.

In 1995, Mandela hosted delegates to the Commonwealth Jewish Council Conference, in his presidential residence. We were joined by many leaders of South Africa's Jewish community; and by Jewish leaders of the ANC. In his speech, Mandela paid tribute to our host, Eric Samson, for providing shelter and succour for ANC leaders, when they returned from exile. 'I am pleased to welcome you here,' he said, 'whether you come from large Jewish communities or small ones. I know that however small your community may be, it is very powerful.'

So here was another leader who believed in the power of the Jewish people. As always, on the one hand, that's good because we only possess such power as others believe us to have. On the other hand, it is a major source of anti-Semitism, but I had learned that there is no point in worrying about that, because anti-Semites will blame us anyway, however large or small our community may be. And that is a problem which the 2001 UN Durban Conference emphasised.

Later, Eric Samson took me with him to a lunch, hosted by the former President and his new wife, in their home. The rest of their guests were major business people, whose mighty companies and corporations were prepared to help Mandela to bring help to people in need, through schools and medical centres in poverty-stricken country areas and to assist his Nelson Mandela's Children's Fund. I presented him with a special award from the Commonwealth Jewish Council, to signal our appreciation and affection for the man who is the world's greatest hero.

In September 2001, I attended the UN Conference Against Racism in Durban. By chance, I ran into Yasser Arafat. The previous day, he had made his expected speech, attacking the Israelis with unremitting venom. '*Kayf halak, ya rais?*' 'How are you, President?' I greeted him, in Arabic. He replied in English: 'Thank you, Lord Janner. And how are you?'

'Fine,' I replied. 'But this week, you have been very wicked. You need to make peace.' No response. 'You will meet Shimon Peres, next week?'

'Yes,' he replied. 'With him, I will make peace.'

'I hope so.'

I phoned my daughter, Laura, and told her of my encounter with Arafat. 'Dad, you're mad,' she said. 'That's just the sort of thing Mum would have said. If you're not careful, they'll kill you.' 'That won't do them any good,' I replied. 'I've met Arafat often enough for him to understand that it's peace that I want and I hope that he and Shimon will make peace. For everyone's sake.'

The Durban Conference was scarcely a harbinger of goodwill. Parades of thousands of local Muslims, with anti-Israel banners, some of them calling for 'Death to the Jews' . . . Arab sympathisers breaking up a Jewish meeting which focused on anti-Semitism and a media conference, organised by Jewish students . . . above all, the handing out of anti-Semitic hate literature, worthy of Streicher and Himmler, including a booklet of caricatures depicting Jews with hooked noses and swastikas and claws dripping with Arab blood. Both at the meetings of the non-governmental organisations and during the conference proper, anti-Israel rhetoric flowed on, often blurring the difference between anti-Zionism and anti-Semitism. After all, Israel is the Jewish State supported by the Jewish people . . .

I watched the bearded Castro, in his Western suit and tie, talking primarily of the inequities of the Americans and of the capitalist world, but not forgetting to castigate what he described as the Israelis' 'genocide of the Palestinians'. The UN Secretary General Kofi Annan tried to heal the wounds, but too many delegates competed to rip them open.

The Israelis were under-represented. Their spokesman was an ambassador who made a speech proclaiming several times in his curiously accented English: 'We in Israel want piss.' The American delegation was disgusted at the way in which the conference was being turned into an anti-US and anti-Israel forum and they announced that they were leaving. They were soon followed out by the Israelis.

I tried to make my voice heard, but failed. 'The Muslim News Online' reported: 'Pro-Zionist peer, Lord Janner, was forced to leave the UK NGO meeting convened to discuss the stance taken by the European caucus on the issue of accusing Israel as a racist state and which was arranged and held after meeting the UK Government official delegation . . .' A delegate told the Muslim News: 'One of us noticed Lord Janner with three Jewish men (one of whom we believed was a security person) had somehow managed to enter the room and were listening to our conversation. One of our delegates in the Black Police Association (UK) went over and asked them to leave,' the delegate said. 'Lord Janner with his colleagues from the World Jewish Congress was not a UK NGO . . . Lord Janner was not contactable . . .' The report was correct, except that the 'security man' was my tough-looking PA, Mitchell Coen. They did not want us to hear any more of their racist rhetoric.

The next day, the Jewish delegations met in the local synagogue hall. Delegates were discussing how they could counter the anti-Israel and anti-Semitic attacks. I intervened. 'You cannot respond,' I said. 'You cannot have any influence over these disgraceful proceedings. Our voice will not be heard and we cannot stay. We cannot remain in this conference after our American and Israeli colleagues have left.'

Eventually, they agreed. We called a press conference, which I chaired. I announced that we were leaving and explained why and I led our Jewish delegations out of that most racist of so-called anti-racist gatherings. It was a disgrace to the good name of the United Nations, and it convinced me that the overflow from anti-Zionism into anti-Semitism was spreading worldwide. I was ashamed that our British NGO colleagues did not raise their voices against these attacks. Had they been levelled against anyone else, they would have been labelled as precisely what they were – viciously racist, besmirching a so-called anti-racist conference. I was pleased to leave. In the words of Nelson Mandela, we could have hoped for better.

In August 2005, I returned to South Africa, this time with the newly appointed Director of our Political Council for Coexistence, Alan Senitt (page 275). At my side was my new political PA, Danny Stone, and with us travelled my daughter, Marion. We stayed first with my friends, the Schneider family, where Marion felt part of the family and a few days later headed off on safari. I gave the keynote address at the annual conference of the South African Jewish Board of Deputies, and my team and I then travelled to Cape Town, for the biennial conference of the Commonwealth Jewish Council, with delegates mainly from the African continent.

As so often with conferences, what mattered most was not what happened during the sessions, but rather the contacts made in the corridors and beyond. Of course we discussed both publicly and privately the concerns of our Jewish communities, but the key moments were our conversations with an outstanding leader of the country's Muslim community, Ebrahim Rasool, Premier of the Western Cape. To our delight, he most willingly agreed to join our Council, and gave us wise advice.

At the end of the conference, we paid our respects to former President F.W. de Klerk, who had bravely joined with Mandela to found the new nation and who remains an outspoken and fascinating advocate of racial unity in his multi-racial land. Then we called on Archbishop Desmond Tutu in his simple office. I thought of my first meeting with him, in the winter of 1990. He had taken me into his dark, dank room on the side of his Cape Town church. Its small heater was scarcely warming the book-lined haven. He told us that he is now no longer physically fit, but clearly his mind and his mission remain unchanged.

That afternoon, a devoted social worker drove us to an awful hutted township, on the outskirts of a town airport. It housed some 20,000 people, who would otherwise have been homeless. Their wooden shacks with corrugated iron roofs were grimly adequate in the summer but would become inhuman during the winter rains. Our host told us that this township was dreadful, but far from the country's worst. Unemployment, poverty and hunger, with crime in its wake, remain horrendous problems in that otherwise glorious land.

PART SIX

Life and Death

TWENTY-EIGHT

Life – It's Magic

With one major exception – Myra's tragic illness and death – most of my life has been a delight. People often ask me: 'How can you stand it? You're always travelling round the world . . . You never stop working . . . Don't you have any fun?' Well, if by 'fun' they mean sitting around on a beach or playing golf, my answer is: No. But I find most of my work today enthralling, challenging and enjoyable, or I would not be doing it. In the past, a major focus of my life was on earning a living. With a wife and three children, that was essential. Today, though, most of my work is voluntary. I have duties in the House of Lords, which I carry out as best I can. The House is my second home and I enjoy the warmth and companionship, along with the political process. That said, I do almost everything else because I wish to – and that, in life, is magic.

As for magic itself, that has been a lifetime's source of major relaxation, of friendship and of pleasure, certainly to myself and hopefully to others. Since my childhood days in Canada, I have always loved both magic and magicians. Magic is the world's best ice-breaker and everyone of every age loves to be fooled. Knowing how to fool has brought many joyful moments; occasional danger and even escape from danger and friendship with the Gandhis.

Then there was the party in the Bucharest synagogue during the festival of Tabernacles ('*Succoth*'). After the service, the local community welcomed our parliamentary group to '*kiddush*', the traditional glass of wine and a biscuit. I showed them an illusion which the great Paul Daniels had taught me, appearing to bend a knife and reconstituting it. I leaned, gently, on the handle but not gently enough. It broke – and the blade shot across the room, mercifully but only just missing a Romanian head!

I often use magic in Parliament, sometimes even to deflect the attention of journalists from an unacceptable course of their questioning, and sometimes to add spice to a dull meal. I only once used it in the Chamber. I was describing how a policy of the then Tory Government was a total deception. Betty Boothroyd, the Speaker, frowned in disbelief when I gave a sample of the art of deception by producing a rubber ball in my hand and then making it disappear. I remembered the words of Shimon Peres, defining the difference between a magician and a politician. 'They both put the lady in a box and cut her in half,' he said, 'but with a magician, she stays alive!' Anyway, magic continues to give pleasure to parliamentary colleagues and, especially, to their guests, and it has brought me incredible contact with some of the world's most famous magicians and mystics.

My interest in magic began in 1940, in Canada (Chapter 2), but the flowering of my magical art emerged when I became friends with that fine magician and former President of the Magic Circle, David Berglas. He did his best to teach me and in the process conferred the greatest compliment of my political life. 'Magic,' he told me, 'is the art of deception. The trouble with you, Greville, is that you are too honest!'

David gave me a photograph of Uri Geller, together with Paul Daniels, himself and me. It was most kindly entitled: 'The world's four greatest magicians', but before Uri was prepared to autograph it, he changed 'four' to 'three' and added: 'and the world's greatest mystic'. Uri may not be a magician but a friend he certainly is, as I have discovered, in good times and in bad and he is a fantastic performer and entertainer.

In March 2001, Uri celebrated his second marriage to his first wife, Hana. Their first was a civil ceremony and this was to be a Jewish religious one, in a marquee in the garden of their Thames-side home. It would be performed by the colourful Rabbi Shmueli Boteach and with Uri's remarkable friend, Michael Jackson, who was flying in from the US. He was to be Uri's best man.

About a hundred guests, mainly stars and celebrities and their partners, gathered by mid-morning. The Rabbi and Jackson arrived about three hours late, which did not matter – we were enjoying the company and the food. Michael Jackson was on crutches. He had broken his foot and was obviously in pain. When he sat beside me, we exchanged only pleasantries, and when the joyful ceremony was over, he was helicoptered away.

That summer, I travelled to the West Coast of the US on a marvellous, Marion-and-her-Dad holiday. First, Las Vegas, to watch the great magician,

Lance Burton, and to meet him after the show . . . Siegfried and Roy, and their vanishing tigers, lions and elephants . . . and 'The Cirque du Soleil', a stage extravaganza on water. Plus, of course, the surreal, clattering, banks of one-armed bandits . . . miraculous, patterned fountains leaping up in the lake outside our Bellaggio Hotel windows . . . a volcano of coloured lights . . . unique, grotesque, over-the-top, and very enjoyable. Then, to San Diego, with its great zoo and Sea World, where Marion spent days with nature while I worked on these memoirs by the hotel pool.

Then on to LA, where the phone rang in my room. It was Uri. 'Why did you not tell me that you were going to LA?' he asked. 'I want you to meet up with Michael Jackson.' 'That would be great. Thank you,' I replied. 'Then stay where you are and he'll phone you.' Which, to my surprise and delight, he did.

The next day, I was off to Universal City. First, to Steven Spielberg's epic creation, The Shoah Foundation, with its recorded, categorised, tragic testimonies of Holocaust survivors. Then my friend Renée Firestone, herself a survivor and activist for the Foundation, drove me to Stage 34, where she dropped me off. Jackson's broad and muscled security man, Henry, awaited me. 'Please come in, Lord Janner,' he said, smiling. 'I'm going to fetch Michael now.'

I had been warned that Michael Jackson's timing is famously erratic, so I was not surprised when he did not arrive for nearly an hour. Meanwhile, Henry's troops allowed me to stroll past Jackson's huge, home-from-home trailer and into the great recording and filming shed. There, four dancers were at work. Live, elastic, brilliant . . . black and Mexican . . . fantastic! When they took a break, they asked me who I was and what I did and I told them that I was an escapee from the House of Lords and then I did magic for them and we became friends. I shared their snacks, fruit drinks and coffee and we talked. Then Jackson appeared and the two of us retreated into a small room and we chatted for forty-five minutes.

Jackson's voice is quiet and gentle. We talked of Uri Geller and of that amazing wedding, when we sat together but he did not speak. 'I hurt that day,' he said. We talked about international peace and suggestions that Uri had asked me to pass on to him about ways that the two of them might work together. We talked of his new 'singles' album and of the book that he intended to write, to raise more money for children's charities. He asked what I did in the cause of peace and charities, so I told him. One of his dancers came in and suggested that rehearsal time had arrived and I asked if I could watch. 'With pleasure,' he said. Uri later told me that this was an unheard-of privilege. Nobody, Uri said, talks with Jackson as I had, nor is allowed into his rehearsals.

I had asked for a batch of his signed photographs for my family and friends. Henry brought them in and Michael autographed them, including one for Marion's learning disabled foster child, Eddie, for whom meeting Michael some years ago had been a high point of his life – and one photo for Maureen and another for me. Then the inside covers of three of his albums, which I had bought locally. 'I had forgotten these songs,' he said. Then he started humming and singing, and moving his arms and body in rhythm. 'How long do you rehearse?' I asked. 'That depends on how it goes – but it could be until midnight.'

So, out into the great shed, where he and his tap dancers set to work with incredible timing and rhythm and body language. Hands up and down . . . heads forward and back – fingers and tongues clicking, but no words while they danced. In a break, I asked Michael and his dancers whether they had been trained, in dance or song or acting, in college or in school.

Jackson replied: 'No. I've never had formal training. You see, dancing is feeling and you cannot teach people to feel.' At which, one of the dancers said: 'Look.' And he did a series of formal, ballet type movements. 'It's too automatic,' he said. 'We create dances, as we feel.'

For nearly three hours, I watched, entranced. Chatting with them during the breaks. Wondering at the feeling of these remarkable professionals. Imprinting on my mind the image of Michael Jackson, with his head thrust back and his arms swinging from his undulating shoulders and working towards total synchronisation with his two colleagues, and the five of them watching their synchronised reflections in those great mirrors.

When I left, I got a hug from each and a promise that we would meet again before long, if not in the United States then in the 'Mother Country'.

A year later, in June 2002, Uri phoned me. 'I have a favour to ask,' he said. 'Michael Jackson is coming over on Friday to do a fundraiser for the Exeter Football Club. As you know, I'm its Chairman and we need money. Can you bring him in the morning to see round Parliament? And would you mind if my old friends, the magician David Blaine and the dancer Patti Boulaye came with us?' Mind? I'd love it. They would arrive by 10.30 and, this time, not late.

Luckily, neither House was sitting that day. My guests arrived on time and I wheeled them through the Palace of Westminster, to the huge delight of the staff, who crowded around and waved and got autographs from our celebrities. It was the birthday of my old friend, Paul Boateng MP (now Sir Paul, our British High Commissioner to South Africa). He cut his birthday cake on the Terrace. We visited the then Lord Chancellor, genial Derry Irvine, in his Residence. Then we were driven to Paddington in a magnificent white stretch limousine, with Jackson leaning out of the window and waving to his fans, who somehow were expecting him. Uri had hired a train for the day. It was packed with shouting, waving, delirious young fans. 'Michael . . . Michael . . . Michael!' they screamed. I shared a compartment with the celebrities and listened entranced as they discussed the problems of their showbiz lives.

After a long period of silence, Jackson turned to me. 'Lord,' he said, 'I want your help. We need a new national day. There's days for everything, from caravans to helping the blind and the deaf. But there's no day when parents are told to hug their children, and say to them: "I love you." My parents never did that to me.' Which explained just about everything that afflicted that sad man.

At Exeter, another white limo awaited us, together with hundreds more fans, adoring and yelling. The football stadium was packed. Michael leapt around the perimeter, umbrella raised to keep the sun away from his strangely off-white features. Then back to London and another entrancing journey, with chat interrupted by long periods of Jackson's contemplative silence. I had always thought that we politicians are the world's most eccentric human beings. That day taught me that I was completely wrong. What an extraordinary day that was! Since then, the life of Michael Jackson has turned into a tragedy. He was and could again become a great entertainer.

David Blaine returned to London that autumn, to spend forty-two days suspended above the Thames, in a glass capsule hanging from a high crane, eating nothing and drinking only water. I was privileged to sit in on one of their preparatory conferences in his West End apartment. Questions: how would they control the crowds? He would only be drinking water, but how would they ensure that his supply would be pumped up safely to the capsule? How would they get top media cover? Once David was aloft, he waved to the adoring crowds below. I paid my respects from within his surrounding security fence.

One evening, I took his producer, Harmony Karin, for an Indian meal, leaving my car some distance away. When we emerged from the restaurant, Harmony spotted three beautiful young women and marched up to them. 'Praise the Lord!' he cried. 'Do you know the Lord? Here is the Lord!' and he signalled to me to bow to the ladies. Yes, show-business people are a rare breed and sometimes highly hilarious.

I was glad when Blaine emerged from his ordeal. He was emaciated but apparently fit. He had achieved the impossible. Was the water pumped up to him laced with sugar or glucose? After all, the man is a renowned magician and he knows how to achieve the impossible with some ingenious deception. Uri's friend and mine, the *News of the World* Chief Executive, Stuart Kuttner, had arranged for the water to be inspected and the newspaper had proclaimed that there was no trickery. Anyway, it was brilliant showmanship and a brave experiment, and we politicians should never criticise celebrities for showmanship, or for magic.

In mid morning on Saturday, 23 July 2005, I was phoned by my close friends, Michael and Linda Falter. Their younger son, Joe, was on holiday in Egypt and they believed that he was in Sharm el Sheikh, where terrorists had struck and two unnamed British men had been blown apart in the market or hotel. Was there any way in which I could check that Joe was OK? Of course, I would try.

I tracked down our Ambassador to Egypt, Sir Derek Plumbly, who was on his mobile phone in Sharm el Sheikh. Yes, two young Brits had been killed. He did not know their names. Certainly, Joe was not among the wounded. He would let me know if he had any news. I contacted the Foreign Office and friends in Egypt and in Israel. I kept in touch with Joe's brother, Gideon, on his mobile and with Michael and his wife, Linda, on the house phone . . . I tried to reassure them.

Late that evening, the Falters told me that they had contacted their son. He was 'chilling out' on some distant beach. His mobile phone was switched off and he knew nothing of the tragedies. That message was magic. Alas, indeed, for the families of those who died. But hurray for young Joe and his family, and for their friends, like me.

I carry unrealities in my pocket. Bouncy balls that move one colour to another, eyeballs of blue, brown and green which transpose, with a flick of the wrist, and magic spot paddles . . . There is no end to the number of people whom these make happy, from small children, with shining smiles, to the senior politicians who accompany them. Magic puts a touch of smiling wonder into life. And life becomes magic, when terror and stress give way in a moment, to sheer joy and relief. If you doubt that, ask the Falters.

TWENTY-NINE

Bereavement and Looking Forward

In the early hours of Monday, 9 December 1996 – the fourth night of the Festival of Chanukah, in the Jewish calendar – Myra passed away. No more pain. But no more life. No more precious time with her children, her grandchildren, her friends . . . for her shopping, her hairdresser, her parties . . . No more time for us, together. Gone. Finished. On the whole, she had led a very good and full life, and she did not want it to end. I was deeply irritated by the kindly meant sermons and messages and addresses about how she could 'now rest in peace'. That is not what she wanted.

I phoned Laura in Israel. Ella's birth was imminent, but Laura could still fly. She arrived at the Willesden Cemetery, just as we were walking into the small hall for prayers.

They buried Myra in her half of a double grave, where I shall join her in due course. Meanwhile: how could I cope, after forty-two years of the deep companionship of marriage? Joyful companionship with a good and generous woman with a highly developed and often mischievous sense of humour. Caring for each other, through personal illness and political crisis. Times of pain and anger of course. But, as Myra told a friend, just a few months before she died: 'As we've got older, we've become closer.' And now she was gone. How would I endure?

Activity was the first essential. Run. I still had the House of Commons, but only for a few more months. Then what? I must hope for the Lords. First, though, there was an election to be won. I must do what I could for Tony and his team. Above all, training in speechmaking and media skills for whichever Labour candidates wanted it. Then: get on with my lecturing and training for JSB. Do as much work as possible.

Travel – especially abroad. Myra holidayed on the basis that there was no point in going away to be more uncomfortable than you were at home. Now I would go to places which were not for her. First, the Lower Galilee town of Sakhnin, chosen for me by my son-in-law David. To learn Arabic and to soak myself in Israel–Arab life, if only for a week. That proved so successful that I wrote a book, half of it in Sakhnin and the rest on my return home. About peace, and using as its title the Arab proverb: 'One hand alone cannot clap'.

Then a joyful two summer weeks with Marion, in the Galapagos, Equador, Peru, the Amazon rainforests and remains of the Inca civilisation of Machu Picchu. The following summer, I spent a week in Alaska, accompanied by Shane Jedeikin, the bright and entertaining son of my South African friends. I should have known that my appreciation for views of bleak scenery and solitude is and was extremely limited. At best, three glorious hours of flight over snow-capped mountains, volcanoes and glaciers in a private aircraft piloted by an elderly and gracious Jewish resident of Anchorage. At worst, fishing for salmon in a swollen river, in pouring rain. Not a bite. The right place to acquire salmon, fresh or smoked, is in the local supermarket.

I worked on with my organisations. Highlight: the Commonwealth Jewish Council Biennial Conference in Gibraltar, followed by a visit to Morocco. It was there that I received the wonderful news of my 'elevation' to the House of Lords. We drank champagne and bubbled with happiness.

So movement was my first recipe for sane survival. Sound was the second. Edmund Cohen, my cousin and oldest friend who had recently lost his own wife, Daphne, told me: 'Keep the radio on at home.' When I was at home, I did just that – but I also kept out of the flat as much as possible. It took two or three years before I could comfortably work there. I considered moving house but a friend told me that if I was happy in the place, I should stay, because moving home is of itself a type of stress, not too far from bereavement. So I stayed in our comfortable Hampstead flat, filled as it was and is with memories of Myra.

Best of all, though, was the love and companionship of my family and friends. After the funeral, Laura flew back to Jerusalem. 'Dad,' she said, 'I want you here when the baby's born. In the room, with me. Like Mum would have been.' On Thursday, 16 January, she phoned. She was in labour. 'Dad, please get moving.' I was on the next flight, certain that Laura's third child would be born before I arrived. I telephoned Laura when we landed. 'Hurry – any moment now,' she said. Into a cab and off to the Misgav Ladakh Hospital. Nothing yet. Laura and I strolled around the grounds and then I went to sleep in an empty upstairs ward. A few hours later, my son-in-law David tapped on my shoulder. 'Let's go,' he said. 'The baby's on its way.' Laura had taken me with her when she had had her scan. It was almost certainly a girl. *She* was on her way. Downstairs into the labour room where the midwife smiled and said: 'She's arriving.'

Moments later, Ella Avigail emerged. Myra had chosen her middle name. Avigail – literally, joy of her father – Laura's father and Ella's father, each of them. I looked at the baby and at Laura and collapsed into a chair, sobbing. Joy and tears, welcome and farewell, care, loss and love, released in an incredible and privileged moment. The miracle of new life, so close to the tragedy of death. Loss of self-control . . . catharsis . . . and then the recognition of my immense and remaining good fortune.

I thought of the birth of Laura's second child, Natan. I had come over for his *Brit Milah* – the traditional, painful and joyful initiation of a Jewish boy. Myra had met me at the airport. 'Darling,' she had said. 'I have a terrible pain in my stomach.' That was the start of her illness, misdiagnosed at the Jerusalem Shaare Zedek Hospital, where they refused to discuss her condition with me. I told Sonia Peres of my agony and she picked up her mobile phone and spoke to her husband, Prime Minister Shimon Peres, who phoned the director of the hospital, who then spoke to me. 'Appendicitis,' he said. 'Let it settle down and then take her home.'

Back to England and into hospital where that great and kind surgeon, Adam Lewis, immediately said: 'We must investigate.' It was cancer.

Then came some two-and-a-half years of operations, of chemotherapy, of incredibly uncomplaining suffering. The most Myra used to say was: 'I hurt.' When Myra was released from hospital after one of her terrible operations, she sat in the car and started singing a Hebrew song: '*Al tishkach et hatikva*' – do not lose hope.

All of the family had coped with Myra's illness as best they could. Daniel tried to block off the reality and phoned her three or four times a day, but succeeded in convincing himself, if no one else, that she would be fine. Marion was busy with her 'Chocolate Paradise' project. She had a room in a business centre and Myra used to go to 'help' her. Myra's packing of chocolates was not efficient, but the laughter was loud and those visits made her very happy. Marion cared for her hugely.

Laura came over from Jerusalem whenever she could. In its own way, it was harder for her, to cope from so far for so much of the time. David and Laura's oldest child, Tali, was nearly four. Old enough to know and to give pleasure to the grandma whom she and little Natan called 'Mimi'. Daniel and Caroline's daughters, Isabel, Esther and Phoebe, were Myra's other joys. When Myra discussed her cancer with a specialist in oncology, he said that the progress of the disease was unpredictable but she could live for several years. 'I want to be at Isabel's batmitzvah' – her religious confirmation – said Myra. 'It's in June of next year. Will I make it?' The doctor assured her that she had an excellent chance. 'Good,' she said. 'I'll work on it.'

On the morning of 10 July 1996, Nelson Mandela addressed a vast crowd from the balcony of South Africa House in Trafalgar Square. Although we had not heard from the oncologist, it seemed that Adam Lewis's optimism had been justified when he had told us that he was 'virtually certain that we have got rid of the cancer'. I cheered with the crowd and Stephen Rubin, distinguished industrialist and friend, brought me to meet Mandela when the world's greatest man unveiled the plaque, donated by Stephen's company, commemorating his visit.

I strolled back to Westminster, filled with happiness. At the Members' Entrance, the policeman said to me: 'Please phone your secretary.' My heart sank. I knew. I dialled Maureen. 'It's better that we meet,' she said.

'No. Please tell me now. It's about Myra, isn't it?'

'Yes.'

'They've found something again?'

'Yes. I'm afraid so.'

We went to see the specialist, who told Myra: 'We can give you chemotherapy. It will be painful.'

'Will my hair fall out?'

'Yes.'

'How long extra would I live?'

'Only about three months, I'm afraid.'

'And you're recommending that I should endure this agony for that purpose?'

'Well, that's a matter for you.'

'How could you be so cruel?' she exclaimed. So that was that. No chemotherapy.

The doctor gave her until the end of the year. Meanwhile, she should get the best quality of life. 'OK,' I said. 'Let's travel, anywhere you want. Where would you like to go?'

'The Accadia Hotel,' she answered, without hesitation. Israel. Herzliya. Where we had enjoyed so many happy holidays with the children. A good hotel by the sea. They fixed us up with a downstairs chalet. Myra's Israeli relatives came to visit. Shimon and Sonia Peres joined us for dinner one evening. We all prayed that the doctors were wrong. They were not.

When I first met Myra, both of us smoked, so it did not affect our courting or our early married relationship. But I got scared of cancer and, after two unsuccessful attempts, I kicked the habit. She did not. From then on, she always said that if we got divorced, the co-respondent would be a cigarette. Apart from hating the smell of tobacco, I was always scared that the habit would kill the woman I loved so much.

When eventually she did contract cancer, it had nothing to do with tobacco. Lying in that dreadful hospital in Jerusalem, she asked me: 'Does my breath still smell of tobacco?' It did not. Myra did not smoke again, even when she was in remission. But a few days before she died, our elder daughter Marion and I were with her and she said: 'I want a cigarette.' We looked at each other and Marion said to her: 'Oh, come on Mum.' And that was that. I have always wondered whether we should have given her a cigarette, especially as after her death we found several packets carefully hidden in her drawers and in the kitchen. 'No,' says Marion. 'She would have coughed and that would have hurt her.'

The funeral and the period of mourning were grim. Myra would have enjoyed some of the bizarre moments. Like the woman who came to our home and reprimanded me: 'Why didn't you tell me the time of the funeral? I wanted to come.' I lost my cool and started yelling at her and Marion ushered me away. 'Come on, Dad . . .' The woman left. Then there was the rabbi with the small white beard, who asked when Myra died. '2.30 on Monday morning,' I said. 'And when was she buried?' he asked. 'At 3.30 on Monday afternoon.' The rabbi nodded. 'Oh, that's excellent!' he said. We Jews follow the ancient customs of hot climates and bury our dead with minimal delay. Then there was the diplomat whom I introduced to Jonathan, sitting alongside me on the family's low stools of mourning. 'This is her brother,' I said. 'Whose brother?' he replied.

When the owner of the dress shop on Hampstead Garden Suburb Market Place expressed her condolences, I told her: 'You gave Myra such enormous pleasure. And your dresses were never too expensive.'

'How do you know that?' she asked.

'Because she paid for them with our joint credit card, which I had to check each month.'

She paused, thoughtfully. 'Well, I think I can tell you now. Myra used to pay half on the credit card and half in cash!'

My political friends rallied round. Gordon Brown and Donald Dewar were among those who came to the funeral. Donald told me later: 'I hope you won't mind me saying so, but I found it very interesting.' Many of our parliamentary friends came to pay their respects at our home. Peter Mandelson, Michael Portillo, Paul Boateng and others who had helped me in those desperate last months. I was moved when the Jordanian Ambassador, my friend Fouad Ayoub, joined us. The '*shiva*' – the week of home mourning – seemed to go on for ever.

I survived. And on the whole, I cope well. In my more pensive moments, I can hear Myra saying impatiently: 'Oh, for heaven's sake, get on with it.' Everything is fine until suddenly something happens and I go under without warning. Our grandchildren used to call her Mimi. I choked when Natan, then aged five, said: 'I do remember Mimi and I loved Mimi but I was only little when I knew her.' Or I come across one of those innumerable notes or shopping lists in some drawer or cupboard. Or I am enjoying myself and suddenly wish she were with me. Down I go, taking care not to let others see it.

Then there are names. I never could remember them and Myra used to remind me. Mainly people, but also: 'What is the name of the hotel we stayed at in Eilat, all those years ago, when it was the only one?' Or: 'What was that terrible joke Daniel made about . . .?' Now I have to answer my own questions. Lord Denning used to say: 'We judges always ask ourselves questions because that's the only way we know that we can get swift and intelligent answers!' Not me. I still need to ask Myra.

Do I believe in life after death? No – but there were some very creepy incidents after Myra left us. Like the night she died. Daniel had parked his almost new car outside our flat. He tried to drive home but the car would not start. The battery was dead. No life. He phoned the AA and their mechanic came round, turned the key in the ignition and the car started without the least difficulty. It gave no sign of trouble then or after.

Myra died in December. Isabel's batmitzvah was celebrated on 4 and 5 July of the following year. The 6th was our wedding anniversary. Laura was staying with me. At 11.20 p.m. on 6 July, right at the end of our anniversary, the telephone rang. Laura was upstairs. I was in bed downstairs. We both picked up the receiver at the same second and we each said: 'Did you phone?' We each replied: 'No.' The line went dead. I pressed 1471 and a disembodied voice told us that the phone call had come from my car phone number. I rushed upstairs and out to the car. It was locked. No one was in the car and there was no problem with the telephone. The last call that I had made on the car phone before arriving home was to my home number. But telephone experts told me that there was no reason whatever why that number should ring again, nor why it should cut off when the call was answered.

Not long ago, Marion asked me: 'Dad, how are you coping?' I replied that I missed her Mum, but otherwise I was fine. She replied: 'Of course you miss Mum. But do understand that if she were here, you would not be doing a lot of the things that you are.'

She was right. I would have been leading a very different life, much of it together with Myra. After all, I retired from Parliament so that we would enjoy life together. But when her life turned to death, I had to decide what to do with mine. It took months before I was able to be happily at home without her. The secret: Myra liked the walls to be neat, smart and tidy. I changed the feel of the place by covering many of them with photographs, paintings and documents. Then I have a new home, in the House of Lords. Thank you, Tony! That is the pivot of my work and also of my entertaining.

So my life's work continues. I am blessed with the vast energy inherited from both of my parents. And since Myra has gone, I have poured much of it into my work, both parliamentary and in the Jewish world, and often the two intertwine. I am both proud and fortunate to be able to serve both.

The power and energy of my life – and, indeed, of my life's work – is an integral part of my world. It comes out of the pores of my skin and is the essence of my existence. I get an attendance allowance from the House of Lords, and I continue to do some professional training in presentational skills and public speaking. But the vast bulk of my life is spent in voluntary public service.

To me, that is life after death. Perhaps, I shall meet a woman with whom not only do I want to spend the rest of my days, but who would be prepared to share and to put up with my way of life. As it is, I am sunk into my work and service, and blessed with a fabulous family and friends. We care for and about each other and I share much of my life with them.

As for public service, there is never a shortage of poignant and crucial issues. I have quietly helped to pull back the Association of University Teachers (the AUT) from the brink of evils, arising out of anti-Israel conference resolutions. As so often happens, hatred against the Jewish State was spilling over into ill-will against our Jewish community. Above all, though, Britain and its diverse communities must either live or die together. So I am deeply involved in work with and in the Muslim world (Chapter 24).

I remain a leader in the service of my Jewish people, in Britain and beyond. As a Vice President of World Jewish Congress, I have top access all over the world. As President of the Commonwealth Jewish Council, I am warmly received by our remarkable Commonwealth family – in 2005, as a guest of the South African Jewish Board of Deputies at their annual conference in Johannesburg, and then chairing and guiding our own Commonwealth Jewish Conference in Cape Town. As Chairman of the Holocaust Educational Trust, I work to keep the hideous memories of Nazi murders alive, in the hope that we shall remind others of the intractable evils of racist dictatorship.

I am often asked: 'Who will take over, when you're gone?' My reply: 'I've no idea. But I do assure you that I have no intention of going for a while yet!' The truth is that the combination of political service to my constituency and to my country and my work for and with the Jewish communities of the world is unique. I wish it were not.

Jews were expelled from Britain in 1290. Oliver Cromwell allowed them back in. Most of these new immigrants were swiftly absorbed into the City of London and other aspects of our national and financial world. Today, we are not only integrated into British society but (in my view, too often) assimilated into it. Instead of retaining pride in our own religious and communal traditions, whether in the home or synagogue, and to whatever extent . . . in recent years some 40 per cent of our young people have 'married out' of the faith. By our sensible ancient rules, which were laid down long before the discovery of DNA, by Jewish law our children take the religion of their mother.

Largely through intermarriage, our community is shrinking. If (God forbid) a latter-day Hitler were to take hold of Britain, there would probably be some half a million whom he would murder because of their Jewish blood. But if you look at the census, you will find that there are only about half that number who declare themselves as Jews or who are Jewish by our religious law (Chapter 18).

This is an extraordinary statistic when you consider the level of service of members of the Jewish community, whether in politics and in Parliament, in science or in literature, in commerce or in voluntary or professional service. We are a noisy lot, which is fine in a vibrant democracy, but, as my parents recognised when they shipped my sister and myself off to Canada during the war, is dangerous when racists could take over.

Now compare those figures against the size of our British Muslim community of some 1.6 million. As a new community, they face to some extent the problems that British Jews had to solve, decades ago. How far should they integrate into our society? And after major terrorist tragedies, should they react as a community? How can they deal with their tiny but dangerous minority, prepared to give up their lives, at least in this world, for what they regard as the cause of Islam?

I believe that we in our stabilised and long-established British Jewish community should work with those Muslims who wish to work with us. There have been bad moments. Like 27 January 2005, when I was flown out, together with Jack Straw and other leaders, to the Auschwitz concentration camp. The same day, the Queen was guest of honour at the commemoration of the liberation of Auschwitz in Westminster Hall. The place was packed with distinguished guests. Sadly, there was one notable and deliberate absentee – Iqbal (now Sir Iqbal) Sacranie, Chair of the Muslim Council.

So there is never a shortage of problems to be solved, of people to be helped or of causes to be served. Boredom has never been my problem and I know that so long as I remain fit to serve, the hours of my days and the days of my life will be too short for the work that I need to cram into them.

Long ago, I visited an old Jewish friend, dying in a Leicester hospital. 'My boy,' he said, 'always remember this. If you have your *gezund* – your health – you've got everything. But if you lose it, it doesn't matter how brilliant or well off you were before, because then you've lost everything.' He died the next day.

I am in my late seventies. Old? Well, I used to regard this age as prodigious . . . ancient . . . one foot in the grave. But not any more. In July 2001, Shimon Peres, who was then Israel's Foreign Minister, visited London. I told him how marvellous it was for me to enjoy the energetic company of a man five years my senior and at the height of his powers and energy. 'Tell me the secret,' I said. 'There is not one secret but three secrets,' he replied. 'First, always look forward, not back. Focus on the future, not on the past. Second, life is short, so there is no time for trifles. Concentrate on serious matters. And above all, don't stop working. If you or I retire, Greville, we will die.'

Well, writing memoirs means looking back. But always with a focus on the future. Concentrating on the serious? Indeed, provided that you include your family and friends within its definition. And stopping work? Never.

Some years ago, Shimon took me with him to an Arab wedding in Nazareth. En route from his home, we passed the Wingate village, named after that brave British soldier Orde Wingate, one of the few of his kind who supported the Zionist effort to create a Jewish state.

'This place must bring back memories for you, Shimon,' I said.

'No,' he replied. 'I don't look back.'

An overstatement, of course. The past provides not only memories of what has gone but guideposts to what is to come and how to make the most and the best of it.

Whenever I visited Vienna, I used to call on Simon Wiesenthal, the most famous of all Nazi hunters, who died in 2005, in his mid-nineties. Once

I asked him whether he could sum up his lifetime's wisdom for success. 'That is easy, Greville,' he replied. 'Know your enemies – and cultivate your friends.' He wrote that out by hand for me, on his office notepaper, and it is framed on the wall of my home, inside the front door.

As I bid farewell to this review of my days, I look back on a varied, exciting and largely privileged and happy life. Sadness, of course. Especially losing Myra. Some people who know that they are terminally ill want to go. Not Myra. A few days before she lost consciousness, she said to me: 'Darling, help me.'

'Help you to do what, my love?' I asked.

'Help me to get well,' she said.

I brought her a glass of milk and said: 'Now drink this. It will give you strength.'

The next day, I found her trying to walk around the bed. 'Will you mourn me when I'm gone?' she asked.

'Of course. But then you'll mourn me when I'm gone – and I may go first.'

'God forbid,' she said.

I still mourn her, much.

There are others I miss, especially my usually wise, always vivacious and often difficult mother. And my Dad, with all the problems he gave me. But we must look forward, not back.

When Rabbi Hugo Gryn was dying, I asked him: 'Hugo, do you believe in an after-life, where you'll be with the people you loved on earth?' He replied: 'No, I don't. But I'd love to be proved wrong!' I hope he has been.

Now for the joys – especially my children and grandchildren, my in-laws and family. And the greatest good fortune, for which I am deeply grateful and much envied by most of my friends – my closest and dearest all live near to me. (See Farewell, in Appendix I.)

Then there is my work. In the House of Lords and with organisations and charities, public and communal. Work which I have chosen to do, and which I can achieve thanks to my remarkable staff, and especially my unique and long-suffering right-hand colleague, Maureen Gold.

Wisdom to pass on? Our children are entitled to lead their lives in their way. We may still have some quiet influence, but the days of control or of passing adverse judgement ended when they left their parents' home. So appreciate and enjoy – which I most certainly do. With robust health, close family and friends and serious work to be done, as I look back on the past I look forward to the future. I bless all those who helped my past to be so bright and especially all those who have cared for me and helped me during bad times. And I thank those around me today who make this life so magic. I am very grateful.

APPENDIX I

Farewell

The appropriate ending to this story of my life so far, is to pay my tribute to those who have helped me so much. I have already recorded direct or indirect appreciation to many of them. Now let me salute them all.

I pay a special tribute to parliamentary colleagues who stand and stood staunchly by me, and have spoken up for and with me, with unremitting kindness and generosity, especially when times were tough. These include: David Ashby, Anthony Beaumont-Dark, Roland Boyes, Martin Brandon-Bravo, Simon Burns, Lord Alex Carlile, Sir Patrick Cormack, Baroness Llin Golding, Gwyneth Dunwoody, the late Sir John Farr, Lord Derek Foster, Nigel Griffiths, Sir Michael Latham, Sir Ivan Lawrence, John Marshall, the late Lord Merlyn-Rees, Clare Short and Keith Vaz.

For much of my life I have been involved in public, political and communal work. Inevitably, I needed resources and finance for my projects. Inducing others to give is usually easier if you can make major financial contributions yourself – 'I give to your charity, you give to mine'. But so very many people have contributed financially towards my work, knowing that I give what I can, which is primarily my work and effort, initiative and time. I am grateful to them all, and I especially salute that outstanding industrialist, Stephen Rubin. He quietly and modestly provides us with the building in which the Holocaust Educational Trust and other organisations labour so happily. He actively supports the Inter-Parliamentary Council Against Antisemitism, and he works with us and provides us with leadership, guidance and support.

In 1996, when Myra was terminally ill, I decided to retire from the House of Commons – which I did, when the House was dissolved for the 1997 election. I hoped that Tony Blair might put me into the Lords, but there was no guarantee. So I needed somewhere to work, near enough to the Palace of Westminster if I was appointed a peer and far enough away from it not to feel daily misery if I remained peerless. I consulted my friend, Jonathan Metliss, who said: 'Why don't you phone Nigel Ross? He's a property man.' I did. 'You couldn't have chosen a better day,' he said. 'I've just bought a building in Strutton Ground.'

'Where's that?'

'It's the market street that leads down from Victoria Street to Horseferry Road. About ten minutes walk from Parliament. Go and have a look and see if you like it.'

It was dreamy. Ever since I was a child and my father took me down Petticoat Lane on Sunday mornings, I have loved markets. The atmosphere, the people, the laughter, the comradeship, the brash, the bawdy, the kindly folk. The stall-keepers, the public – the best of fun places. Especially good medicine for a lonely man. 'How do I thank you?' I asked him. 'You don't,' Nigel replied. 'I thank you for the work that you do for other people.'

Which reminded me of the only other occasion I had received that fantastic response to appreciation. In the 1980s, the Labour Friends of Israel and the Trade Union Friends of Israel were about to run into serious financial difficulty. So, at the suggestion of Sir Sigmund Sternberg, I telephoned one of our community's most loveable people, Davide Sala. At that time, I scarcely knew him. He was a Sephardi who had come to Britain from Iraq via Italy and made a fortune in shipping. He invited me to breakfast at the Dorchester Hotel.

'What can I do for you?' he smiled at me. I told him of the travails of the two organisations. 'How much do you need?'

'Five thousand pounds for each.'

'When do you need it?'

'As soon as possible. Preferably now.'

He took out his cheque book and wrote out two cheques, each for £5,000.

'How do I thank you?' I asked.

'You don't,' he replied. 'I thank you for asking me. I am fortunate to be able to perform this *mitzva*.' '*Mitzva*' is the Hebrew word for a commandment and one of the major commandments is to give to charity. It helps to earn you a place in heaven.

For years after, Davide Sala helped me with every organisation I worked for. He never said no. And he never made you feel like a '*shnorrer*' – a beggar – for asking. You were doing him the favour by asking.

Davide's wife, Irene, was killed in a plane crash in Chile. Soon after, Davide was diagnosed with cancer. He fought the disease with courage and with good humour. Then one day I was called in to say farewell. He opened his eyes and smiled at me. I kissed him on his forehead. A few hours later he was gone. I miss him.

Sami Shamoon is another Sephardi leader whose support I deeply appreciate. He and his wife Angela and their daughter Alexandra are wonderful friends and great people. There are many other generous benefactors, without whom I would not have been able to carry out my charitable projects and communal work. I thank them all. To each of them, I extend my deepest gratitude.

One of the joys of my parliamentary years has been and remains the pleasure of working with my own staff. Especially with the wonderful Maureen Gold, who to me is far more than my personal secretary and the Director of the Commonwealth Jewish Council. When she applied for the job, she said: 'I'm forty-six. Is that too old for you?' At that time, I was sixty-five and was pleased to assure her that I regarded her as a very young person. Since then, she has not only been the pillar of care and concern and support for me and her colleagues, but also and especially the fount of laughter and fun. In our office, she has had the support and comradeship of many assistants and volunteers. We tracked down over a hundred and twenty of them for my seventy-fifth birthday celebration and eighty-seven arrived for my party.

Jon Mendelsohn, who once worked under my command, is now my respected guru. Another is Douglas Krikler, who is now the Chief Executive of the United Joint Israel Appeal (UJIA). The crew of the Holocaust Educational Trust and of the Commonwealth Jewish Council are among my appreciated colleagues, supporters and constructive critics, who criticise me privately but support and defend me in public. Friends, indeed.

I have always enjoyed working with very bright, young people and, where possible, running them off their feet. One who turned the tables and for years ran me off mine was Paul Secher. Paul first visited Parliament when he was Chairman of the Leicester University Law Society. I showed him round Parliament and immediately offered him a job as a research assistant – which he took. He spent a happy year working for and with me, together with Simon Henderson, who later became and remains a distinguished financial journalist.

About four years after Paul had moved on, I was lecturing on law at the Café Royal. I wandered downstairs to an exhibition of trampolines and other indoor equipment. To my amazement, there was Paul, their sales director. 'What a pity you've got this job,' I said to him. 'I'm building up a training operation and would have loved you to work with me.' He paused, thoughtfully – as he normally does, when faced with a key moment. 'Do you mean it?' he said.

'Of course,' I replied. 'I don't make jokes like that.'

'Well, perhaps we can meet. I'm about to be made redundant.'

So meet we did. After we had discussed terms, Paul said: 'I need a week to think about this because if I take it on, it will be my career.' He did and it is. He is the most loyal, diligent and meticulous of partners, whose persistent good nature, good humour and tact made my business life so contented. I was proud when he and his wife, Sue, made me godfather of their firstborn son, Joe.

Paul Secher and I started our training organisation as simply JS Associates. In 1986, we were joined by Leslie Benson. I had been in Israel for a World Jewish Congress meeting and wandered outside for some fresh air. There was a young man selling copies of Israel's equivalent to the *National Geographic* magazine. We chatted. He was from South Africa. He would like to come to England and do journalism. He travelled to London to meet Paul and myself and has stayed ever since. JS became JSB and then JSB Limited.

Paul and Leslie are the ultimate proof that in business as in marriage, opposites can form a joyful team. Paul – cautious, careful and meticulous. Leslie – the entrepreneur, ambitious and more concerned with the whole than the detail. When I hear from others of troubles with their partners, I bless the gods of chance that brought me into the exhibition at the Café Royal to meet Paul, and out of the World Jewish Congress meeting to run into Leslie.

Another parliamentary assistant was a bright and slightly solemn young man called William Sandover. After two years with me, he opted for diplomacy and applied for the Foreign and Commonwealth Office. I was asked to see one of their investigators. A rather pompous, middle-aged and fat man arrived at my office in Dean's Yard, complete with fawn raincoat and spectacles. I received him in the drab interview room. 'Good of you to see me,' he said.

'Not at all. A pleasure.'

'Tell me.' He paused. 'Does William Sandover drink?'

'I expect so. But if you're asking whether drinking has ever affected his work, the answer is – certainly not. Just a pint in a pub . . .'

'Is he in debt?'

'Probably. Most young people are, aren't they? But I don't know anything about it. If he is, it certainly hasn't affected his work or his morale.'

A long pause. 'Is he a homosexual?'

'I've no idea. I shouldn't think so. I've never discussed it with him. If he is, so what?'

Pause. 'Blackmail, Mr Janner.'

'Well, I wouldn't worry about that. As far as I know, he's completely straight. In all respects.'

'Ah, you mean integrity?'

'Yes. That, too.'

'One final question, if you don't mind.' Pause. 'Do you think it would do him harm in the Diplomatic Service that he has spent two years working for a Zionist leader?'

I couldn't believe it. With uncharacteristic cool, I said to him: 'I think it would do the Diplomatic Service a lot of good to have someone working for it who understands Zionism and the view of Jewish people like myself. As far as I know, there are very few at the moment.' After a not too warm, farewell handshake, my guest left. I told William that I had probably blighted his prospects, but to give the FCO its due, they took him and he is still there and doing well.

Mitchell Coen was my first PA in the House of Lords. I have two key memories of his time with me. First, there was his watchful protection, as we walked through the ruins of Jenin. And second, when he stood behind the President of Latvia and me, in the corridor outside her Riga office. She turned around and looked at him, then said to me: 'I am glad that you have brought the intimidator with you!' Mitch looks very tough, but is one of the kindest of men.

Mitch was followed for the next two years by the very bright and delightful Edward Lewin. He was about the same age as Mitch, but looked five years younger. One day, Edward and I were walking together when a man asked me: 'How old is your son?' Edward snapped at him: 'Lord Janner's too old to be my Dad!' Well, maybe.

My crew suffered one horrendous tragedy. Alan Senitt, who was Director of the Coexistence Trust (Chapter 24), left my office in June 2006. Two weeks later, we received the terrible, unbelievable, shattering news. Alan and a lady friend were outside her home in Georgetown, Washington DC, early on a Sunday morning. They were mugged by three men, who assaulted his friend. Alan intervened and they stabbed him to death.

The following day, a parcel arrived in our office, by express mail from the United States. Alan's handwriting was on the outside. My birthday was the next day and this was obviously a present for me. So on the Tuesday morning, we opened the package and we wept. It was a baseball cap with my name and the crest of the House of Lords on it. With it was a handwritten card of good wishes. I have no words adequately to express our sorrow at the vicious, senseless and terrible destruction of the young life of this outstanding young man.

I deeply appreciate a joyful, laughing office, overseen by the wondrous Maureen Gold, and until recently with Jo Silverman alongside her. My remarkable typists and friends, Pat Garner and Margaret Lancaster, modernised from typewriter to computer – both at my right hand for some forty years. So yes, I am working – but where, when and how I choose. Two pensions, Myra's and mine, built up over nearly half a century and now, alas, for me alone. And as that great American financier, Bernard Barou said: 'Old age is ten years older than I am at any particular time.' I spend the precious time where and with whom I choose – especially with my family and with my friends, of every age . . . with interesting colleagues and lively people . . . and giving service, here and overseas.

Other bright assistants who became my friends and who have not appeared in the pages of this book include Jerry Lewis, who became a Vice President of the Board of Deputies and a freelance journalist; and Jonathan Prichard, who went from me to become an assistant to the Bishop of Chichester – an unlikely progression of faiths. There are many others. My fond appreciation to them all.

As for this book – I have finished it with the help of Simone Girson, Colum Lipsith, Michael Livingston, Janice Lopatkin, David Lewy, Ben Radstone and especially of David Korn, Gideon Wittenberg and my daughter Laura. Without them, you would not be reading these Memoirs.

Ultimately, it is my closest family who remain the bastions of my existence and the great joy of my days.

My son, Daniel, achieved his proud professional success in 2002, when he 'took Silk' – when he was appointed Queen's Counsel. Although some of his work is far away, his family remain joyfully close. His wife, Caroline and his three daughters – Isabel, Esther and Phoebe – are at the centre of his world and, of course, of mine. And their family Friday evening Sabbath dinners are highlights of so many of my weeks.

In-laws are an unhappy source of misery jokes. Happily, not mine. George and Evelyn Gee, father and mother of Daniel's wife Caroline, were friends of Myra and myself, long before Daniel had the good sense to marry Caroline. And so they have remained.

Marion is an inspiration. She throws herself into involvement in issues and in helping people – often those who need it most and get least. She successfully initiated the lobby group, called Payback, to influence the justice system to reduce the number of prison sentences for non-violent offences. Now, she is involved in setting up and developing a new communications charity called Bright, to help people with mental health and other problems. And for many years, she has fostered and helped immensely a young man called Eddie, now twenty-four. Despite his learning difficulties, Eddie has a very full and relatively independent and satisfying life. I am very proud of Marion.

Our youngest daughter, Laura, studied to become a rabbi. In 2004, to my delight, she was consecrated in her new role. She became Rabbi Janner-Klausner. With the ready consent of her brilliant husband, David, they had included the name of Janner in their surname. Otherwise, it could well eventually disappear, as all three of Daniel's children are girls.

On Laura's great rabbinate day, I missed Myra hugely. She would have been sitting at the ceremony, setting us all laughing with her incisive and often wonderfully inappropriate jokes. What would Chief Rabbi Israel Brodie have thought about it all, were he still alive? My guess: that he would have chuckled and said nothing. At least one of his family had followed his trail, in however surprising a direction.

David has a fine mind – and a great attachment to his brother, one of Israel's most famous writers, Amos Oz, and to his sister Marganita, and their children. David has always put his family first and enabled Laura to study and to work by sharing their family duties. Their children, Tali, Natan and Ella are fabulous. Sadly, David lost his father, Yehudah Arieh Klausner, when he was still a youngster and his mother, Rosa Lida, in 2001.

Most years, I take my grandchildren away for long weekends. We travel wherever they want – to Paris or to Venice, to Rome or to Budapest. What a privilege for me. I often think of how I never spent a day away, still less a weekend, alone with my father or with either of my grandfathers.

As for my sister Ruth, she is a fantastic friend. From the time that we were evacuated together to Canada until today, she has been a pillar of my life. Ruth qualified as a solicitor and for many years worked together with our father in his office – not a role with which I could cope. She has long been President of a Jewish youth organisation, called Habonim Dror. Rightly, she is proud of her input into this remarkable organisation, which has so much influence on the lives of so many youngsters. For many years, Ruth was happily married to Philip (Lord) Morris of Kenwood, who passed away in 2004. Like me, she is blessed with children and grandchildren who are at the core of her life.

So my family world keeps changing. I wish nothing more than God's blessing on them all. To life!

APPENDIX II

UK Speech at UN General Assembly on 60th Anniversary of Liberation of Auschwitz

The Nazis murdered my entire family in Lithuania and Latvia – every one of them. My immediate family were so very fortunate that we were British, and I am now so very fortunate and proud to stand here today, representing the British government and the British Parliament.

In 1946 I was a national serviceman in the British Army of the Rhine. At the second anniversary of the liberation of the Belsen concentration camp, by the British Army, I first felt the true horrors of the Nazi killing machine and I soon became the youngest war crimes investigator in our army. So I know that today, whatever our nationality, we must all do everything in our power to ensure that the next generation learns these lessons – the lessons of the Holocaust . . . learns from the history of the Holocaust . . . and does everything in its power to fight genocide – whenever, and wherever, it appears.

Today, we commemorate the 60th anniversary of the liberation of the Auschwitz concentration camp – the deepest and most revolting symbol of Nazi evil. Today, as the Secretary General has so eloquently said, we remember the Jews and the Roma . . . the physically and the mentally disabled . . . the gays, the political prisoners, the prisoners of war . . . the millions of human beings murdered by the Nazis. Yes, in Auschwitz and yes in Belsen. Yes, in dozens of other terrible concentration camps – liberated by Allied Forces. But also those – like my family – slaughtered in their towns and villages, in their homes, and in their places of worship.

The Nazis sought to exterminate people – men and women, children and babies – people whom they regarded as inferior. They exterminated millions. But their evil did not stop with those whom they murdered. They embedded in tragedy the scarred lives of survivors and of their families.

It took many painful years for our international community to recognise that we must never allow future generations to forget. So our first challenge today is to do all in our power to ensure that the victims and their families are honourably and permanently remembered. Many nations now work effectively together to achieve this remembrance.

In 1998, Britain and other lands established the Task Force for International Co-operation on Holocaust Education, Remembrance and Research. This task force now includes twenty member countries. All support the Declaration of the 2000 Stockholm International Forum on the Holocaust. We work together to establish national programmes to create and to develop Holocaust education, remembrance and research. Countries with little tradition of commemorating the Holocaust have drawn on the experience of Britain and many other lands in raising public awareness of these tragedies.

The Holocaust was a crime unknown to mankind. It had no name. Today, the word embodies the vision of murders and mass graves, and the Nazis' grim efforts to wipe out people whom they despised. The 1951 UN Convention on the Prevention and Punishment of the Crime of Genocide established a legal base to ensure that the most horrendous of crimes should no longer go unpunished.

We said: Never Again. But, tragically, the world still suffers from the evils of genocide and ethnic cleansing. The international community has not learned enough from the Holocaust. So the United Kingdom fully supports and salutes the aims of today's special session of the General Assembly.

The Nazi killings were war crimes – heinous crimes of war and of unique inhumanity. In 1991, the British Parliament passed the War Crimes Act. Our schools include Holocaust education in their curricula. And in Lithuania, Estonia and Latvia, the British government together with the Holocaust Educational Trust and the governments of the Baltic countries have developed a project to access and to mark, to map and to signpost hundreds of Holocaust mass graves. These graves contain the bodies and bones of victims whom the Nazis, and their local allies, dragged from their homes and massacred without mercy, and buried in pits.

In Britain as in some other nations – Holocaust Memorial Day, 27 January – Thursday of this week – marks the anniversary of the liberation of Auschwitz. It has become a key national event. The Day serves two purposes. First, to remember those who suffered and died in the tragedy of the Holocaust. Second, we reflect on the lessons to be learned, and we remember other human tragedies and intolerance. Non-governmental organisations, together with teachers and educators, have been most active and effective participants.

Lord Janner of Braunstone QC, 24 January 2005

Index